"Anywhere So Long As There Be Freedom"

Charles Carroll of ye Inner Temple Esqr. Second
Son of Daniell Carroll of Litterlouna Esqr. in the
Kings County in the Kingdom of Ireland 1702

"Anywhere So Long As There Be Freedom"

Charles Carroll of Carrollton, His Family & His Maryland

An Exhibition and Catalogue Organized By Ann C. Van Devanter

THE BALTIMORE MUSEUM OF ART

Art Museum Drive
Baltimore, Maryland 21218

Library of Congress Catalogue Number 75-27470

DATES FOR THE EXHIBITION
September 30 - November 30, 1975

The Exhibition and Catalogue were generously supported through a grant from the National Endowment for the Arts, Washington, D.C. The Maryland Bicentennial Commission and the Archdiocese of Baltimore provided funds to augment the scope of the catalogue. The Maryland Historical Society, Baltimore, and the Peale Museum, Baltimore, are co-sponsors of the exhibition.

In addition to the portraits and decorative arts in this publication, the exhibition includes books, documents, maps, views, and plats which relate to the Maryland of the Carrolls. Many of these will be found as illustrations to the essays.

COVER:
Cat. No. 37, Thomas Sully, *Charles Carroll of Carrollton*

HALF TITLE PAGE:

BOOK PLATE

English, 1702

Engraved paper; overall size: 4 1/4 x 4 1/16 inches; plate size: 3 3/8 x 2 3/4 inches

Carroll arms within a shield surrounded by elaborate mantling and with the Carroll crest (Hawk with wings elevated); ribbon empty

Engraved at the bottom of the plate: *Charles Carroll of Ye Inner Temple Esqr. Second/Son of Daniell Carroll of Litterlouna Esqr in the/Kings County in the Kingdom of Ireland 1702*

Private Collection of a Descendant

PAGE 101:

BOOK PLATE

English, 1763

Engraved paper; overall size: 3 15/16 x 3 3/16 inches; plate size: 3 1/8 x 2 3/16 inches

Carroll arms within a shaped cartouche flanked at the right by a standing putto and with the Carroll crest (Hawk with wings elevated)

Engraved at bottom of the plate: *Charles Carroll*

Private Collection of a Descendant

On September 20, 1763, Charles Carroll of Annapolis had written to Charles Carroll of Carrollton in London, "You may get a fresh plate of our arms, styling yourself the only son of Charles Carroll, Esq. of the city of Annapolis in the Province of Maryland . . . get at least 1000 stamps from the plate to be pasted in all the books" (CCA to CCC, MS 220, MdHi) and on December 8, 1763, Charles Carroll of Carrollton replied. . . . "Before the receit of yr last I had a plate of our arms engraved & 200 stamps with only my name at the bottom, & had ordered 400 more. I shall leave the plate with the engraver to supply me with more stamps if wanted: the plate is too short to have the words you direct inserted" (Carroll Papers, MS 206, MdHi)

Table of Contents

Foreword vii
TOM L. FREUDENHEIM

List of Lenders xi

Acknowledgments xiii

Abbreviated Chronology of Charles Carroll of Carrollton xv

Genealogical Charts xvii

Preface 3
ELLEN HART SMITH

Charles Carroll of Carrollton and His Family 1688-1832 9
SALLY D. MASON

Charles Carroll of Carrollton: Conservative Revolutionary, 1776-1781 35
RONALD HOFFMAN

Charles Carroll of Carrollton: English Aristocrat in an American Setting 43
EDWARD C. PAPENFUSE

The Carroll House in Annapolis and Doughoregan Manor 59
WILLIAM VOSS ELDER, III

Catholicism and The Carrolls in Early Maryland 83
JOSEPH T. DURKIN, S.J., AND ANNABELLE M. MELVILLE

CATALOGUE OF THE EXHIBITION

The Face of a Family 103
ANN C. VAN DEVANTER

Charles Carroll of Carrollton and American Independence 113

Portraits of the Carroll Family 119
ANN C. VAN DEVANTER

The Carroll Family: An English Lifestyle in America 277
WILLIAM VOSS ELDER, III

Furniture, Silver, Memorabilia, and Other Household Objects
Relating to the Carroll Family 285
WILLIAM VOSS ELDER, III

Selected Bibliograhy and Index of Artists 303

Foreword

The opportunity to celebrate sometimes carries with it special obligations. This is certainly the case with respect to our Bicentennial era. For this reason, *Anywhere, So Long As There Be Freedom* (the motto on the Carroll Family crest) is a particularly appropriate vehicle for The Baltimore Museum of Art to initiate its Bicentennial celebration. The core of this exhibition is the works of arts through which an extraordinary American family is portrayed. Charles Carroll of Carrollton is certainly not among the best known of our Founding Fathers, even in his own Maryland. Yet few figures in our early history provide such insight into aspects of that history.

Charles Carroll of Carrollton lived a long and productive life, even by the standards of our own day, spanning the Colonial, Revolutionary, and Federal periods of American history, and he was deeply involved in a multitude of pivotal factors about that history. Although perhaps best known as one of the four Maryland Signers of the Declaration of Independence (and then as the last living Signer), his life and that of his family carries far greater significance. For in studying the Carrolls we gain a special insight into the political, social and economic milieu of their times. Their dealings in property and business range from the accumulation of land by the first generation of Carrolls in America and the establishment of one of the greatest fortunes by the second generation to the financial undertakings of Charles Carroll of Carrollton in the early days of the Republic: The First and Second Bank of the United States, the Bank of North America, the Baltimore and Ohio Railroad and the Chesapeake and Ohio Canal — the latter two being important factors in the development of commerce and settlement of inland America.

The Carrolls' role in the history of religious toleration in this country is also characteristic of an aspect of our past. Subjected to severe discrimination because of their Catholicism, they eventually played a major role in seeing their Church gain equality in a nation dedicated to principles of toleration. In addition Charles Carroll of Carrollton's political influence in Maryland immediately preceding, and immediately after, the signing of the Declaration of Independence, as a State Senator and as a framer of the Maryland Constitution, was significant.

Perhaps most remarkable, however, is the fact that we can study a subject of this kind in such depth and do so in the context of an art exhibition. The extant records of the Carrolls are an almost unique example of contemporary documentation for an American family. The existence of many letters, documents, and other rare materials in family archives as well as in various libraries and museums provides a range of information not ordinarily available in the study of an historic figure. Even more extraordinary however, is the existence of family portraits which enable us to come literally face-to-face with this family — from two generations before Charles Carroll of Carrollton through his grandchildren — and which provide us with a unique history of portraiture in this region from the early 18th century into the mid-19th century.

A project of this kind is not easily assembled, and the number of people involved is obviously great. However, one person has been primarily responsible for the conception of the exhibition and its direction. Ann Van Devanter approached the Museum almost two years ago with the idea for an exhibition based on the Carroll family portraits and was invited to be Guest Curator for the exhibition in honor of America's Bicentennial. She has managed the project from its most modest inception all the way through extensive phases of research, culminating in both the exhibition and in the detailed catalogue of family portraits included herein. Much new information has been uncovered, so that this project of celebration might become a process of learning, not only for those who worked on the exhibition, but also for those who view it. There is no adequate way of thanking Ann Van Devanter for all her work, her affection for the subject matter, or her creative genius in assembling and making sense of this documentation of a family.

Many other people have been involved in making certain that the exhibition and publication would be as important as they are. William Voss Elder, III, Curator of Decorative Arts and the Museum's coordinator for the project has brought to it his vast knowledge of Maryland and of the periods covered by the exhibition; in addition, I am grateful for his two essays on architecture and decorative arts. Ann Boyce Harper, Managing Editor, has pursued this publication project with her usual thoroughness, becoming a collaborator in the assembling of this vast array of materials. Anne Mastin, Assistant Guest Curator, has ably and devotedly served the entire project in every phase of its development. Indeed, the number of persons whose roles have been essential is too great for inclusion here and will be found in the acknowledgments which follow. I am deeply grateful to all of them for making the exhibition happen. The several essays contained herein represent the various views of scholars who have worked on Carroll material in some of the specialized areas of its involvement. I am delighted to thank Joseph T. Durkin, S.J., Professor Emeritus, Georgetown University, Washington, D.C.; Dr. Ronald Hoffman, Associate Professor, University of Maryland; Sally D. Mason, University of Maryland; Dr. Annabelle M. Melville, Commonwealth Professor, Bridgewater State College, Bridgewater, Massachusetts; Dr. Edward C. Papenfuse, Archivist for the State of Maryland; and Ellen Hart Smith, author of the first biography of Charles Carroll of Carrollton. Each essay captures a particular facet of Charles Carroll and his family, thus expanding on the visual documentation of the exhibition and catalogue itself.

The exhibition would obviously not take place without the cooperation of very generous lenders. Many of them are listed elsewhere, but, in addition, this exhibition required the cooperation of a large number of Carroll Family descendants, some of whom have asked to remain anonymous. We are especially grateful for their interest in sharing with us not only their works of art but also information and documentation which made it possible to unravel a variety of mysteries surrounding works connected with the Family.

This project has been supported by a generous grant from the National Endowment for the Arts, a Federal Agency created by Act of Congress in 1965. It is yet another of the Endowment's major ways of supporting exhibitions whose scope would otherwise be considerably less ambitious. The Maryland Bicentennial Commission and the Archdiocese of Baltimore provided funds toward the publication of this catalogue, enabling us to expand its scope.

The exhibition is being co-sponsored by The Maryland Historical Society and the Peale Museum, our sister institutions in Baltimore, without whose cooperation it would have been even more difficult to assemble an exhibition of this scope. We are very pleased for the support of The Maryland Historical Society, its Director, P. William Filby, and its Assistant Director, Romaine Somerville, in making available so much of the documentation which lies behind the exhibition. Director Wilbur Hunter of the Peale Museum provided his special knowledge of Baltimore history, and we are grateful to him as well.

The Baltimore Museum of Art is offering this exhibition and publication as a contribution to the celebration of our Bicentennial. We celebrate not only our nation but also the opportunity to learn more about our past. We also celebrate Maryland and its role in the early period of American history. And we celebrate a family whose contributions are still visibly with us. Perhaps most characteristically, the cooperative effort that this exhibition represents, between countries, institutions, private individuals, professional colleagues, and, finally, viewers, is a microcosm of the interdependence of people which America's independence really celebrates.

Tom L. Freudenheim
Director

List of Lenders

Archdiocese of Baltimore
Archives of the State of Maryland, Annapolis
Trustees of The British Museum, London
Musee Carnavalet, Paris
Catholic University, Washington, D.C.
Historical Society of Delaware, Wilmington
Detroit Institute of Arts
Mr. and Mrs. Harry B. Dillehunt, Jr.
Her Majesty Queen Elizabeth II
Mrs. Marion Poor Fisher
Georgetown University, Washington, D.C.
Georgetown Visitation Convent, Washington, D.C.
Groton School, Groton, Massachusetts
Hammond-Harwood House Association, Annapolis
Thomas O'Brien Hanley, S.J.
Sir Frederick Hervey-Bathurst
Mr. Frederick John Hervey-Bathurst
The Johns Hopkins University, Baltimore
Mr. and Mrs. Bryden B. Hyde
Independence National Historical Park, Philadelphia
Kennedy Galleries, Inc., New York
Mr. Edward Norriss Kimball, Jr.
Mr. Richard Fuller Kimball
Duchess of Leeds Foundation, London
The Trustees of the Tenth Duke of Leeds Will Trust
Mr. Lester S. Levy
Library of Congress, Washington, D.C.
Library of the Defense Ministry, Paris
The Maryland Historical Society, Baltimore
The Massachusetts Historical Society, Boston
Mrs. Andrew Matthew McCrone
Mr. and Mrs. Paul Mellon
The Metropolitan Museum of Art, New York
Mr. and Mrs. LeRoy Morgan
National Gallery of Art, Washington, D.C.
National Portrait Gallery, Smithsonian Institution, Washington, D.C.
The New York Historical Society, New York
The New York Public Library, Arents Collection, New York
Estate of Miriam Perkins Carroll Norris
Mr. and Mrs. Robert O'Donnell
Joan Pennington Overturf
The Peale Museum, Baltimore
The Historical Society of Pennsylvania, Philadelphia
Enoch Pratt Free Library, Baltimore
The Art Museum, Princeton University, Princeton, New Jersey
Mrs. Edmund R. Purves
Mr. John Beverly Riggs
Dr. Leonard M. Rothstein
Mrs. John R. Sabina

Mr. John D. Schapiro
Mrs. Sloan Simpson
Mr. and Mrs. Walter A. Slowinski
Mr. and Mrs. Richard L. Staples
The State of Maryland, State House, Annapolis
Mrs. T. Gaillard Thomas
Mr. and Mrs. C. Edward Walter
The Walters Art Gallery, Baltimore
The Wellington Museum, London
The Eighth Duke of Wellington
Colonial Williamsburg Foundation, Williamsburg, Virginia
Victoria and Albert Museum, London
Yale University Art Gallery, New Haven, Connecticut

Acknowledgments

An undertaking of this magnitude is composed of many parts, each one essential to its success. In planning this exhibition and in preparing this catalogue we have incurred numerous debts for assistance and advice and it is extremely difficult to thank adequately all individuals and institutions involved.

In the spring of 1971 Mrs. Hermann W. Wunderlich of Kennedy Galleries, Inc., New York, suggested it was time that someone pay long overdue tribute to Charles Carroll of Carrollton. The seed once planted, grew, and by the Spring of 1974 Tom Freudenheim, Director of the Baltimore Museum, and William Voss Elder III, Chief of Curatorial Services and Curator of Decorative Arts, were enthusiastically endorsing *Anywhere So Long As There Be Freedom.* It is the vision of these three that gave birth to this exhibition.

An idea does not really exist, however, until it is implemented. I am fortunate in being able to cite three collaborators who are largely responsible for this project. The role of our Assistant Guest Curator Anne Nye Mastin can never be given adequate credit. Without her creative, devoted and tireless efforts above and beyond the call of duty this exhibition and the accompanying catalogue would never have seen the light of day. William Voss Elder III has piloted the undertaking through many difficult months with warm good humour and his enormous talents and abilities are evident in every detail of the finished product. Ann Boyce Harper's brilliant abilities as editor of this catalogue can never reveal her true role in this exhibition as advisor in many aspects of the installation and the educational adjuncts of the project. It has been a privilege and a pleasure to work with these three exceptionally talented people.

To M. B. Munford, Assistant Curator of Decorative Arts must also go very special tribute. M.B. personally undertook the burden of a thousand important details, held the fort, and smiled while we demolished her office, pilfered her pens, tied up her telephone and generally disrupted her environment. Not one of us could have survived without her. Nor could we have managed without the exceptional talents of Jennifer Goldsborough, who, with charm and grace fulfilled the roles of researcher, writer, editorial assistant and trouble shooter without equal.

We were most fortunate in having as our co-sponsors for the exhibition The Maryland Historical Society and the Peale Museum. The entire staffs of both institutions contributed endless amounts of time and energy to this endeavor. To each and every one I extend my most sincere thanks.

The nature of this exhibition as a personal tribute to one of America's outstanding founding fathers has resulted in an enormous debt to a very special and distinguished group of people: Charles Carroll's descendants, who as lenders, researchers, advisors and morale boosters have added the dimension which makes this enterprise a very special and rewarding one. My deepest gratitude goes to these gracious and generous individuals.

Charles Carroll has taken us out of the traditional realm of the art museum into historical waters uncharted for us. Some exceptionally distinguished scholars have assisted us in this aspect of the project, adding their knowledge and their experienced scholarship to the catalogue in the forms of essays, and to the exhibition in the form of research. My sincere thanks to the authors in this volume: Father Joseph T. Durkin, Dr. Ronald Hoffman, Mrs. Sally D. Mason, Dr. Annabelle Melville, Dr. Edward Papenfuse, and Miss Ellen Hart Smith. We are privileged to be able to publish their opinions and interpretations of much of the background of the exhibition.

Equally important on the historical front and not nearly as recognizable are the talented researchers who spent countless hours — too many on a volunteer basis — ferreting out, checking, and corroborating the mountains of material essential to the interpretation of our subject. Behind every word on each page of this catalogue and each label in the exhibition stand the superb work of Mrs. Wrexie Agan, Mr. Stiles Tuttle Colwill, Mrs. Maya Donelan, Mrs. Alex Hart Green, Mrs. Doris Himelfarb, Mrs. Jean F. Knight, Mrs. Vivian F. Logan, Mrs. Grace R. MacMillan, and Mrs. Mary Washington Newhall. Thank you all, more than I can say.

A very special thank you also goes to the owners and lenders whose generosity made this exhibition possible. Not only have they graciously agreed to part with their treasures for the duration of this exhibition, they have also given us valuable information without which the catalogue would not have been possible.

The Frick Art Reference Library, New York, essential to any and every art historical project, went far above and beyond the call of duty for me and for Charles Carroll, as did the Catalogue of American Portraits, Smithsonian Institution, Washington, D.C. and the Archives of American Art also located in the Smithsonian. One other archive also deserves special mention: The J. Hall Pleasants Studies in Maryland Painting on deposit at the

Maryland Historical Society. It goes without saying that no consideration of painting in Maryland at any period would be possible without the magnificent work of Dr. J. Hall Pleasants. His work is the foundation of this exhibition, and it, in turn, is a constant reflection of his scholarship.

It has, however, taken far more than these superb archives to get the job done. Many individuals gave generously of their time and their expertise, by letter and by telephone and cheerfully stepped into the breach checking dozens of necessary details, often at zero hour. Again my thanks to Mr. William R. Best, Director, Thomas Gilcrease Institute of American History and Art, Tulsa, Oklahoma; Miss Mary Black, Curator, the New York Historical Society; Mr. John Brannigan, Stack and Reader Division, Library of Congress; Mr. William P. Campbell, National Gallery of Art, Washington, D.C.; Nelson R. Coleman, III, expert on clocks and watches; Dr. Andrew Cosentino, Assistant Professor of Art, Franklin & Marshall College, Lancaster, Pa.; Mrs. Worth B. Daniels, Jr.; Dr. Harold E. Dickson, Professor of Art History, The Pennsylvania State University; Mr. Edward Dwight, Director, the Munson-Williams-Proctor Institute, Utica, New York; Dr. Roland Fleischer, Professor of Art History, The Pennsylvania State University; Ernest S. Freudenheim, gem specialist; Thomas O'Brien Hanley, S.J., Editor, The Carroll Papers; Miss Claudia Kidwell, Associate Curator, Division of Costume and Furnishings, the Smithsonian Institution; Dr. Aubrey Land, University of Georgia; Mr. James Mulcahey, Curator, National Park Services; Mr. Peter Parker, Historical Society of Pennsylvania, Philadelphia; Dr. John Beverly Riggs, Eleutherian Mills-Hagley Foundation, Inc., Greenville, Delaware; Miss Helen Sanger of the Frick Art Reference Library; Dr. Charles Coleman Sellers; Mr. Robert Stewart of the National Portrait Gallery, Smithsonian Institution; Mrs. Florian Thayn, Office of the Architect, U.S. Capitol; The Reverend John J. Tierney, Archivist, Archdiocese of Baltimore; and Mrs. Joan Wilson, Archivist/Curator, Stratfield Saye House, nr. Reading, England.

The addition of "The Three American Graces" added an exciting new dimension to the Carroll story and also presented the difficulties of overseas research and loans. One person in particular has smoothed our path at every turn, worked tirelessly on our behalf and endured with the utmost calm and good humour the many roadblocks we have unwittingly placed in his way: Mr. H. V. T. Percival, Director of The Wellington Museum, London. I thank him here with gratitude, affection and the greatest admiration.

To the Director of the Baltimore Museum, Tom Freudenheim, whose vision and encouragement have been a constant guide, I am eternally grateful for the opportunity to make this exhibition a reality. To each member of his staff, and every one who has made a contribution, I would like to express not only my gratitude but my sincere admiration. Working with a team of this quality has been both a joy and an inspiration. Without the enthusiastic and creative assistance and advice of each and every one, the job would have been less than impossible. I would particularly like to mention Geoffrey Lemmer, Senior Conservator and Margaret Ash, Conservator, who skillfully and willingly prepared many of the works for exhibition; Installation Designer Robert Zimmerman who with Melanie Harwood and Margaret Powell (doubling as indefatigable proof-reader par excellence) creatively and patiently worked to bring the exhibition alive; Dr. Glenn Long's Education Department, and especially Rose Mary Glennon who, with the creative assistance of Frank DeCato brought her very great talents to bear on the educational adjuncts so important to this exhibition; Duane Suter, Museum Photographer, whose high quality work can be seen on almost every single page of this catalogue; Audrey Frantz and Barbara Fine who typed their fingers to the bone and wore out their ears on the telephone; Diana Schramm, Registrar and Carrie DeCato, Assistant Registrar whose efficient operation and meticulous care of each item has been a mainstay in the realization of the exhibition; Judy Frost, Librarian (now of the Cleveland Museum of Art) and Joan Robison, Assistant Librarian, who were indefatigable in their pursuit of research materials essential to the project; and Emily Laisy (now of Cleveland), Martha Parkhurst and Theo Easter who kept the financial ship afloat so ably; and Kim Hallfrisch who spent hours on the road collecting the items for the exhibition.

Last but not least my gratitude to a very special asset to The Baltimore Museum of Art: the Women's Committee who contributed more than I could ever list here to this exhibition not only in material and moral support, but in hours of telephoning, research, transcribing of documents — it goes on and on. What a group they are!

A.C.V.D.

Abbreviated Chronology of Charles Carroll of Carrollton

CCA — Charles Carroll of Annapolis
CCC — Charles Carroll of Carrollton
CC IV — Charles Carroll of Homewood

1737 Sept. 19: Born in Annapolis, son of Charles Carroll and Elizabeth Brooke.

1747-1749 Studied at Bohemia Manor School in Cecil County, Maryland.

1749 Sent to Jesuit College of St. Omers in French Flanders with cousin John Carroll.

1753 Studied classical and modern literature at Jesuit College in Rheims.

1755 Left Rheims for Paris; studied philosophy and science at College of Louis-le-Grand.

1757 Studied in Paris at College of Louis-le-Grand late summer: CCA visited him in Paris.

December: At Bourges studying civil law.

1758 Summer: Met and courted Miss Alcock in Bourges.

1759 CCC returned to Paris to complete degree in Civil Law.

Late August: Left France for London.

Sept. 2: Arrived in London to study English Law at the Middle Temple.

1761 March 12: Death of Elizabeth Brooke Carroll, CCC's mother.

1763 Fall: Began courting Louisa Baker; proposed marriage; Miss Baker refused.

1764 Sept.: Embarked from England for Maryland aboard the *Randolf* under Capt. Walker.

1765 Feb. 14: Reported in *The Maryland Gazette* that CCC had arrived in Annapolis.

1766 Engaged to Rachel Cooke who died in November.

1768 June 5: Married his cousin Mary (Molly) Darnall in Annapolis. CCC accepted into Homony Club; Paca and Chase were also members.

1773 Jan.-June: Antilon-First Citizen debates in *The Maryland Gazette* over Gov. Eden's fee proclamation. Daniel Dulany (Antilon) defends the governor; CCC (First Citizen) defends right of assembly to set fees.

1774 Member of Annapolis Committee of Correspondence.

Sept. 5: Continental Congress met in Philadelphia; CCC attended as an observer since Md. delegation valued his opinion. His religion prevented him from being an elected member.

Oct.: Continental Congress adjourned.

Oct. 19: Brig *Peggy Stewart* burned at Annapolis.

1775 Member of Md. Committee of Correspondence, Committee of Safety.

May: George Washington appointed Commander-In-Chief of Revolutionary forces; CCC describes him as "a cool prudent man."

Nov.: CCC voted onto Committee "to represent and act for this county and city, and to carry into execution the association agreed."

1776 March-June: Mission to Canada to obtain support for American cause; traveled with Benjamin Franklin, John Carroll and Samuel Chase.

May 21: Md. Convention issued anti-independence instructions to Congressional Delegation.

June 28: Md. Convention's anti-independence instructions rescinded; CCC instrumental in achieving this.

July 18: Took seat as Md. delegate to Continental Congress (until 1778). Made member of Board of War.

July 19: CCC voted in Congress to authorize engrossment of Declaration of Independence on parchment in preparation for its signing.

Aug. 2: Signed Declaration of Independence with 49 other delegates.

CCC drafted Md. Constitution.

Aug. 27: Md. Constitution presented to Assembly.

Nov. 3: Md. Constitution amended and accepted.

1777-
1800 Maryland State Senator.

1782 May 30: Death of CCA.

June 10: Death of Molly (Mrs. CCC).

1784 One of three committee members appointed to draw up instructions for the newly formed Potomac Co., later the C&O Canal Co. of which CCC was a Director.

1787 CCC elected to serve as delegate to Federal Constitutional Convention; declined.

1788 Prepared address urging Maryland's ratification of Federal Constitution.

1789-
1792 Nov. 3: CCC and John Henry elected as first U.S. Senators from Md. after ratification of Federal Constitution. First U.S. Congress in New York City.

1792 Law passed which prohibited serving in both Federal and State Senates. CCC resigned from the U.S. Senate.
CCC proposed as candidate for president against Washington.

1800 "Ousted" from State Senate by Democrats.
Founder of First Bank of United States.

1816 One of the major founding stockholders of the Second Bank of the United States.

1826 July 4: Adams and Jefferson died; CCC became last surviving signer of Declaration of Independence.

1828-
1831 President of the American Colonization Society.

1828 Member of the Board of Directors of Baltimore and Ohio Railroad.

July 4: Laid 1st cornerstone of the railroad.

1832 Nov. 14: CCC died at house of his daughter Mary Caton; buried at Doughoregan.

CHART I

This chart shows the interrelationships between the line of Charles Carroll of Carrollton and that of the Carrolls of Duddington, of Upper Marlboro, and of Rock Creek. The four lines were closely related by ties of blood and marriage through the Darnalls and the Carrolls. The Carrolls of Anne Arundel and the Barrister line are not represented here, as their relationship to the Carrolls on this chart is so distant. In the case of the Barrister, the relationship has not been determined; the common ancester of the Barrister and the Signer seems to be Teige O'Carroll, chief of Ely, who lived prior to the 13th century A.D. Daniel and John Carroll, the progenitors of the Anne Arundel line in Maryland, were nephews of Daniel Carroll of Litterluna and thus first cousins of Charles Carroll the Settler and first cousins twice removed of the Signer.

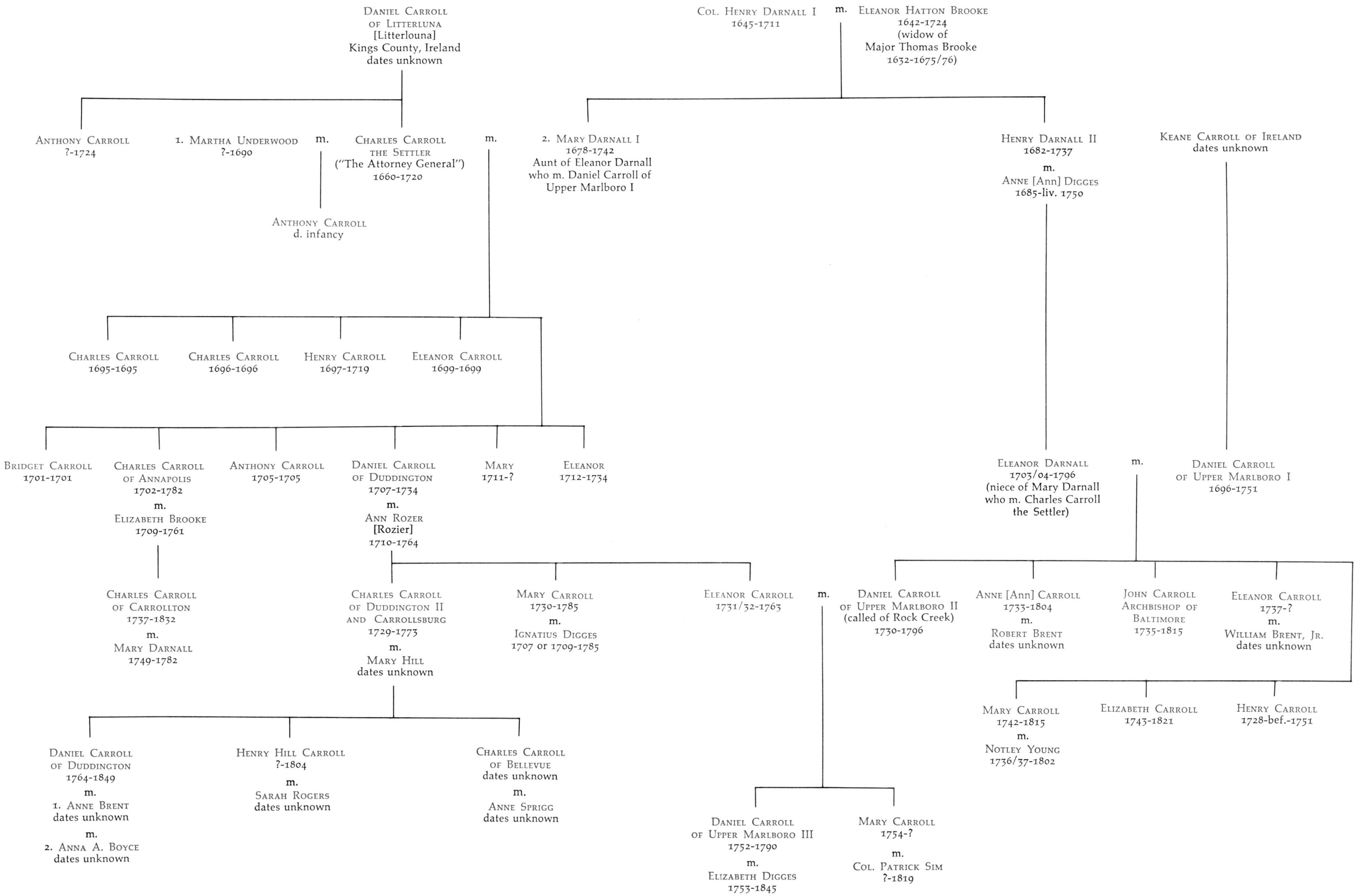

CHART II

This chart illustrates both the immediate antecedents and descendants of Charles Carroll of Carrollton and his wife Mary Darnall Carroll from great-grandparents through grandchildren. The dual relationship of Charles Carroll of Carrollton to his wife Mary Darnall II, is also indicated. The Signer's maternal grandparents, Clement Brooke (ca. 1676-1735/37) and Jane Sewall (?-1761), were Mrs. Charles Carroll of Carrollton's maternal great-grandparents. Thus, Charles Carroll of Carrollton and his wife were first cousins once removed through the maternal line. The Signer's grandmother, Mary Darnall I (1678-1742), was the great-great aunt of Mrs. Charles Carroll of Carrollton; therefore, Charles Carroll of Carrollton and his wife were second cousins once removed through the paternal line.

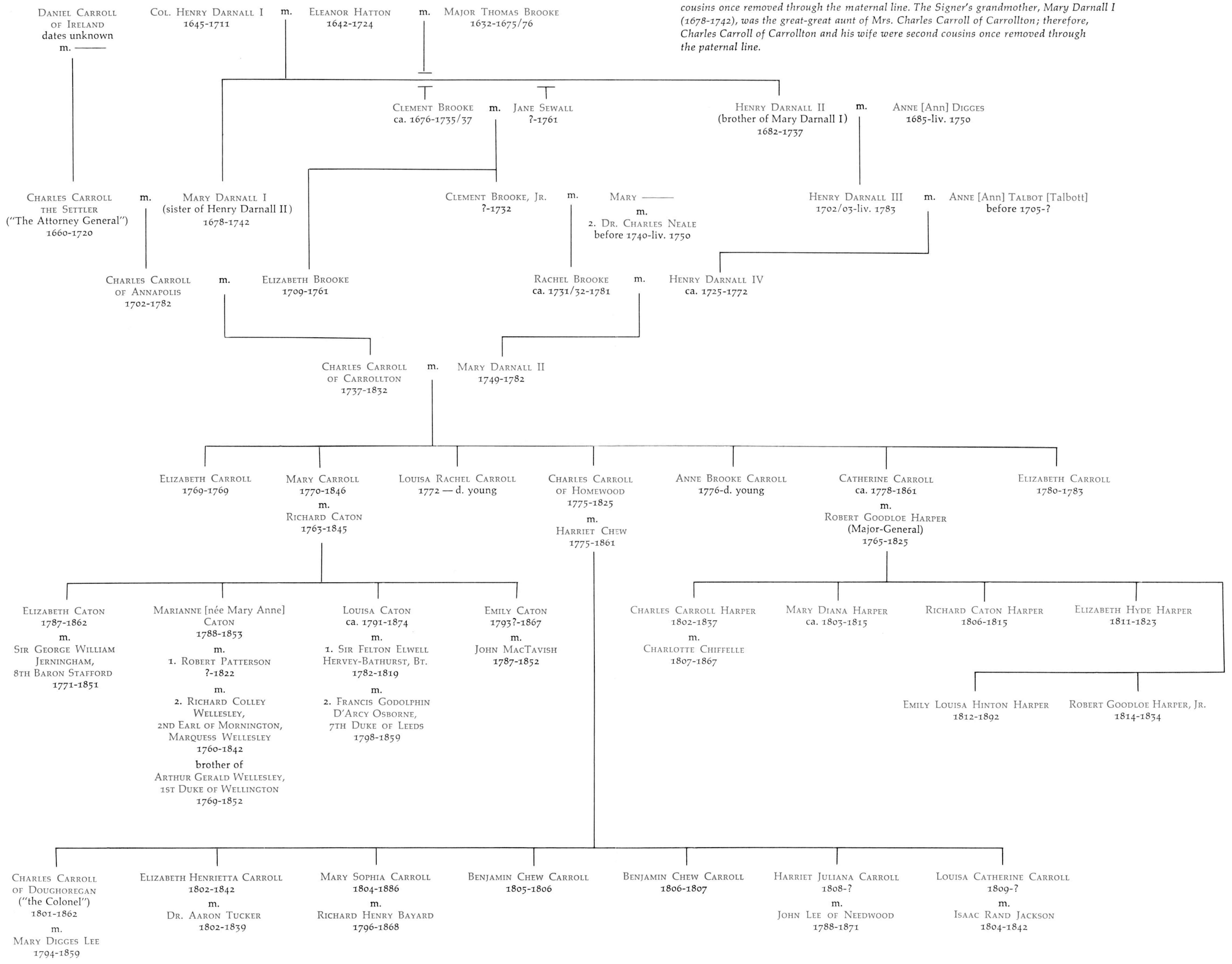

CHART III

This chart illustrates the interrelationship of members of the Carroll and allied families whose portraits (in red) are included in the exhibition. The catalogue numbers are cited under the family members' name.

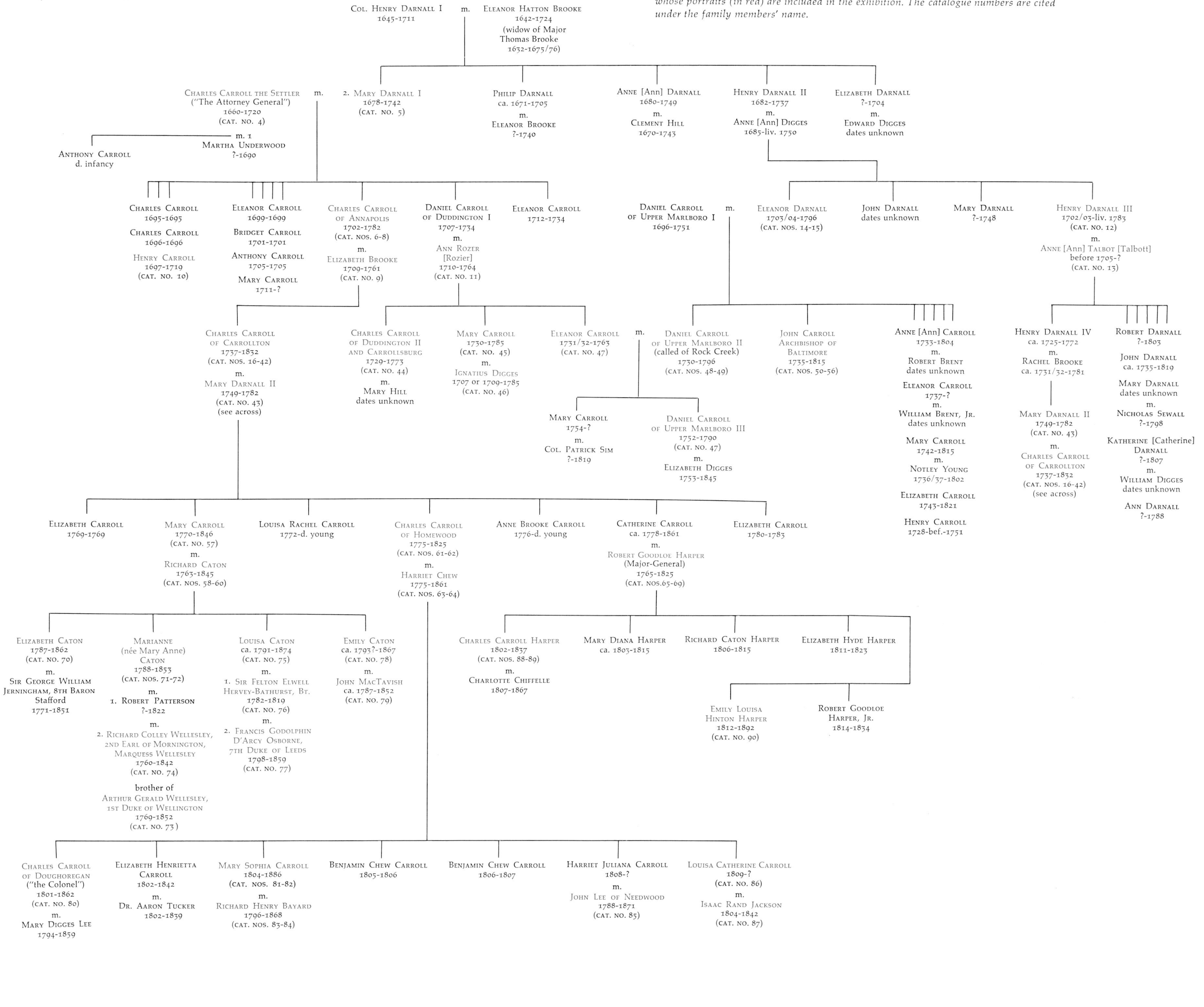

Col. Henry Darnall I
1645-1711
m.
Eleanor Hatton Brooke
1642-1724
(widow of Major Thomas Brooke 1632-1675/76)
Charles Carroll the Settler
("The Attorney General")
1660-1720
(cat. no. 4)
m.
2. Mary Darnall I
1678-1742
(cat. no. 5)
Philip Darnall
ca. 1671-1705
m.
Eleanor Brooke
?-1740
Anne [Ann] Darnall
1680-1749
m.
Clement Hill
1670-1743
Henry Darnall II
1682-1737
m.
Anne [Ann] Digges
1685-liv. 1750
Elizabeth Darnall
?-1704
m.
Edward Digges
dates unknown
m. 1
Martha Underwood
?-1690
Anthony Carroll
d. infancy
Charles Carroll
1695-1695
Charles Carroll
1696-1696
Henry Carroll
1697-1719
(cat. no. 10)
Eleanor Carroll
1699-1699
Bridget Carroll
1701-1701
Anthony Carroll
1705-1705
Mary Carroll
1711-?
Charles Carroll of Annapolis
1702-1782
(cat. nos. 6-8)
m.
Elizabeth Brooke
1709-1761
(cat. no. 9)
Daniel Carroll of Duddington I
1707-1734
m.
Ann Rozer [Rozier]
1710-1764
(cat. no. 11)
Eleanor Carroll
1712-1734
Daniel Carroll of Upper Marlboro I
1696-1751
m.
Eleanor Darnall
1703/04-1796
(cat. nos. 14-15)
John Darnall
dates unknown
Mary Darnall
?-1748
Henry Darnall III
1702/03-liv. 1783
(cat. no. 12)
m.
Anne [Ann] Talbot [Talbott]
before 1705-?
(cat. no. 13)
Charles Carroll of Carrollton
1737-1832
(cat. nos. 16-42)
m.
Mary Darnall II
1749-1782
(cat. no. 43)
(see across)
Charles Carroll of Duddington II and Carrollsburg
1729-1773
(cat. no. 44)
m.
Mary Hill
dates unknown
Mary Carroll
1730-1785
(cat. no. 45)
m.
Ignatius Digges
1707 or 1709-1785
(cat. no. 46)
Eleanor Carroll
1731/32-1763
(cat. no. 47)
m.
Daniel Carroll of Upper Marlboro II
(called of Rock Creek)
1730-1796
(cat. nos. 48-49)
John Carroll Archbishop of Baltimore
1735-1815
(cat. nos. 50-56)
Anne [Ann] Carroll
1733-1804
m.
Robert Brent
dates unknown
Eleanor Carroll
1737-?
m.
William Brent, Jr.
dates unknown
Mary Carroll
1742-1815
m.
Notley Young
1736/37-1802
Elizabeth Carroll
1743-1821
Henry Carroll
1728-bef.-1751
Henry Darnall IV
ca. 1725-1772
m.
Rachel Brooke
ca. 1731/32-1781
Mary Darnall II
1749-1782
(cat. no. 43)
m.
Charles Carroll of Carrollton
1737-1832
(cat. nos. 16-42)
(see across)
Robert Darnall
?-1803
John Darnall
ca. 1735-1819
Mary Darnall
dates unknown
m.
Nicholas Sewall
?-1798
Katherine [Catherine] Darnall
?-1807
m.
William Digges
dates unknown
Ann Darnall
?-1788
Mary Carroll
1754-?
m.
Col. Patrick Sim
?-1819
Daniel Carroll of Upper Marlboro III
1752-1790
(cat. no. 47)
m.
Elizabeth Digges
1753-1845
Elizabeth Carroll
1769-1769
Mary Carroll
1770-1846
(cat. no. 57)
m.
Richard Caton
1763-1845
(cat. nos. 58-60)
Louisa Rachel Carroll
1772-d. young
Charles Carroll of Homewood
1775-1825
(cat. nos. 61-62)
m.
Harriet Chew
1775-1861
(cat. nos. 63-64)
Anne Brooke Carroll
1776-d. young
Catherine Carroll
ca. 1778-1861
m.
Robert Goodloe Harper
(Major-General)
1765-1825
(cat. nos.65-69)
Elizabeth Carroll
1780-1783
Elizabeth Caton
1787-1862
(cat. no. 70)
m.
Sir George William Jerningham, 8th Baron Stafford
1771-1851
Marianne (née Mary Anne) Caton
1788-1853
(cat. nos. 71-72)
m.
1. Robert Patterson
?-1822
m.
2. Richard Colley Wellesley, 2nd Earl of Mornington, Marquess Wellesley
1760-1842
(cat. no. 74)
brother of
Arthur Gerald Wellesley, 1st Duke of Wellington
1769-1852
(cat. no. 73)
Louisa Caton
ca. 1791-1874
(cat. no. 75)
m.
1. Sir Felton Elwell Hervey-Bathurst, Bt.
1782-1819
(cat. no. 76)
m.
2. Francis Godolphin D'Arcy Osborne, 7th Duke of Leeds
1798-1859
(cat. no. 77)
Emily Caton
ca. 1793?-1867
(cat. no. 78)
m.
John MacTavish
ca. 1787-1852
(cat. no. 79)
Charles Carroll Harper
1802-1837
(cat. nos. 88-89)
m.
Charlotte Chiffelle
1807-1867
Mary Diana Harper
ca. 1803-1815
Richard Caton Harper
1806-1815
Elizabeth Hyde Harper
1811-1823
Emily Louisa Hinton Harper
1812-1892
(cat. no. 90)
Robert Goodloe Harper, Jr.
1814-1834
Charles Carroll of Doughoregan
("the Colonel")
1801-1862
(cat. no. 80)
m.
Mary Digges Lee
1794-1859
Elizabeth Henrietta Carroll
1802-1842
m.
Dr. Aaron Tucker
1802-1839
Mary Sophia Carroll
1804-1886
(cat. nos. 81-82)
m.
Richard Henry Bayard
1796-1868
(cat. nos. 83-84)
Benjamin Chew Carroll
1805-1806
Benjamin Chew Carroll
1806-1807
Harriet Juliana Carroll
1808-?
m.
John Lee of Needwood
1788-1871
(cat. no. 85)
Louisa Catherine Carroll
1809-?
(cat. no. 86)
m.
Isaac Rand Jackson
1804-1842
(cat. no. 87)

"Anywhere So Long As There Be Freedom"

Charles Carroll of Carrollton, His Family & His Maryland

Charles Carroll of Carrollton
by Sir Joshua Reynolds (1723-1792)
Cat. No. 16

Preface

It was 1776 when fifty-six American colonists, Charles Carroll of Carrollton among them, signed the Declaration of Independence. But Carroll had won his own personal independence earlier — actually in 1773 when he bested Daniel Dulany in the controversy over Maryland officials' fees. Replying to Dulany, known as "Antilon" in the public debates, Charles Carroll had signed his newspaper letters "First Citizen," and this is what he literally became.

Acclaim was a very new thing for him, who had been all of his thirty-five years an outsider. The barrier was not money, since his father, Charles Carroll of Annapolis, was the richest man in America. Instead it was a matter of religion. His grandfather, Charles Carroll, the Settler (also known as the Attorney General) had come to Maryland expecting religious freedom. Hopefully, he changed the family's motto from "Strong in Faith and War" to "Anywhere So Long as There Be Freedom." But it did not work out that way. Soon after he arrived from Ireland, in 1688, discriminatory laws against Catholics echoed the English Protestant Revolution. This was why his grandson, Charles Carroll of Carrollton, had to be educated abroad; this was why he could not enter a political controversy under his own name; this was why he was happy to sign the Declaration of Independence, which would lead to equal rights for those of all faiths.

What was Charles Carroll of Carrollton really like? His impeccable self-control, his dignity, tact, and reserve all stand (as he intended them to do) between us and really knowing. He wanted to be, and he remained, in spite of fame, his own man. Fortunately, he wrote many letters during his lifetime, notably when he was still young and unguarded.

The third-generation Charles Carroll, he went off, at age ten, to Bohemia Manor Academy run by the Society of Jesus near the Pennsylvania line. Since Catholic churches and schools were forbidden, it was rather like going underground. Charles, always a happy, adjustable child, did well. He easily passed the pre-Binet test for intelligence; he "took to" Greek and Latin. In other subjects — but these were less important and not a real test — he was no perfect student. He would have trouble even with "little figures" and to the end of his life he had difficulty spelling certain words. The number of ways he managed to spell "pamphlet" shows a certain ingenuity and virtuosity.

What the Jesuit fathers did not teach him seems as creditable as what they did. They might well have explained discrimination, bitterly, to their pupils; they refrained. Charles Carroll was grown before be really understood the religious issue in Maryland, and even then he was not, his father thought, half as upset and indignant as he should have been.

Bohemia was only a stop-gap. With his second cousin John — Jacky — Carroll, the future Archbishop of Baltimore, Charles was preparing for the Jesuit College of St. Omers, in French Flanders. Within a year, Jacky, a fine student and two years older, was ready and Charles at least able to go along.

He was very young to be sent abroad, and delicate, and small for his age — small-boned and slight and noticeably straight. In his new school, not an easy one either physically or academically, he was younger than most of the other boys. Yet he did well here, too. ". . . I have got the fifth place in my school, among three & twenty boys," he wrote home. His tutor had only one criticism, that Charles was inclined to be "giddy." Exacty what he meant by this is a question. Probably it was a tendency to laugh and talk behind his slate. He got over it, anyway. Anyone less giddy than Charles Carroll of Carrollton grown up is hard to imagine; he was critical of "little levities" in his young wife, and his letters to his children are ponderous with platitudes. It is nice to think he was a little giddy, at least, when young. For later, everything Carroll did was constructive and for a purpose. He had a mind that was cultivated every day and, as he said of himself, he had "perseverance, and the habit of business" and the respect for excellence. "The uncluttered, stimulating environment of the clerical, academic world" had given him attitudes and a set of habits he would always value and never lose.

After St. Omers, he went to the College of French Jesuits at Rheims, then to the College of Louis-le-Grand in Paris. Personally, by this time, he would have liked to come home. But his father was against ending his education. He wanted him to start studying law. Accordingly, Charles Carroll began in Bourges in 1757 with "ye civil, or Roman law," continued it back in Paris and went on to the Middle Temple in London, where he stayed five years. It was the last place in the world he wanted to be. He hated law from the very first. Dry, dry, dull, dull, he wrote home over and over again.

Besides, there was no chance of his ever being another Attorney-General. Maryland Catholics, not allowed to vote, were not admitted to the bar. Of course, as his father pointed out, the manager of a big estate would find knowledge of the law useful; he was less likely to be imposed on or cheated. Perhaps one of the reasons his father, Charles Carroll of Annapolis, was so insistent was that he had always wanted to study law himself; at eighteen, when his brother Henry died, he had had to give it up. His son needed to achieve this in his place.

It was a risk, of course, to keep Charles in the wicked city of London. Until he entered the Middle Temple he had been safe with the Jesuit priests. Charles Carroll of Annapolis knew — he hoped — that his son had a level head and good judgment. But he had had a nasty scare in 1758, when a perfectly strange Miss Alcock, the "young, pretty, witty," daughter of some Englishman who had a button factory in France, almost became his daughter-in-law. Level-headed Charles had had every immediate *"dessein de l'epouser si elle avait voulu. . . ."* It was just pure luck that she had not.

By the winter of 1763-1764 Charles was twenty-six; his law studies and his stay abroad were almost over; and it was high time, really, for the marriage he was to arrange himself. Charles felt very strongly about this. Of an exemplary dutifulness in things like the law, he announced that he would rather be disinherited than married against his will. He was, of course, just talking. He was in neither danger. He had probably got the idea from one of the high-flown romantic plays he saw in London, finding them considerably less obscene, incidentally, than his father did. But he did know what disinheritance would, in the unlikely event, involve — the greatest estate in America. His father had sent him an inventory of it, which he soon had occasion to show.

Charles met Louisa Baker while he and a Middle Temple friend were touring

View of Annapolis, 1794
by C. Milbourne
Watercolor on paper; 10 x 16 5/8 inches
Hammond-Harwood House Association, Annapolis

Europe. She was a pupil in the Ursuline convent in Paris. The interlude was simple, painful and interesting. He pursued her for six months and was turned down. Frankly, he wrote home, "had I known the mother before I opened the affair to Mr. Baker I should have entirely dropt the thoughts of that marriage." But his opinion of Mr. Baker remained high, even after the refusal, and his opinion of Louisa grew, if anything, with time. "A greater commendation I cannot make of the young lady than by pronouncing her no ways inferior to Louisa," he would write of the next girl he wanted to marry, Miss Rachel Cooke of Maryland. Of Molly Darnall, who, like Louisa, had no dowry, "I prefer her thus unprovided to all the women I have ever seen — even to Louisa," he said with a flourish. And this girl he really did marry. But then he rather spoiled the flourish by giving one of their daughters — nine years after Louisa — the unforgettable Louisa's name.

Charles Carroll had thought his life in Maryland would follow the classic formula of "rural amusements such as farming . . . united to Philosophy. . . ." But the estate his father made over to him was no little Sabine farm, and he soon found that he was not exactly a rural type. Fresh from London, he was at home in crowded, competitive, cheerful Annapolis, where there were parties all the time and somebody was always suing somebody else. From the manor, Carrollton, which his father now made over to him, he took the "appellation" Charles Carroll of Carrollton which he used the rest of his life.

Some of the friends he made in Maryland were, of course, in the close-knit, little Roman Catholic society, many of them cousins. Partly because they were afraid of being slighted and excluded by their political masters, partly because they enjoyed relaxing in each other's company, Maryland Catholics had always pretty much flocked together. It was the easiest, safest way. But this Catholic joined two clubs which expanded his social horizons greatly.

One was the Jockey Club; as breeder of the chestnut racehorse Marius, sired by Governor Sharpe's imported Othello, Charles Carroll not only contributed to "the improvement of the breed of horses," which was the club's purpose then and now, but thoroughly enjoyed himself. He was also taken into the celebrated Homony Club of Annapolis. Roman Catholics had never before been considered for social clubs. There was too much bad blood, too many chips on too many shoulders. But Charles Carroll of Carrollton slipped into place easily, and the Homony Club was extremely good for him. In this company, which cut across class as well as political and financial and now religious lines, he got to know more about Annapolis and Maryland than he had ever suspected in his sheltered, "different," only-child boyhood.

Soon, however, politics was taking most of his time. He had always been of a "puny Constitution" but he did not spare himself. Also his father could not forget that Charles Carroll of Carrollton was supposed to be managing the biggest estate in America. He worried about his neglecting that and his family.

It was not that Charles Carroll of Carrollton altogether liked politics. (For one thing, it was too much like law.) But public service was a right he had not always had. It had been hard to come by, and it behooved him now not to give it up. From 1773, when he emerged as the First Citizen, he served well first his province, then his nation and his state. Finally, however, the decision was no longer in his hands. He had always been a Federalist. The Federalist disaster in 1800 was strong enough to take even the First Citizen with it. He was out of politics at last, and the taste in his mouth was far less sweet than back in 1773 when he had stood on his porch in Annapolis and received the whole Lower House of Assembly, adjourned for the purpose of thanking him for the First Citizen letters. "Public gratitude, sir, for public services, is the patriot's dues. . . ." It had not, in the long haul, proved quite that simple.

Suddenly, leaving politics, he saw himself an old man. He was sixty-three. His father and his wife were both dead; his three surviving children were grown. The eldest, Mary, was married to Richard Caton; Catherine — Kitty — to Robert Goodloe Harper. The only son, named, of course, Charles, married Harriet Chew and became Charles Carroll of Homewood. They were all gone by 1801. Left alone in Annapolis, Mr. Carroll found it rather dull. Baltimore was the booming town now, the interesting place to be. At the house of Richard and Mary Caton, he settled down (paying board, of course) to enjoy his old age.

Everybody wanted to pay respects to Mr. Carroll of Carrollton. Old friends came; newcomers; tourists. Many of his callers came to solicit money for worthy causes, and they had come to the right place. From youth he had had a "Charity acct." "This money we must place to the Charity acct," his father wrote tersely about a borrowing relative. But most of the charities were less involuntary. His Church was, of course, his chief beneficiary; his Church's schools and colleges came next.

One interesting private charity was the manumission of his own slaves—never all of them, only those he thought could handle freedom if they had it, but there were a good many of these. He was president too, between 1828 and 1831, of the American Colonization Society, founded in 1816. But there were too few slaveholders who wanted to give up valuable property, and too few (if any) critics of slavery who wanted to buy this property from them and settle it in Liberia.

More likely to succeed were the business enterprises that were burgeoning in Baltimore, the B & O Railroad, the C & O Canal, the Second Bank of the United States; and there was still his own Baltimore Iron Works. Mr. Carroll took an interest in all of these, and in his balance at the bank, until he died.

He was never bored. The habits of study and self-improvement that he had learned at the College of St. Omers kept him busy reading. He was still reading Theocritus and Molière — never, of course, novels. He was convinced that "the frequent lecture of novels unfits the mind for solid improvement," and very sorry indeed, incidentally, that solid improvement did not interest even one of his children. Surely he suspected a matter of too much money and his own fault, but he had been called hard and stingy all his life, like his father before him, and in indulging his family and, as in the underwriting of many charities, he was perhaps answering his critics.

He did not live too long, although ninety-five would be far too long for most people. He was still riding horseback and taking cold plunges in his eighties, retained his interest in many things, retained his faculties to a remarkable degree, always had somebody who loved him ready to read aloud to him when his eyes did begin to fail.

In his extreme old age he was constantly being honored — riding in parades, sitting on platforms, accepting scrolls, listening to speeches. These ceremonial occasions were a little tiring — so much alike, so bombastic, so embarrassing to this oddly modest politician. After the death of Adams and Jefferson, who had died dramatically on the same day, the fiftieth anniversary of the Declaration of Independence, the Last Surviving Signer could not, however, refuse.

But after his own death the legend he had been in his own time began to fade. Unlike Adams and Jefferson, he was recalled chiefly by special groups — Marylanders, Roman Catholics. This was not right. Charles Carroll of Carrollton was a man for all Americans. One of the purposes of this exhibition and this publication is to give him the wide recognition due him.

ELLEN HART SMITH

Charles Carroll's Thesis from the College of Louis-le-Grand
July 8, 1757, Paris
Engraving; 41 1/8 x 26 3/4 inches
Private Collection of a Descendant

Charles Carroll of Carrollton and His Family, 1688-1832

Charles Carroll of Carrollton has always been most widely acclaimed for an honor he received by default: on July 4, 1826 with the almost simultaneous deaths of John Adams and Thomas Jefferson, he became the last surviving signer of the Declaration of Independence. That he should have reached his eighty-ninth year, the age which brought him this distinction, was remarkable and somewhat ironic. His "thin and puny habit of body" had from his youth convinced him that in a world beset with such pestilences as smallpox, yellow fever, and the "bilious cholick," he was destined for an early grave.[1] Meticulous attention to physical health was almost a fetish with him throughout his life, and he persistently urged his children and grandchildren to observe the regimen to which he attributed his longevity: "due exercise of body and mind . . . going to bed at nine o'clock and rising by five o'clock in the morning" followed by a cold bath, a brisk horseback ride, and prayers or mass. Above all, as he advised his son Charles Carroll of Homewood in 1809, one must avoid "lounging in bed after waking in the morning," for such a habit "I believe . . . to be very injurious to health, particularly to persons inclined to a corpulent habit."[2]

Veneration of Charles Carroll of Carrollton for simply outliving the other bold men who assembled in Philadelphia in the summer of 1776 to repudiate 169 years of American dependence on Great Britain, has unfortunately obscured the real significance of his having been one of that select and hopeful company. Had the Declaration been presented to the First Continental Congress, which convened in September 1774, Carroll's name would not have appeared at all, for although he had been sufficiently esteemed in Maryland since 1773 to make him an obvious choice as a delegate, Charles Carroll was a Roman Catholic, and, in Maryland, Roman Catholics had been legally barred from voting and from holding office since 1718.

He went to Philadelphia in 1774 anyway, at the request of the official Maryland delegation who valued his opinion in spite of his religion. He was hopeful that Congress, "composed of men of strong sense," would be able to "steer a proper course between Independency and subjection," noting with some relief that, in this regard, "the New England and Maryland deputies are as moderate as any."[3] Should civil war come, however, "there is and ought to be no neutrality — indeed were I permitted to remain neuter I would disdain the offer. I will endeavor to defend the liberties of my country or die with them."[4] In the light of his noble sentiments in support of, and his obvious identification with the American cause, it is startling to realize that in "An Address to the British People," one of the products of the First Continental Congress's secret deliberations, men who had *pointedly* sought Carroll's company in the social whirl precipitated by the sitting of the Congress declared the Roman Catholic religion to be "inimical to liberty and a danger to the state."[5] They were

[1] CCC to CCA, May 1, 1774. MS 206. MdHi.

[2] CCC to Charles Carroll of Homewood, July 1, 1809. MS 203. MdHi.

[3] CCC to CCA, September 9, 1774. MS 206. MdHi.

[4] CCC to CCA, September 7, 1774. MS 206. MdHi.

[5] Joseph Gurn, *Charles Carroll of Carrollton 1737-1832* (New York: P. J. Kennedy & Sons, 1932) p. 51.

"astonished," they maintained in that Address, that Parliament, in passing the Quebec Act of 1774 guaranteeing freedom of religion to Canadians, had " 'established' " in that neighborhood province, " 'a religion that has deluged your island [Britain] with blood, and dispersed impiety, bigotry, persecution, murder, and rebellion through every part of the world.' "[6]

Within eighteen months, the Second Continental Congress, faced with the imminent probability of a protracted war with Great Britain, suddenly found the support or, failing that, at least the neutrality of the Catholic Canadians crucial to the American cause. By resolution in February 1776, the Second Congress assigned to Charles Carroll of Carrollton, his second cousin Father John Carroll (later Archbishop), Samuel Chase, and Dr. Benjamin Franklin the critical task of mollifying and turning to American advantage the hostile sentiments which the First Congress's ill-conceived Address had ignited along the northern border. Chosen because of his religion and of his fluency in French to undo an insult as applicable to him as to those with whom he was to treat, Charles Carroll apparently never considered refusing the commission and set off from New York on April 2, 1776, with high hopes of serving both his country and "the poor Canadians."[7]

Despite the beautiful scenery which Carroll appreciatively described in the Journal he kept of the trip and the "interesting, uncommon, and captivating" company of the inimitable Dr. Franklin, Carroll's initial ardour for "rendering important services to my country" was rather quickly dampened.[8] Fatigue, absence from "my dearest connections," and an increasing pessimism about the mission's chances for success led him to write to his father in April 1776 in what was to become a familiar refrain whenever politics refused to yield to his "integrity . . . perseverance, and habit of business" and to assume the mathematical tidiness and rational order he preferred:[9]

> *These public honors set very heavy on me; I think I am fitter for a private station, at least such a one is more suited to my feelings and inclination . . . yet having accepted this employment, it is incumbent on me to execute it as well as possible: I must not therefore grudge time or labour.*[10]

The eventual failure of the Canadian mission to produce either an alliance or an appreciable modification of anti-American sentiments did not reflect adversely on the commissioners themselves. Charles Carroll was regarded in Maryland as having been of great service to his country in Canada,[11] and his official presence in the political arena, at the national as well as at the provincial level, was thereafter accepted as a matter of course.

Immediately upon his return in mid-June 1776 he took his place in the Maryland Convention where he was instrumental in rescinding the anti-independence instructions that body had issued to the Maryland congressional delegation on May 21. On July 5 (with overtones of the Canadian refrain), he wrote to his

[6] *Ibid.* p. 59.

[7] CCC to CCA, March 26, 1776. MS 206. MdHi.

[8] CCC to CCA, March 29, 1776; CCC to Molly, April 15, 1776, MS 206. MdHi.

[9] CCC to CCA, May 5, 1776. MS 206. MdHi.

[10] CCC to CCA, March 29-30, 1776. MS 206. MdHi.

[11] Daniel of St. Thomas Jenifer to CCA, June 16, 1776. MS 206. MdHi.

father: "Contrary to my expectations I am appointed a Deputy to Congress, and much against my inclination I find myself obliged to set off for Philadelphia in a week at fartherest." [12] He took his seat in the Second Continental Congress on July 18, was appointed to the Board of War, and voted the next day to authorize the engrossment of the Declaration — the document itself had been unanimously passed on July 15 when the objections of New York and three Pennsylvania counties were overcome — on parchment, in preparation for the signing. On August 2, along with forty-nine others, Charles Carroll of Carrollton, Roman Catholic, placed his life, his sacred honor, and a fortune described by John Adams as the "first in America" on the line by inscribing his name on the Declaration of Independence.

What the occasion meant to Carroll is difficult to say; more practical and businesslike than introspective on paper, there is no reference to it at the time in the voluminous correspondence he maintained with his father, always his most intimate confidante and associate, and scant reference to it thereafter. On July 4, 1777, Carroll remarked to his father in a letter from Philadelphia: "This day the Congress dines at Smith's Tavern: you will see by the enclosed paper it is to be celebrated as the anniversary of Independence." [13] To an overture made to him in 1829 by the District of Columbia chapter of The Friends of Civil and Religious Liberty of Ireland he is reported to have asserted that in signing the Declaration he " 'had in view not only our independence of England but the toleration of all sects professing the Christian religion and communicating to them all equal rights.' " [14]

Whether Carroll really gave much thought to religious freedom in 1776 — and the evidence suggests that he did not — his interpretation of the significance of his signing from the vantage point of his ninety-second year is quite accurate from the perspective of the present. Carroll, as the only Roman Catholic signer of the Declaration of Independence in 1776, signified the long overdue rejection of the religious persecution that had marred colonial life practically from the beginning and symbolized as well the emerging commitment of the founding fathers to freedom of conscience as a cornerstone of the "liberty" in whose name they justified their actions. In terms of the familial ambitions of the Carrolls — the relentless desire for stability and permanence which had brought Carroll's grandfather, Charles Carroll the Settler, to Maryland in 1688 and which had driven his irascible father, Charles Carroll of Annapolis, not only to amass the greatest fortune in the colonies but also to create a suitable heir to inherit it — Charles Carroll of Carrollton's signature on the Declaration of Independence was the consummate victory. It constituted the long-sought political guarantee that the Catholic Carrolls were to be at least as secure as their Protestant neighbors.

The prospects of achieving that kind of security in his native Ireland must have appeared increasingly tenuous to Charles Carroll's grandfather throughout the 1680's. The abolition of many anti-Catholic laws by Catholic Stuart monarchs, who were restored to the English throne in 1660, the year of grand-

[12] CCC to CCA, July 5, 1776. MS 206. MdHi.

[13] CCC to CCA, June 26-July 4, 1777. MS 206. MdHi.

[14] Joseph Gurn, *Charles Carroll of Carrollton*, p. 261.

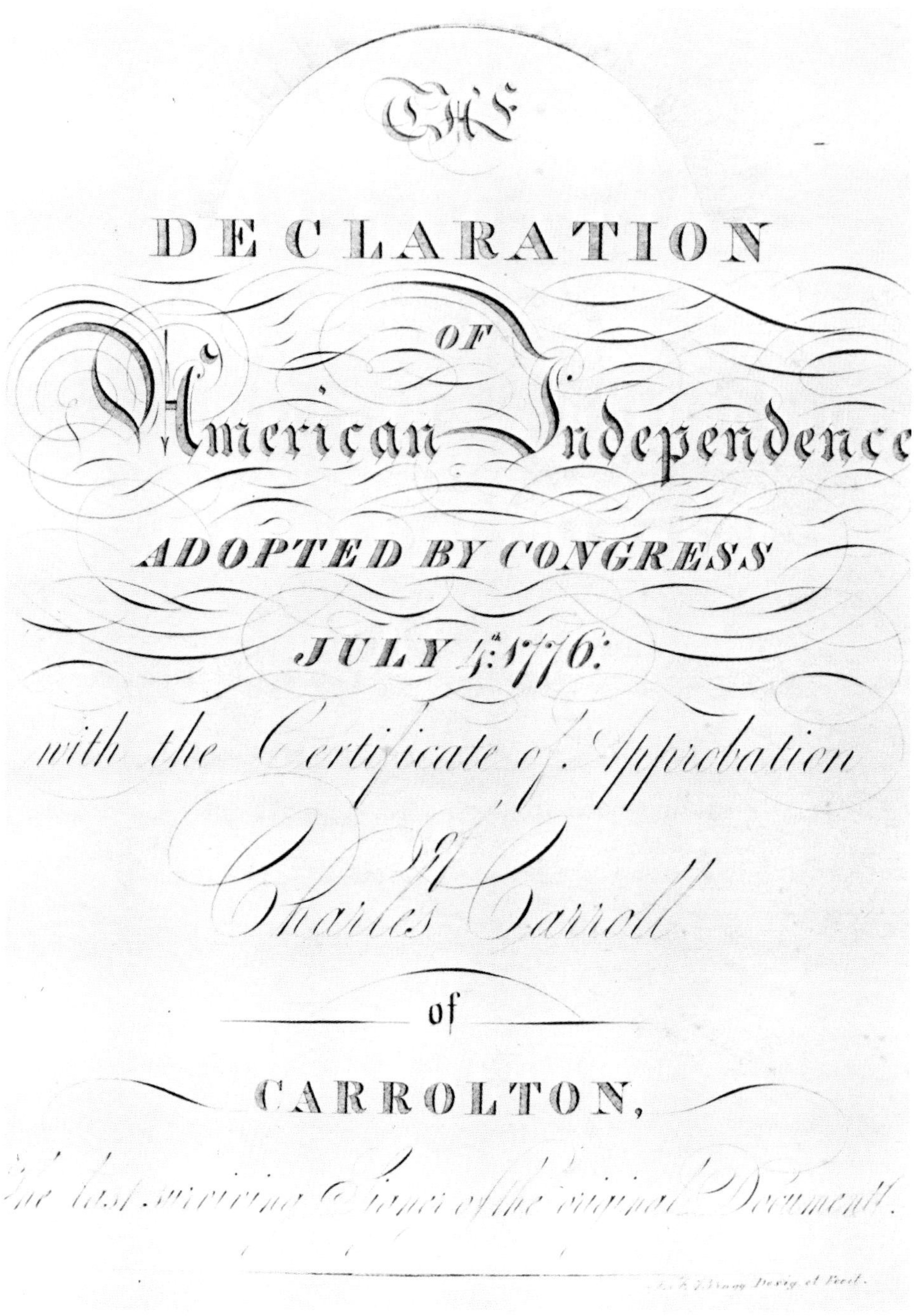

The
DECLARATION
of
American Independence
ADOPTED BY CONGRESS
JULY 4th 1776:
with the Certificate of Approbation
of
Charles Carroll
of
CARROLTON,
The last surviving Signer of the original Document.

The Declaration of American Independence with the Certificate of
Charles Carroll of Carrollton the Last Living Signer of the Original Document
One volume, 32 pp., designed and executed by Isaac Bragg of Connecticut, bound by Joseph Forster of New York City; 15 13/16 x 12 7/8 inches
Presented to the Common Council of New York, July 4, 1828
Received by the New York Historical Society from the Common Council of New York City, March 14, 1889
New York Historical Society, New York

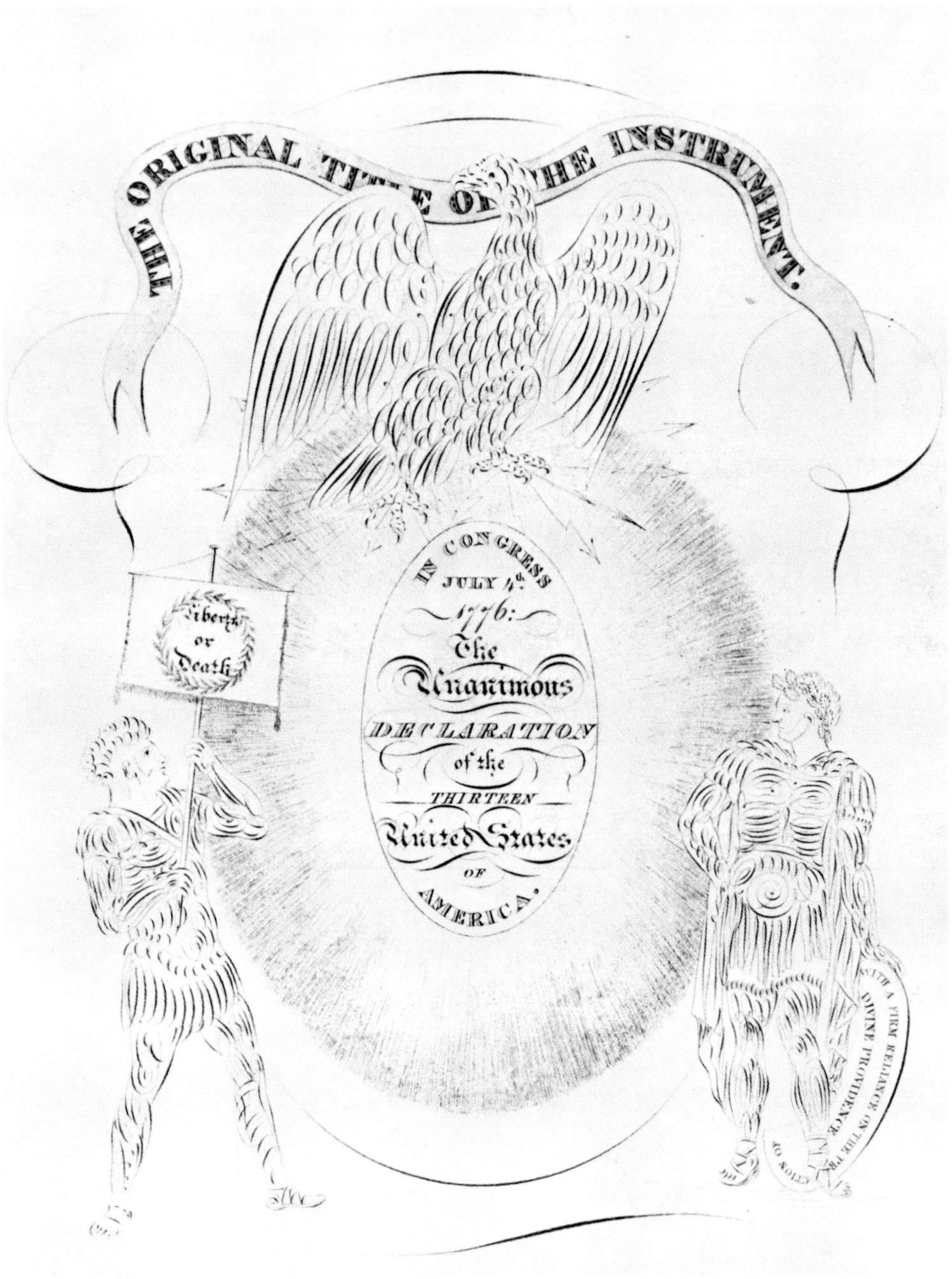
THE ORIGINAL TITLE OF THE INSTRUMENT.
IN CONGRESS JULY 4th.
1776:
The
Unanimous
DECLARATION
of the
THIRTEEN
United States
OF
AMERICA.
Liberty or Death

father Carroll's birth, could not erase from Irish consciousness the scars of the century of religious persecution which Henry VIII had begun when he secured the English throne to the House of Tudor by creating a national church. The English monarchy's "plantation of Ireland" policy, whereby estates were seized from non-conforming Irish nobles and bestowed on members of the Anglican English gentry, had produced generations of landless Irishmen whose acute awareness that the traditional hostility seethed just below the surface made them mistrust the permanence of the Stuart reforms. Therefore, when Carroll's grandfather, Charles Carroll the Settler, an urbane and erudite young man, educated at the Jesuit College of St. Omers in French Flanders and trained in law at London's Inner Temple, was given the chance to enter the service of the Calverts, Lords Baltimore and Proprietors of the Province of Maryland, he accepted it with alacrity. In 1688, armed with a commission as Attorney General of the colony, Charles Carroll the Settler set out for Maryland, determined to secure in the new world the place denied him in the old.

He had been in Maryland approximately a month when the Glorious Revolution installed the Protestant William of Orange and his wife Mary on the English throne, an event which jeopardized the position of Catholics in Maryland and threatened the power of their benefactor, the Lord Proprietor. The haven for English Catholics envisioned by the First and Second Lords Baltimore had never materialized in Maryland. Catholics did not emigrate in sufficient numbers to offset the Protestant influx, and many of the Catholics who did settle in the province were, like Charles Carroll the Settler, members of an elite. Their enjoyment of the economic and political privileges bestowed on them by the Proprietor tended to irritate and focus the frustrations of two factions within the Protestant majority — the economically less fortunate colonists struggling to wrest a bare subsistence from the new environment and the more affluent gentry rankling at its exclusion from most of the powerful and prestigious provincial offices. In the months following the Protestant ascension to the English throne, while the provincial government in Maryland temporized, awaiting the Proprietor's instructions to acknowledge the legitimacy of the new regime by issuing a proclamation of loyalty, rumors of Papist plots and Catholic/Indian conspiracies against Protestants inflamed the colony. Eager to manipulate the longstanding political, economic, and religious jealousies to their advantage, John Coode, Henry Jowles, Kenelm Cheseldyne, Nehemiah Blackiston, and other leaders of the Protestant gentry encouraged the social turmoil. In August 1689, at Coode's direction, delegates to an Associators' Convention were elected and upon convening simply took over governing the colony. In 1691 William III, in response to the appeals of this group, removed Maryland from the control of the Proprietor and appointed Sir Lionel Copley, a Protestant, governor.[15]

Infuriated by the victory of "such profigate wretches and men of scandalous living as Code" whose "absurd lyes" had simultaneously deprived Lord Baltimore of his colony and the Attorney General of his offices, Charles Carroll

[15] Lois Green Carr and David William Jordan, *Maryland's Revolution of Government 1689-1692*. (Ithaca: Cornell University Press, 1974).

the Settler publicly protested.[16] His impassioned objections and insults to the personnel of the new colonial government finally landed him in jail from which he emerged, after several terms, no less loyal but a good deal more discreet. He was ready to capitalize on the economic opportunities still available to him instead of further penalizing himself by lamenting the political ones he had lost. He practiced law in the Chancery and Prerogative Courts, retaining the Calverts as his clients, and embarked on an increasingly lucrative career as a planter/capitalist. This combination of agriculturalist and money-lender became both a characteristic occupational pattern in the Chesapeake economy and a major factor in the creation of the Carroll fortune.[17] His success was remarkable. By the end of his life, he possessed more than *sixty thousand acres of land.*[18]

The Settler's political ambitions, however, were not dead. In 1714 he traveled to Great Britain to visit his dying benefactor Charles Calvert, Third Lord Baltimore, fully cognizant of the recent conversion of Calvert's son and heir Benedict Leonard to the Church of England which would likely return Maryland to its former proprietors. Carroll was confident that Benedict Leonard's apostasy would not invalidate the rewards due such a faithful and diligent protector of Calvert interests as himself. These happy prospects were only temporarily complicated by the sudden death of Benedict Leonard while the Settler was still at work settling the father's estate. The Fifth Lord Baltimore was a minor, and it was probably gratitude for timely assistance in their unexpected current situation as well as for two and a half decades of loyal service that led young Charles Calvert and his guardian Lord Guilford to send the Settler back to Maryland commissioned as the Proprietor's Agent and Receiver General of their newly regained province.

To the Protestant governor of Maryland, Captain John Hart, the appointment of an unrelenting Papist to collect the colonial revenues from which his salary would be paid and to conduct *all* Lord Baltimore's public and private business in the colony was both a personal insult — he had long been irritated by the Settler's arrogance — and a threat to his administrative powers. Determined to remove Carroll from his positions, Hart demanded that he swear the oaths of allegiance, abhorrence, and abjuration which the Maryland Assembly had voted in July 1716 to require of all officeholders. Hart knew full well that no Catholic could possibly ascribe to the repudiation of Papal authority and denial of transubstantiation which the oaths contained.[19] By 1718 Carroll's provocations and Hart's retaliations had resulted in the passage of laws by the Maryland Assembly which effectively excluded Catholics from participation in the political life of the colony until 1776 when the reputation of the Settler's grandson overcame them. Catholics were forbidden, on pain of fines and imprison-

[16] *Archives of Maryland,* vol. VIII (Baltimore: Maryland Historical Society, 1890), pp. 124-125.

[17] Aubrey C. Land, ed., *Bases of Plantation Society* (New York: Harper and Row, 1969).

[18] Thomas Meagher Field, ed., *Unpublished Letters of Charles Carroll of Carrollton . . .* (New York: U.S. Catholic Historical Society, 1902).

[19] J. Thomas Scharf, *A History of Maryland.* 3 vols. (Hatboro, Pennsylvania: Tradition Press, 1967), pp. 378-383.

ment, to vote, to hold office, to practice law, to educate their children, or to worship publicly.

The Settler died in July 1720, leaving his wife, Madam Mary Carroll, and four of the ten children she had borne him: Charles Carroll of Annapolis, his legal heir (an elder son Henry had died in 1719), two daughters, Mary and Eleanor, and another son, Daniel Carroll of Duddington. The Settler's estate, which was divided among his widow and the children, was a considerable one in both real and personal property as indicated by the fact that its executors were required to post bond of £60,000 sterling — or approximately 2/3's the value of the whole — the largest bond ever required in Maryland up to that time. In 1723 Charles Carroll of Annapolis reached his majority and came home from school in France to assume control of his family's fortune.

Denied access to political power, Charles Carroll of Annapolis turned his considerable energies to attaining wealth as the only available means of securing the Carroll foothold in Maryland. With considerable acumen he set about re-assembling the Settler's estate which had been parceled out to his mother, his sisters, and brother, since by consolidating their portions he controlled considerably more working capital than that which would have been available to him from his share alone. For this ultimately self-serving administrative task, which included collecting rents and interest on money lent, he charged his relatives a flat 5% commission per transaction. Within a few years, the Settler's estate was £600 in debt to its administrator. By 1731, Charles Carroll of Annapolis, in partnership with Benjamin Tasker, Daniel Dulany, and a Protestant cousin Dr. Charles Carroll, was able to invest £3,500 in establishing the Baltimore Iron Works on the banks of the Patapsco River. By 1764 this venture was yielding him about £400 annually.[20] In addition, he continued to expand his father's money-lending operations and estimated by the mid-1760's that he had in excess of £24,000 at interest.[21]

Charles Carroll of Annapolis' management of his family's finances was publicly questioned in 1757 by his nephew, Charles Carroll the Younger, a son of his brother Daniel who had died in 1734. More irritated than injured by his nephew's charges that he had been defrauded of part of the inheritance due him from the estates of his grandmother, his aunts, and his father, Charles Carroll of Annapolis demanded that the suit be submitted to arbitration. Messrs. Hill and Waring, the arbitrators, were not convinced by the account book the accused prepared for his defense nor by his justifications of the fees he had charged his family for administering their funds, and they ordered him to reimburse his nephew in the amount of £900![22]

Charles Carroll of Annapolis' extraordinary drive to enlarge his fortune was matched by his determination to fashion an heir mentally and morally fit to receive and preserve that grand legacy. The relationship through which this goal was achieved so absorbed both the father and the son for forty-five years that neither ever had another human involvement of comparable intensity.

[20] Florence Reynolds, "Charles Carroll of Annapolis, Colonial Capitalist." Master's Thesis, Johns Hopkins University, 1970; CCA to CCC, April 10, 1764. MS 220. MdHi.

[21] CCA to CCC, January 9, 1764. MS 206. MdHi.

[22] Florence Reynolds, "Charles Carroll of Annapolis"; MS 211 and MS 211.1. MdHi.

CHARLES CARROLL OF ANNAPOLIS
John Wollaston? (Fl. 1736-1767) or John Hesselius? (1728-1778)
Cat. No. 8

The relationship began on September 8, 1737 with the birth of their only child — the son they affectionately called "Charley" — to Charles Carroll of Annapolis and his common-law wife, Elizabeth Brooke. The relationship of Charley's parents, as indicated by their marriage certificate dated February 15, 1757,[23] was not legalized until their son was twenty years old. Since no document containing specific reasons for the delay has yet come to light, an explanation must be postulated on the basis of Charles Carroll of Annapolis' *modus operandi* within the legal framework of his time.

The intensity of Charles Carroll of Annapolis' economic ambitions, as suggested by his administration of the estates of his nearest relatives, indicates an economic motive — namely the protection of the Carroll fortune from both

[23] MS 1893. MdHi.

the dower right, which entitled a widow to one-third of her husband's estate, and the guardianship right, which placed her in charge of the other two-thirds on behalf of minor children. A widow with access to such a fortune the size of Carroll's would be irresistible, and upon remarrying might carry the Carroll legacy into "a strange family," a circumstance against which Charles Carroll of Annapolis was careful to warn his son.[24] If, however, Charles Carroll of Annapolis died unmarried, with or without issue, his estate would at least remain in Carroll hands, probably, as indicated by his will, circa 1760, in those of his kinsman Daniel Carroll of Rock Creek.[25]

When Charles Carroll of Carrollton reached his majority, fully formed in accordance with all the standards by which his father measured worth, it was necessary, prior to the marriage ceremony which legitimatized him, to nullify his mother's dower right; otherwise, upon his father's death, one-third of the inheritance would still go to her. This was done in the agreement signed by Elizabeth Brooke and Charles Carroll of Annapolis on November 7, 1756, in which, in exchange for the sum of £100 sterling a year — less than a tenth of his annual income, Miss Brooke waived her dower right and relinquished all claims on any part of her husband's estate, either real or personal.[26]

Why, given his wealth, did she willingly settle for so little? She had no reason to doubt either his affection or that of her son or that they would provide for her, as is revealed by her husband's will[27] and by the last letter she wrote to Charley before her death:

> *Yr tender affection for my welfare & health put me in mind of what you used to tell me when a little Boy lolling and fondling about me — that you loved me dearly & should always have ye same fondness and affection for me during life. Yr behaviour & yr regard ye have shewn me hither to convince me of the truth of those words which I assure you, my dear, gives me no small comfort.*[28]

Charles Carroll of Annapolis was sufficiently sensitive to her feelings to reprimand Charley in 1754 for not beginning his letters "*Dr Papa and Mama* as I formerly directed" and for not having written "to your Mother this year. Although she is not, she has reason to be displeased. I attribute it to inattention, but for the future, be more considerate."[29] Loved or not, however, she had little real choice about signing the settlement, for she was completely dependent upon her husband and her son financially as well as emotionally. In June 1737, three months before her child was born, the will of her father Clement Brooke was proved. She was not mentioned in the disposition of his fairly sizeable estate, indicating that she was left with no material resources of her own.[30]

Charles Carroll of Annapolis' attitude toward his son was based on a single-minded conviction that he alone knew what was best for his son and that he

[24] CCA to CCC, January 5, 1762. MS 206. MdHi.

[25] MS 206. MdHi.

[26] MS 2018. MdHi.

[27] MS 206. MdHi.

[28] Elizabeth Brooke Carroll to CCC, September 10, 1760. MS 431. MdHi.

[29] CCA to CCC, September 30, 1754. MS 220. MdHi.

[30] Hall of Records, Annapolis.

was always capable of acting in conformity with that knowledge—convictions that his son accepted without question. There were times when Charley might complain about, or protest against, some paternal instruction that caused him unhappiness — like that which kept him in London so long against his "inclination" — but he never rebelled. Only once, in the controversy over the legal tender bill in 1777, did he refuse to do something that his father very much wanted him to do, and then he refused, not because he thought his father was wrong, but because "Papa" could not see that what was *right* and what was *necessary* were not the same.

Within the relationship between father and son this basic conviction was manifested in a juxtaposition of affection and expectation that produced, without rancor or hostility, precisely the heir that Charles Carroll of Annapolis' dream demanded. There is no evidence to suggest that the long delayed marriage was used as a weapon to coerce his son's progress toward acceptability; Charley's earnest desire to please and satisfy his father, though undoubtedly accentuated both by his being sent so far from home at such a tender age and by his constant awareness of the money — which he must have always known how his father valued — invested in his development, is too obviously sincere and consistent not to have been congenital. "You may be assured Dr. Papa I shall strive not to turn into an abuse the confidence you put in me. I shall endeavor to manage my little affairs with all the care and attention I am capable of by avoiding the extremes of affectation and meanness. I keep strick accounts and shall send them to you at the end of the year so you will be able to Judge yourself whether I have spent foolishly or no."[31] The books Charley read, the places he visited, the people he met and observed, all contributed to his erudition, his social grace, and his gentility, but it was his relationship with his father and his father alone that made him who he was.

The fascinating correspondence between Papa and Charley which reveals Charles Carroll of Annapolis' attention to every aspect of his son's physical, intellectual, moral, and social development began in 1749 when Charley at age 11 was sent to the college of St. Omers in France along with several other sons of the Maryland Catholic gentry — Robert Brent, and his cousins Watty Hoxton and Jacky (John) Carroll — to begin an educational odyssey that lasted sixteen years.

In 1753 upon completion of the formidable curriculum at St. Omers — English, Latin, French, and Greek grammar, "great and little figures," spelling and penmanship — Charley moved on to the Jesuit College at Rheims where the year he spent studying classical and modern literature deepened his affection for authors whose works he had first encountered at St. Omers. "I find no conversation more agreeable," he later wrote, "than that of a Horace's, a Virgil's, or a Raine's," though at times he would

> *forsake the . . . melodious harmony of the muses for the profitable and faithful lessons of History where I learn to be wise at the expense of others and to attain to true glory by the example of the great, good, and Just.*[32]

[31] CCC to CCA, February 4, 1758. MS 206. MdHi.

[32] CCC to CCA, June 14, 1758. MS 206. MdHi.

Since the society in which Charley would move in Rheims was different from that at St. Omers, Charles Carroll of Annapolis thought it time to instruct him on how to determine and assume appropriate behavior in a variety of situations:

> *You must view everything worth notice carefully and with Attention, especially the behaviour of all about you. What may become a man in one country may be very ridiculous in another. Before you act, observe the actions of others. None but brainless thoughtless people do otherwise . . . but be not so servile an Imitator as to let it be seen that you Copy, but let your actions be your own, Natural, and Set easy on you. . . .*[33]

Besides Charley's behavior, Papa also gave his attention to the boy's physical progress, specifically to his posture, his hair, and his teeth. He hoped, he wrote rather severely, that Charley had broken himself of his habit of "stooping and pokeing" out his head, as "it is absolutely inconsistent with yr. carriage! Unless you have grown since I last saw you, you cannot afford to lose the least of yr. height. I remember you measured 5 ft. 5 inches [summer 1757]. What do you measure now?"[34] In regard to his hair, Papa recalled that he had had "good hair when a child, if it continues so, pray wear it, it will become you better than a wig, and besides you will be more in the fashion."[35] And, if Charley did not want to wind up like Papa who had already lost "several" teeth to "scurvy" in the gums he had better heed Mama's advice on dental care![36]

In 1755 he left Rheims for Paris where he was to spend two years at the College of Louis-le-Grand concentrating on philosophy and science. His mother, writing to him in September 1756, feared her news of home would seem "insipid" to him in comparison with "le beau monde" of Paris, but Charley, eagerly anticipating the visit from Papa planned for late summer of 1757, found instead that time passed all too slowly, although, he hastened to add he was not "idle," but busy studying French and preparing his graduating thesis.[37]

In December 1757, miserable that the long-awaited visit with his father had ended, Charley set out for Bourges, grumbling irritably about the inadequacies of the "publick coach" to which he chose to attribute the "slow, dull, melancholy" nature of the journey and via which he swore never to travel again.[38] During the summer of 1758 he laid aside his Roman and French civil law books and refreshed himself with a short trip through the Loire Valley on which he met Miss Alcock, the "young, pretty, witty daughter" of a button manufacturer who, much to Papa's consternation, "amused" Charley even more than the "curious and amusing" method by which her father made buttons! Could it have been Miss Alcock, whom Charley rather quickly discovered to be "very mediocre though spirited and beautiful" who prompted Papa's terse command to his son at the end of that summer — "Avoid any intimacy or

[33] CCA to CCC, September 30, 1754. MS 220. MdHi.

[34] CCA to CCC, ca. 1759. MS 220, MdHi; CCA to CCC, August 20, 1758. MS 206, MdHi.

[35] CCA to CCC, September 30, 1754. MS 220. MdHi.

[36] CCA to CCC, September 30, 1754. MS 220. MdHi.

[37] Elizabeth Brooke to CCC, September 8, 1756. MS 206. MdHi; CCC to CCA, July 26, 1757. MS 206. MdHi.

[38] CCC to CCA, December 19, 1757. MS 206. MdHi.

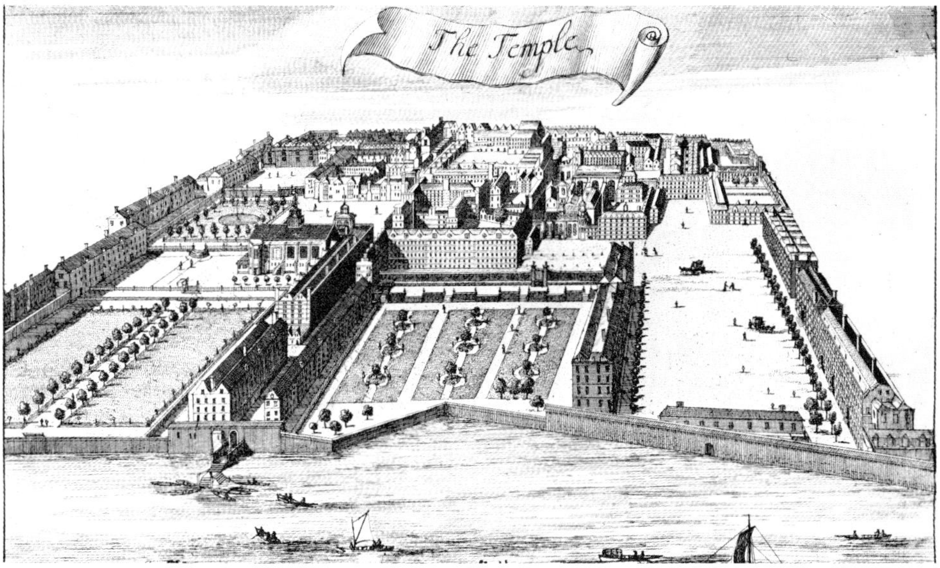

THE TEMPLE
Engraving, 1755
Legend: *The Temple / Published Recording to Act of Parliament 1755 for Stow's Survey / 54*
8 x 13 inches
From the book: *A Survey of the Cities of London and Westminster . . .* by John Stow, 1698, vol. I, 6th ed., 1954, p. 744, plate 54
Library of Congress, Washington, D.C.

familiarity with ye fair Sex, especially Visits or Conversations without Witnesses!"[39]

The death of his tutor Mr. Champion and "the stingy behaviour of my landlady" led Charley to quit Bourges in 1759[40] and return to Paris to complete his study of civil law. In late August of that year, he left France for London, arriving on September 2 to begin five years of training in English law.

Eighteenth century London was a far different world from any Charley had lived in before — a sophisticated, and, in his father's judgment (he had visited there in 1757 after seeing his son in Paris), a corrupt metropolis, teeming with such subtle temptations and such clever traps that only resolute and constant vigilance could keep a young man from being ensnared. Always before, even in Paris, Charley had lived and studied under the watchful care of the Jesuits; now, by his own admission, he was "in an open sea." "My present situation," he wrote Papa in January 1760,

> *is the most dangerous I have ever been in . . . a young person's passions are strong of themselves and need no outward encouragement; but when roused by occasions, strengthened by example, fired with wine and jovial company become almost irresistable . . . the greatest resolution, prudence, & virtue are requisite to protect me from such contagion . . .* [yet] *who can promise to others, even to himself to remain always virtuous?*[41]

[39] CCC to parent, June 14, 1758. MS 206. MdHi; CCC to parents, August 30, 1758. MS 206. MdHi; CCA to CCC, August 10, 1758. MS 206. MdHi.

[40] CCC to CCA, February 17, 1759. MS 206. MdHi.

[41] CCC to CCA, January 29, 1760. MS 206. MdHi.

It is doubtful that Papa, whose concern with Charley's behaviour had increased in intensity as the boy grew into young manhood, took much comfort from his son's self-doubting candor. Determined that the naive and inexperienced lad in whom he had invested so much psychic energy and so much money should not be swept off his feet into marriage by some alluring London temptress whose father, he darkly suspicioned, would be leering greedily at the renowned Carroll fortune, Papa began an intensive campaign designed to put Charley on his guard in all association with females. For his pains, he finally received a rather unsettling letter of reassurance from Charley who seems, for maybe the only time in his life, to have been twitting Papa just a little:

> *I can't close this letter without touching on that part of your precautioning me against too great familiarity with women. A most necessary precaution indeed for what is so deceiving, so engaging as women! I have often wondered why Providence has bestowed such art, such sagacity on that sex and at the same time so much beauty. . . . I have frequently remarked that the most beautiful are always the most powerful, at least with me. . . . Ye strongest, wisest, best of men have been ensnared by women and brought to utter destruction: what then have I not to fear who am so weak? Great no doubt are the charms of that pleasing deceitful sex, and surpassed by nothing but their art in setting them off to ye best advantage & in rendering them more fatal. However to be serious I hope to satisfy you in this point as in all others, & never will, you may depend on it, think of marriage without your previous consent and knowledge.*[42]

Charley's general unhappiness with his London situation had little to do with women, however; the causes of his discontent were far less exotic. The Inns of Law, located near the old Globe Theatre, were "deficient" in "the choice of good company." "The genteelest company" was "confined to the upper end of town," too far away — and too expensive a society — for the law student.[43] Matters were further complicated by the fact that he quite simply hated the law: its "intricacies" and "subtleties," its endless difficulties of "interpretation" alternately "frightened," "perplexed," "dismayed," and finally "disgusted" him. His mind had been trained in classical literature, after all, impressed with the purity of rational thought and reinforced by Papa's constant iteration of the principles and standards of acceptable conduct. Small wonder that he found the common law uncertain and obscure, "founded upon and still subsisting by villainy." [44] In addition to its relativism the law possessed another major defect, at least from Charley's point of view: he was barred from ever practicing it because of his religion. Why, he beseeched Papa, must he endure "perpetual banishment" in order to learn a profession that, practically speaking, would be useless to him?[45]

Charley was also kept in a state of anxiety by his father's continuing threats to quit Maryland entirely in order to escape religious persecution. The endurance of Maryland Catholics, and especially of Charles Carroll of Annapolis, had been tested to the limit when the Maryland Assembly, on the pretext of insuring their

42 CCC to CCA, January 29, 1760. MS 206. MdHi.

43 CCC to parents, November 13, 1759; CCC to CCA, July 16, 1761. MS 206. MdHi.

44 CCC to CCA, April 29, 1763. MS 206. MdHi.

45 CCC to CCA, April 10, 1760. MS 206. MdHi.

loyalty to the English side in the hostilities which began against the Catholic French and their Indian allies in 1756, had saddled them with a double tax! It was almost more than Charles Carroll of Annapolis could stand; nothing, until the passage of the infamous legal tender bill in 1777, ever infuriated him more. His son quite agreed that the law was merely a clever ruse on the part of "an ignorant, base, contemptible rabble" to get its hands on "other men's property," and he was willing to confront William Calvert, Lord Baltimore, and Mr. Sharpe, brother of the current Maryland Governor, at a dinner party with the injustice of the law (although to no avail).[46] However, Charley could not see any point in leaving Maryland for a Catholic province like Louisiana for then "you will only exchange religious for civil Tyranny, and in my opinion of ye two the greatest evil." He knew of no Catholic state, he told Papa, in which "the greatest blessing, civil liberty, is enjoyed." [47]

The general malaise compounded of all these factors deepened into depression when in June 1761, three months after the events, Charley received his father's letter telling of his mother's final illness and death. He was stunned at the "afflicting" news:

What comfort can there be for so great a loss . . . I loved my Mama most tenderly . . . What fond delusive hopes have I entertained of seeing her again! I was too credulous: all my imaginary Joys are vanished in an instant: they are succeeded by the bitter cruel thoughts of never seeing more my loved lost mother: The greatest blessing I wished for in this life was to see, to enjoy my Parents after so long a separation, to comfort, to support them in advanced age; one is for ever snatched from me! May God Almighty Dr Papa preserve yr health & grant you a long life: Were you to leave me too, oh then I shou'd be completely miserable indeed. . . I wish you wou'd permit me to return to Maryland in the next fleet. I am only doing here what I cou'd do as well at home. . . . I can apply as closely to the law in yr. house as in the temple: what more distractions shall I meet with in Annapolis than in London? [48]

Charley's desires for an early return to Maryland were suddenly mitigated in the fall of 1763: "If I meet with success in this enterprise it will be absolutely impossible for me to return to Maryland this spring; I am afraid that my voyage must be put off to the spring following." [49] "This enterprise" was the courting of Miss Louisa Baker, a seventeen year old, convent-educated girl made known to Charley through his old tutor Mr. Crookshanks during the Paris portion of a continental trip. His father had, characteristically, provided Charley with the criteria for choosing a wife a year and a half earlier when his son was in the depths of his despair with no thoughts of marriage, much less of a specific girl. Charles Carroll of Annapolis' cardinal rule in wife-picking — as in everything else — was that the head must rule the "passions!" That point established, there were three categories to be considered: her character and physique, her family background, and her fortune. On the first count, she must be "Virtuous, Sensible, good-natured, complaisant, complying, & of a Cheerful Disposition,"

[46] CCC to CCA, September 16, 1760; CCC to CCA, April 10, 1760. MS 206. MdHi.

[47] CCC to CCA, April 10, 1760. MS 220, nos. 48, 49. MdHi.

[48] CCC to CCA, June 10, 1761. MS 206. MdHi.

[49] CCC to CCA, October 11, 1763. MS 206. MdHi.

and Catholic, of course, (Charley had already sworn never to marry a Protestant.) She should also be "of good size and well-proportioned and free from any natural defects of Lameness, Deafness, Squinting, Stammering, Stuttering" for such disorders might imply "gout" or "consumption" and might be "in the blood." She must be of a good family, considering that the Carrolls, as he was in the process of having a genealogist verify, were "descended from princes;" moreover, "the character . . . of ye father and mother & the Regularity of the Family are seriously to be weighed, for you will not geather Grapes from Thorns!" And, finally, there was the fortune, which, "in Prudence ought not to be overlooked," but at the same time,

> *ought not to be preferred or even put in competition with ye other qualities I have taken notice of & which I wish you may find in a wife . . . A nobleman would not suffer an undersize, Pyebale, Walleyed, Spavined Mare at Stud, and he shall urge his love to marry a Hump Back Puny woman with a great fortune, had he not a greater affection for his beast than his family?* [50]

It was not long before Charles Carroll of Annapolis began to worry that Louisa's attractions and her family might combine to persuade his son to remain abroad; ". . . see you I must," he insisted, "& when my eyes are closed live where you please. You know I have long been impatient to be with you & for yr good have long deprived myself of the Pleasure." [51] He needn't have been concerned for Charley had made it clear early on in his suit that he would never live apart from his father and that "the situation of our affairs absolutely require my residence in Maryland." He would never "sacrifice the future aggrandisement of our family to a woman!" [52]

The negotiations, which ultimately were fruitless, lasted approximately six months, most of which time Charles Carroll of Annapolis was distraught because Charley's letters were not sufficiently informative: "could you not learn what Mr. Baker is supposed to be worth, where his Estate lays, of what it consists, what fortune you suppose he may be able to give his daughter?" [53] he wrote Charley plaintively in February 1764. By this time, however, Mr. Baker had decided that Louisa was too young and sheltered to marry, and he suggested that Charley return in a few years to try again.[54] Stung by the rejection, Charley decided he was well out of the suit; "had I known the mother before I opened the affair to Mr. Baker, I should have entirely dropt the thoughts of that marriage." Miss Baker's "notions" exceeded her fortune anyway; "a domestick wife not so fond of show and parade, who is not above the business of her family will best suit me." [55]

It was time to come home to Maryland; Charley's odyssey was over at last. He booked passage on the Randolph due to sail under Captain Waller in September 1764 for the James River, and by mid-February 1765, as noted in

[50] CCA to CCC, September 1, 1762. MS 206, nos. 83, 84. MdHi.

[51] CCA to CCC, January 9, 1764. MS 206. MdHi.

[52] CCC to CCA, November 12, 1763. MS 206. MdHi.

[53] CCA to CCC, February 28, 1764. MS 206. MdHi.

[54] John Baker to CCC, December 15, 1763. MS 206. MdHi.

[55] CCC to CCA, March 21, 23, 1764; CCC to CCA, July 17, 1764. MS 206. MdHi.

The Maryland Gazette, "Charles Carroll Junr, Esq." had arrived at his father's house in Annapolis. As his father had promised during the courtship of Louisa, he gave his son upon his return the 10,000 acre manor, Carrollton, located in what is now Frederick County from which his son took the name which distinguished him.

The Annapolis to which Charley returned was entering what William Eddis, secretary to Governor Eden and an observant diarist, styled her "golden age," and was a gay little town with a polished and affluent society. The fine houses and splendid horses and carriages attested to the wealth of upper class Annapolitans whose frequent and sumptuous amusements seemed so profuse at times to Eddis that he wondered how pocketbooks and health could stand them! In addition to the balls, dinners, and performances staged purely for the social elite by such exclusive groups as the Maryland Jockey Club, the Governor, in order to increase his popularity, frequently financed public balls and provided purses for horse races. Governor Ogle had given an impetus to breeding fine horses in 1748 by importing some thoroughbreds, and other upper crust families like the Taskers had followed suit.[56] Charles Carroll of Carrollton had himself brought two mares home with him from London and had received from his father as a homecoming gift a fine horse named Nimble worth more than £100. With fortnightly assemblies, "routs," races, plays, and balls the returned traveler who had written in 1761 that London had "certainly more amusements, more avocations" than Annapolis must have been pleasantly surprised![57]

He must also have been pleasantly surprised at the increased social access enjoyed by members of his faith. His father as a young man had been far more restricted in his social life than Charles Carroll of Carrollton found himself to be. Religion was not an impediment to his inclusion in the Homony Club, a pseudo-literary gentlemen's group, although in the 1740's its predecessor the Tuesday Club had excluded Catholics from membership. For several years until the dispute with Great Britain divided them into Tories and Patriots and ended their pleasant interludes forever, Charles Carroll of Carrollton regularly enjoyed the society of the other Homony Club members: Governor Eden, his secretary Mr. Eddis, the prominent Anglican rector, the Reverend Mr. Jonathan Boucher, Lloyd Dulany, Richard Sprigg, John Brice, John Hall, Thomas Jennings, Anthony Stewart, Charles Wallace, and Robert Couden. The economic power represented by the fortune Charles Carroll of Annapolis had accumulated and the emerging sense among Marylanders after the Stamp Act crisis in 1765 that the new loyalties which were forming cut across old religious divisions combined to smooth Carrollton's way into the echelon of society for which he was so admirably qualified.

Within a year after his return, Charles Carroll of Carrollton was engaged to be married to his cousin Rachel Cooke, a girl of "good sense", a "Sweet temper", and "a modesty that would charm a rake". She was, he wrote to a friend in

[56] Julia Cherry Spruill, *Women's Life and Work in the Southern Colonies.* (New York: W. W. Norton Company, 1972), pp. 91-95.

[57] CCC to CCA, June 10, 1761. MS 206. MdHi.

London, in "no ways inferior to Louisa!" [58] In November 1766 before the ceremony could take place, Miss Cooke fell sick, and within three weeks, to the surprise of her doctors who had not believed her illness to be serious, she was dead. At twenty-nine and of a "puny constitution" himself with two unsuccessful courtships to his credit and as far from producing the next Carroll heir as he had ever been, Charles Carroll of Carrollton secluded himself at Doughoregan Manor, the family seat. He planned to "submit patiently" if not "cheerfully" to "the crosses and trials of this life," to "drink up the very dregs of it." [59]

Either the cup was more shallow than he anticipated or he was a very fast drinker! At any rate, by August 1767 he was writing his English friend William Graves of his intention to marry another cousin, nineteen-year-old Molly Darnall who, with her mother Rachel, had been members of Charles Carroll of Annapolis' household since April 1761. This arrangement had resulted from the scandalous career of Henry Darnall III, Molly's grandfather, whose habit of living beyond his means brought him to public disgrace and his family to financial ruin. In 1755, Mr. Darnall, aided by Charles Carroll of Annapolis who provided the £1000 sterling security bond, obtained the position of Naval Officer of the Patuxent. In the spring of 1761, Darnall was found to have embezzled £1600 sterling from the public till and was hastily removed from office. Implacably angered, Charles Carroll of Annapolis moved swiftly to recover the £1000 sterling the "ungrateful" gentleman's malfeasance had cost him, and on April 22, 1761, Henry Darnall III and his eldest son, Henry Jr. (Molly's father) signed an indenture forfeiting to Charles Carroll of Annapolis their rights to the remainder of their once sizeable fortune. "We can," Charles Carroll of Annapolis assured Charley with grim satisfaction, "hold ye lands during ye lives of ye Father & Eldest Son at least, by wh. we can so destroy them as to make ye 2nd Son's chance of ye reversion not worth anything." His reputation and finances in shambles, Henry Darnall III fled to Europe where he lived for a number of years on the brink of poverty. The career of his eldest son, Henry Jr. remains tantilizingly obscure. Although his signature appears on the marriage settlement of his daughter and Charles Carroll of Carrollton dated June 4, 1768, he is mentioned in the family correspondence only once. In September 1772, the Carrolls were informed that he had been executed. His crimes are to date unknown.[60]

Molly brought no more to her marriage with Charles Carroll of Carrollton than Elizabeth Brooke had brought to Charles Carroll of Annapolis; her lack of any financial resource of her own made her completely dependent on her husband. It is interesting to note in this connection the care which Charles Carroll of Carrollton took in writing his will to assure that neither of his daughters nor any of his granddaughters would ever find themselves in such a vulnerable position. His bequests to each of his female descendants were invari-

[58] CCC to William Graves, November 27, 1766; CCC to Christopher Bird, September 17, 1765. MS 203.1, MdHi.

[59] CCC to Christopher Bird, March 8, 1767. MS 203.1, MdHi.

[60] CCA to CCC, April 16, 1761, MS 220, MdHi; CCA to CCC, May 21, 1761, MS 220, MdHi; Provincial Court Deeds, BT 4: 1759-1762, folios 280-281, MdHi; CCA to CCC, May 21, 1761, MS 220, MdHi; CCC to CCA, August 17, 1763, MS 206, MdHi; CCA to CCC, September 6, 1772, MS 206 MdHi.

ably styled "for her sole and separate use free from the control of power of her present or any future husband".[61] Thus dignity and security, benefits of being born to "an independent fortune" which Charley had perceived while a student in London, were extended to two generations of Carroll female offspring.[62]

What was she like, the girl Charles Carroll of Carrollton succeeded in marrying on June 5, 1768? She suited her father-in-law — after all he had practically raised her and asserted proudly that during her seven years in his house he had "never had reason to chide her." Their mutual affection was deep and genuine, though he hastened to assure people that she was his son's "Choice!" [63] The bridegroom described her to his friend Graves as being of "a good family without any money," but insisted that even so he preferred her "to all the women I have ever seen — even Louisa!"[64] Molly was pretty and spirited, and the young Carrolls led an active social life in Annapolis where they lived in "Papa's" house, Papa and Mrs. Darnall having removed to Doughoregan. Molly was, at least in her father-in-law's frugal opinion, somewhat extravagant; noting the orders and bills that flowed between Annapolis and London, and the quantities of plate and furniture which kept arriving, he expressed a "wish" that Molly would not order any "Superfluities!" "Enjoy your fortune, keep an hospitable table," he advised the junior Carrolls, "But lay out as little money as possible in dress, furniture, and show of any sort; decency is the only point to be aimed at." [65]

The first baby, a daughter named Elizabeth after Carroll's mother, was born in 1766 and lived less than a year. Six more pregnancies followed in rapid succession, and by 1780, Molly had borne seven children and buried three — her first, her third, Louisa Rachel, and her fifth, Anne. Her last baby, named Eliza, born in 1780, survived her by only a year. The second child, "Little Pol," as her doting grandfather called her, was born in September 1770, and became her father's favorite. In 1775, the long-desired son and heir, another Charles Carroll, later called of Homewood, arrived, "ye finest Boy in the world, as Molly says to her Mama!"[66] Catherine, nicknamed Kitty, the third Carroll child who lived to maturity, was born in 1778.

The rigors of child-bearing did not enhance Molly's health. By the time Kitty was born, she was more and more frequently "indisposed," with pains in her breast and in her stomach. To ease her discomfort — the "tar water," emetics, and other available remedies having been of no help — Molly turned to laudanum, an opium derivative, which she was using with such frequency by 1778 that both Papa and Charley were alarmed: "tell her I beg her never to touch laudanum which I hear she still takes; it is as bad as dram drinking," Papa urged Charley. In the spring of 1779, she resolved, Charley wrote his father, "not to

[61] Will of Charles Carroll of Carrollton, in Kate Mason Rowland, *Life and Correspondence of Charles Carroll of Carrollton,* vol. II (New York: G. Putnam and Sons, 1898), Appendix C, pp. 393-431.

[62] CCC to CCA, January 29, 1760. MS 206. MdHi.

[63] CCA to William Graves, December 23, 1768. MS 206. MdHi.

[64] CCC to William Graves, August 27, 1767; CCC to William Graves, January 16, 1768. MS 203.1, MdHi.

[65] CCA to CCC, November 30, 1772; CCA to CCC, June 1, 1772. MS 206. MdHi.

[66] CCA to CCC, May 17, 1775. MS 206. MdHi.

take any more opium," and in an effort to improve her health, he took her to Bath that summer to take the "waters." Though she gained weight there as both her appetite and digestion improved, the springs had no lasting effect, and by May of 1781 Charles Carroll of Annapolis was terribly concerned: "I think she cannot hope for health if she will not resolve to overcome her strange appetite for Chalk & Opium. I earnestly begg it for the sake of her family and children, and as I love her." A certain air of resignation crept slowly between the lines of the letters as the days passed and Molly's addiction continued — "Molly is some better," "Molly is indifferent," "Molly is about as usual." [67]

In spite of her uncertain health, she oversaw a good portion of the domestic economy at Doughoregan as well as at the Annapolis house. She seemed to pull herself together if a social occasion were in the offing. She would go to the Sharpes at Whitehall or the Lloyds at Wye in the most inclement weather for a visit or a party, taking severe cold in the process, much to Papa's annoyance. In April 1781 she and her husband hosted a dinner party for the Marquis de LaFayette, General Smallwood, and some other officers while Pol, Charles, Kitty and Eliza were quarantined in the nursery suffering from smallpox inoculations.[68] No doubt her malaise was accentuated by her mother's death in the summer of 1781.

It was unfortunate that Charles Carroll of Carrollton's political career preoccupied his mind and called him away so frequently at the very time when his presence and support at home would have been most important. By the time the Revolution was over, Molly was dead; she had witnessed her beloved "Papa's" fatal misstep and fall from the porch of the Annapolis house in May 1782, and the shock was finally more than she could bear. She withdrew to her room and never left it again, dying barely two weeks after her father-in-law. Overwhelmed by his double loss, and by the demands of the paternal role he had been too busy — and perhaps temperamentally unsuited — to assume, Charles Carroll brought in his cousin Nancy Carroll to tend his four motherless children, the oldest of whom was Pol, now called Mary, aged twelve, while he threw himself whole-heartedly into his political and business career. With Eliza's death in 1783, he was left with the three children who grew to adulthood — Mary, Charles, aged eight, and Kitty who was five.

Charles Carroll of Carrollton served as a state senator from February 1777 until he along with his Federalist colleagues were ousted in the election of 1800 by the Democrats, whom he cordially despised and who, he was convinced, were about to "precipitate . . . a . . . revolution that will subvert our . . . social order and the rights of property." [69] Although he declined to serve when elected a delegate to the Constitutional Convention of 1787, he was one of the Constitution's most ardent supporters. He was elected to the United States Senate in 1788 as one of Maryland's first two representatives to that body and served until 1792 when it became illegal to sit simultaneously in federal and state legislatures.

[67] CCA to CCC, April 28, 1778; CCC to CCA, May 14-15, 1779; CCA to CCC, May 7, 1781. MS 206. MdHi.

[68] CCC to CCA, April 5, 1781. MS 206. MdHi.

[69] CCC to Charles Carroll of Homewood, November 3, 1800. MS 203. MdHi.

Charles Carroll of Carrollton
James B. Longacre (1794-1869) after Robert Field (ca. 1769-1819)
Cat. No. 18

His public involvements did not distract him from his strict attention to his private business, and he managed to preserve and enlarge the fortune his father had left him while at the same time financing the rise of his children and grandchildren to national and international social prominence. His political, economic, and social successes were enormous, but he had one very poignant personal failure, and that was his son Charles Carroll of Homewood.

"Exercise of the mind" never interested the young Charles Carroll very much, nor, as indicated by his father's references to his "corpulent" tendencies, did "exercise of the body." The reputation for charm and good looks which the young man had acquired by the time he was twenty did not impress his father who instead found it "painful . . . to recall past transactions and repeated admonitions to improve yourself while you remain single which were not attended to." [70] Charles Carroll of Carrollton was hopeful that his son's marriage in July 1800 to Miss Harriet Chew of Philadelphia, daughter of the Chief Justice of the state court of Pennsylvania and sister of Colonel John Eager Howard's wife Peggy, would have a settling effect, but again he was to be disappointed. Young Charles' refusal to keep the "exact and clear accounts" his father believed so essential was reflected in the cost of building and furnishing the house at Homewood which the elder Carroll had promised the newlyweds. It cost $40,000, four times what Carroll had intended to be spent!

[70] CCC to Charles Carroll of Homewood, July 17, 1801. MS 203. MdHi.

View of Apsley House
Engraving published in 1853 in a book by Richard Ford; 23 x 17 inches
Victoria and Albert Museum, London

Young Charles' inability or unwillingness to restrain his financial appetites foreshadowed another more tragic indulgence — an inability to partake temperately of "wines and fermented liquors." In 1814 his perseverence in this "degrading habit" led his father to forbid his presence at Doughoregan, and in June 1816, Harriet and her four daughters — Elizabeth, Mary Sophia, Harriet, and Louisa (her son, Charles Carroll V was shortly to leave for school abroad with his first cousin Charles Carroll Harper, Kitty's eldest child) — moved permanently to Philadelphia to escape, in her father-in-law's words, "the afflicting scene she has daily witnessed." [71] The abstinence that his father advised him was essential to a reconciliation was never permanently achieved, to his father's bitter disappointment: "I wish I could conclude this letter by subscribing it with the name of an affectionate father, but your course of life has nearly extinguished my affection. A return of it you are not to expect without an entire and permanent reformation." [72]

Mary, Charles Carroll of Carrollton's eldest daughter, initially disappointed him in her choice of a husband; Richard Caton's dashing good looks appealed to Mary far more than his indebted financial status did to her father. Mr. Carroll gave his consent on the condition that the young Englishman get out and secure employment "sufficient to maintain himself and a family." [73] The wedding took

[71] CCC: "Requests and Directions to Col. Howard and Messrs. Caton and Oliver," June 11, 1816. MS 203. MdHi; CCC to Robert Goodloe Harper, June 8, 1816. MS 431. MdHi.

[72] CCC to Charles Carroll of Homewood, May 15, 1814. MS 203. MdHi.

[73] CCC to Daniel Carroll, March 13, 1787. MS 431, MdHi.

Detail from a View of Brooklandwood
Early 20th century photograph; 4 x 6 5/16 inches
Private Collection of a Descendant

place in 1786, and the bridegroom fulfilled the second condition by going to work for his father-in-law.

Richard Caton never got out of debt; his speculative instincts and grand dreams far exceeded his business abilities and judgment. He and Mary did produce four exceptional daughters, three of whom — Marianne, Elizabeth, and Louisa — dazzled society on both sides of the Atlantic with their brilliant marriages to titled Englishmen: Marianne, widow of Robert Patterson, Madame Jerome Bonaparte's brother, to Richard Colley, Marquess Wellesley; Louisa, first to Sir Felton Elwell Hervey-Bathurst, aide-de-camp to the Duke of Wellington, and after Hervey's death to Francis Godolphin D'Arcy Osborne, 7th Duke of Leeds; and Elizabeth, in 1836, to Sir George William Jerningham, 8th Baron Stafford. Emily, the youngest Caton daughter, married a Scotsman named John MacTavish, and after living in Montreal for a short time, they returned to Maryland where John went to work for his grandfather-in-law, and Emily managed the Doughoregan and Baltimore households with an economy and attention to strict accounts that were the joy of Carroll's declining years.

The suitor of Carroll's youngest child Kitty reminded him of Mr. Caton. Having already overlooked that indebtedness for the sake of Mary's happiness, he was twice as determined to forestall the suave South Carolinian, Robert Goodloe Harper. Harper, however, was more than a match for him. A consummate politician, a clever and persuasive lawyer, and an irresistible suitor, Harper managed to marry Kitty in 1801, gain employment as her father's lawyer, acquire both a Baltimore house and a country plantation, Oakland (largely at Mr. Carroll's expense), and to win the lifelong affection of his initially disapproving father-in-law! He and Kitty had six children, three of whom — Richard, Mary Diana, and Elizabeth — died in childhood. Of the three who reached maturity — Charles Carroll Harper, Emily Harper, and Robert Goodloe Harper, Jr. — only Emily enjoyed long life; Robert died at twenty en route to Maryland from school in France, and Charles Carroll Harper died in 1837 in his mid-thirties. Kitty herself was rarely in good health, and, while she remained at home or at Doughoregan, her husband, who served in Congress, was lionized by Washington society. It made "your poor Catharine" very suspicious! "I was so pleased, my dear husband, to hear from the Vice-President, Mr. Clinton . . . you were so well and so much in company, no man younger or more attentive to the Ladies than you!" [74]

The accomplishments of these post-Revolutionary Carrolls — the brilliant marriages, the elegant style of life at Doughoregan and at the Catons' Lombard Street house where, after 1821, Charles Carroll of Carrollton spent his winters — were substantively different from those of their forebears, Charles Carroll the Settler, Charles Carroll of Annapolis, and, for half his life, Charles Carroll of Carrollton. In a very real sense everything that could be achieved in terms of their ambition to plant a family in the new world was achieved by the time Cornwallis surrendered at Yorktown in 1781 and the guarantee of political security Charles Carroll signed at Philadelphia in August 1776 became an undeniable reality. After that there was no proud legacy of religious persecution to hand down to the next generation, no high sense of purposeful survival to refine the mind and subdue the passions. All that remained was to enhance, to embellish, to enjoy, and to spend what had already been won, and for these tasks, the Carroll children and grandchildren were admirably equipped.

[74] Catherine Carroll Harper to Robert Goodloe Harper, March 1, 1810. Ms 431. MdHi.

SALLY D. MASON

MANUSCRIPTS CONSULTED

Maryland Historical Society

MS 203 — CCC to his Son
MS 203.1 — CCC Letterbook 1765-1768
MS 203.2 — CCC Letterbook 1770-1774
MS 205 — Inventory of CCC's Estate
MS 206 — CCA/CCC Correspondence — also called CCA Papers
MS 209 — CCC Journal 1792-1802
MS 211 — CCA Accounts
MS 211.1 — CCA Accounts as Administrator of the Affairs of Daniel Carroll and Charles Carroll of Duddington
MS 214 — CCA Letterbook to Hill and Waring
MS 216 — Miscellaneous Carroll Papers
MS 220 — Carroll-MacTavish Papers
MS 430 — Mary Diana Harper Papers
MS 431 — Harper-Pennington Papers
MS 645 — Perine Papers, Box 14
MS 1029 — Charles Carroll Harper Letterbook
MS 1225 — Carroll-Harper Papers
MS 1227 — Carroll-Purves Papers (also listed as MS 215)
MS 1229 — Caton-Hoffman Papers
MS 1893
MS 2018

Browne, William Hand, ed. *Archives of Maryland.* Baltimore: Maryland Historical Society, 1890.

Library of Congress
Carroll Family Papers
Jonathan Meredith Papers

Maryland Hall of Records, Annapolis
Proceedings, Baltimore County Orphans Court, 1833-1837

New York Public Library
The Arents Collections: Charles Carroll of Carrollton Letterbook, 1771-1835 (Arents Tobacco Supplement 767).

Books Consulted

Carr, Lois Green, and Jordan, David William. *Maryland's Revolution of Government 1689-1692.* Ithaca: Cornell University Press, 1974.

Thomas Meagher Field, ed. *Unpublished Letters of Charles Carroll of Carrollton . . . .* New York: U.S. Catholic Historical Society, 1902.

Gurn, Joseph. *Charles Carroll of Carrollton 1737-1832.* New York: P. J. Kennedy & Sons, 1932.

Hanley, Thomas O'Brien. *Charles Carroll of Carrollton: The Making of a Revolutionary Gentleman.* Washington, D.C.: The Catholic University of America Press, 1970.

Hoffman, Ronald. *A Spirit of Dissension: Economics, Politics, and the Revolution in Maryland.* Baltimore: Johns Hopkins University Press, 1973.

Land, Aubrey C. ed. *Bases of Plantation Society.* New York: Harper and Row, 1969.

Reynolds, Florence. "Charles Carroll of Annapolis, Colonial Capitalist." Unpublished Master's Degree Thesis, Johns Hopkins University, 1970.

Rowland, Kate Mason. *Life and Correspondence of Charles Carroll of Carrollton.* 2 vols. New York: G. Putnam and Sons, 1898.

Scharf, J. Thomas. *A History of Maryland.* 3 vols. Hatboro, Pennsylvania: Tradition Press, 1967.

Semmes, Raphael. *Baltimore As Seen by Visitors, 1783-1860.* Baltimore: Maryland Historical Society, 1953.

Smith, Ellen Hart. *Charles Carroll of Carrollton.* Cambridge: Harvard University Press, 1942.

Spruill, Julia Cherry. *Women's Life and Work in the Southern Colonies.* New York: W. W. Norton Company, 1972.

XXVIIIth YEAR.) THE (N°. 1430.)

MARYLAND GAZETTE.

THURSDAY, FEBRUARY 4, 1773

The FIRST CITIZEN *to the editor of the Dialogue between* TWO CITIZENS.

SIR,

THE intention of this address is not to intice you to throw off a fictitious, and to assume a real character: for I am not one of those who have puzzled themselves with endless conjectures about your mysterious personage; a secret too deep for me to pry into, and if known, not of much moment; of as little is it in my opinion whether your complexion be olive or fair, your eyes black or gray, your person stout or *incarvated*, your deportment easy and natural, insolent, or affected; you have therefore my consent to remain concealed under a borrowed name, as long as you may think proper, I see no great detriment that will thereby accrue to the publick; *you* will be the greatest! nay! the only sufferer; your fellow citizens, ignorant to whom they stand indebted for such excellent lucubrations, will not know at what shrine to offer up their incense, and tribute of praise; to you this sacrifice of glory will be the less painful, as *you are not actuated by vanity or a lust of fame*, and in obscurity you will have this consolation still left, the enjoyment of conscious merit, and of self applause. Modest men of real worth are subject to a certain diffidence, called by the French *la mauvaise honte* [a], which frequently prevents their rising in the world; you are not likely, I must own, to be guilty of that fault; *in vitium ducit culpa fuga* [b]; you seem rather to have fallen into the other extreme, and to be fully sensible of the wisdom of the French maxim, *il fault se faire valoir* [c], which for the benefit of my English readers I will venture to translate thus—"*A man ought to set a high value on his* "*own talents.*" This saying is somewhat analogous to that of Horace—*sume superbiam quaesitam meritis* [d]. As your manner of writing discovers vast erudition, and extensive reading, I make no doubt you are thoroughly acquainted with the Latin and French languages, and therefore a citation or two from each may not be unpalatable.

Having paid these compliments to your literary merit, I wish it were in my power to say as much in favour of your candour and sincerity. The editor of the dialogue between two Citizens, it seems, is the same person, who *overheard and committed to writing the conversation*. I was willing to suppose the editor had his relation at *second hand*, for I could not otherwise account for the same, mutilated, and imperfect part of the conversation attributed to me, without ascribing the publication to downright malice, and wilful misrepresentation. Where I can, I am always willing to give the mildest construction to a dubious action.—The editor has now put it out of my power of judging thus favourably of him, and as I have not the least room to trust to his impartiality a second time, I find myself under the necessity of making a direct application to the press, to vindicate my intellectual faculties, which no doubt, have suffered much in the opinion of the publick (notwithstanding its great good nature) from the publication of the abovementioned dialogue.

The sentiments of the first Citizen are so miserably mangled and disfigured, that he scarce can trace the faintest likeness between those, which really fell from him in the course of that conversation, and what have been put into his mouth.

The first Citizen has not the vanity to think his thoughts communicated to a fellow citizen in private, of sufficient importance to be made publick, nor would he have had the presumption to trouble that awful tribunal with his crude and indigested notions of politicks, had they not already been thus egregiously misrepresented in print. Whether they appear to more advantage in their present dress, others must determine; the newness of the fashion gives them a quite different air and appearance; let the decision be what it will, since much depends on the manner of relating facts, the first Citizen thinks he ought to be permitted to relate them his own way.

1st Cit. I am sorry that party attachments and connexions have induced you to abandon old principles; there was a time, Sir, when you had not so favourable an opinion of the integrity and good intentions of Government, as you now seem to have. Your conduct on this occasion makes me suspect that formerly *some men, not measures*, were disagreeable to you. Have we reason to place a greater confidence in our *present rulers*, than in those to whom I allude? Some of the present set (it is true) were then in power, others indeed were not yet provided for, and therefore a push was to be made to thrust them into office, that all power might centre in *one family*. Is all your patriotism come to this?

2d Cit. I do not like such home expostulations, convince me that I act wrong in supporting Government and I will alter my conduct, no man is more open to conviction than myself——(Vide Dialogue to the words —"*would be all fair argument*.")

1st Cit. I am not surprised that the threadbare topics of arbitrary princes, and proclamations, should give you uneasiness; you have insinuated that the repetition of them is tiresome, but I suspect the true cause of your aversion proceeds from another quarter. You are afraid of a comparison between the *present ministers* of this province, and *those*, who influenced Charles the first, and brought him to the block; the resemblance I assure you would be striking. You insinuate that "*The* "*opinions of the greatest Counsel in England*" are come to hand, in favour of the proclamation, and 40 per poll, and you seem to lay great stress on those opinions. A little reflection, and acquaintance with history will teach you, that the opinions of *Court Lawyers* are not always to be relied on; remember the issue of *Hambden's* trial; "*The prejudiced or prostituted Judges (four* "*excepted*") (says Hume) "*gave sentence in favour of* "*the Crown.*" The opinion even of a Camden, will have no weight with me, should it contradict a settled point of constitutional doctrine. On this occasion I cannot forbear citing a sentence or two from the justly admired author of the Considerations, which have made a deep impression on my memory. "*In a ques-* "*tion*" (says that writer) "*of publick concernment, the* "*opinion of no Court Lawyer, however respectable for* "*his candor and abilities, ought to weigh more than the* "*reasons adduced in support of it.*" He then gives his reasons for this assertion; to avoid prolixity I must refer you to the pamphlet; if I am not mistaken you will find them in page 12. Speaking shortly after of the opinions of Court Lawers upon "*American affairs*," he makes this pertinent remark—"*They*" (Court Lawyers opinions) "*have been all strongly marked with the same* "*character: they have been generally very sententious, and* "*the same observation may be applied to them all, they* "*have declared THAT to be LEGAL which the minister* "*for the time being has deemed to be EXPEDIENT.*" Will you admit *this to be fair argument?*

2d Cit. I confess it carries some weight with it; I cannot with propriety dispute the authority, on which it is founded; make therefore the most of my concession; should I admit your reasoning on this head to be just, does it follow, that the Court and Country interests are incompatible; that Government and Liberty are irreconcilable? Is every man, who thinks differently from you on publick measures, influenced or corrupted?

1st Cit. "*God forbid it should be the case of every indi-* "*vidual.*" I have already hinted at the cause of your attachment to Government; it proceeds, I fear, more from personal considerations, than from a persuasion of the rectitude of our Court measures; but I would not have you confound Government, with the Officers of Government; they are things really distinct, and yet in your Idea they seem to be one and the same.

Government was instituted for the general good, but Officers intrusted with its powers, have most commonly perverted them to the selfish views of avarice and ambition; hence the Country and Court interests, which ought to be the same, have been too often opposite, as must be acknowledged and lamented by every true friend to Liberty. You ask me, are Government and Liberty incompatible? Your question arises from an abuse of words, and confusion of ideas; I answer, that so far from being incompatible, I think they cannot subsist independent of each other. A few great and good princes have found the means of reconciling them even in despotic states; Tacitus says of Nerva, "*Res* "*olim dissociabiles miscuit, principatum, ac libertatem**." a wicked minister has endeavoured, and is now endeavouring in this *free government*, to set the power of the supreme magistrate above the laws; in our mother country such ministers have been punished for the attempt with infamy, death, or exile; I am surprised, that he who imitates *their* example, should not dread *their* fate.

2d Cit. This is not coming to the point, you talk at random of dangers threatening liberty, and of infringements of the constitution, which exist only in your imagination. Prove, I say, *our ministers* to have advised unconstitutional measures, and I am ready to abandon them and their cause; but upon your *ipse dixit*, I shall not admit those measures to be unconstitutional, which you are pleased to call so, nor can I allow all those to be Court hirelings, whom you think proper to stigmatise with that opprobrious appellation, and for no other reason, but that they dare exercise their *own judgment in opposition to yours.*——(Read the 2d Citizen's harangue from the last words *(opposition to yours)* to the following inclusively, *sweat of his brow.*)

1st Cit. What a flow of words! how pregnant with thought and deep reasoning! if you expect an answer to all the points, on which you have spoken, you must excuse my prolixity, and impute it to the variety of matter laid before me; I shall endeavour to be concise, and if possible, avoid obscurity—you say—*I know not what or whom I mean by we, and the friends of the constitution*—I will tell you, Sir, whom I do not mean, from whence you may guess at those, whom I do.—By friends of the constitution, I mean not those, whose selfish attachment to their interest has deprived the publick of a most beneficial Law, from the want of which by your own account, "*Our staple is fallen* "*into disgrace in foreign markets and every man's proper-* "*ty is in a degree decreasing and mouldering away.*" I mean not *those few*, out of tenderness and regard to whom, the general welfare of this province has been sacrificed; to preserve *whose* salaries from diminution, the fortunes of all their countrymen have been suffered to be impaired; I mean not *those*, who advised a measure, which cost the first Charles his crown and life, and who have dared to defend it upon principles more unjustifiable and injurious than those, under which it was at first pretentedly palliated. You see Sir I adopt the maxim of the British constitution—*The King can do no wrong*, I impute all the blame to his ministers, who if found guilty and *dragged to light*, I hope will be made to feel the resentment of a free people. But it seems from your suggestion that we are to place an unlimited trust in the men, whom I have pretty plainly pointed out, because they are men of great wealth and have "*as deep a stake in the safety of the constitution* "*as any of us.*" Property even in *private* life, is not always a security against dishonesty, in *publick*, it is much less so. The ministers, who have made the boldest attacks on liberty, have been most of them men of affluence; from whence I infer, that riches so far from insuring a minister's honesty, ought rather to make us more watchful of his conduct.

You go on with this argument, and urge me thus —"*Do I conceive that such men can possibly be hired un-* "*less they be overtaken by infatuation, to engage to pull* "*down a fair and stately edifice, with the ruins of which,* "*as soon as it is levelled to the ground, they and their fa-* "*milies are to be stoned to death.*" I have read of numberless instances of such infatuation; there are now *living examples* of it; the history of mankind is full of them; men in the gratification of sensual appetites, are apt to overlook their future consequences; thus for the present enjoyment of wealth and power—liberty in reversion will be easily given up; besides, a perpetuity in office may be aimed at; hopes may be entertained that the *good thing*, like a precious jewel will be handed down from *father* to *son*. I have known men of such meanness, and of such insolence, (qualities often met with in the same person) who exclusive of the above motives, would wish to be the first slave of a sultan, to lord it over all the rest; power Sir, power is apt to pervert the best of natures; with too much of it, I would not trust the mildest man on earth; and shall we place confidence in a *minister* too long inured to rule, grown old, callous, and hackneyed in the crooked paths of policy?

2d Cit. "*I do not chuse to answer this last question*—" you grow warm and press me too close. but why is all your indignation poured out against our ministers, and no part of it reserved for the lawyers—those cut-throats, extortioners—those enemies to peace and honesty, those *respublicae portenta, ac paene funera* [e], to use the energic words of Tully, because I can find none in english to convey my full meaning, but by comparing *our harpies* to those two monsters of iniquity —Piso, and Gabinius.

1st Cit. From this vehemence of yours, I perceive you are one of those, who have joined in the late cry against lawyers; from what cause does all this rancour and animosity against those gentlemen proceed? is it a real tenderness for the people, which has occasioned such scurrility and abuse? or does your hatred, and that of your kidney, arise from disappointment and the unexpected alliance between the lawyers and the people, in opposition to officers—This alliance, I know, has been termed unnatural, because it was thought contrary to the lawyer's interests, to separate themselves from the officers; since a close and firm union between the two, would probably secure success against all patriotic attempts to relieve the people from their late heavy burthens, of which too great a part still subsists.

2d Cit. "*For heaven's sake to what purpose is all this* "*idle talk? you well know it does not touch us, we are* "*not galled and therefore need not wince.*" But reconcile, if you can the inconsistency of conduct, with which some of your favourites may be justly reproached; I have one or two in my eye *(great patriots)* whose conduct, I am sure, will not bear a strict scrutiny; "*I* "*can tell them with truth*——(Vide dialogue from the last words, to these)—"*glorious and patriotic particu-* "*lars.*"

[a] *An awkward bashfulness.*

[b] *The avoiding one fault is apt to lead us into another.*

[c] *In the text these words have received a liberal interpretation; they mean strictly—That a person should assume proper consequence.*

[d] *May be translated—Assume a pride to merit justly due.*

* *(Thus translated by Gordon.) Nerva blended together two things, once found irreconcileable—Publick Liberty and sovereign Power.*

[e] *Mr. Melmoth, the elegant translator of Cicero's familiar letters, makes this remark in his notes on the 8th letter of the first book, Vol. I*——"*Cicero has delineated the cha-* "*racters at large of these consuls (Piso and Gabinius) in* "*several of his orations, but he has in two words given* "*the most odious picture of them that exasperated eloquence* "*perhaps ever drew, where he calls them* "*duo reipublicae portenta ac paene funera*"——*an expression* "*for which modern language can furnish no equivalent.*"

THE FIRST CITIZEN LETTER FROM THE MARYLAND GAZETTE
February 4, 1773
The Maryland Historical Society, Baltimore

Charles Carroll of Carrollton: Conservative Revolutionary 1776-1781

Charles Carroll of Carrollton's role during the Revolution is fascinating and instructive. It is also widely misunderstood. During the conflict ridden years of the 1760's he did not play an active part in opposing British taxation policies although he clearly sympathized with the colonial protest. But regardless of his feelings, being Catholic prohibited him from holding public office — a matter that both rankled and deeply troubled all Catholics — and so, after his return from England, he devoted his time to business and personal concerns. Suddenly in 1773 he emerged as a controversial political figure. A serious economic depression gripped the colony during the first half of that year, and in the midst of this problem there developed the most celebrated newspaper controversy fought in Maryland before the Revolution. The argument focused on the validity of a decision taken without the consent of the legislature by the colony's governor, Robert Eden, to increase the rate of fees charged for government provided services. Out of this debate a new coalition of "popular leaders" including Carroll emerged to hold power. From that moment on they led the colony to independence and statehood.

In the 1773 newspaper debate the chief protagonists were Charles Carroll of Carrollton and Daniel Dulany. Both men had private as well as public motives for engaging in the argument. Daniel Dulany, probably the most powerful political figure in Maryland, had gone through several unsettling experiences during the past year and his once unassailable position seemed now to be eroding. His deepest problem involved the strained relations with Robert Eden, and he had even traveled to England in an effort to shore up his position with the proprietary family. Though receiving some partial reassurances, Dulany returned to Maryland still troubled. Shortly after arriving in Annapolis, he became impressed with the storm of protest over Eden's actions and the opportunity afforded him by the confrontation. On January 7, 1773 Dulany published in the *Maryland Gazette* an articulate defense of the governor's actions.

Charles Carroll of Carrollton correctly believed that Dulany decided to defend Eden specifically with the intention of increasing his standing with the governor. He also maintained that Dulany expected to increase handsomely his private fortune. Probably this personal conviction on Carroll's part, rather than any deep seated ideological conviction, influenced him to attack Dulany, a man he personally loathed. Bad blood, it must be emphasized, had long existed between the two aristocratic families. The Carrolls had often been humiliated — both publicly and privately — by the scornful Dulanys. On one occasion Daniel Dulany purposefully delayed the litigation involved in Charles Carroll's marriage to Molly Darnall. Carroll requested the assembly to pass an enabling act giving Molly, who was still a minor, the status of an adult. He asked for the measure so that Molly might legally sign a disclaimer stating that if her husband died she would have no right to claim the fortune. Normally such a request passed in routine fashion, but on this occasion Daniel Dulany, wanting to irritate the Carrolls, attempted unsuccessfully to block the act. Though the judical issue was complex, the substance of the matter was generally known, and the following poem published anonymously in the *Maryland Gazette* in 1773, some years after the enabling act had been secured, suggests vividly the bitter pattern of personal antagonism that underlay the public debate.

When your letter I read my heart
leap'd for joy
That I on occasion so apt
might employ
My rancour, and venom innate to
let fly
At a man I abhor — and I'll tell
you why
I could not be married (you've heard
of the fact)
Before I got an enabling act,
For a man you'll allow, would cut a
poor figure
Tho big as myself, or perhaps
somewhat bigger,
Who to any fair virgin his
honor shou'd plight
Without being enabled to do — what
is right
In this he opposed me.[1]

As the newspaper debate proceeded, supporters gathered around Carroll, and two men, Samuel Chase and Carroll's father, Charles Carroll of Annapolis, soon molded these individuals into a vigorous political faction determined to destroy Dulany's standing with the electorate. The testing ground for the controversy came in the 1773 election and to the Carroll family's satisfaction Dulany's followers suffered a crushing defeat. That evening Charles Carroll of Carrollton wrote enthusiastically to his father of the victory. After receiving the letter the elder Carroll immediately replied: "I am obliged to you for your account of yesterday's transactions. They must be mortifying indeed to the Dulanys. Their pride and insolence," he rejoiced, "is humbled, and what is still more galling they have great reason to fear an end of their powers, influence and future promotions." [2]

The faction of men who coalesced around Carroll in 1773 was destined to guide Maryland during the Revolution. Their general character must be understood in order to appreciate properly the context in which Carroll acted. Fundamentally all of them — Charles Carroll of Carrollton, William Paca, Samuel Chase, Matthew Tilghman, Thomas Johnson — were conservative. Known by their contemporaries as the "popular party" they were elated with their ascension to power, and they anticipated enjoying the traditional benefits of power — money, prestige, and influence. The strain in Anglo-American relations, it should be understood, had not been a direct or immediate cause in their rise to power, although Britain's indifference to the colonies' political sensitivities and economic problems certainly enhanced their appeal. Still, with the exception of Chase and Tilghman, their attitudes on the imperial dispute with Parliament

[1] *Maryland Gazette,* June 24, 1773.

[2] CCA to CCC, May 15, 1773. MS 206. MdHi.

State House, Annapolis
Engraving [1789]
3 5/8 x 6 3/8 inches
The Maryland Historical Society, Baltimore

were not widely known. Chase deservedly enjoyed the reputation of an incendiary, while Tilghman's conduct as a leader in the lower house was steady and cautious. The feelings toward England of Johnson and Carroll were not matters of public record, and, although Paca was close to Governor Eden, all three were regarded as warm friends of the colonial cause.

Yet once in power the Maryland leaders were forced to contend with the Anglo-American conflict. The structure of politics required them to take a stand because other ambitious political elements hoped to exploit the imperial controversy in their bid for power. Thus the very shape of the confrontation with Parliament and the prodding of internal political forces anxious for violence caused the popular leaders to make decisions and take actions which most of its members regretted. Ultimately the Revolution came to most of the Maryland leadership, including Carroll, as an unwelcome development. Anxious to seek reconciliation with Britain, most of them privately lamented that events beyond their control constantly required the adoption of increasingly dangerous positions. Their truest conviction was expressed on May 21, 1776 when the Maryland Assembly voted unanimously not to seek independence, a decision they reluctantly reversed on June 28th when reports from the Continental Congress indicated all in favor of separation except Maryland and New York.

The fears that underlay the Maryland leadership's reluctance were well founded. Since the previous fall, disorder of a wide variety had mounted within the colony. Reports from all parts of the province told continually of insurrectionist activities among blacks and whites, servants and slaves, some indigenous, others instigated by the British. Accompanying the accounts were communiqués from frightened militia commanders emphasizing the extent of desertion and disobedience which threatened their commands' effectiveness. Many among the revolutionary leadership saw these developments as confirmation of the suspicion that the rebellion would unleash those convulsive social tensions previously restrained by the old system of authority. Within their society a host of suppressed dissensions existed — the uneven distribution of wealth, the potential of servile insurrection, the clash within the church. From each of these factors had developed deeply embedded animosities and the revolutionary leaders correctly recognized that the rhetoric about liberty and their attacks on royal privilege might well come to be used on themselves just as they had used them against England. In sum, the most perceptive of the Maryland leadership realized that there was hardly anything Britain could do which would prove so threatening to their class as did the Revolution itself.

After independence the disorder worsened in Maryland and in many areas of the state a condition of near anarchy prevailed. And yet amidst the shattering turmoil the revolutionary leaders demonstrated considerable flexibility and intelligence in controlling the discontent. Desperately hoping to stabilize the situation, they pursued two very different strategies. To insure the framework of institutional control they voted a variety of control measures and composed an extremely conservative state constitution which theoretically guaranteed the rule of a propertied elite. But the unrestrained deterioration they confronted convinced them of the need to go much further and, in fact, to reverse the elitist philosophy of the constitution.

During the new government's first assembly session in early 1777 the state's leaders anxiously sought to save both their class and the Revolution by popularizing the movement for independence. Believing these elements to be mutually entwined, the political elite designed a state fiscal program aimed at subduing the class antagonisms that underlay much of the internal protest. Two major measures were enacted. The new tax system shifted the burden of assessment from polls to land and slaves, in essence from the majority to the planter elite. The tender law was even more radical. Its purpose was plain — by authorizing the payment of all pre-war debts, including sterling obligations, with depreciated paper money, the legislation voided the bulk of all internal credit obligations. For the revolutionary leaders — sensible though frightened men — these measures constituted an extreme financial sacrifice in order to maintain power. Practically all of them were large creditors, and they now faced the prospect of seeing as much as one-third of their fortunes wiped out. A few who were debtors would benefit, but the majority would suffer considerably. Yet they unanimously endorsed the proposal as a fundamental prerequisite to save their class and the Revolution. Recognizing what the "temper of the times" demanded, they accepted reality with sorrow but without dissent.

The experience of Charles Carroll of Carrollton during these years is especially instructive. At first he enthusiastically embraced the movement for independence. Carroll had entered the political arena in his contest with Dulany and, as a young man of thirty-six whose Catholic religion had frustrated any political aspirations, was swept up in the imperial protest. Now the movement for imperial reform offered him an exciting role which included a diplomatic assignment for the Continental Congress. Leaving in March 1776 with Benjamin Franklin, Samuel Chase and his cousin, John Carroll, on a poorly conceived and totally unsuccessful mission to Canada, he did not return to Maryland until mid-June to argue for independence.

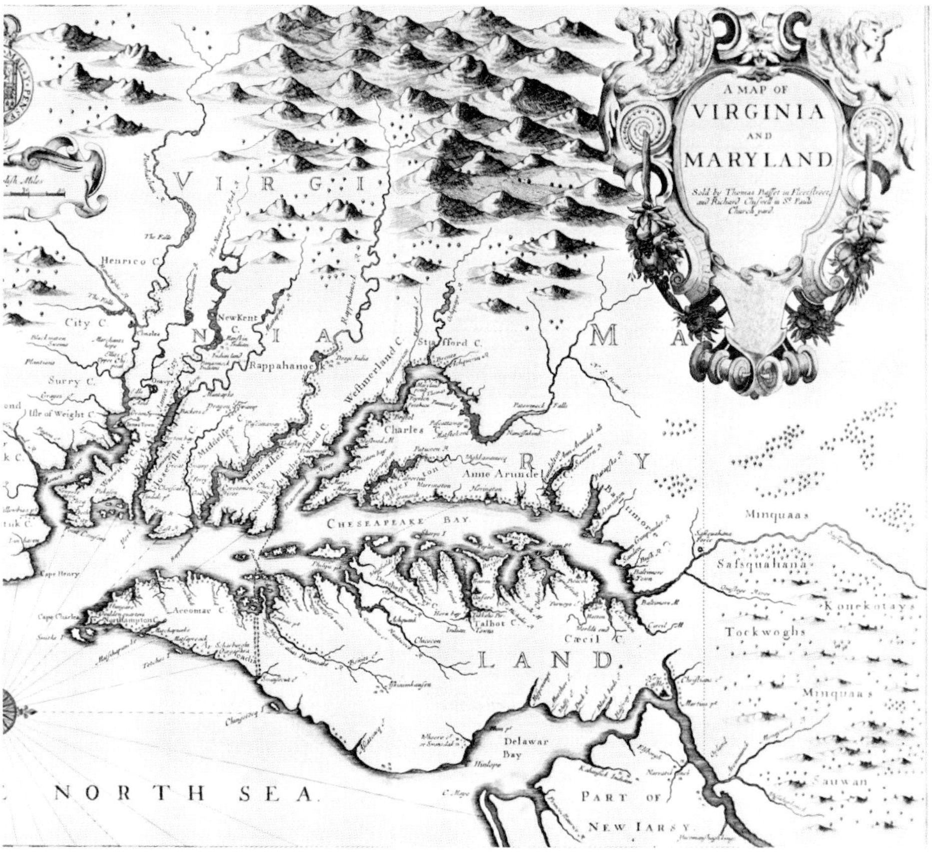

A Map of Virginia and Maryland
John Speed
Engraving, 1676
From: John Speed. *The Theatre of the Empire of Great Britaine.* New edition, folio, London: T. Basset, 1676, opposite p. 43.
This map is derived from John Smith's map of 1612. Speed's book of 1676 is the first English atlas to have any detailed maps of this region of America.

For several weeks after the decision for separation and his signing of the Declaration of Independence Carroll remained euphoric. But as the summer wore on he began to appreciate more fully why many had so vigorously opposed leaving the empire. The disintegration of society into the state of anarchy that many feared seemed to be fast approaching. Independence had indeed proved a tragic mistake, and none became more convinced of this than Carroll who, in words laced with horror and anger, condemned the Revolution. Nothing but a return to the British Empire, he contended, could bring stability and prevent the onset of social upheaval. Should reconciliation not take place, he warned, the colonies "would be ruined not so much by the calamities of war as by the intestine divisions and the bad governments which I foresee will take place in most of these united states; they will be simple Democracies, of all governments, the worst, and will end as all other democracies have in despotism." [3]

[3] CCC to CCA, October 18, 1776. MS 206. MdHi.

The fall and winter of 1776-1777 were difficult for Carroll. Reluctantly he acknowledged that rapprochement with England was not imminent. And so, with the faint hope of some institutional authority established by the constitution, he lobbied hard during the first assembly session for the popular fiscal program. His political colleagues agreed with its necessity, but not his testy seventy-six year old father, Charles Carroll of Annapolis, who single-handedly had built an immense fortune, much of it based on usury, and who now railed at the financial sacrifices occasioned by the impending flood of worthless money. For the next several years hundreds of letters flew between the two as they strenuously argued their points in private, with total honesty. Loving each other deeply, their words rang with anger in one paragraph and affection in the next. The elder Carroll regularly censured his son as a "panderer" of popularity, a "courter" of the rabble and challenged him to cast off his "meekness of temper."[4] And yet he would also implore "Charley" to "drudge not since nothing is dearer to me than your health." The younger Carroll, while castigating his father's behavior as "meddlesome" and certainly "out of season," would simultaneously plead with the old man to forego his long walks in the "chill" winter air.[5]

The younger Carroll tried to convince his father that the act was an essential concession demanded by a popular revolution; the elder Carroll saw nothing but dangerous leveling in the measure: if the assembly would pass such a bill, what was to stop them from deciding "that no man shall hold above 500 acres of land — that he shall sell all above that quantity at the rate of £100 current per thousand? Why should not the land-holder be obliged to part with his land as well as the sterling money holder be obliged to part with his sterling?"[6] Admitting both the personal cost and the unjust effect of the bill, the son repeatedly tried to educate his father about revolutionary necessities: "the law suits the multitudes, individuals must submit to partial losses; no great revolution can happen in a state without revolutions or mutations of private property."[7] "There is a time when it is wisdom to yield to injustice and to popular heresies and delusions,"[8] the son instructed the father; if the populace was not legislatively placated in revolutionary times, "they commonly have recourse to violence and greater injustice towards all such as have the temerity to oppose them, particularly when their unjust proceedings are popular."[9] Carroll and his legislative colleagues reasoned well, even though he could never convince his father who vowed, "I will not let the tender law sleep, nor the rogues who have taken advantage of it, nor the men who ought to repeal it."[10]

Only in late 1780, with the state's convulsions markedly diminishing, did the assembly repeal the tender act. For Charles Carroll of Carrollton the return of

[4] For example, see CCA to CCC, December 8, 1779. MS 206. MdHi.

[5] For example, see CCC to CCA, November 13, 1777. MS 206. MdHi.

[6] CCA to CCC, March 18, 1777. MS 206. MdHi.

[7] CCC to CCA, November 8, 1777. MS 206. MdHi.

[8] CCC to CCA, November 13, 1777. MS 206. MdHi.

[9] Ibid.

[10] CCA to Daniel of St. Thomas Jenifer, July 20, 1779. MS 206. MdHi.

stability constituted a great political triumph. He and his allies in a very real sense were the architects of a successful campaign to win legitimacy, support, and popular approval in a very trying and dangerous situation. Also aiding a restoration of order were the fading of Britain's military fortunes in the Chesapeake and the cautious methods by which the courts gradually reasserted their judicial authority. But basically, the Maryland elite believed they had prevailed by acquiescing in those sacrifices necessary to appease the "revengeful democracy" [11] that had been unleased by the Revolution. None except the elder Carroll showed any sign of daring to think differently.

Inevitably the intense chaos of the war years deeply affected the value structure of Charles Carroll of Carrollton. After his initial "breakdown" he rapidly recovered and developed considerable insight into the social impact created by the Revolution. Recognizing that the vast majority of the public had little reason to support the War for Independence — a war which placed much greater demands on them than the comparatively mild tyranny of England — Carroll fully appreciated the need for making the movement a matter of self interest to the people. Similarly, he realized that the war's dislocation required the leadership class to bend and make great sacrifices if it were to remain in power. And most important, Carroll emerged from those years with limited faith in the people and with a determined conviction that his class would never again be placed in such a precarious position. His subsequent career, at both the state and national level, reflected his commitment to the maintenance of stability and — ironically — to the suppression of the powerful egalitarian forces unleashed by the American Revolution.

[11] CCC to CCA, August 20, 1776. MS 206. MdHi.

Ronald Hoffman

62

have to this my Last Will and
Testament set and Subscribed
my Hand and Seal, this Second
day of September, One Thousand
Eight Hundred and Twenty five.

Ch. Carroll of Carrollton

Signed, Sealed, [illegible]
Declared by the Test[illegible]
Last Will and [illegible]
the presence [illegible]
request, in [illegible]
the presence [illegible] each other,
have [illegible] our Names
as Wit[illegible] thereto, the 4
following [illegible]
Correc[illegible] being first made,
That [illegible]
[illegible] first inserted 4
[illegible] "of" and "my"
[illegible] of the fifth
[illegible] last men[illegible]
four"

Will of Charles Carroll of Carrollton
Maryland Hall of Records, Annapolis
Accession Number 19968

Charles Carroll of Carrollton: English Aristocrat in an American Setting

To Charles Carroll of Carrollton, the epitome of the good life was a financially secure place in the landed aristocracy of England. Although his children were to disappoint him in not marrying well enough, and in not living up to his expectations, by the end of his life two of his Caton grandchildren had married British nobles and the third was to do so in 1836, four years after his death. Later in the nineteenth century such alliances of American wealth with English titles would become commonplace, but at the time they were virtually unique accomplishments attributable to the influence and, above all, money of an indulgent grandfather. The effect Charles Carroll of Carrollton had on his grandchildren is clear from the fantasies of Elizabeth Caton, especially the letter she wrote to her aunt in 1818:

> *Is not England a paradise? I cannot help telling you a foolish thought that has come into my head & which never can be realized unless we make Grandpapa twenty years younger . . . go and see Houghton, a magnificent seat of Lord C — and you will not be surprised when I tell you that I always longed for it to be Grand Papas & that it could be bought for what Carrollton* [Manor] *would sell for and that if Grandpapa would sell Doughoregan etc., he could live in it like a prince and give his children three or four thousand a year each besides. . . . absurd as the wish is, I can not get it out of my head — We could have our townhouses and spend all the autumn and winter with him.*[1]

Charles Carroll of Carrollton perceived himself to be an aristocrat and, he felt strongly that an aristocracy was essential to the good governing of society even if, in America, it was untitled. It wasn't that he was unhappy about living in the new world, although at times he was distressed by the desire of some to "subvert our . . . social order and the rights of property."[2] Except perhaps during the War of 1812, he manifested no interest, as his father once had, in selling out and moving elsewhere, nor did he dream of a place in the House of Lords. He was far too business oriented and realistic for that. Instead, Carroll dedicated himself to ensuring that the government of his state and nation gave proper deference to what John Adams referred to as "the well-born." For twenty-three years he was moderately successful, serving in the State Senate where he exercised considerable influence and power, but when Jefferson's Democratic party won the election of 1800, Carroll abandoned all efforts at directing public affairs and turned to the pressing problems of managing his fortune in order that he and his family could continue at least to live like aristocrats, even if they could no longer govern like them.

In the years immediately following his return to America in 1765, and during the Revolution, Carroll served as a willing apprentice to his father, Squire Carroll, in the management of the family fortune. Even while abroad in school, at his father's behest, he applied himself to learning the Italian method of bookkeeping and on one occasion even disputed with his father about whether or not the Squire was extracting illegal compound interest from one of his debtors. Apart from the political differences that they would have during the Revolution, the sharp exchange over the matter of compound interest was perhaps the greatest strain their otherwise close and usually tender relationship suffered.

[1] Elizabeth Caton to Catherine Carroll Harper, June 19, 1818. MS 431. MdHi.

[2] CCC to Charles Carroll of Homewood, November 3, 1800. MS 203. MdHi.

Obviously, from the Squire's standpoint his 'Charley' had been working *too* hard on his bookkeeping exercises, a fact young Carroll freely admitted: "I am still going on with my Italian bookkeeping. I think it a too tedious and prolix a method for a gentleman. The Multiplicity and intricacy of a Merchant's transactions require greater method and the nicest exactness." It was in the same letter that he turned his newly acquired skills to the accounts of Mr. Clifton, one of his father's debtors whose debt was then in suit in England. "You cannot be ignorant that compound interest is deemed usury," Charley wrote; "the Law looks upon it in that light and has endeavoured to restrain that illegal practice by severe & heavy penalties, by forfeiture, if I am not mistaken, of treble value of the money lent." [3] The Squire's response was immediate and irate. As far as he was concerned, in any legal sense it was not compound interest he was charging, and Charley would soon learn that in order to secure debts with people who might otherwise be expected to default, it was necessary to treat interest unpaid as principal to be added to the original loan. Charley backed away from the issue and the temporary breech between father and son was soon healed, probably because Charley found on his return that his father was right. On the balance sheet for 1798 there is a notation that the actual amount of principal out on loan might be less than that given on the sheet because "of the difference in many cases between simple and compound interest, for where more than one years interest remains unpaid the amount of interest [that] accrues is added to the principal and if not paid by the debtors, will lessen the . . . balance." [4]

By 1773 Carroll was devoting a significant portion of his time and energies to advocating the American cause, but he was not to disappoint his father's desire for a son well-schooled in the arts of a landed gentleman, who managed his finances with extreme and "prudent" care. Even though trained in both continental and English law, at 27, when Carroll arrived home, his first loves were geometry and the cautious increase of the family fortune. He was disgusted by the "subtleties of law," and preferred the "strict reasoning" of geometry, although he never considered pursuing it seriously.[5] Even after the outbreak of hostilities with Britain, when it was legal for Catholics to practice law, Carroll preferred attending to his own financial affairs and forsook both geometry and the profession his father had chosen for him. So prudent was he in managing his expenses abroad that one of his father's friends expressed a prophetic fear that he would always he devoted to financial matters to the exclusion of other gentlemanly activities. As William Graves explained in a letter to Squire Carroll written in 1770:

> *Your saying they* [Charley and Molly] *cannot wont if they are tolerable economists will procure me pardon for remarking on this part that the only matter I used to caution your son against was too much economy. In truth the only quarter in which I wish to remold his mind was the prudential part . . .*

Graves expressed the hope that Charley would "spend the whole of his present income among his tenants, manufacturers & neighbors, by doing principally

[3] CCC to CCA, July 4, 1762. MS 206. MdHi.

[4] List of Assets, 1798. MS 220. MdHi.

[5] CCC to CCA, July 2, 1763, April 29, 1763. MS 206. MdHi.

what none but a man of affluence can do. The advantage will finally redound to himself." Charley should not "lay by money" but improve his lands. Being out of doors will be good for his health, especially if he supervises the work and thus rides a great deal. "I know your son well enough to know he will never spend your fortune; my only fear is that he will be too sollicitous about the increase of it." He is good at figures

> *but he ought to guard against a timid & pecuniary aeconomy by being large in his views, expenses, conduct, & by all means to beware of encouraging a desire of money for the sake of laying so much more at interest & not for purposes of pushing in any vein of trade or new project; or bettering or ornamenting his estate, improving roads, erecting farmhouses or of beautifying his own habitation in walks, gardens, plantations, pleasure grounds, etc. etc.*[6]

Although Charley was to heed some of Graves' strictures with respect to the improvement of his own and his children's lands and life styles, he would never overcome a tendency to cautious investment and "pecuniary aeconomy," particularly as it related to annually increasing the principal of his fortune. Without a doubt he never squandered his father's fortune, and from the day of his father's death in 1782 until his own fifty years later, he did everything within his power to keep it on the increase.

In 1764, by his own estimate, Squire Carroll had a net annual income of £1,800 sterling a year, which in 1832 dollars, adjusting for inflation, amounted to $10,715. It was derived from 40,000 acres of land, some of which was cultivated by 285 slaves or leased, 1/5 interest in an ironworks worth ca. £400 sterling a year, and £24,230 sterling ($140,937) in loans at interest. In 1788, his son had approximately the same assets in land, including the fifth interest in the Baltimore ironworks property, approximately the same number of field slaves, but had increased the amount of principal (plus accruing interest) invested in bonds and mortgages to $375,800.28, and according to George Washington by 1790 had become "the most monied man" Washington was acquainted with.[7]

Although no lists of assets have survived for the years prior to 1798, it is clear from what is known about Carroll's investments prior to that time, and the scattered papers extant from the sixteen years following his father's death, that 1788 was a private financial watershed, as much as it also was a significant public turning point in the development and growth of a national economy. To Carroll, the six years prior to 1788 had been difficult ones as he and other likeminded people had attempted to control the forces advocating easy credit and inflated paper money. It must have been with a great sigh of relief that he read the final product of the Philadelphia convention. In January 1788, probably not long after he had balanced his books from the previous year, Carroll penned a long (34 page) defense of the Constitution which he fully expected to give to the Maryland Ratifying Convention as one of the representatives from Anne Arundel County. At the last minute the anti-

[6] William Graves to CCA, January 14, 1770. MS 206. MdHi.

[7] George Washington to Charles Carter, September 14, 1790. *Writings of George Washington*, vol. 36, p. 114.

federalists staged a successful campaign against him. He lost the election and probably did not give the speech as planned. Nevertheless, his observations on the virtues of the proposed new government form a clear statement of how he perceived the nation and creditors like himself would fare if the Constitution were to be adopted.

It would be splendid, he wrote, if the science of government could be "reducible to a few elementary principles as obvious & certain as the axioms of geometry," but it could not. The best that could be expected is that proposed by the Philadelphia convention which, through checks and balances, would curb the "excesses of an uncontrolled Democracy" to produce "respectability abroad and stability at home . . . I hope, Sir, the day is fast approaching when no nation will remain so degraded as to crouch under the yoke of entire servitude, yet none I fear (such is the condition of humanity) can long enjoy the exuberance, the excess of Liberty."

> *Let it not be feared that these multiplied checks will impede the motion of the great machine: they will equally prevent too much, & too little & produce that due admixture of energy, & caution, of action and repose, wich constitute the true, the invigorating health, and perfection of government. . . .* Spiritus intus alit: totamque infusa per artus Mens agitat molem, et magno se corpore miscet [The spirit within nourishes and flowing through the limbs animates the whole mass, and mixes itself with the great body].

To Carroll, what the country needed was a strong central government that would oversee and insure the revival of public credit.

> *In consequence of the several powers vested in Congress by the 8th Sec. 1st Art., particulry the power to lay & collect taxes, duties, imposts, & excises, we have every reason to expect that the public securities will rise in value; that by having the interest in all considerable transfers of property. If this event should take place, every one must perceive the advantages which those meritorious citizens will derive from it, who lent their money to the Public in a critical time, or whose effects were forced from them to support the army in its greatest need. Then Sir, will the Public be able to requite in some measure, tho much too late, unexampled sufferings & patience of that patriotic army by whose perseverance & virtue exerted under the pressure of accumulated distress, we are now enabled to decide whether we shall be a happy & free People, or through our own fault draw down upon ourselves & our posterity all the calamities attendant on, & consequent to Anarchy, civil discord, & war.*
>
> *Another advantage, Sir which will surely result from the adoption of this Constitution will be the revival of public & private credit. The energy of the federal govt will gradually infuse a portion of its spirit into the State governements; the regularity with which the taxes will be collected, the introduction of a better system of taxation more productive and less oppressive than the present, the order with which the public revenue will be administered, the punctuality with which the debts and engagements of the Public will be discharged, all these causes co-opperating with others, which it would be too tedious to particularise, will unquestionably restore public credit, & the restoration of public credit will soon be followed, if not accompanied by, private confidence. The latter is the sure consequence of a good administration to private property. The provisions contained in the 10th Section 1st article, will greatly contribute to remove those appre-*

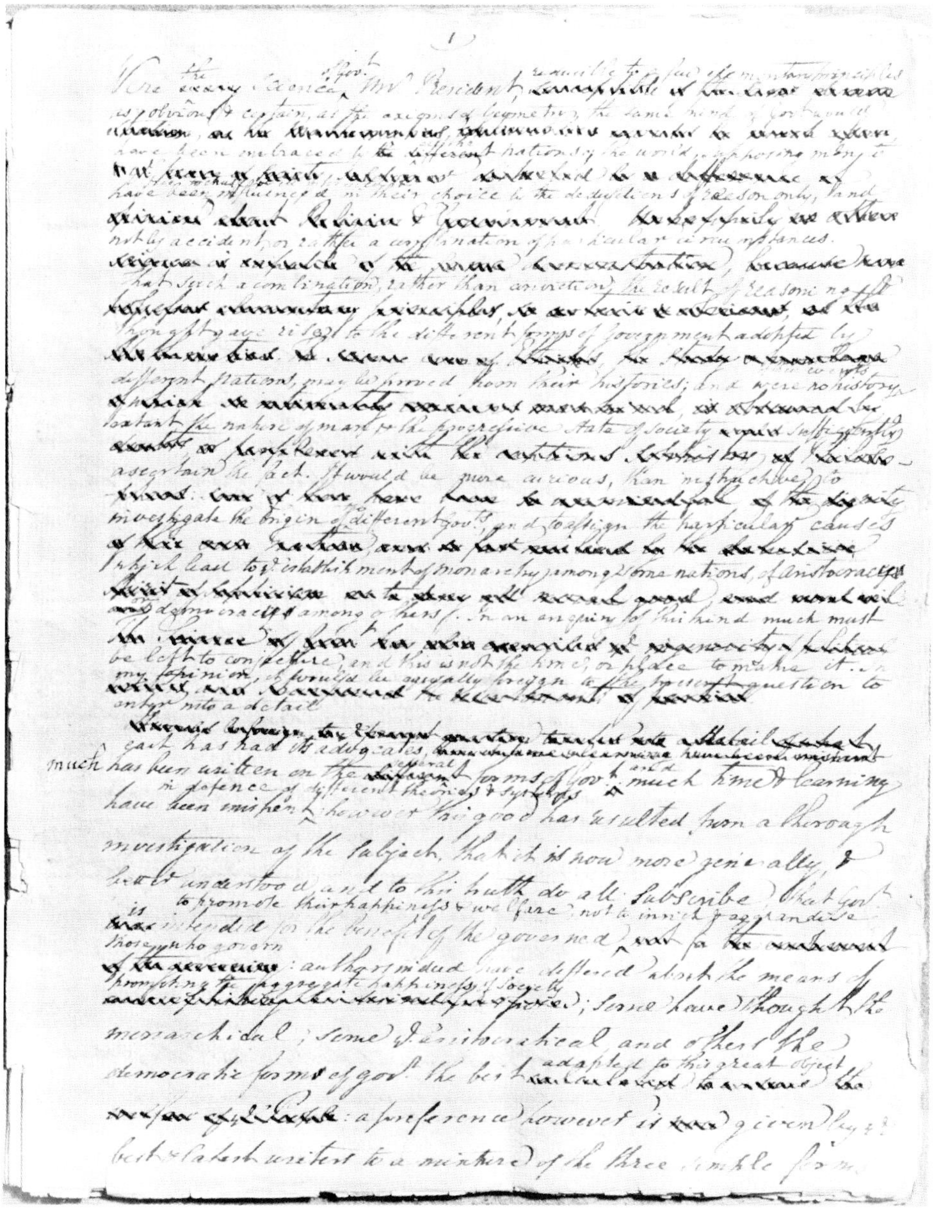

Address to the President of the Maryland Convention for the Ratifying of the United States Constitution, prepared by Charles Carroll of Carrollton
Maryland Hall of Records, Annapolis
P-937, Special Collections

hensions wich have banished private confidence, occasioned hoarding of the coin, a languid curculation, and consequent fall in the value & price of lands.[8]

How much Carroll invested in public securities prior to the 1790's is not known, but he had little cause to be dissatisfied with the economic policies of the new government and, as one of the first two U.S. Senators from Maryland, happily supported Hamilton's proposals to fund the National debt and to establish National credit. After 1788, apart from briefly serving in Congress (1789-1792) and continuing in the State Senate as an outspoken advocate of

[8] P-937, Special Collections, Maryland Hall of Records, Annapolis.

sound fiscal policy until his ouster in 1800, Carroll concentrated almost the whole of his energies on the care and increase of his fortune. As he explained to his family in two letters written in 1790 while he was attending the Senate in New York, with the exception of considering a means of securing the National debt, "I am already tired of my situation and wish to be at home where I would employ my time more to my satisfaction than in this place. . . . When I am at home, I can not only give directions but see them executed. . . ."[9] When he returned to Maryland to stay in 1793, he would never cease overseeing the execution of his affairs until the year before he died at 95, when undoubtedly with reluctance, he activated a Power of Attorney that in effect relinquished control of his fortune to his sons-in-law. Even then, characteristically, there was a clause that reserved him the right to make up his own mind about how his money was to be spent if he found their management wanting.

THE LANDED ESTATE

The Carroll fortune can be divided easily into two parts: land and money at interest. Even as early as 1764 bonds, mortgages and the 1/5 interest in the Baltimore ironworks constituted by far a better source of income than land. In that year, Squire Carroll estimated his net annual income at £1,800 sterling and his gross revenue was probably not more than £2,500 sterling. Of the gross, approximately £1,050 was derived from land. About 4,000 acres of his 'dwelling plantation' 'Dooghragen' was tenanted and earning about £258 sterling a year. Another 3,900 acres of the Frederick County tract "Carrollton" was also leased, returning £250 sterling a year. In addition some of Doughoregan and a portion of the lands near Annapolis were worked by 285 slaves, which, in 1764, had a market value of £8,550 sterling. Assuming that the slaves returned approximately 6.4% of their market value (what they were earning on Doughoregan in 1819) then the cultivated lands not leased to tenants were grossing £547 sterling a year, bringing the landed income to £1,050 or 42% of the total earned annually.

The point that he was making approximately £325 sterling a year more from bonds and mortgages than from his combined landed income was not lost on the Squire. By 1764 he virtually had ceased investing heavily in the purchase or patenting of new land. While it is true that he bought and sold property for the remaining 18 years of his life, some of which came to him through foreclosures on mortgages, he concentrated on developing those lands already partially cultivated in 1764: Carrollton and Doughoregan Manors. In that year Carrollton, on the Monocacy and Potomac rivers, had approximately 39 tenants cultivating approximately 3,900 acres. Over the next decade the number of tenants rose to 63, increasing the annual rent from £250 to c. £565 sterling. The Squire followed the same pattern of developing his lands, although less successfully, at his main dwelling plantation, Doughoregan, where in addition to leasing to tenants, he also cultivated some of the land himself with slave labor. Leaseholders on both manors, but particularly on Carrollton, were

[9] Thomas O'Brien Hanley, *Microfilm Edition of Charles Carroll of Carrollton Papers.* Item 995 — CCC to Mary Caton, April 14, 1790; Item 966 — CCC to Mary Caton, July 11, 1790.

'Tenants at Will' which meant that their leases were renewed annually and they could be forced to change crops, pay higher rents and in general adopt methods of agricultural improvement. On both Manors such leases proved to be a means of shifting from tobacco to wheat as the market for the latter commodity grew profitable.

After the Squire's death and perhaps before, his son took great care to husband resources even to the extent of not raising the rent and he forbade tenants from depleting the soil. For example, in 1784 when he was considering renewing William Hobbs' lease to 40 acres of 'Dooheragen & Howard's Resolution' which Hobbs' father had leased from the Squire, Carroll noted on Hobbs' account: "n.b. wrote to Messrs Macbee & Warfield ye 11th May 1784 that if Wm. Hobbs would enter into bond with security to pay the above balance in three years . . . I would lease him for 7 years the 40 acres which my father agreed to lease his father and at ye same rent . . . he is not [to] till corn or tobo on any part of the land to be leased to him: clauses for manuring will be inserted in the lease."[10]

Of all the approximately 40,000 acres that the Squire held in 1764, and which he passed on to his son in 1782, the principal income producing properties were Doughoregan and Carrollton. A slave-worked plantation was also maintained at Poplar Island, in the Bay near Talbot County, but it proved increasingly unproductive and by 1816, Carroll manumitted his slaves there, possibly in an effort to cut costs without selling slaves that had long been in his family, a course he never repeated elsewhere. Annapolis and Baltimore City property produced some income with Baltimore by far the more important of the two. By 1804, Baltimore City lots, bought, developed and leased by Carroll, were earning about $2,500 (£550 sterling) a year. But neither Annapolis nor Baltimore City lands provided as much income as either Doughoregan or Carrollton. Of the two, Doughoregan was larger in acreage (14,000 as opposed to 13,000), but returned less. By 1819, its net revenue was $6,900 (£1,554 sterling) a year, which when inflation is accounted for, is probably even less than what it was producing in 1764. Carrollton was farmed exclusively by tenants and in time became a major source of income. By 1832, it was returning about $18,000 a year, second in importance only to annual stock dividends. To increase the rents from the approximately $3,500 (£565 sterling) that the Squire received in 1770's to the $18,000 (£4,054 sterling) of 1832 took considerable time and hard work. As Richard Caton explained in a pamphlet published shortly after the signer's death in 1832, it was not until 1812 that the rents from Carrollton reached a point sufficient to sustain his father-in-law's household expenses estimated by 1819 at $12,000 a year and before 1812 Carroll "drew largely on his moneyed Estate" to meet them.[11]

Both the Squire and his son assiduously attended to the detail of land management. Even in 1822 at the age of 85 Carroll overlooked few particulars of the daily operation of Doughoregan. In that year, he wrote his overseer Wil-

[10] Loose paper found in Carroll Account Book, Liber X, MS 211. MdHi.

[11] Richard Caton, "A Brief Statement of Facts in the Management of the Late Mr. Carroll of Carrollton's Moneyed Estate." Baltimore: 1832. MdHi.

VIEW OF BALTIMORE ca. 1800
Watercolor on paper, 12 3/16 x 16 inches
The Maryland Historical Society, Baltimore

liam Gibbons careful instructions on bottling cider including the perhaps unnecessary, "let it be bottled off in a cool clear day, the wind westly, or north east." While apparently always fair with his tenants, Carroll, nevertheless, watched their tenant accounts closely. In the same letter where he instructed the faithful Gibbons on cider-making, he also took note of one tenant who was attempting to abscond without paying his rent:

> *Mr. Caton tells me you could not find Macklefresh. If he did not sell his tobacco to some person in the neighborhood, he must have deposited it in the Tobacco house of some confidential friend, or carried his tobacco to the inspection house at Elkridge landing, or to some of the inspecting houses in this city/Baltimore/ I suspect he carried his tobacco in bulk to be packed & prized at some neighbor's tobacco house, as I believe he had nothing on his tenement to prize his tobacco. It would be well to find out, if you can, who lent his aid to cover the fraud committed by Macklefresh.*[12]

As Gibbons was to testify later, until almost the last months of his life, Carroll never relinquished control over the management of his lands, and while always

[12] CCC to William Gibbons, April 27, 1822. Gift of Richard Webster to the MdHi, March 20, 1975.

his "moneyed estate" occupied the greater share of his time, attention and energies because it was more profitable, like the English aristocrat he emulated, Carroll never allowed his "landed estate" to be neglected.

One major factor in estate management with which Carroll's English counterparts did not have to contend was slavery. It must have been apparent very early to both Carroll and his father that tenanting land could be more profitable than cultivating it themselves with slaves, not that they would ever willingly abandon slaves altogether. The social significance of owning large numbers was too great for that. But not until the Squire's death in 1782 was any effort made to prune the slave population on Doughoregan to at least make it more productive. Between 1773 and 1782, the number of slaves on Doughoregan rose from 330 to 427, a growth rate of 29% that is easily attributable to natural increase. But, beginning in 1782 Carroll launched a major campaign to reduce his slave holdings that lasted until at least 1800. During those years, 245 slaves disappeared from the Manor, when, given the 1773-1782 growth rate, they ought to have increased to well over 600. How Carroll rid himself of so many slaves is not altogether clear. In 1798, only one of his children, Mary, was married and her plantation, Brooklandwood, in Baltimore County had but twenty slaves. The most probable explanation is that Carroll sold his slaves to people who gave him their interest-bearing bonds or securities that did not have to be recorded except when placed in suit and which even then never specified the purpose for which they were executed.

Carroll managed his remaining slaves much as his father had done, permitting them to live in family units on 'quarters' supervised by overseers, where slaves were housed as well, if not better, than the bulk of the white tenant and freehold population. The basic policy difference between father and son was that Carroll never let his slaves increase beyond the point where they quite literally consumed all the profits, a situation other large slaveholders like George Washington failed to prevent and which in many cases brought them to the verge of bankruptcy. While Carroll undoubtedly sold slaves, he was not so mercenary as to sell only the lame, the young, and the old. From the age structure of those left on the Manor he apparently kept his sales to good field hands and possibly their wives, leaving the family structure much as it always had been.

After 1800, Carroll did not sell as many slaves and allowed the population to grow to between 250 and 300. In effect he seems to have been willing to allow his slaves to live quietly and multiply as long as they produced an income equivalent to what he might have gotten if they had been sold on bonds. Proportionately, the amount of time necessary to extract 6% return from slaves worth $44,000 in 1832 was much greater than that involved in managing the same amount of capital out at interest. Doughoregan was the only such indulgence Carroll allowed himself, and even there he did not fall victim to reckless abandon. The slave reductions made before and after 1800 enabled him to manage the remainder and their progeny well enough that as late as 1819 his 195 field slaves were producing a net return of 6.4% of their market value.

THE MONIED ESTATE

If Carroll had a maxim by which he lived it was the admonishment he wrote his son in 1808 about spending one-half years' allowance in one quarter: "Fortunes are as frequently dissipated by negligence and inattention to pecuniary concerns as by vice and extravagance."[13] Throughout his long life no one was able to accuse him of negligence and inattention to his financial affairs. At 84, when others of his generation were either dead or retired to their gardens, Carroll would write his son that "my time is so taken up with settling accounts, writing letters, and the cares of complicated estate and the attention requisite to prevent as much as possible things getting into disorder, that I really have not sufficient leisure to devote to gardening even as an amusement." Under only rare circumstances did he allow his children or grandchildren access to the principal of the family fortune. In 1803 he bitterly complained to his son about his lavish expenditures which had eaten into the "monied capital of the estate." "I am determined not to proceed in breaking in upon the capital as I have done for these three years past. This would be eating the calf in the cow's belly. I have the interest of my grandchildren too much at heart to persevere in so inconsiderate a course of expenditure."[14] By the time of his death Carroll had literally taken over most of their assets as well as his own. In 1832, he held title not only to all of his son's lands, but also those belonging to *both* his sons-in-law, including the Catons' townhouse and their estate Brooklandwood, the Harpers' estate, Oakland, and 45,302 acres of land in New York and Pennsylvania that Caton and Harper had acquired through various speculative ventures and had been forced to turn over to their father-in-law as security for debts which he had assumed.

There is no question that Carroll inherited a large fortune in investments other than land. By 1764, over half of the Squire's annual income was from money at interest. Through careful re-investment of the net revenue in bonds and mortgages the principal of £24,675 sterling in 1764 rose to about £85,000 sterling in 1788, an average annual increase of £2,358 sterling. During the next decade, Carroll further increased the principal of his investments to £128,705 sterling, an average of £4,642 sterling a year. He was able to do so largely because of new investment opportunities such as bank stocks and U.S. government securities made sound by the assumption of state debts. By 1798, 22.6% of his monied estate was in such high interest stocks with the remainder still in fragile bonds and mortgages bearing at best 6% annually. Six years later in 1804, the principal only had grown to £143,001 sterling (£1,430 a year), but Carroll had divested himself of such a considerable portion of his bonds and mortgages (reinvesting in bank and other stock that yielded interest as high as 10%) that approximately 46% of his money was tied up in these securities and his income had risen significantly.

From their inception, Carroll evidenced a strong faith in banks. By 1804, he held shares in the Bank of Maryland worth £5,993 sterling, shares in the 1st Bank of the United States worth £2,827 sterling, and shares in the Bank of

[13] CCC to Charles Carroll of Homewood, April 7, 1808. MS 203. MdHi.

[14] CCC to Charles Carroll of Homewood, August 8, 1803. MS 203. MdHi.

Baltimore worth £2,686 sterling. He was a vociferous supporter of the 1st Bank of the United States and served from its inception as one of its directors. He also favored internal improvements and public service schemes and held shares in a number of the most important, including the Susquehanna and Potomac Canal Companies, the Frederick, Reisterstown, and Jones Falls Turnpike Companies, the Georgetown Bridge Company, and the Baltimore Water Company. While some of them ultimately proved failures and Carroll lost money on a few, others, like the Baltimore Water Company proved successes. In 1807, on the advice of his son-in-law, Richard Caton, Carroll sold his Water Company stock which cost him $5,915 for $36,270 and in a fit of generosity, gave Caton half the profits.

Until 1807, Carroll invested exclusively in American businesses, but in July of that year he ventured into the London securities market sending Barings £500 sterling as "merely an experiment with a view to learn the form and expence attending purchases of stock in London."[15] His curiosity about British investments undoubtedly stemmed from his intense disillusionment with American foreign policy. To Carroll, Jefferson was a 'short-sighted man' who "from fear of, or predilicition for France and antipathy to England is too much inclined to favor the views of Napoleon against that country, the bulwork of this and the Independence of Europe."[16] What Carroll feared most was that America would allow the Naval power of England to be so reduced that the "empire of the seas devolved on France" so "that the United States would become in reality, if not in name a province of that nation."[17]

Carroll apparently did not invest any considerable funds in British stock for four years but in 1811 when Congress, contrary to expectations, failed to renew the Charter of the 1st Bank, he wrote his agent in London, William Murdoch, instructing him to begin buying "the stocks of Great Britain" on his account.[18] Murdoch did as he was directed and by July 1814, with Carroll's explicit approval, Maryland's sole surviving signer of the Declaration of Independence held £6,150 sterling ($27,306) in five percent British Navy Stock. To what extent this money aided and abetted the attacks on Washington and Baltimore in August and September of 1814, is difficult to say, but it certainly demonstrates a certain disenchantment on Carroll's part with his own country and the way it had "been woefully governed for several years past by a french faction."[19] To be fair, however, the bulk of Carroll's capital assets did remain in America during and after the war and a considerable portion was invested in securities that ultimately aided the American war effort.

Thanks to Stephen Girard, a Philadelphia Banker, who took over and successfully managed the assets of the 1st Bank of the United States, Carroll was

[15] CCC to Barings, July 1, 1807. CCC Letterbook: Arents Collection. New York Public Library.

[16] CCC to Charles Carroll of Homewood, March 13, 1807. MS 203. MdHi.

[17] Ibid.

[18] CCC to William Murdoch, 1810-1811. CCC Letterbook, Arents Collection. New York Public Library.

[19] CCC to William Murdoch, March 15, 1811. CCC Letterbook, Arents Collection. New York Public Library.

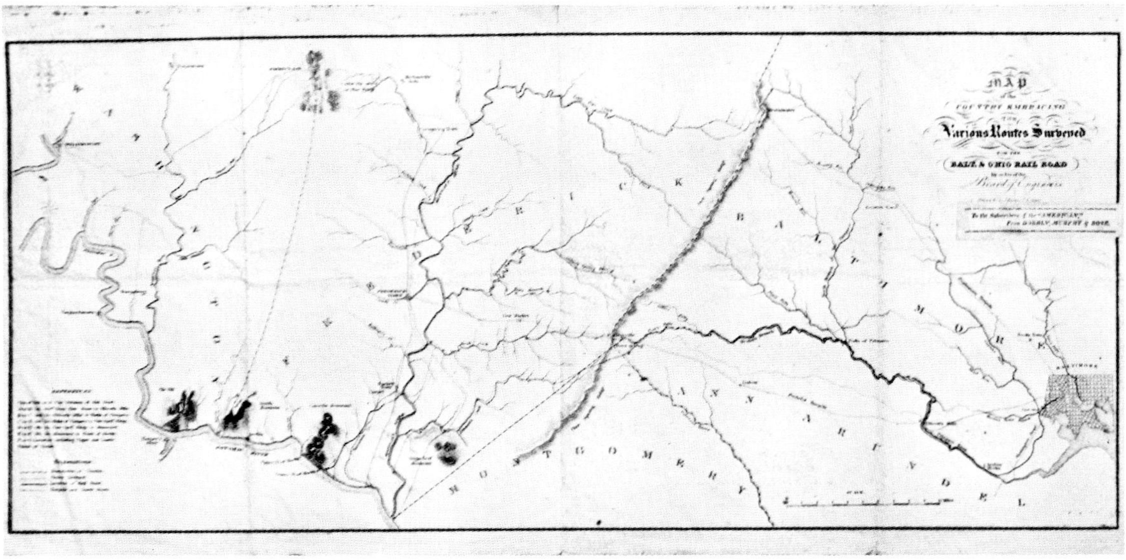

Baltimore and Ohio Railroad Map ca. 1831
Engraving, 10 7/8 x 5 1/2 inches
The Maryland Historical Society, Baltimore

not to lose on that enterprise. In May 1812, he received $43,345, 70% of his principal. With these funds and money derived from further liquidating his bonds and mortgages, Carroll temporarily invested in a number of securities for the duration of the war, including the purchase of $80,000 in Bank of North America Stock which he held for about a year. All such investments were expedients designed to hold and perhaps increase his principal until such time as a second U.S. Bank was established. As Carroll explained to his New York broker, Roswell Colt, in August 1814, it was alright to invest $17,000 in bonds bearing 7% but the rest of the proceeds from the sale of the Bank of North America Stock should be laid out in U.S. stock so that he could easily convert to cash if peace came and a 'new bank' on sound principles was established.[20]

A year and a quarter after the Treaty of Ghent was signed in December 1814, ending the 'second American war of independence,' a second Bank of the United States was chartered. Carroll was almost eighty and eagerly embraced the new bank as the safest and most profitable means of securing the bulk of his 'monied estate.' As quickly as possible he converted the temporary investments made during the war and other securities into stock of the Second Bank. By the time he died in 1832 he held 2,683 shares worth $295,130, more than the total value of all his other stocks combined. He even liquidated his 5% British Navy Stock, although he didn't withdraw from the British empire altogether, reinvesting the proceeds in the Bank of Montreal stock worth $44,850, and bearing 8.5% interest annually.

Apart from the purchase of U.S. Bank Stock and shares in the Bank of Montreal, the only other major investment Carroll made in his last years was in

[20] CCC to Roswell Colt, August 1, 1814. CCC Letterbook, Arents Collection. New York Public Library.

the Baltimore and Ohio Railroad. Although he did not purchase more than 300 shares (worth $6,600 in 1832) of stock in the B & O, he did buy $42,444 in State backed securities that helped build the railroad, and he was very enthusiastic about the railroad's prospects. In February of 1828, when he was 90, Carroll wrote his granddaughter, Elizabeth Caton:

The public prints will inform you what rapid improvements are going on in New Jersey, New York, and the New England States. Baltimore is not behind any of them, the Railroad to the Ohio is an arduous & magnificent enterprise; this great work, it is expected, will be completed in the course of six years for six millions. . . .[21]

Carroll never abandoned altogether loaning money out on bonds and mortgages, but after 1814 he never allowed the principal to rise above £40,274 sterling, half of the amount he had in similar securities in 1788. By 1832 when he died, only 26% ($172,888) of his monied estate was in bonds and mortgages, the rest being in interest bearing bank accounts or stocks.

Carroll certainly had reason to be pleased with his management of his monied estate. From approximately £2,500 sterling ($11,000) in 1764, the Carroll family annual income had risen to £12,145 sterling ($53,973.66) in 1832, or when inflation is accounted for, nearly four fold. Such was more than sufficient to live nobly. According to Jane Austin, in England "a £10,000 a year man was as good as a Lord," and Carroll more than adequately met this criteria. If he had any disappointments in his last years it was that he would not have more to leave to his family. A visitor in April 1832 noted how visibly shaken he was when told of the large fortune recently left by Stephen Girard:

As Philadelphia had been my late residence Mr. Carroll asked me a number of questions on the late Stephen Girard and his immense estate. 'How much did he die worth?' he asked me several times. I said, I had heard it reported that Mr. Girard's estate was estimated at between 8 and 10 millions of Dollars. 'A great deal of money made in one man's life' was the remark everytime that I gave him the same answer to the same question — which he repeated perhaps five or six times in the course of the evening.[22]

DIVIDING THE SPOILS

In the early hours of November 14, 1832, Charles Carroll of Carrollton died peacefully in his sleep at the age of 95. He left an estate worth about 1.6 million dollars all of which he carefully dispensed in a will and three codicils that when printed filled 35 pages of small type. It was his intent that the three branches of the family be treated equally, taking into account what they had already received over the years since each was established.

Throughout his life Carroll provided well for his family and he kept accurate accounts of *every* expenditure to prove it. From the day of their marriages, each of his children received an average of about $10,000 a year in gifts and

[21] CCC to Elizabeth Caton, February 26, 1828. MS 220. MdHi.

[22] Mr. J. J., "My Reminiscences of the late Venerable Charles Carroll of Carrollton," September 1833. MS 206. MdHi.

The Carrollton Viaduct 1831, Endicott & Swett (in Balto. 1830-1831; N.Y. 1831-1834)
Legend: *Lith of Endicott & Swett / CARROLLTON VIADUCT, / BALTO. & OHIO R.R. / Published by Endicott & Swett Graphic Hall Balto. / for the Methodist Protestant*
Lithograph, 6 1/2 x 9 inches
The Hambleton Collection, The Peale Museum, Baltimore

annuities or a total of $1,128,514. Carroll built their homes, maintained 'millenary' accounts for the women, and was constantly bailing various family members out of debt. In relative terms the Harper branch benefited most from his largess, mostly because Carroll was forced to assume a very large debt (over $40,000) in order to keep Robert Goodloe Harper from bankruptcy. In absolute terms, however, because Mary was married the longest, the Caton branch received the most money.[23]

Money Dispersed by Charles Carroll of Carrollton in his Lifetime to the Three Branches of his Family and the Amounts to which Each was Entitled by his Books

Branch	*No. of Years*	*Amount Received*	*Amount Entitled to*	*Difference*
Caton	45	445,119	375,943	79,176
Harper	31½	343,957	219,719	121,461
Carroll	32½	339,438	230,270	108,168
Totals:		1,128,514	825,932	308,805

Source: Carroll Account Books, Library of Congress

[23] Raphael Semmes, *Baltimore As Seen by Visitors, 1783-1860* (Baltimore: Maryland Historical Society, 1953), p. 71.

Estimate of the Value of Mr. Carroll's Entire Estate ca. 1832		
Carrollton Manor	12,000 Acres	$ 480,000
Doughoregan Manor	13,500 Acres	270,000
Oakland Farm		25,000
Poplar Island		6,000
Pennsylvania lands	27,691 Acres	55,382
New York lands, "Moreland Manor"	17,611 Acres	30,000
Houses, Lots, etc., in Annapolis		5,000
"The Farm" near Annapolis inclusive of "Eager Addition" and "Advance"		4,000
"Trusty Friend" farm or *Halfway House,* Anne Arundel County		2,000
Ground Rents, Houses lots, etc., Baltimore, except		25,000
Gay Street House, late residence of General Harper		12,000
Personal Property of every sort (stocks, money, slaves, cattle, utensils, crops, furniture, plate)		750,000
Total		$1,654,382

Source: Private Papers of a Descendant

Although he tried hard to prevent it by leaving an intricate will and codicils, there was inevitable dissension and acrimony about some of the provisions of the will and the division of the "general residium." Harriet Chew Carroll, widow of Carroll's only son Charles, was the source of the most difficulty. She and her lawyers tried desperately to overturn the third codicil on the grounds that Carroll was unduly influenced by his granddaughter, Emily McTavish, but to no avail. Even Harriet's attorneys could find little complaint about Emily. From depositions that they themselves secured, but for obvious reasons did not present in Court, it is clear that Emily was devoted not only to her grandfather, but also to all her family, lavishing attention and care indiscriminately on anyone who needed it. If she got "Folly" Quarter on Doughoregan instead of Harriet by virtue of the third codicil, she probably deserved it and the Courts upheld that view.

Approximately seven years after Carroll died, the controversy surrounding the disposition of his estate was at last resolved and the survivors retired to partake of the spoils. From the point of view of his family, Carroll's fortune was a spectacular and most beneficial achievement, although in terms of Carroll's contemporaries, many, especially merchants like Robert Oliver and bankers like Stephen Girard, accumulated considerably more wealth in their lifetimes. None of the subsequent generations of Carroll's descendants would do as well, although some would continue to observe many of the customs and traditions of the English landed aristocracy that Carroll so openly admired. Late in Carroll's life one visitor remarked that he kept the most English household in America. Other epitaphs might be more noble, but none could be more appropriate especially to one who, only four years after the close of the Revolution, defended the proposed United States Constitution on the grounds that it was closely modeled on well-tested and universally admired British principles.

Edward C. Papenfuse

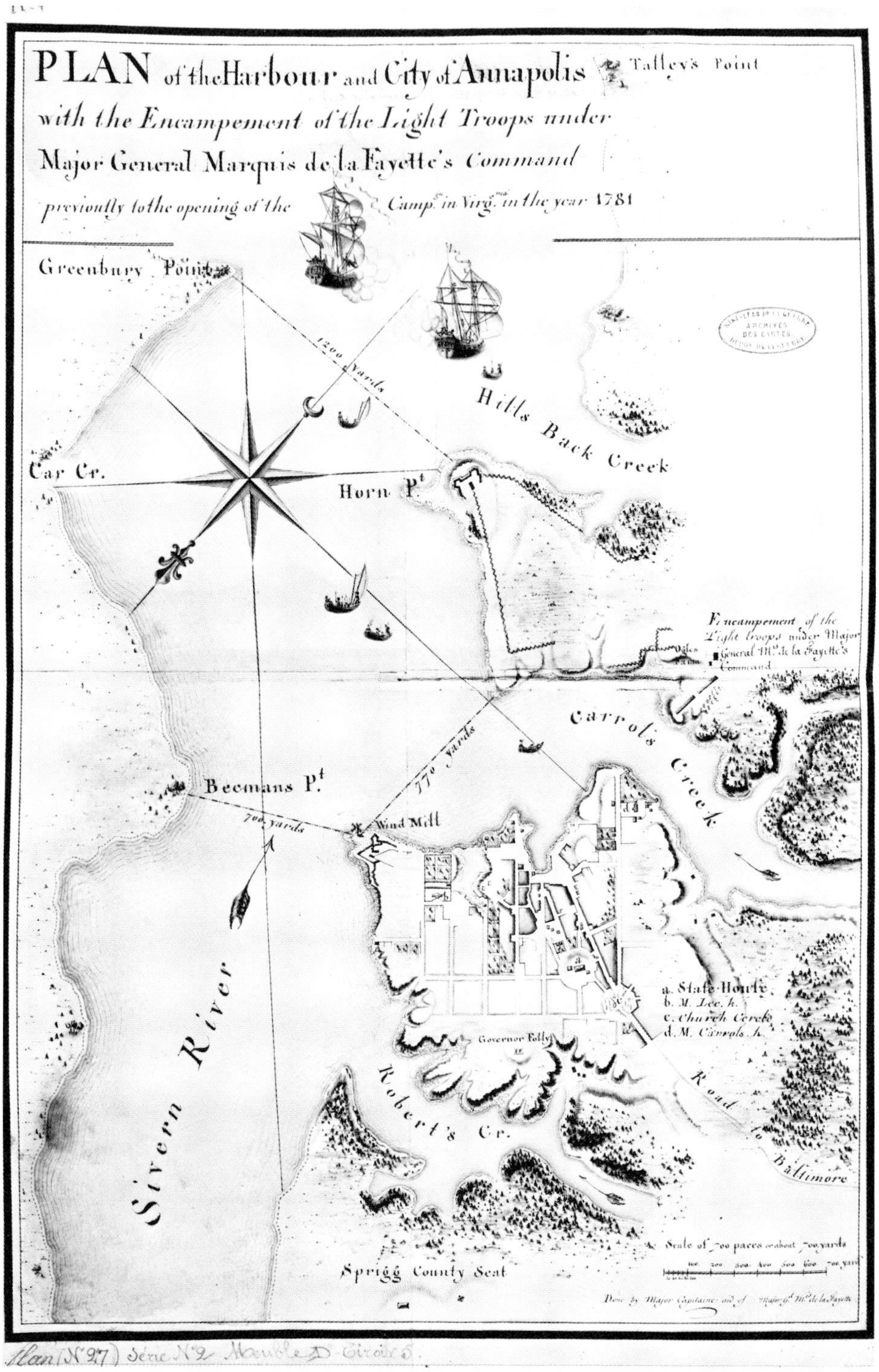

PLAN OF THE HARBOUR AND CITY OF ANNAPOLIS
Ink and watercolor on paper; 27 1/2 x 18 7/8 inches
The Library of The Ministry of Defense, Dépôt de la Guerre, Paris
This plan of the harbour and city of Annapolis was drawn in 1781 by a Major Capitaine, aid of Major General Marquis de Lafayette. The French troops' camp was just across Carroll's Creek (now Spa Creek). The Carroll House is one of the four landmarks in the map's legend.

The Carroll House in Annapolis and Doughoregan Manor

The first of his family in America, Charles Carroll the Settler, through the patronage and friendship of the Lords Baltimore, established in the late 17th century and early 18th century the extensive land holdings that were to be the basis of the Carroll fortune in the 18th and 19th centuries. He arrived in Maryland in 1688 and, in the early years, would have lived in the capital of the Maryland colony, Saint Mary's City. In the year 1694 when the provincial capital was moved to Annapolis, we can assume that Charles Carroll the Settler would soon follow. In December 1695,[1] for the sum of £60 sterling, he acquired 180 acres of land which included "all dwelling houses, barns, stables, gardens, orchards, etc."[2] and which was called "Goffes Increase." This property, increased to 822 acres by 1738 and known as "The Farm," was about three miles from Annapolis near the South River. In the last decade of the 17th century, Charles Carroll the Settler also purchased a 500 acre tract called "Carroll's Forest"[3] in Prince George's County, as well as received warrants for survey of "Ely O'Carroll"[4] and "Litterluna"[5] in Baltimore County.

In 1701 Charles Carroll the Settler made his first purchase within the confines of the new capital on the Severn River.[6] This was a lot of one and three-quarter acres of land, listed as Lots 1, 2, and 3 on the Stoddert Map of 1718, which was acquired from the widow of the postman John Perry and was on the southwest corner of Market and the Duke of Gloucester Streets. Adjoining land, named as Lots 4 and 5 on the Stoddert Map of 1718, was purchased from a Henry Ridgely in 1706.[7] According to the deed, a brick tenement with the dimension of 24 feet was included with the purchase.[8] These two Stoddert lots are particularly important as they represent the site of the present Carroll house in Annapolis. In 1717, three more lots, 6, 7, and 8 on the Stoddert Map, were acquired.[9] This is where the famous Carroll gardens of the latter half of the 18th century would have been. This latest purchase made by Charles Carroll the Settler extended the Carroll property from the western side of Market and Duke of Gloucester Streets down to Spa Creek. Of equal importance as the purchase of the Annapolis lands would be the acquisition in 1702 of the 7000 acre tract called "Doughoregan Manor" in what was then Baltimore County, later Anne Arundel, and now Howard County.[10] The next year Charles Carroll

[1] Provincial Court Deeds. W.R.C., No. 1, Deed 737. Hall of Records, Annapolis.

[2] Anne Arundel County Deeds. Liber E.I. #2, folio 663. Hall of Records, Annapolis.

[3] Kate Mason Rowland, *Life and Correspondence of Charles Carroll of Carrollton* (New York: G. Putnam & Sons, 1898), p. 6.

[4] Patent Records. Liber B.B., folio 339. Hall of Records, Annapolis.

[5] Ibid. Liber C.D., folio 55.

[6] Anne Arundel County Deeds. Liber W.D., folio 370. Hall of Records, Annapolis.

[7] Ibid. Liber W.T. #2, folio 372-373.

[8] Federal Tax Assessment of 1798 for the Middle Neck Hundred, Anne Arundel County, includes in the listing of the structures on Charles Carroll of Carrollton's Annapolis property "one old brick dwelling house 40 x 24 feet, single story." This may have been the house mentioned in the deed from Henry Ridgely.

[9] Anne Arundel County Deeds. Liber I.B. #2, folio 364-366. Hall of Records, Annapolis.

[10] Patent Records. Liber P.L. #4, folio 370. Hall of Records, Annapolis.

the Settler patented 3000 adjoining acres, known as the "Addition."[11] It was the lands in Annapolis and at Doughoregan Manor that would be the focal point of Carroll family life for the next two generations. Other purchases made by the Settler include that of 1705[12] when he acquired by patent 1600 acres called "Enfield Chase" in Prince George's County and later[13] the 10,000 acres in Frederick County called Carrollsburg or Carrollton Manor which ultimately lent itself to the name Charles Carroll of Carrollton.

Unfortunately, none of the houses known to have been occupied by Charles Carroll the Settler survive. From litigation in the Chancery Court in 1761, when Charles Carroll of Annapolis, the Settler's son, entered suit against a Thomas Rutland for infringing on his property, it is known that there was a house owned by the Settler on the property known as "The Farm."[14] For the proceedings, a plat was drawn up, now lost, which, according to the court records, specified "the dwelling house of the plaintiff's father," referring to the Settler, and "the dwelling house of the plaintiff," meaning that of Charles Carroll of Annapolis. It seems likely that the houses here were only for occasional occupancy by the owners or for those who were providing the foodstuffs and other necessities for the large household of family and servants living in the primary abode in Annapolis. In any case, this plantation had special meaning for the Carrolls as the earliest family graveyard was located there; it too was mentioned in the lost plat in the Rutland suit. When James Carroll, who had been executor of Charles Carroll the Settler's will and guardian of Charles Carroll of Annapolis until he became of age, died in 1729, the *Maryland Gazette* reported that he was interred in the Carroll graveyard about three miles from Annapolis.[15] Both Charles Carroll the Settler and Charles Carroll of Annapolis and their wives would appear to be buried there, and in 1825 when Charles Carroll of Homewood died seven years before his father from acute alcoholism and was refused the right to be buried in the Chapel at Doughoregan Manor, he too was buried in this family graveyard. Here in 1961 his grave was discovered in an open field, and his remains were removed to the terraced garden of the house on Spa Creek in Annapolis.

The location and the appearance of the house of Charles Carroll the Settler in Annapolis cannot be firmly identified. From the Stoddert Map of 1718, it is known that the Settler occupied geographically one of the most desirable parts of the city and owned lots that were equal to nearly 1/4 of the city's total acreage.[16] In the early decades of the 18th century, there must have been many important houses in Annapolis. They were probably built in the middle of joined lots with ample lands around them, much as the country style plantation houses

[11] Ibid. Liber D.D. #5, folio 712.

[12] Ibid. Liber C.D., folio 317.

[13] Ibid. Liber I.L. #A, folio 405.

[14] Chancery Court Records. #11, D.D. #2, folios 2, 21, 31, and 34, Hall of Records, Annapolis.

[15] *The Maryland Gazette*, June 17 and 24, 1729. Hall of Records, Annapolis.

[16] Ground Plat of the City and Port of Annapolis, from the 1718 Survey by James Stoddert. Archives of the State of Maryland, Annapolis.

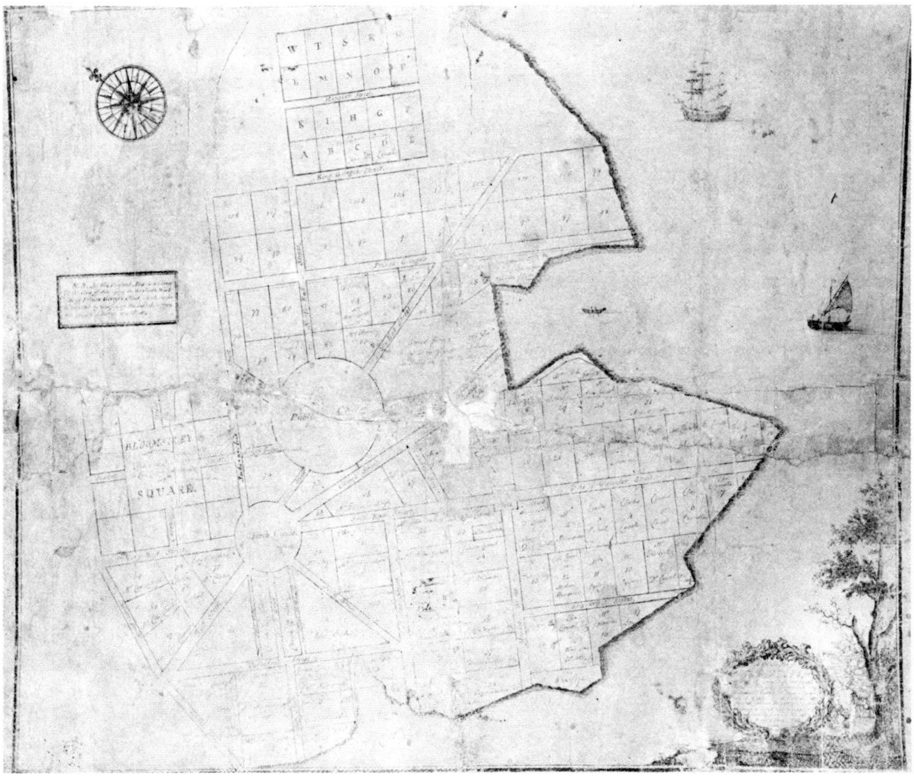

1743 PLAT OF ANNAPOLIS
Ink on paper; 18 x 26 inches
Map Collection, Hall of Records, Annapolis
This early map and plat plan of Annapolis, drawn in 1743 from Stoddert's 1718 survey, indicates the extensive holdings of the Carroll family, perhaps as much as one-fourth of the town. The peninsular site of the Carroll House exceeded any other in Annapolis.

were built around Annapolis. The Settler's house would have been one of the most important of these houses. An inventory of his estate dated 1720, shortly after his death, enumerates the rooms and furnishings of his house, which appears to have been large for its time as well as luxuriously furnished.[17]

The Carroll house which stands in Annapolis today and commands such a presence facing Spa Creek was built by Charles Carroll of Annapolis with alterations being made by his son Charles Carroll of Carrollton. Neither stylistically nor from the inventory of the Settler's estate could this house have been built by Charles Carroll the Settler. A recent study sponsored by a grant from the National Endowment for the Humanities indicates that the Settler's house was probably on Lot 5 of the Stoddert Map of 1718 which would be next to the site of the present house and where the church of Saint Mary's now stands. Before the study, it had been thought that his house was on the northwest corner of Market and the Duke of Gloucester Streets where a mid 18th century dwelling remains. The Carroll name had been associated with this land, but the land belonged to James Carroll, executor of the Settler's estate, not to the Settler. After James Carroll's death, the land was left to Charles Carroll of Annapolis who subsequently sold it to the Hall family. The study

[17] Inventory of Charles Carroll, the Settler. MS 220, Liber X, Box 16, MdHi.

sponsored by the National Endowment for the Humanities indicates that the dwelling on this land was probably built by the Hall family.[18]

Assuming then that the Settler's house was near the present site of the Carroll house, several possibilities arise. In the 1798 tax assessment for the property owned along Duke of Gloucester Street, two structures are listed which might have been on the lots when Charles Carroll the Settler lived in Annapolis.[19] One is listed as an "old stone house 40 x 20, single story;" the other as "one old brick dwelling house, 40 x 24, single story." Even though a one and a half story house was often recorded in these tax records as being of one story, both of these houses appear to be too small to accommodate the seventeen rooms, passages, or storage rooms which are listed in the inventory of the Settler's estate in 1720. In addition, it is almost impossible to imagine the furnishings listed in the inventory as fitting into a house with the dimensions of 40 x 24 feet. For example, in the dining room, named as such in the inventory, are listed twelve tall back leather chairs, three oval tables, one tea table, and two card tables. If these houses were not occupied by the Settler, then there is one more possibility regarding the house of Charles Carroll the Settler. Also listed in the 1798 tax assessment is "a framed addition 52 x 22 feet, two story." This addition was on the eastern end of the present brick house and originally was joined to the same by a passageway. Its later appearance is shown in a View of Annapolis done ca. 1858.[20] Since only the foundations for this wing survive, it is impossible to determine if this was definitely the house of Charles Carroll the Settler. For instance, it is known from the accounts and letterbooks of Charles Carroll of Carrollton that he was to make extensive alterations to the brick house in Annapolis.[21] Is it possible that he had this built as an addition in the 1760's or 1770's? It seems unlikely that an addition would have been frame and not actually attached to the existing brick house. In 1735 accounts, produced by Charles Carroll of Annapolis there is a curious debit entry against his mother, Mrs. Mary Carroll, which sheds some doubt as to whether the original house of the Settler was frame.[22] For the services of Patrick Creagh, she was charged five pounds and ten shillings for painting the outside of the house and the sum of two pounds for painting the dining room. This would indicate that the house referred to was of brick or stone and that the charge was for painting its wooden trim — windows, cornices doors, etc. Mr. Creagh also charged Mrs. Mary Carroll 25 pounds for the 20,000 shingles he provided for shingling the house, passage, and meat house, and for 20,000 shingle nails. There is an entry for 1000 feet of plank for the said repairs, indicating that he was replacing an older roof. Other entries for 1000 feet of both scantling and feather edged siding for the passage and entry, as well as that for twenty-eight

18 Annapolis Lot Histories, NEH Grant #H69-0-M8, 1971. Edward C. Papenfuse and Jane McWilliams.

19 Federal Tax Assessment of 1798 for Middle Neck Hundred, Anne Arundel County. Hall of Records, Annapolis.

20 *View of Annapolis*, E. Sachse & Co. publishers, Baltimore, ca. 1858. MdHi.

21 New York Public Library, Arents Collection 50767.

22 CCA Accounts. MS 211.1. MdHi.

Southern or garden facade, the Carroll House, Spa Creek, Annapolis

The original brick house of ca. 1725-1735 is contained within the confines of the two massive chimneys. A perhaps earlier frame structure, mentioned in late 18th century correspondence and shown in a mid-19th century view, was connected to the eastern end of the house. Remains of the stone sea wall and the terraced gardens can be seen in the photograph.

panes of 8 x 10 crown glass, indicate that this passage was a new connection. If these are references to the house in Annapolis, then they would preclude the possibility that Mrs. Carroll was living in a frame house built on the Annapolis property by the Settler. Instead she was in a brick dwelling that was included in the original purchase or would have been built by the Settler. However, by terms of the Settler's will, Mrs. Carroll received the right to be provided with foodstuff, firewood and other necessities of life from the old dwelling plantation known as "The Farm" near Annapolis.[23] It was still owned by the family at the time of the 1798 tax assessment where there are mentioned "one brick dwelling house, 28 x 28 feet, single story, and one brick house, one and one half story 35 x 28." Even though the accounts of Mrs. Carroll seem to preclude her residence at the dwelling plantation, perhaps Charles Carroll of Annapolis was charging her for making the necessary improvements on the buildings there. Another, very unlikely, possibility is that the references in these accounts could have referred to a plantation house on the property known as "Enfield Chase." By terms of the Settler's will, if a house was built on this property in Prince George's County, she was to move there. Since Mrs. Carroll remained a part of

23 Anne Arundel County Wills. Box C, Folder 11. Hall of Records, Annapolis.

the Annapolis scene until her death, it seems more likely that she lived in the house in Annapolis which was built or purchased by her husband.

The building date for the monumental brick house still standing in its beautiful situation in Annapolis can perhaps be found in the aforementioned accounts against Mrs. Mary Carroll. In 1723, she is credited with nails "for C.C.'s brick house." This early date is in accord stylistically with the brick house and, as Charles Carroll of Annapolis would have reached his majority in 1722, he would have had control of his father's estate. However, since references to C.C.'s brick house continue to appear until 1729, it seems likely that the actual construction of the house did not begin until 1726 or 1727. Even with the leisurely construction schedules of the 18th century, it seems improbable that it took almost seven years to build Charles Carroll's brick house. In addition, 1726 or 1727 seems a more logical time as it marks the beginning of the alliance between Charles Carroll of Annapolis and Elizabeth Brooke.[24] Although the accounts have not survived in their entirety, the frequency of references in the accounts of Mrs. Carroll to C.C.'s brick house between 1726 through 1729 also indicates that the most active building was taking place at that time. In 1726 "diamond glass, window lead, and sodder" are provided for C.C.'s brick house; this is repeated again in 1727. In August, October, and November of 1729, nails by the thousands are listed as well as more windows and "sodder." What is hard to explain is the use in the 1720's of leaded diamond casement windows since guillotine sash windows had been introduced in Maryland and elsewhere in the colonies in the first decades of the 18th century. In fact, this same account book at corresponding dates contains entries for glass for such sash windows. If casement windows were used in the house in Annapolis, then they must have been replaced later in the 18th century since no evidence of them survives today.

In any case, the Carroll house on Spa Creek as it survives today is actually a structure of three different dates. The earliest structure of four bays is flanked by a wing, most likely made in the last quarter of the 18th century, on the eastern end and a mid-19th century addition on the western end. The original house rises three and one half stories on the creek side and two and a half stories on the land or approach side. The ground level basement or first floor contained the kitchen, pantry, other service and store rooms, and perhaps offices connected with the family shipping interests at the nearby wharves. On the northern or land side of the house, the original ground level was higher than it is today. The house was entered by a small entrance porch with two columns as shown in the Sachse print *Bird's-Eye View of Annapolis*, published in 1858. There is evidence today, both in an original doorway and two side lights or small windows which still contain early sash and their original steel barring, that a well or stairway under the entrance porch provided access to the basement or first floor level. The interior arrangement of the house is the same on its two principal levels with partitions rising from the basement to the attic story. The central

[24] Charles Carroll of Annapolis was, according to his own account, born April 2, 1702, and Elizabeth Brooke Carroll, his wife, was christened on May 17, 1709, and, he thought, born on May 9, 1709. Considering the early marriages of the day their alliance could have begun in 1726-27. Their only child Charles Carroll of Carrollton was born when his mother was 28 years of age. Letter CCA to CCC, November 10, 1761. MS 206. MdHi.

Stairway, the Carroll House, Annapolis
The massive handrails, newel posts, closed stringcourse, and the turning of the balusters, corroborate the suggested building date of the late 1720's or early 1730's. There were originally twice as many turned balusters. The stairway winds from the basement or ground level to the third floor.

entrance hall is flanked by two rooms, each with a corner fireplace. Through the entrance hall and under the curve of the stairway, one originally entered one of the two large parlors on the south or creek side of the house. The other parlor was joined to the smaller room to the left of the stairhall. The partitions that divided these rooms on both the first and second floor of the house were removed many years ago.

Little of the original interior woodwork or decoration survives in the Annapolis house with the exception of chair rails in certain of the first floor rooms. In the third and attic stories that were less susceptible to the 19th century renovations, some early panelled doors can be found. However, the most important surviving feature in the interior of the house is the curving stairway that rises

Interior, the Carroll House, Annapolis
Photograph, courtesy of M. E. Warren, Annapolis
This late 19th century photograph of the fireplace wall of one of the first floor double parlors in the Carroll House in Annapolis shows the heavy fielded plaster panelling and cornices also found in the dining room at Doughoregan Manor. The early 19th century mantelpiece is not original to the room.

from the ground floor level to the third floor. Here the heavy newel post and hand railings with evidence of pendant drops and boldly turned balusters on a closed string course all speak of the 1720's and 1730's in Maryland domestic architecture. Further evidence for this date of construction can perhaps be found in the massive timber roof and beam construction in the attic as well as the existence of horizontal summer beams supporting the floors of all rooms. The later plaster panelling of the first floor drawing rooms or parlors will be discussed in relationship to similar panelling at Doughoregan Manor.

In 1756 there is an indication that Charles Carroll of Annapolis made some improvements on the grounds of the large brick house that he had built. In a letter dated September 8 of that year, Elizabeth Brooke wrote from Annapolis to her son Charles Carroll, later to be known as of Carrollton, in Paris of the various changes:

> *This place as I write you in mine that miscarryed is greatly improved — a fine flourishing young orchard with a variety of choice fruit, ye garden inlarged & a stone wall around it, two fine large meadows, several houses built, all this done since you left it it is really a pretty place, but I suppose it would seem insipid to you after being in Paris and seeing Le Beau Monde.*[25]

[25] Elizabeth Brooke Carroll to CCC, September 8, 1756. MS 206. MdHi.

Nine years later, Charles Carroll of Carrollton would return from Europe to Maryland and would soon make improvements to this brick house in Annapolis. By the time he arrived in America, his mother had died, and his father was still living in Annapolis, although perhaps dividing much of his time now between the brick house and Doughoregan Manor where a comfortable plantation house had been erected.

Charles Carroll of Carrollton's arrival in America in 1765 coincides with the greatest building period in Annapolis domestic architecture which had begun in the 1760's with such important surviving houses as those built for the Ridout and Scott families. It was actually in the 1770's, just on the eve of the American Revolution, that there was an almost feverish building activity employing the architectural services of William Buckland, William Noke, Joseph Horatio Anderson, and others, and it seems that Charles Carroll of Carrollton was caught up in the tide. Besides the addition of more service structures and out buildings to the ample grounds on Spa Creek and the alterations to the existing brick house of the 1720's, he was making other improvements in the general landscape of the site, including a necessary sea wall. Would Charles Carroll of Carrollton have sought out the services of an architect, such as Buckland or Anderson, or would he have thought that his own European experience made him his own master? It is known, for instance, that he took courses in drawing and design and that he had traveled, in the 18th century terms, quite extensively both in England and on the Continent. He also had the advantage that no one else had in Annapolis — the immense resources of laborers and workmen, in some cases, skilled workmen, from his father's huge plantation, Doughoregan Manor. The construction of the sea wall in 1770 and the parapet wall by 1774 would have required both design and some knowledge of construction methods. Both would present an ideal introduction for an architect knowledgeable in "land skip" design, such as Joseph Horatio Anderson of Annapolis.

Anderson is credited by documentary evidence as the architect of numerous houses in Annapolis and his best known work is the Maryland State House of 1772.[26] In a letter of May 5, 1774, Charles Carroll of Annapolis wrote to his son:

> *Mr. Anderson called here* [Doughoregan] *on his way to Frederick on I think ye 29 or 30th past and told me his people who would be here next day with a cart would call and leave the plan of my house. I have not seen him or his people. If he does not want ye plan to make out a bill of scantling or any other purpose pray send it in ye chariot with the child.*[27]

The mentioned plan must have been for the house in Annapolis as the dwelling house at Doughoregan Manor dates most decidedly from an earlier building period. Was it a master plan incorporating the existing structures, laying out the grounds, improving the terraced gardens that still remain, adding earthen para-

26 For a fuller discussion of Joseph Horatio Anderson see Morris L. Radoff's *The State House of Annapolis* (Hall of Records, Annapolis, 1972) and Charles Scarlett, Jr., "Governor Horatio Sharpe's Whitehall," *Maryland Historical Magazine,* Vol. XLVI March 1951, no. 1):8-26.

27 CCA to CCC, May 5, 1774. MS 206, MdHi.

pets and supporting walls as well as creating the sea wall or was it merely for a minor addition, such as that of a portico to the eastern framed wing? No conclusive evidence has come to light regarding the employment of an architect, but with further study perhaps more credit can be given to the neglected Mr. Anderson.

Through the lengthy correspondence between Charles Carroll of Annapolis and his son it is possible to trace the construction of some of the improvements initiated by Charles Carroll of Carrollton. In a letter written in August of 1770, an exact date is established for the beginning of building the sea wall on Spa Creek.[28] Such a sea wall is unique in Annapolis and perhaps in other coastal towns both in terms of its survival, quality, and early date. Charles Carroll of Annapolis wrote the following from Doughoregan:

> *I do not approve of ye Susquahanna stone for ye walls in ye water. It is true it will be cheaper and ye work will sooner finished but I am morally certain you will have to do it over again; no joint you can make with ye stone will prevent ye earth washing through it so I am afraid you will be pennywise and pound foolish. I had if necessary rather be 40 years a doing it than not do it well and I am pursuaded it cannot be well done without stones squared as we proposed.*

The stones were indeed squared and most of the original sea wall survives today, attesting to the value of the elder Mr. Carroll's advise and to the proficiency of the workmen who constructed it. The stones are not Susquehanna stone but rather are of ferruginous sandstone, a local rock found in many areas of Maryland, especially Anne Arundel County. In fact in another letter the elder Carroll mentions "ye severn stone."[29] Some of the remaining garden walls at the Carroll house in Annapolis, though rough cast, are made of this same stone. Work on the wall obviously progressed very slowly. Most likely the work was seasonal and was done when the stone cutters were not occupied in building projects related to agricultural or other mercantile pursuits at Doughoregan. In November 1772, Charles Carroll of Annapolis wrote that because of the low tides he expected to see the first two courses of the stone wall completed.[30] Finally in a letter dated April 2, 1775, Charles Carroll of Annapolis advised his son "to take down the stone cutters shop & wall & to level all the earth along the 1st rise or slope, you will then have yr work regularly before you."[31]

The same correspondence indicates that by August 8, 1771, a stable had been built.[32] In the same month, instructions and suggestions are seemingly given for the erection of a coach house.[33] In September of the same year, it is indicated that these instructions pertained to an addition to an already existing coach house.[34] Charles Carroll of Annapolis approved of the addition and wrote

28 CCA to CCC, August 12, 1770. MS 206, MdHi.

29 CCA to CCC, April 25, 1770. MS 206, MdHi.

30 CCA to CCC, November 7, 1772. MS 206, MdHi.

31 CCA to CCC, April 2, 1775. MS 206, MdHi.

32 CCA to CCC, August 8, 1771. MS 206, MdHi.

33 CCA to CCC, August 30, 1771. MS 206, MdHi.

34 CCA to CCC, September 4, 1771. MS 206, MdHi.

"money layed out in usefull & lasting improvements is well layed out, when it is layed out on things in show it is flung away." The existence of still another building is confirmed by the following observation of the elder Carroll in the same letter. He wrote " if you intend to ever put carriages in yr cow house will not ye 6 feet folding doors be too small."

In 1772 Charles Carroll of Carrollton was shaping and grading the slopes from his entrance gate to the wash house.[35] Two years later, in April of 1774, Charles Carroll of Annapolis is offering fatherly advice regarding the parapet wall:

> *If ye raise ye earth three feet above ye stone wall will not ye parapet wall be too high? By leveling ye yard I suppose you will be obliged to add 1 or two steps to the steps going down to ye middle store.*[36]

From the letterbook of Charles Carroll of Carrollton, now in the Arents Collection of the New York Public Library, it is possible to have an insight into a particular living scale in America and specifically in 18th century Annapolis.[37] It is an unparallelled document from the late 18th and early 19th century America. Contained therein are the extensive orders to English agents of every imagineable foodstuff, article of household furnishings, dry goods, hardware, farm tools, and implements, among other things. Throughout the book are references to the remodeling and architectural projects in Annapolis or at Doughoregan Manor. The very first order on October 18, 1771, is for a white marble mantelpiece for which the dimensions are given.[38] On June 4, 1772, an extensive order for the best stock locks of different sizes with pipe keys as well as small locks for cabinet doors and "two bells with rings in different sounds with cranks for four rooms, also spare cranks and wires, some of the wire will be used on the outside of the house." Included are also orders for nails, white lead, and 300 squares of glass, 8 x 10 inches, plus 24 leather aprons for masons, carpenters, and brick-layers. Perhaps these materials were for a major renovation of the existing brick house. Further study is needed to clearly distinguish those references to architectural undertakings or alterations at Annapolis from those at Doughoregan. For example, on November 13, 1773, a sketch of a marble mantelpiece for "a small study Mr. Carroll has lately built" was sent to Mr. William Tyler, statuary maker in London. Was this for the Annapolis or Doughoregan Manor house? And on March 1 of the same year, directions were sent to the London agent to "send as soon as possible to a vessel bound to this port or to Patapsco the glass ordered for the enclosed design. I shall want this glass early in the fall. Let the glass be cut in London to fit the angular panels in the circular heads of these windows." Could these glass windows have been for a coach house now destroyed? Certainly no such windows survive at Doughoregan Manor. Could they have been for windows in the now destroyed eastern frame wing?

[35] CCA to CCC, September 17, 1772. MS 206, MdHi.

[36] CCA to CCC, April 10, 1774. MS 206, MdHi.

[37] CCC letterbook, New York Public Library, Arents Collection 50767.

[38] Ibid. October 18, 1771. This letterbook contains no pagination. This and following references can be located in the date sequence of letters and orders.

There are, however, very specific references in the correspondence that persisted year after year between Charles Carroll of Carrollton in Annapolis and his father at Doughoregan Manor. In the 1858 Sachse *Bird's-Eye View of Annapolis,* there is shown a portico or frontispiece on the land or approach side of the framed wing to the brick house. This is very similar to that added in the late 1760's at Mount Clare, the house built by Charles Carroll the Barrister on the outskirts of Baltimore. Such porches or piazzas could best be described as a projecting portico with a second floor chamber above an open first floor porch. In a letter of May 4, 1770, Charles Carroll of Annapolis wrote to his son from Doughoregan Manor:

> *As to yr molds Robert is not clear nor could Timothy make ye matter plain to him, if you intend 4 pillars it is plain the bases, capitals and astracals must be all alike for each pillar, but if you intend only 2 pillars in front and pilasters adjoining to ye house, then ye bases, capitals and astracals to ye pilasters will only be in work. The way to satisfy Robert is to draw and send a plan of yr pillars with ye bases. et al. Robert says you had better have yr pillars in stone.*[39]

The stone columns for Charles Carroll the Barrister's porch at Mount Clare and the marble paving were ordered through agents in Bristol, England,[40] but the stone columns for the porch in Annapolis and their bases, capitals, and astragals were apparently fashioned by the stone masons permanently employed in the Doughoregan Manor complex. Leather aprons were needed for the stone cutters at Doughoregan for in Charles Carroll of Annapolis' words, "ye stone rubs on their britches and clothes."[41] In another letter of April 2, 1771, it was stated that the stone cutters were working on fashioning the columns for a porch at Doughoregan Manor, and they were too busy at that particular time to come to the house in Annapolis to hang the gates.[42] What might be such a porch appears in an early 19th century print of Doughoregan Manor.[43]

The Carroll house as it must have appeared after the various improvements of the 1770's is reflected in the cited 1798 tax assessment:

> *one brick dwelling house, two story, 100 x 34 feet with a framed addition 52 by 22 feet, two story; and an old stone house, 40 x 20 single story; wash house (brick), 20 x 24 single story; wood house (brick) 56 x 16; poultry house, framed (18 x 14); stable (brick) 20 x 44; coach house (brick) 20 by 60 feet . . . one old brick dwelling house 40 x 24 single story on the same Lot.*

The first dimension of 100 feet given in the tax assessment is inaccurate. Actually in taking the dimensions of the Carroll house as it stood in 1798, the original brick house as built by Charles Carroll of Annapolis measures 45 feet in length. The width of the passage or connector to the eastern wing is 9 feet

[39] CCA to CCC, May 4, 1770. MS 206, MdHi.

[40] Doctor Charles Carroll of Annapolis Letterbooks, MS 208. MdHi.

[41] CCA to CCC, May 4, 1770. MS 206, MdHi.

[42] CCA to CCC, April 2, 1771. MS 206, MdHi.

[43] This print of Doughoregan Manor was made by Charles Louis Hullmandel (1789-1850), an English lithographer, about 1830, after a sketch by W.G.O., an unidentified artist. Collection of The Maryland Historical Society, Baltimore.

Detail from View of Annapolis

Lithograph on paper; 14 1/8 x 19 inches. Inset entitled "Charles Carroll's Residence," 2 x 3 inches

The Maryland Historical Society, Baltimore

This view of the Carroll House in Annapolis is inset into the border of a larger view of Annapolis. Lithographed and published by Sachse, Baltimore, this print with the 1858 *Sachse Birds-Eye View of Annapolis* provides most information regarding the early appearance of the house.

and 9 inches, and the conjectural length determined from the partial remaining foundations of the eastern wing is 51 feet and 9 inches. These three dimensions total more than 106 feet. The depth of the brick house is also miscalculated as it measures 35 rather than 34 feet. These inaccuracies merely reaffirm the known fact that the tax assessors of the period were often rather cavalier in their measurements.

The evaluation of the dwelling house and lot was $2900. The value of the Carroll holdings on Spa Creek can be revealed by comparing its tax assessment to that of other houses which still stand in Annapolis. The assessment for the Brice House is only $1800 while that of the Chase-Lloyd House was $2500.

Pictorial evidence of the Carroll property is revealed in a manuscript map of the *Harbour and City of Annapolis* in 1781 which was drawn by a French cartographer.[44] It is shown with some obvious inaccuracies, but the Carroll property, because of its location, is one of the four lettered and thus designated landmarks in the town. The outline of the house is inaccurately depicted at a right angle, rather than in its true oblique position, to Duke of Gloucester Street. Numerous other structures are shown in outline — perhaps the old stone house, wash house, wood house, poultry house and stable of the 1798 tax assessment. A large structure is shown across Duke of Gloucester Street and from Charles Carroll of Carrollton's will of 1832, it is identified as the true location of the coach house which was left to Emily Caton MacTavish.[45] A

[44] Plan of the Harbour and City of Annapolis, 1781. The Library of the Ministry of Defense, Dépôt de la Guerre, Paris.

[45] Will of CCC, 1832, Acc. No. 19968, Hall of Records, Annapolis.

neat shore line is depicted with the sea wall beginning at the foot of Duke of Gloucester Street where it met Spa Creek and running in front of the garden and house. Projecting from this sea wall into the water or over the water are shown two structures at each side of the terraced hillside gardens at the eastern end of the house. These would seem to be indeed the pleasure pavilions, referred to in a letter written by William Sharrett to Charles Carroll of Carrollton at Doughoregan. Sharrett wrote: "one of the pavillions [sic] is almost roofed . . . the brick layer won't begin on the other pavillion till about 15 days time."[46] Only one project which was undertaken before the tax assessment of 1798 does not seem to be reflected in these records, that is the enlargement of the connection between the brick house and the frame eastern wing. From a letter dated November 1771, it is known that a passage connected two houses.[47] Charles Carroll of Annapolis wrote from Doughoregan Manor to tell his son where he could find some legal documents that had been misplaced.

> *I had ye opinions about Escheats wh you mention, it was in ye walnut tree press wh stood in ye passage between ye two houses; if you have moved it thence it may be ye old scrutore in ye chappell, if you did not with other papers move it into Deard's press in the study. . . .*

The filler or two story connection between the original brick house and the frame eastern wing must have been built in the 1780's or 1790's. The brick work of this part of the surviving Carroll House, and the arched brick window on the land side seem to date from this period. The later date of this addition is also reflected in the numerous and different ways in which the brick work of the addition is joined to the earlier house at the first and second story levels.

After Charles Carroll of Annapolis' death in 1783 and when the entire economic and even cultural center of the Chesapeake Bay after the Revolution shifted from Annapolis to the booming port of Baltimore on the Patapsco, Doughoregan Manor came to be the principal residence of Charles Carroll of Carrollton. The tax records reveal that until 1820 the house in Annapolis was still furnished, and letters and other documents show that it was occasionally used by Carroll, his children, and his grandchildren.[48] The 1820 tax assessment, however, reveals that the house was emptied of its contents and on May 12, 1821, the house was rented for a term of one year to a "Major Richard Jones of the said city of Annapolis."[49] The indenture or agreement offers the following description of the buildings:

> *. . . two dwelling houses aforesaid, the stable and the coach house also the garden annexed to the wooden house, also the three lots lying between the dwelling house of said Carroll and the house of Clotworthy Bernie enclosed with post and rail fences. . . .*

Rent was not paid in advance, but at the end of each six month period, $250 was collected, making a total rent of $500 per year. Rental of such a desirable

46 William Sharrett to CCC, July 5, 1777. MS 206, MdHi.

47 CCA to CCC, November 1771. MS 206, MdHi.

48 Annapolis City Records, Tax Assessments.

49 Charles Carroll Papers, Hall of Records #1499, Scholarly Resources, Inc., Ed. Thomas O'Brien Hanley, Wilmington, Delaware, 1971.

house and location must have been continued for many years. In the *Baltimore American and Daily Commercial Advertiser,* on March 25, 1844, the following advertisement appeared:

> *CHARLES CARROLL HOUSE ANNAPOLIS*
> *For sale, lease or rent that large and commodious brick dwelling house in Annapolis containing eleven fine rooms with out houses, gardens, and stables, It is beautifully situated on an eminence commanding a delightful prospect of the bay and surrounding country and for those fond of pleasure there is fine fishing and ducking in the vicinity. It was the former residence of the late Charles Carroll of Carrollton and devised by him to his daughter Mrs. Mary Caton.*

The house obviously did not sell for it was left by Mrs. Mary Caton to her daughters who in 1852 presented the house and its grounds to the Redemptorist Fathers of the Catholic Church who still retain ownership.[50]

The largest agricultural operation at the time of Charles Carroll the Settler seems to have been at Doughoregan Manor. This is determined by comparing it to the other plantations and by the number of slaves listed as working there. As indicated in the inventory of the Settler's estate in 1720, Doughoregan Manor was a working plantation only as there are no listings for household furnishings. It would be Charles Carroll of Annapolis who would begin the existing plantation house at Doughoregan Manor and who would make the first and most important improvements.

Even though according to the marriage settlement made between Charles Carroll of Annapolis and Elizabeth Brooke on November 15, 1757,[51] Elizabeth Brooke received £100 sterling per year. Charles Carroll of Annapolis in addition provided very well for her in his will.[52] From the wording, it is clear that it was made after the marriage settlement, although the exact date is not known. Apparently unrecorded, the will reads as follows:

> *to my dear wife . . . over and above what I have engaged to give her as a marriage settlement, my dwelling on Chance or Dooreghan with all that tract of land called Chance by me resurveyed with all the buildings and improvements thereon with so much of Dooreghan as is now cleared and makes part of my dwelling plantation so as not to take in any part of Valentines, Jacobs or John Reed's plantations or the woods adjacent thereto being part of Dooreghan. . . . I also bequeath to my said loving wife all the household goods, and Goods Furniture, and kitchen utensils in my said house and kitchen thereto adjacent with all the beds, bedding, rugs, quilts, blankets, counter panes, sheets, table linen, etc. during her natural life . . . also 50 head of sortable black cattle, 50 head of hog, 50 head of sheep, 6 good working horses, two yoke of oxen, two breeding mares, two of my best chair horses, the chair, etc., etc. . . and further:*
>
> *I bequeath to my said wife during her natural life 7 negro men and 7 negro women which negro shall not be above forty or under 15 years old.*

In addition to the sum specified in the earlier marriage settlement, Elizabeth Brooke Carroll would also receive annually for the rest of her natural life, £150 sterling.

50 Anne Arundel County Deeds. Book NHG 1, folio 341. Hall of Records, Annapolis.

51 MS 2018. MdHi.

52 Will of CCA. MS 206, MdHi.

From the wording of the will, a suitable house at Doughoregan Manor had been built, and we learn that a separate kitchen was also in existence. Although Doughoregan Manor was extensively remodelled by Charles Carroll of Doughoregan when he inherited the property from his grandfather in 1832, the early 18th century story and a half brick plantation house, typical of the Maryland tidewater area, is still contained within the fabric of the surviving house. The brick house was flanked on either side by symmetrically placed dependencies — one containing kitchens and store rooms and the other a private chapel for Catholic worship. The descriptive and revealing tax assessment for 1798 records the following for Doughoregan Manor in the Elkridge Hundred in Anne Arundel County:

> *One brick dwelling, 66 x 32 feet one story; one brick kitchen 59 x 27 feet, one story; one stone vineyard house 31 x 18 feet, one story; one framed ice house, 18 x 18 feet; one stone bathing house, 19 x 19, the evaluation of the above $4,000.00.*[53]

There is no mention of the flanking chapel which originally by present measurements had the same dimensions as the kitchen dependency. As a place of public worship, it was the property of the Catholic Church in 1798 and was, therefore, untaxable and unlisted. It should also be noted that such a tax assessment would only cover those structures immediately around the dwelling house. The farm buildings, dairy, wash houses, slaves' quarters that were located nearby received separate listings. Also, the kitchen, as was the chapel, was "T" shaped and should have received more than the two overall measurements of the tax assessment.

The separate kitchen building consisted of four rooms and a stairhall leading to the chambers above. Two rooms of nearly equal size, each with a large cooking fireplace, were on the first floor with a smaller room next to the stairhall referred to as the buttery. The fourth room was the largest and did not have a fireplace. In the 19th century it was used as a billiard room, but in the 18th century it most likely served as a store room for the necessities of a plantation far from Annapolis. In the mid-18th century, some of the space of the chapel dependency was probably taken up by other rooms, although it is an undivided space today.

The exact height of the original walls can be traced in the brick work at Doughoregan Manor, and its early appearance is confirmed by a 19th century print that shows the house as it must have appeared just prior to Charles Carroll of Carrollton's death in 1832.[54] The known dates of two manuscript plats made in the years following the death of Carroll when the estate remained in litigation indicate that the print shows Doughoregan as it appeared in the 1820's or early 1830's.[55] These plats are both drawn by a William Dawson, Jr. of Baltimore. One of the plats dated 1840 documents that, with the exception of

53 Federal Tax Assessment for 1798 for Elkridge Hundred, Anne Arundel County. Hall of Records, Annapolis.

54 See the illustration of *Doughoregan Manor* printed by C. Hullmandel.

55 The plat dated 1832 was presented to The Maryland Historical Society by the Carroll descendant who still possesses the 1840 plat.

DOUGHOREGAN MANOR, HOWARD COUNTY
From a sketch by W.G.O., printed by C. Hullmandel
Lithograph; image size: 8 5/8 x 12 7/8 inches
The Maryland Historical Society, Baltimore

Doughoregan Manor, as it appeared at the time of Charles Carroll of Carrollton's death in 1832. The ink inscription *The Carroll Manor Md / Residence of the Hon Chas Carroll of Carrollton* indicates that the print was executed prior to 1832 and correspondingly prior to the death of the English lithographer Charles Joseph Hullmandel in 1840.

SKETCH OF DOUGHOREGAN MANOR, HOWARD COUNTY
Ink on paper; approx. 61 x 51 1/2 inches
Private Collection of a Descendant

This ink sketch of the house at Doughoregan Manor appears on an 1840 plat drawn by William Dawson, Jr. With the exception of the story and a half chapel and kitchen wings, the house by 1840 had assumed its present appearance.

East Facade, Doughoregan Manor, Howard County
From the Photographic Collection of The Maryland Historical Society, Baltimore
Doughoregan Manor measures in excess of 270 feet in length. The house stands today unchanged in appearance from this late 19th century view of the entrance facade.

Garden Facade, Doughoregan Manor, Howard County
Here giant catalpa trees and boxwood survive from the 18th century landscaping.

SERVICE BUILDING, DOUGHOREGAN MANOR, HOWARD COUNTY
From the Photographic Collection of The Maryland Historical Society, Baltimore
This story and half brick house, one of the many other 18th century buildings at Doughoregan Manor may well be the Weaving house known to have been built after the Revolution. By family tradition it has also been called the laundry house.

the raising of the roofline of the kitchen and chapel wings, the present size of Doughoregan had been achieved by that time. However, the plat drawn in 1832 shows that the kitchen had been connected to the main house with a passage, but the chapel still stood as a separate dependency. This separation is also shown in the print which would indicate that this addition was made between 1832 and 1840.

According to Carroll family tradition, the house at Doughoregan Manor was begun in 1735. This early date is borne out in some of the architectural remains such as the large size brick employed in the central block and in both the chapel and the kitchen dependencies, as well as the Flemish bond of all the walls. The interior more clearly reflects this early construction date. Early 18th century panelling, chair rail, and cornice are used in the main parlor and in the small room adjoining the stair hall on the first floor. Fielded plaster panelling and cornices are found in the room in the southwest corner of the house, now employed as a dining room. This panelling is very similar to that on the first floor of the Carroll house in Annapolis, and the work is most likely by the same hand. On September 3, 1763, Charles Carroll of Annapolis wrote to his son:

> *I am making an addition to my house at Elkridge I want to stucko it but we have not here a workman who can do it, I wish you could by yr self or by a crimp procure such a one, I would be content he shd only serve 2 years for ye charges of his passage, etc., but let him procure a certificate from some master builder or undertaker that he is a good workman, if he cannot go on other terms I would pay his passage if he would work for me on reasonable terms, & you may assure him he would not want good business here*[56]

[56] CCA to CCC, September 3, 1763. MS 206, MdHi.

In 18th century terms, the use of the word "addition" could be interpreted to mean an improvement, and the stucco workman would be the master plaster worker who could create such panelled rooms that now appear both at Doughoregan and at the house in Annapolis. In January of 1764, Charles Carrollton wrote his father: "I have spoke to Mr. Bird about the stoko man. He will endeavor to find one to go on the terms proposed; but he doubts whether a good workman can be engaged to leave England on such terms."[57] Whether the stucco man came from England is unknown, but the remaining panelling indicates that the work was done.

There were originally, as now, four fireplaces on both the first and second floors of the original Doughoregan Manor house. However, only the one in the present dining room retains its original surrounds or mantelpiece. An examination of the first floor joists and flooring reveals that the stairway was always in its present position in the small hallway to the right of the entrance doorway. This original stairway occupied a relatively small area and would, therefore, like the stairway in Annapolis have wound to the second floor. The stairway was rebuilt in the latter half of the 19th century, but it may have had the same early character as that in the Carroll house in Annapolis.

The inventory of Charles Carroll of Carrollton's estate, made by an appraiser on the first of April 1833, helps to reconstruct the use of the first floor rooms and those in the passage or the connector leading to the kitchen dependency.[58] Specified in the central or main block are a dining room, most likely in its present location, a sitting room, Mr. Carroll's bedroom, a passage (perhaps the large central hallway), a small room, the servants' hall, a large store room, a small store room, a kitchen, a lumber room, and a passage. Upstairs there are listed nine separate bedrooms.

A most revealing description of Doughoregan Manor in 1827, the later years of its occupancy by Charles Carroll of Carrollton is contained in a letter written by Henry D. Gilpin to his father in Wilmington.[59] His physical description of the house and the hospitality of the Carroll family is of great interest:

> . . . [We] *got into the carriage & drove up to the Manor which is sixteen miles from Baltimore, near the road I traveled to Harper's Ferry. We found the family there expecting us, and joined old Mr. Carroll & two or three other gentlemen at the dinner table; he is a nice little old man, with a sharp face, not very thin, & gay benevolent face — his hair is very white & long being tied with a ribbon behind. He wears drab breeches & worsted stockings, with an old fashioned waistcoat with long pockets hanging down, a large wrapper or cloak, silk in summer & cloth in colder weather, which he tucks up & holds round him as he walks, so as to look quite funny. His conversation is very lively & pleasant though not very profound, and he seems to take great interest in all that is going on, mixing a great deal with the family . . . he has on the ground floor, his library, chamber & closet, where he remains when he does not feel inclined to join in the bustle which*

[57] CCC to CCA, January 27, 1764. MS 206, MdHi.

[58] CCC, Inventory of Estate. MS 205, MdHi.

[59] The Gilpin Papers, Historical Society of Pennsylvania; "A Glimpse of Baltimore Society in 1827: Letters by Henry D. Gilpin," *Maryland Historical Society Magazine*, Vol. 69 (Fall 1974, no. 3):266-268.

is usually going on in the rest of the house; in the former room are some family portraits which I think wd. make Elizabeth laugh pretty loudly — consisting of ladies in enormous draperies, craped hair, long waists, garlands of flowers &c. — little boys in pink purple or scarlet knee breeches, standing in the midst of banks of flowers, venerable faces peeping from among robes of state & enormous wigs &c. The whole place is a sample of southern hospitality on its greatest scale as to carelessness & kindness though not as to splendour which certainly never is thought about. . . . The house is an old one or at least the gradual growth of several generations, parts having been from time to time added — some one story, some two — some rough cast, other brick — so that although full of rooms, it is quite an insignificant place — it has two uniform wings — almost the only parts that are so, one being a chapel & the other a kitchen. On one front is an old fashioned porch opening on the road or entrance — on the other a similar one looking on the garden, which is large, with broad 'closely-shave-green' walks that are very pleasant although the flower beds & fruit trees along side of them, have but little pretension either to beauty, variety or excellence. The interior besides the chambers which are very numerous both up & down stairs, and Mr. Carroll's rooms, consists of a large wainscoated irregular hall, and two parlours; presenting in their furniture a singular medley of old and modern fashions — there are here fine new curtains of the gayest colours; there are sofas & chairs, covered with glorious old cushions, and so deep that you cannot sit, but must really lie back in them — there is perhaps a large fire in one room, & none in another — a card table in full operation in one — a harp, guitar, and songs sounding in another — in one people eating away, in another chattering or whispering in corners. Everybody seems to catch in ten minutes all the freedom & ease of the place. When you arrive there is generally a crowd in the porch to welcome you, the old gentleman comes out to shake hands, & either stays & talks or if busy goes back in a few minutes to his room — every body is glad to see you, but no body takes any trouble — you get up if you choose when the chapel bell rings at seven, & hear prayers & on feast days, mass — if the old gentleman has not appeared, you wait until he is ready for breakfast, but any time after that the breakfast table remains & you eat it when you choose — on a large table in the hall, through the middle of the day, there are punch, toddy, lemonade, wine cakes, & all that sort of thing, with heaps of newspapers, new novels & You may loll on the sofa & read them, & nobody expects you to rise, even ladies, unless inclined — you meet little parties in the garden, but you need not join them unless you like — there are guns, & you may go to shoot, there are horses and you may ride — a bath & you can bathe. You stay a day or a week, welcomed when you come, & going away at any hour you choose.

The description of the wainscoted entrance hall where the walls are now fully plastered leads one to believe that perhaps the other rooms on the first and second floors were fully or partially panelled when the house was first built in the 18th century.

A complete study of Doughoregan Manor as an agricultural complex in the late 18th century and early 19th century should be pursued. Undoubtedly the 18th and early 19th century farm and service buildings at Doughoregan are the greatest survival of their kind. They stand without the activity that must have surrounded them in the years that Doughoregan Manor was occupied by Charles Carroll of Annapolis and Charles Carroll of Carrollton. In the 1770's and 1780's, there were nearly five hundred slaves on the plantation and nearly a quarter again as many artisans and craftsmen in such varied areas as the

TOMB OF CHARLES CARROLL OF CARROLLTON
Charles Carroll of Doughoregan placed this monument above the remains of his grandfather in the chapel at Doughoregan Manor. It was executed in Rome in 1852 by Edward S. Bartholomew.

vineyard, the flour mill, the saw mill, work house and the weaving manufactory, among others.

In 1832, at the age of 95, Charles Carroll of Carrollton died in Baltimore at the residence of his daughter Mary and her husband Richard Caton. Funeral services were held at Baltimore's Catholic Cathedral and the funeral cortege then carried his body back to his beloved Doughoregan Manor. He was buried beneath the altar in the chapel, and the marble monument and memorial executed by Edward S. Bartholomew in Rome in 1852 was placed in the chapel by his grandson Charles Carroll of Doughoregan.

After Carroll's death, Charles Carroll of Doughoregan, his grandson, made alterations to the dwelling house which are reflected in the present day appearance of Doughoregan Manor. However, the preestablished plan of a central block flanked by symmetrically placed dependencies was maintained. After receiving the inheritance in the late 1830's Charles Carroll of Doughoregan would raise the central block to a full two stories, make improvements to and also raise the roof of the chapel to match that of the kitchen dependency, build a wing to connect the chapel to the main house in accordance with the similar connecting wing built by Charles Carroll of Carrollton on the other side of the house. He would add the decorative balustrade to the roofline, a cupola on the roof of the central block as well as the Greek Revival porticos on the entrance and garden facades. Extensive alterations to the interior of the chapel also seem to have been made at this time although some of these were already underway in 1822.[60]

By the time of his death, Charles Carroll of Carrollton owned all the houses of his children and their spouses which included the Harper plantation of Oakland, the Caton's house in Baltimore, and their plantation Brooklandwood,[61] as well as Homewood, the house built by his son Charles Carroll.[62] In addition, he is known to have owned a plain two story house with an L- or T-shaped wing at Bath or Warm Springs, the fashionable late 18th century spa currently known as Berkeley Springs, West Virginia.[63] Just prior to his death in 1832 he was to begin construction of Folly Quarter for his favorite granddaughter Emily Caton MacTavish and her husband John MacTavish.[64] These houses are also part of the architectural history of the Carroll family, and will be treated fully in the exhibition, but they have been more adequately discussed by architectural historians and it is really Doughoregan Manor that even today remains as the symbol of Charles Carroll of Carrollton and his family in Maryland. The result of the research undertaken for this exhibition and publication is the light which has been cast on the architectural history of both this house and the earlier one in Annapolis. As these were the two principal houses occupied by Charles Carroll of Carrollton, this seems appropriate. In the past, little interpretation has been made from the vast amount of material found in the Carroll papers at The Maryland Historical Society and in such documents as the letterbook of the Signer in the Arents Collection of the New York Public Library as it relates to the architectural history of the Carroll family. The possibility of further study is extensive, but even this initial effort indicates the elaborate and aesthetic tastes of one of the leading families of Maryland. No other Maryland family, through three generations, has left us such an architectural legacy.

William Voss Elder, III

60 CCC to William Gibbons, November 1, 1882. Appeals and Issues, DMP 2, p. 44. Hall of Records, Annapolis.

61 The "Caton House" on Lombard Street in Baltimore, now called the Carroll Mansion, is an historic house museum, administered by the Peale Museum. "Brooklandwood" was the subject of an article by Robert Erskine Lewis in the *Maryland Historical Society Magazine*, Vol. XLIII, (December 1948,):280-293.

62 "Homewood," still standing on the Campus of Johns Hopkins University in Baltimore, has been a subject of numerous articles, especially that by J. G. D. Paul entitled "The History of Homewood," privately printed by The Johns Hopkins University.

63 CCA and his son owned lots 24 and 25. A letter written in 1778 by Daniel of St. Thomas Jenifer to CCA reveals that Carroll's house was recently completed. Daniel of St. Thomas Jenifer to CCA, August 3, 1778. MS 206, MdHi.

64 Folly Quarter is discussed in an article by Robert L. Alexander, "William F. Small 'Architect of the City'," *Journal of the Society of Architectural Historians*, Vol. XX (No. 2, May 1961):63-77. However, additional Folly Quarter material, including the contract for the building of house and the numerous outbuildings has recently been located among the Carroll-MacTavish Papers, MS 220, MdHi.

Archbishop John Carroll
William S. Leney, F.S.A. (1769-1831) and Benjamin Tanner F.S.A. (1775-1848) after Jeremiah Paul (?-1820)
Cat. No. 53

Catholicism and the Carrolls in Early Maryland

Together with Rhode Island and Pennsylvania, Maryland ranks as one of the foremost contributors to the American heritage of religious liberty, a heritage which traces its origins to the early Stuart era in England. When George Calvert, First Lord Baltimore, forfeited a promising political career to become a Roman Catholic in 1625, he began almost at once to dream of a New World haven for persecuted English Catholics. Although George Calvert did not live to see this dream materialize, his sons benefited from their father's influence with the Stuart rulers when in June, 1632, King Charles I granted Cecil Calvert (Cecilius, if one uses the formal Latin name) a generous charter making him First Lord Proprietor of the Maryland colony.

Cecil, the Second Lord Baltimore, was not only a devout Catholic; he was an astute businessman as well. He saw at the very outset that, to succeed, his Maryland Venture, as it was called, could not be exclusively Catholic and he therefore insisted that full religious toleration be assured Christians of all persuasions.[1] Ten days before his colonists set sail on November 22, 1633, he wrote out a set of instructions to that effect.[2]

The *Ark* and the *Dove* which made the four-months' voyage carried between 200 and 300 passengers, among whom were sixteen Catholic gentlemen-adventurers and their families, and many indentured servants, predominantly Protestant. The leader of the colonists and first Governor of Maryland was the brother of Cecil, Leonard Calvert, who was accompanied by four Jesuits — two lay brothers and two priests: John Altham and Andrew White. It is from the latter's account that so many of the details of Maryland's founding have been preserved.[3]

The colonists landed first on an island in the Chesapeake Bay, which they named St. Clement's and there Father White offered the first Mass for the Catholics, while the Protestants held their own services of thanksgiving nearby. The date was March 24, 1634, a landmark in the history of our nation. As one historian has remarked, this experiment in religious equality and toleration gives Maryland "a unique place in the history of English colonization."[4]

This felicitous beginning was soon marred, unfortunately, by subsequent events. As John Tracy Ellis has pointed out, "A universal anti-Catholic bias was brought to Jamestown in 1607 and vigilantly cultivated in all thirteen colonies from Massachusetts to Georgia."[5] This bias emerged in Maryland even in the time of Leonard and Cecil Calvert and had its sources in the bigotry both encroaching from neighboring Virginia and welling up within Maryland

[1] Although Pennsylvania and Rhode Island conferred religious liberty on Jews as well as Catholics and Protestants, the formal grant in Maryland was restricted to Christians. It is true, nevertheless, that a Maryland Jew named Jacob Lumbrozo after meeting some preliminary difficulties in 1658, was allowed to settle down peacefully and participate in the political life of the colony. Cf. William T. Russell, *Maryland, the Land of Sanctuary* (Baltimore, 1907), pp. 271-274.

[2] John Tracy Ellis, *Documents of American Catholic History* (Milwaukee, 1956), pp. 100-103. Baron Baltimore's instructions were dated November 13, 1633.

[3] Andrew White, S. J., *Relation*, reprinted in *Woodstock Letters*, I, 16ff.

[4] Charles McLean Andrews, *The Colonial Period of American History* (New Haven, 1936), II, p. 291.

[5] John Tracy Ellis, *American Catholicism* (Chicago, 1956), p. 19.

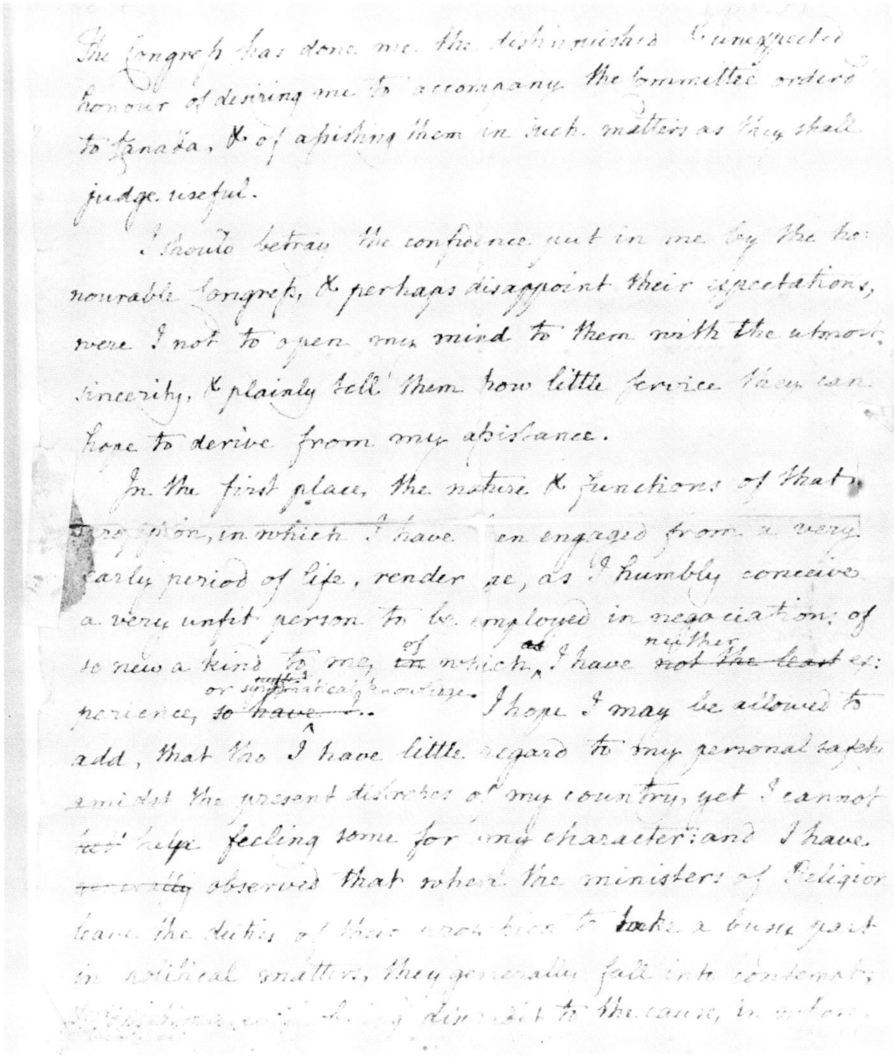
The Congress has done me the distinguished & unexpected honour of desiring me to accompany the Committee ordered to Canada, & of assisting them in such matters as they shall judge useful.

I should betray the confidence put in me by the honourable Congress, & perhaps disappoint their expectations, were I not to open my mind to them with the utmost sincerity, & plainly tell them how little service they can hope to derive from my assistance.

In the first place, the nature & functions of that profession, in which I have been engaged from a very early period of life, render me, as I humbly conceive, a very unfit person to be employed in negociations of so new a kind to me, of ~~in~~ which I have neither ~~not the least~~ experience, or sufficient political knowledge ~~to have~~. I hope I may be allowed to add, that tho I have little regard to my personal safety amidst the present distresses of my country, yet I cannot help feeling some for my character: and I have observed that when the ministers of Religion leave the duties of their profession to take a busy part in political matters, they generally fall into contempt, & sometimes bring discredit to the cause, in whose

Letter from John Carroll to the Continental Congress 1776
6 3/4 x 8 1/4 inches
The Archdiocese of Baltimore

itself where, from the beginning, Protestants were always the majority. On March 25, 1655, the Catholic-Calvert forces were defeated decisively in the "Battle of the Severn," and from that time until after the American Revolution, Catholics in Maryland were never to have the complete religious freedom that had been outlined by the Act Concerning Religion of 1649 in which all residents were allowed to practice freely their religion. Maryland law would not only proscribe political participation as in voting and holding office, it would also forbid the erection of churches or the employment of Catholic teachers as well. A law of 1704 made it a crime for "Popish priests" to baptize children in the faith or to offer Mass. Catholics who were disenfranchised in 1718 for their supposed sympathies toward the Jacobite cause were further penalized in 1754 by double taxation. Most keenly felt was the discrimination which aimed at the very roots of the faith: the education of the children. Since English penal law prevailed in the colonies, Maryland as well as English Catholics suffered under the law of 1700 which stipulated that parents who tried to send their children abroad for a Catholic education should forfeit £100 and face the possibility of being accused of treason.[6] Maryland Catholics, nevertheless, remained undaunted in the face of these restrictions and persisted in seeking ways to circumvent them both within the colony and on the continent of Europe.

The most notable attempt to provide a Catholic elementary education in eighteenth century Maryland was the school at Bohemia Manor, near the Pennsylvania border, where the Carrolls, Neales, Heaths, and Brents all sent their sons. When the future Archbishop and the future Signer, John and Charles Carroll, attended Bohemia Manor, it consisted of a small brick building standing a few feet south of the manse or rectory where their Jesuit teachers resided. It had opened during the pastorate of Father Thomas Poulton (1742-1749) and at one time housed twenty boarders and gave instruction to as many more day students. At Bohemia John and Charles Carroll could take courses in reading, writing, simple figures, and beginning Latin; until 1748 it was the scene of their first formal education.

Beyond Maryland, the nearest English Catholic schools were those run by English Jesuit exiles in the Low Country towns of Saint-Omer, Liège, and Bruges. The College of Saint-Omers, which had been founded in the late sixteenth century by Father Robert Parsons, had, by the mid-eighteenth century, become quite competent in turning out Jesuit novices or gentlemen's sons, and the fame of the Flemish school had spread to distant lands. Spartan in its regime, the daily life at the *collège* must have seemed strange to the young American cousins who had been accustomed to the leisurely luxury of a Maryland manor. Nevertheless, Carrolls had been going to Saint-Omers ever since they settled in Maryland, and this was the school to which both John and Charles were sent in 1749 to "lay a foundation for other studies which might hereafter be profitable" to themselves and "useful" to their friends. From little figures they passed to rudiments or great figures; from middle grammar to upper grammar or syntax. In rhetoric and the humanities, the crowning achievements of the curriculum, the Carroll cousins developed the trenchant expression and polished precision of writing and public speaking which marked the later careers of both men.[7]

After four years at Saint-Omers the paths of the Carroll cousins began to diverge. In later life Charles admitted he had found the school better suited to educating priests than men destined for commerce or politics. At the age of fifteen he was eager to leave and obtained his father's permission to study in Rheims after which he went to Paris. He then studied law at Bourges, returned to Paris, and finally completed his study of law at the Inner Temple in London.

[6] Annabelle M. Melville, *John Carroll of Baltimore* (New York, 1955), pp. 6-7. This work was first printed in a condensed version under the title *Archbishop John Carroll, Priest and Patriot* (Washington, D.C., 1953).

[7] For a detailed account of life at Saint-Omers cf. John Gerard, *Memorials of Stonyhurst College* (London, 1881), pp. 2-38.

John, on the other hand, found his vocation at Saint-Omers. In 1753 he "went up the hill" to Watten, the Jesuit novitiate seven miles away.

It is appropriate here to say something of the relationship of Maryland's three notable Carrolls: Daniel Carroll of Upper Marlboro II (more often called of Rock Creek); John Carroll, Archbishop of Baltimore; and Charles Carroll of Carrollton. The brothers Daniel and John were Charles Carroll's second cousins, but the kinship stemmed from their mother, Eleanor Darnall, not their father, Daniel Carroll of Upper Marlboro I. Daniel and John were descendants of Keane Carroll of Ireland whose relationship to Daniel Carroll of Litterluna, Ireland, the father of Charles Carroll the Settler, is so distant that it cannot exactly be defined. The two lines of Maryland Carrolls developed contemporaneously in the colony. The third generation of Keane's line followed much the same pattern as the third generation of Charles Carroll the Settler. Both Daniel II and Charles III, as well as John were sent abroad to study; while Charles returned to sign the Declaration of Independence, Daniel became famous in his turn as a signer of the Constitution of the United States. John became first bishop and then archbishop of the Catholic Church of the United States.

Through their mother, Eleanor Darnall Carroll, the brothers were related to the Darnall family whose American branch had been founded by the brother-in-law of Lord Baltimore, Colonel Henry Darnall I, Eleanor's grandfather. He had come to Maryland in 1672 and had quickly risen in wealth and reputation. Her own father, Henry Darnall II, inherited much of this wealth and acquired more by his marriage to Anne (Ann) Digges. Henry II's sister Mary Darnall, Eleanor's aunt, married Charles Carroll the Settler. Through that marriage, Eleanor Darnall became a first cousin to Charles Carroll of Annapolis, making her children second cousins to Charles Carroll of Carrollton. Eleanor's son Daniel of Rock Creek married Eleanor Carroll, who was Charles the Signer's first cousin, thus making Charles Carroll a first cousin by marriage to Daniel. When one reads that Charles the Signer himself married a Mary Darnall, it becomes evident that the Carrolls and Darnalls were related in ways enough to dismay even the most ardent genealogist.[8]

Their respective careers in adult life naturally separated John the Bishop and Charles the Signer; nevertheless the Carroll family ties generally remained strong and, on occasion, led to close involvements. When the Second Continental Congress decided to send a mission to Canada in 1776 in an effort to persuade that province to throw in its lot with the Thirteen Original Colonies in establishing independence from Britain, the two cousins were both members of the mission which journeyed to Montreal that spring in company with Samuel Chase (later a Maryland signer of the Declaration of Independence) and Benjamin Franklin.[9] After the Republic was firmly established under the Constitution, the Carroll cousins worked together to persuade President Wash-

[8] The best genealogical material on the Carrolls of Upper Marlborough and Rock Creek is found in Sister Mary Virginia Geiger, *Daniel Carroll, a Framer of the Constitution* (Washington, D.C., 1943), pp. 2-21.

[9] For an account of this Canadian Mission, See Melville, *John Carroll of Baltimore*, pp. 38-53.

ington's administration to support Catholic priests as missionaries among the Indians of the Northwest Territory.[10] From time to time the Bishop of Baltimore found a haven for clerical refugees in his cousin Charles' chapel at Doughoregan Manor.[11] When Charles the Signer's son in July 1800 precipitated a family crisis by planning to marry Harriet Chew of Philadelphia in an Episcopalian ceremony, Bishop Carroll joined the family protests and, in the end, presided at the Catholic ceremony in old St. Joseph's Church in one of the season's most talked-of marriages.[12] When Charles the Signer became interested in comparative religion in the last year of the prelate's life, Archbishop Carroll still found time and energy enough to draw up a list of books suited to such a study.[13] The letters of the prelate show clearly how deeply concerned he remained about all that related to the Carrolls of Carrollton. He always regarded the Signer's granddaughters as his own grandnieces and in spite of the worldly pleasures some of them pursued — most notably the Catons so famous as the "Three American Graces" — they could always rely on his office and the affections he held for his "very dear relations."

Although John Carroll's ties with his brother Daniel were cut short by the latter's death in 1796, almost two decades before the prelate's own demise, they were far closer by reason of both blood and affection. Apart from the bishop's mild impatience with his brother's Masonic affiliation, history shows no evidence that the two were ever at odds. Daniel's will not only left the bishop the "two acres of land comprehending and contiguous to the Roman Catholic Church," charming old St. John's Chapel on Daniel of Rock Creek's estate, but it also made the bishop co-trustee of the family properties bequeathed to Daniel's grandsons.[14]

John Carroll had every reason to revere his brother's memory, as did the state and nation. As a senator in the Maryland legislature (1782-1792), as state delegate to the Continental Congress (1781-1783), as chairman of the Maryland-Virginia project to promote navigation of the Potomac River (1785), and as a member of the Philadelphia Convention of 1787, Daniel Carroll served his state well. In working to secure Maryland's ratification of the Constitution, as a member of the House of Representatives (1789-1791) and as one of the first three Commissioners appointed by George Washington who planned and implemented the nation's capital (1791-1795), he served the Republic. As his biographer has so justly asserted, Daniel Carroll of Rock Creek "contributed his ardent belief in the value of a strong and centralized government, and his deep conviction that religious liberty was a proper attribute of the dignity of man."[15]

The story of Maryland Catholicism, however, in the days of the early Republic will always remain principally centered around the career of John Carroll

[10] Ibid., pp. 166-167.

[11] Ibid., p. 159.

[12] Ibid., pp. 131-132.

[13] Ellen Hart Smith, *Charles Carroll of Carrollton* (Cambridge, 1942), p. 271.

[14] These grandsons were William and George. Daniel Carroll's children had predeceased him. The will is found in Geiger, *Daniel Carroll*, pp. 181-182.

[15] Ibid., pp. 180-182.

of Baltimore. After entering the Jesuit novitiate in 1753 and completing his training, he taught in Jesuit schools in Flanders — possibly at Saint-Omers, certainly at Liège — and was ordained to the priesthood, probably in 1769. When the Jesuit Order was suppressed by Rome in 1773, Carroll was Prefect of the Sodality at Bruges. In October of that year, he was briefly arrested after which he took refuge with Lord Arundell of Wardour Castle in England. He returned to Maryland in the late spring of 1774 to find his homeland inexorably moving toward revolt. After playing his part in the Canadian Mission in 1776, he returned to Maryland and settled down with his mother at Rock Creek, where he took up a quiet ministry in St. John's Chapel and the surrounding countryside. He was, in this limited way, joining a pastoral effort which merits our respect — the devoted and often heroic service rendered to the Maryland Catholics by their priests, most of them Jesuit, during the colonial period and afterward. Covering many miles daily over the primitive roads, these men celebrated the Mass in small secluded chapels or in private homes, offered spiritual comfort to the sick and dying and gave religious instruction to both children and adults. Typical of the clergy whose lot Carroll now shared was Father Joseph Mosely who, racked with pain from an internal ailment and, in the course of a day's journey, forced periodically to alight from the saddle for rest, still persevered. Saint Ignatius' Church at Chapel Point, Charles County, which can claim to be the oldest parish still active in the United States, is part of the legacy bequeathed by the valor of those eighteenth century missionaries.

With independence from Britain assured in 1783, Father Carroll turned his organizing abilities to the most urgent problems faced by his fellow clergy: the need for overall discipline and some means of regular material support now that they were deprived of both their Jesuit superiors and the supervision of their former English Vicars General. On June 27, 1783, he met with deputies from the clergy at Whitemarsh, the former Jesuit residence on the road to Annapolis, to plan for reorganization. His efforts were crowned with success the following year with the creation of the "Select Body of Clergy" and a request to Rome that Father John Lewis be empowered to act as their ecclesiastical superior. Father Lewis, the last Jesuit superior in the Colonies, had been made Vicar-General by the Vicar Apostolic of London before the war.

Rome, after taking into consideration the age of Father Lewis (he was sixty-four at the time), John Carroll's warm friendship with Benjamin Franklin, and the information gained through France of the American situation, decided to name John Carroll. His youth, his renowned family connections, and above all his reputation for learning and virtue, made him the logical choice to assume the role of "Superior of the Mission in the provinces of the new Republic of the United States of North America" in 1784.

The powers attached to this office were not those of a bishop, the Roman authorities believing that they were not yet needed for the governance of the American mission. It soon became evident, however, that a full-scale Catholic bishopric was required for the new nation, and negotiations for this purpose were inaugurated between the American clergy and Rome. The matter provided an opportunity for Carroll to display an attitude for which his whole

Engraved by H. B. Hall (1808-1884) after Duplessis (1725-1802), Benjamin Franklin 1868
Legend: *BENJAMIN FRANKLIN. / Engraved by H. B. Hall, from the original / Picture in pastel, painted from life by J. A. Duplessis in 1783, and now / (1868) in the possesion of John Bigelow Esq.*
Engraving, 6 7/8 x 3 7/8 inches
Library of Congress, Washington

previous experience had prepared him — his vigorous insistence on freedom and accommodation to American democratic procedure even in a matter of such high religious importance.

He warned the Roman authorities that "in our free and jealous government . . . it will never be suffered that [the Catholic] Ecclesiastical Superior . . . receive his appointment from a foreign State." He and his clergy were convinced that "we neither must request or admit any other foreign interference than such, as being essential to their religion, is implied in the acknowledgment of the Bishop of Rome, by divine appointment, head of the universal Church." Therefore, he stressed, the American clergy must be allowed to choose their bishop, and Rome should merely ratify that selection.[16] Rome accepted this reasoning and when, by an almost unanimous vote of the American clergy, John Carroll was nominated by the Brief of November 6, 1789, Pope Pius VI confirmed him as First Bishop in the United States. The apostolic bull was prepared and dispatched to the United States with the words:

> *Nothing more acceptable and pleasing could happen to us, than . . . that you should have nominated, by almost unanimous consent, John Carroll as the first Bishop of the new See of Baltimore. For since our Holy Father Pius VI was fully aware of the unblemished reputation of Mr. Carroll and*

[16] Peter Guilday, *The Life and Times of John Carroll* (New York, 1922), pp. 209-210.

LULWORTH CASTLE April 1, 1875, Lord Duncannon (Frederick George Brabazon Ponsonby, 6th Earl of Bressborough) (1850-1895) and William Watts (1752-1851)
Legend: *Lord Duncannon, del; / W. Watts, Sculp.*
Engraving, 6 x 8 inches
Victoria and Albert Museum, London

> *of the remarkable zeal with which for many years he has strenuously laboured there for the salvation of souls, His Holiness has confirmed . . . this first election . . . which you have exercised with such rectitude and wisdom.*[17]

In choosing the place for his consecration as bishop, John Carroll was honoring old ties dating back to his days on the Continent. While on his last Jesuit assignment in Bruges, he had formed warm friendships with Charles Plowden and Thomas Weld, the sixth possessor of Lulworth Castle in Dorset, England, and a personal friend of King George III. Weld insisted that the ceremonies must take place in St. Mary's, the charming circular family chapel which was the first Catholic church built in England since the Reformation. John Carroll was pleased to accommodate and by July 1790 was ready to leave on his trip to England.

The consecration took place on August 15, 1790, the feast of the Assumption of the Blessed Virgin, a fitting day for the consecration of the first bishop of the nation whose patron she was to be. Charles Walmesley, Bishop of Rama, was assisted by James Parter and Charles Plowden, chaplain at the Castle who preached the homily. The munificence of Thomas Weld "omitted no circumstance which could possibly add dignity to so venerable a ceremony."[18] Young Thomas Weld, who would one day be a cardinal, held the missal over Carroll's

[17] Quoted in Melville, *John Carroll*, p. 109.

[18] Charles Plowden, *A Short Account of the Establishment of the New See of Baltimore* (London, 1790).

shoulder during the ceremony. To those present the event symbolized a new era for the Church in the United States, a land where English-speaking Catholics enjoyed fuller participation in human rights among their neighbors than in any other portion of the English-speaking world.

A notice of December 10, 1790 in the *Maryland Journal and Baltimore Advertiser* informed the public that Carroll had returned to America and "on the landing of this learned and worthy prelate he was respectfully waited on by a number of his fellow citizens of various denominations who conducted him to his residence."[19] The complexities of Carroll's episcopal jurisdiction during the twenty years that he presided over the entire United States virtually single-handed are too numerous to be described in so brief an essay.[20] There were exasperating flauntings of authority by both clergy and lay trustees from Boston to Savannah; there were nationalistic tempests in Philadelphia and Baltimore; there were even threats of outright schism in Charleston. Carroll perceived that the very blessings of his beloved nation, blessings which contributed so marvelously to the progress of the Church, also involved dangers. Religious liberty and the government's unshakeable belief in the protection of private property could be misinterpreted by the Irish, the Germans, the French — by the clergy and the laity alike. Coming as they did without any experience in democratic procedures and lacking the heritage which the colonists had so valiantly preserved both during and after their War for Independence, the newcomers felt suddenly loosed from their former bonds of poverty, political subservience, and religious proscription. It required patience and tact, and above all a limitless charity, to deal with the countless conflicts of Carroll's rapidly growing flock.

On April 8, 1808, Pope Pius VII created Baltimore a metropolitan see and named the four suffragan sees as Boston, New York, Philadelphia, and Bardstown, Kentucky. It was not until 1810 that Carroll had the pleasure of consecrating three of the suffragan bishops at Baltimore (New York's bishop would come later). Carroll himself was not invested with the pallium, symbolizing his position as Archbishop of Baltimore, until August 18, 1811. The creation of the sees, however, did not diminish Carroll's responsibilities. He was constantly called upon between 1810 and his death five years later for advice and direction by the new sees, particularly New York which did not have an actual bishop until 1815. His own Diocese of Baltimore included, besides the states of Maryland, Virginia, North and South Carolina, and Georgia, the Territory of Louisiana as well. The purchase of Louisiana in 1803 had added vast lands beyond the Mississippi River in addition to the city of New Orleans, a hotbed of multinational intrigues. It was not until October 1812 that Carroll finally had an able Apostolic Administrator in the person of William Dubourg to accept the burdens of Louisiana and the Two Floridas.

It was scarcely possible that a man of Carroll's intellect, family background, and influence should not participate from time to time in events of some po-

19 Quoted in Melville, *John Carroll*, p. 122.

20 The bishops of the new dioceses of New York, Boston, Philadelphia and Bardstown, Kentucky, were not consecrated until late autumn, 1810; and Carroll's coadjutor bishop, Leonard Neale, was a negligible factor in the administration of the Diocese of Baltimore.

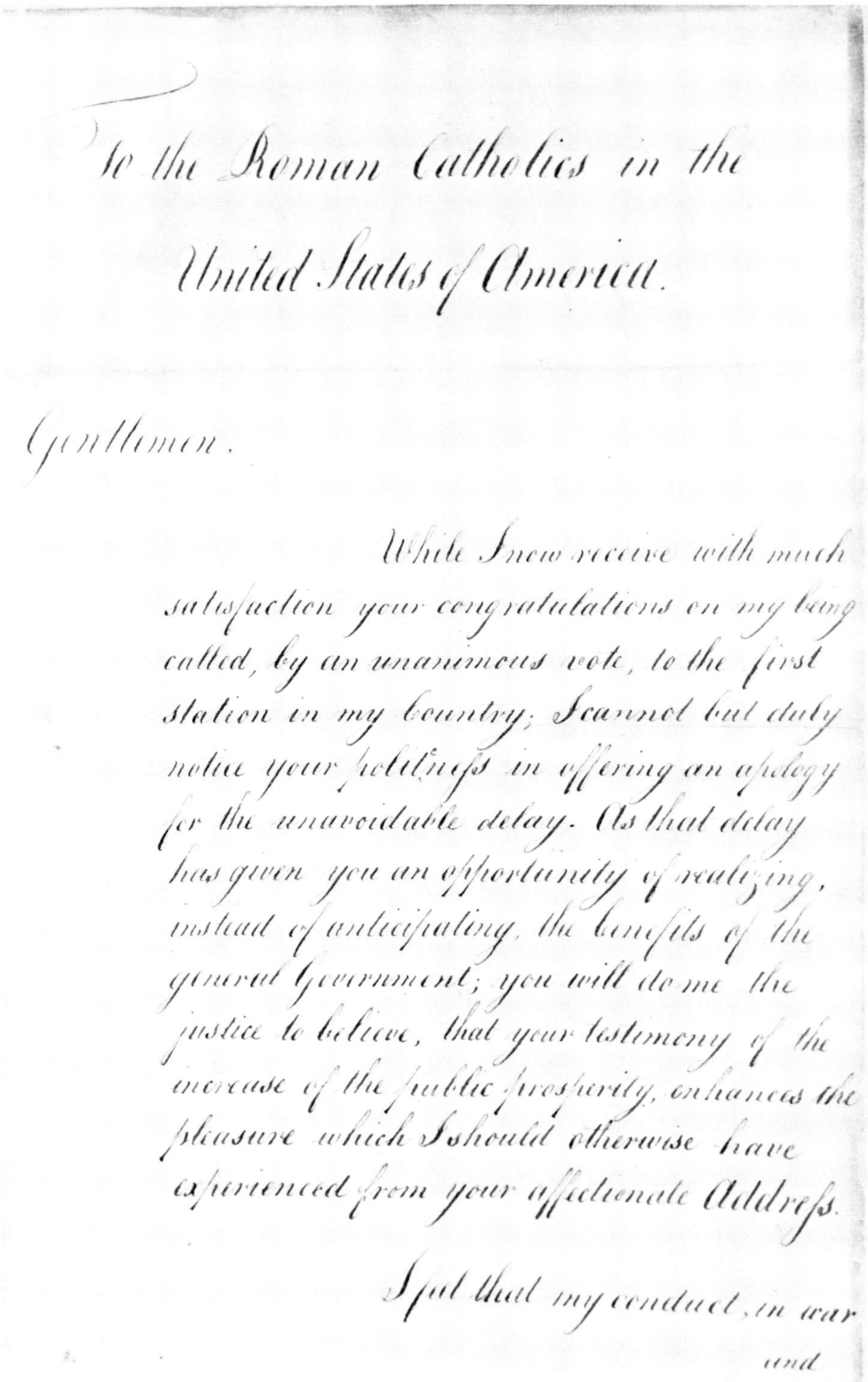

To the Roman Catholics in the United States of America.

Gentlemen.

While I now receive with much satisfaction your congratulations on my being called, by an unanimous vote, to the first station in my country; I cannot but duly notice your politeness in offering an apology for the unavoidable delay. As that delay has given you an opportunity of realizing, instead of anticipating, the benefits of the general Government; you will do me the justice to believe, that your testimony of the increase of the public prosperity, enhances the pleasure which I should otherwise have experienced from your affectionate Address.

I feel that my conduct, in war and

Letter from George Washington to the Roman Catholics In The United States of America
March 12, 1790, 12 3/4 x 8 1/6 inches
The Archdiocese of Baltimore

litical significance. As early as 1776 he had stated his conviction that clergymen ought to confine themselves to ecclesiastical affairs. While he was still Superior of the Mission he had zealously defended the principle of religious liberty when he replied to an article which appeared in the *United States Gazette* in May 1789. Using the name "Pacificus," Father Carroll, on June 10, 1789, asserted that Catholics had every right to participate fully in the new government. The establishment of the United States was not the work of this or that religion. It arose, rather, from the "generous exertion of all her citizens to redress their wrongs, to assert their rights, and to lay its foundations on the soundest principles of justice and equal liberty."[21] Carroll was not defending one profession but all religions.

Father Carroll had a second occasion in 1789 to express his belief in complete religious liberty. This time he addressed the President of the United States, George Washington. In conjunction with his brother Daniel, his cousin Charles of Carrollton, Dominick Lynch of New York, and Thomas FitzSimons of Philadelphia, John Carroll tendered the new executive the congratulations and joy of the American Catholics upon Washington's election. Then he continued: "While our country preserves her freedom and independence we shall have a well-founded title to claim her justice, the equal rights of citizenship. . . . We pray for the preservation of them where they have been granted, and expect the full extension from the justice of those States which still restrict them."[22] Washington's reply on March 12, 1790, acknowledged the claims of Catholic citizens to equality and added, "I hope to see America among the foremost Nations in examples of justice and liberality."[23]

Both the first President and the first Bishop in the United States held the same concept of liberty and justice. Carroll admired Washington and took a keen interest in the success of his policies. At the first synod held after he became bishop, Carroll initiated the custom of public prayer for the government at the close of the Mass. Washington was in turn sympathetic to the requests of the bishop and his cousin Charles that priests be supported by federal funds to serve among the Indians of the Northwest Territory.[24] Both John and Charles were active in getting Maryland to reprint Washington's *Farewell Address*, and the bishop and chief executive remained on friendly terms after the latter's retirement. The very last summer of Washington's life he entertained at Mount Vernon the bishop and his niece, Elizabeth Carroll. No finer sermon ever emanated from Carroll's lips than his eulogy for Washington at the President's death in 1799.[25] It is not surprising that when the nation came to dedicate a monument to Washington in July 1815, it was to John Carroll they turned for heartfelt tribute. It was one of the great regrets of his last year of life that Archbishop Carroll had to decline because of failing energies and voice.[26]

[21] Guilday, *Life and Times of John Carroll*, pp. 113-114.

[22] Ibid., pp. 365-366.

[23] Ibid., p. 366.

[24] Melville, *John Carroll*, p. 166.

[25] John Carroll, *Eulogy on George Washington* (New York, 1931).

[26] Melville, *John Carroll*, pp. 279-280.

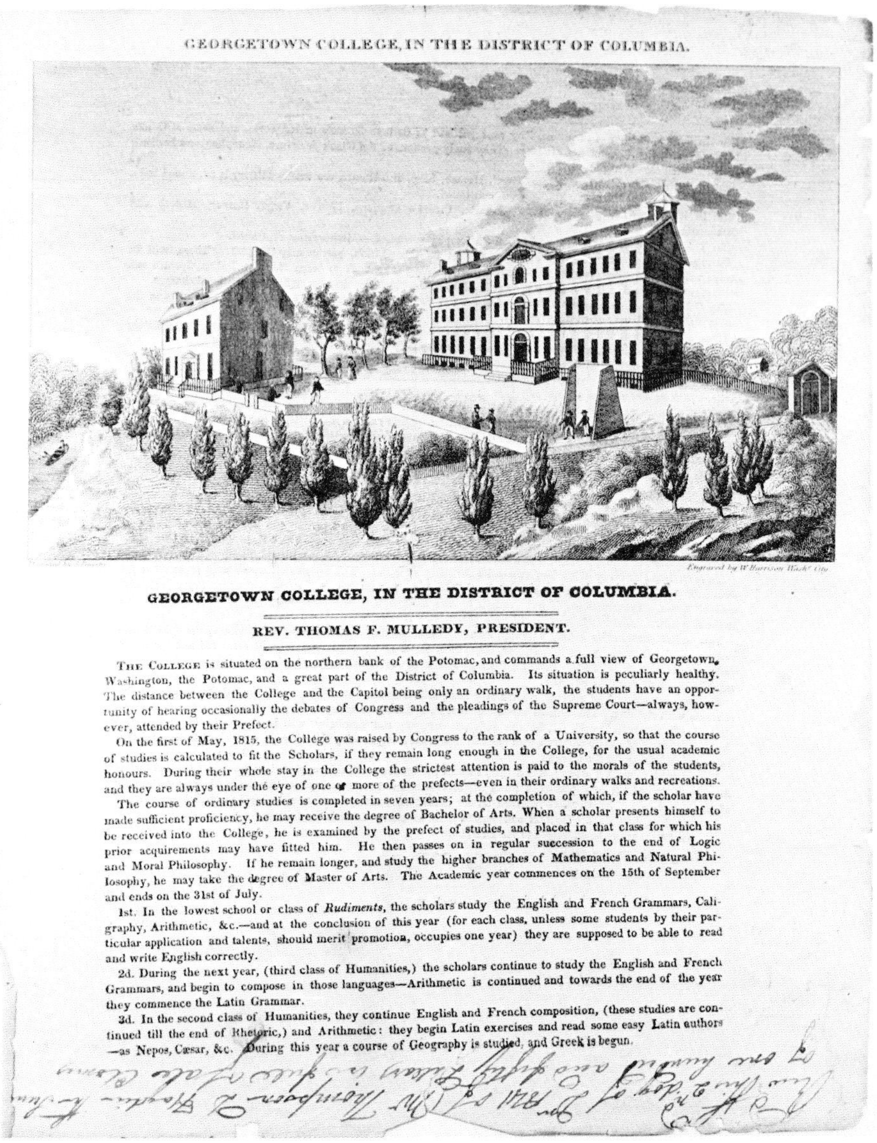

GEORGETOWN COLLEGE, IN THE DISTRICT OF COLUMBIA.

Engraved by W. Harrison Wash. City

GEORGETOWN COLLEGE, IN THE DISTRICT OF COLUMBIA.

REV. THOMAS F. MULLEDY, PRESIDENT.

THE COLLEGE is situated on the northern bank of the Potomac, and commands a full view of Georgetown, Washington, the Potomac, and a great part of the District of Columbia. Its situation is peculiarly healthy. The distance between the College and the Capitol being only an ordinary walk, the students have an opportunity of hearing occasionally the debates of Congress and the pleadings of the Supreme Court—always, however, attended by their Prefect.

On the first of May, 1815, the College was raised by Congress to the rank of a University, so that the course of studies is calculated to fit the Scholars, if they remain long enough in the College, for the usual academic honours. During their whole stay in the College the strictest attention is paid to the morals of the students, and they are always under the eye of one or more of the prefects—even in their ordinary walks and recreations.

The course of ordinary studies is completed in seven years; at the completion of which, if the scholar have made sufficient proficiency, he may receive the degree of Bachelor of Arts. When a scholar presents himself to be received into the College, he is examined by the prefect of studies, and placed in that class for which his prior acquirements may have fitted him. He then passes on in regular succession to the end of Logic and Moral Philosophy. If he remain longer, and study the higher branches of Mathematics and Natural Philosophy, he may take the degree of Master of Arts. The Academic year commences on the 15th of September and ends on the 31st of July.

1st. In the lowest school or class of *Rudiments*, the scholars study the English and French Grammars, Caligraphy, Arithmetic, &c.—and at the conclusion of this year (for each class, unless some students by their particular application and talents, should merit promotion, occupies one year) they are supposed to be able to read and write English correctly.

2d. During the next year, (third class of Humanities,) the scholars continue to study the English and French Grammars, and begin to compose in those languages—Arithmetic is continued and towards the end of the year they commence the Latin Grammar.

3d. In the second class of Humanities, they continue English and French composition, (these studies are continued till the end of Rhetoric,) and Arithmetic: they begin Latin exercises and read some easy Latin authors—as Nepos, Cæsar, &c. During this year a course of Geography is studied, and Greek is begun.

GEORGETOWN COLLEGE IN THE DISTRICT OF COLUMBIA 1829, Designed by S. Pinistri and engraved by W. Harrison (dates unknown)
Legend: *GEORGETOWN COLLEGE, IN THE DISTRICT OF COLUMBIA. / Designed by S. Pinistri / Engraved by W. Harrison Wash. City. / . . . .*
Engraving, 9 3/4 x 7 3/4 inches
Georgetown University, Washington

Carroll's relations with President Thomas Jefferson were equally cordial, even though the Bishop of Baltimore was less sympathetic to the Republican Party which brought Jefferson to office. In facilitating the transfer of Louisiana to American jurisdiction, Carroll worked with Jefferson and his Secretary of State, James Madison, to ensure harmonious relations between the political and ecclesiastical authorities in that Territory and to safeguard Church properties there — particularly those of the Ursuline nuns.[27]

[27] Henry C. Semple, S.J., *The Ursulines of New Orleans* (New York, 1925), pp. 59-62.

In 1812, when Madison was himself in the White House and war with England was declared, the Archbishop of Baltimore gave the President his firm support in setting aside a day of national prayer.[28] Although he would never have chosen war as a means of settling grievances, John Carroll was an ardent patriot. Once the decision for combat was made, his whole public support was given to Madison's government. When peace finally came Carroll was eighty years old, but his devotion to his country was as vigorous as it had been throughout his entire career, and so it remained to the end of his days.

The great men of our early Republic were marked with a breadth of vision and a diversification of activities which continue to amaze the twentieth-century specialist with his narrow-range of interests and his microscopic point of view. John Carroll was no exception to this earlier pattern of genius, and he left a lasting imprint on the social life of the nation. In Baltimore, for example, he took an active part in the foundation of the Library Company, incorporated on January 20, 1796, which became a valuable asset to the city's cultural life.[29]

In the field of education, his influence was extensive. The opening of classes in Georgetown College in the fall of 1791 was the realization of a dream Carroll had cherished for nearly a decade. He had written to Charles Plowden in 1782, "The object nearest my heart is to establish a college on this continent for the education of youth, which might at the same time be a seminary for future clergymen." While in England for his consecration, he worked assiduously to arouse interest in the American college, and he returned to the United States with many pledges of financial assistance. The school was begun under the headship of Robert Plunkett, a graduate of the English college at Douay; by 1798 the future of Georgetown was assured.[30]

Opening almost simultaneously with Georgetown was a second Catholic educational institution, which has also remained to this day. While Georgetown on the Potomac was begun with the primary intention of preparing young men for the "study of the higher sciences in the university of this or neighboring states," St. Mary's Seminary in Baltimore was intended to educate men for the priesthood. The Baltimore seminary, like the Potomac college, owed some of its origins to Carroll's London sojourn in 1790. While in England Carroll discussed plans with a French Sulpician for bringing to the United States members of the Compagnie de Saint-Sulpice to train American clergy for the Diocese of Baltimore. Once it opened its doors under Charles François Nagot in 1791, it attracted to Maryland such incomparable French Sulpicians as Ambroise Maréchal, Jean Marie Tessier, Antoine Garnier, John Baptiste David, and others. Carroll reported to Rome, "The establishment of a seminary is certainly a new and extraordinary spectacle for the people of this country. The remarkable piety of these priests is admirable, and their example is a stimulant and spur to

[28] Melville, *John Carroll*, pp. 273-275.

[29] Stuart C. Sherman, "The Library Company of Baltimore, 1795-1854," *Maryland Historical Magazine*, XXXIX (March 1944):6.

[30] John M. Daley, S.J., *Georgetown University: Origin and Early Years* (Washington, D.C., 1957), pp. 29-64.

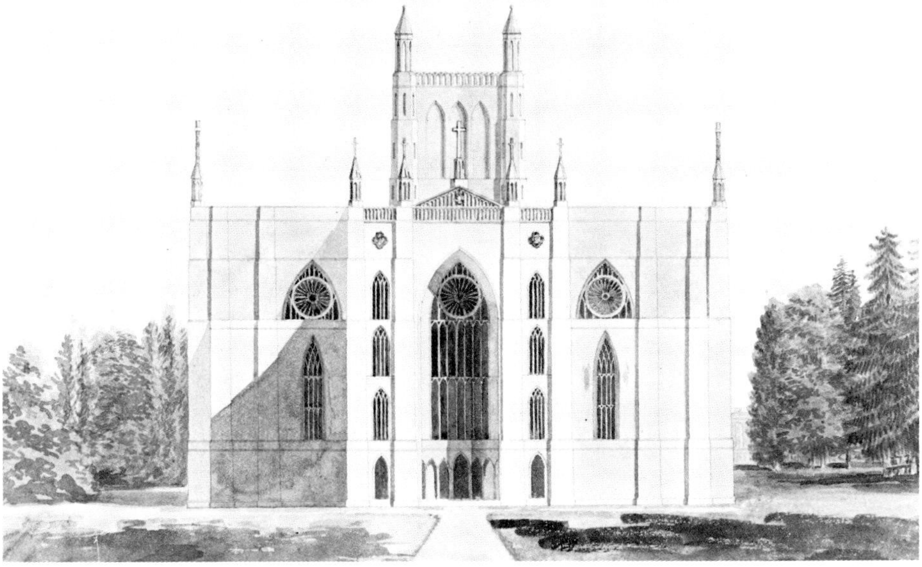

Drawing for the Catholic Cathedral, Baltimore. Sketch of the West Front, 1805
Benjamin Henry Latrobe (1764-1820)
Signed and dated: *BH Latrobe 1805*. Inscribed: *Sketch of the West Front, being the first / Design, corrected in the proceeding / Elevations.*
Ink and wash on paper, 12 3/4 x 16 inches
The Archdiocese of Baltimore

Drawing for the Catholic Cathedral, Baltimore. South-North Elevation, 1805
Benjamin Henry Latrobe (1764-1820)
Signed and dated: *BH Latrobe 1805*. Inscribed: *South-North Elevation*
Ink and wash on paper, 12 3/4 x 16 inches
The Archdiocese of Baltimore

all. . . ."[31] Maréchal became in time Carroll's second successor, the third Archbishop of Baltimore.

The next most pressing need was to encourage Catholic education for young women. Although the Visitandines made the first successful start in that direction, the success of their school was the work of Carroll's coadjutor, Bishop Leonard Neale. The work of female education was from the very beginning undertaken by the community of Saint Elizabeth Seton under the aegis of John Carroll. Carroll had confirmed her in New York before she ever came to Baltimore; he had directed pupils to her school on Paca Street; he had administered her first vows as a Sister of Charity of St. Joseph in Baltimore; and it was the Archbishop who guided her uncertain footsteps during the painful adjustment to responsibilities as Superior of the first truly American religious community. He and his family befriended her children and secured entrants to her Emmitsburg academy. It was Carroll who insisted that the Rules of St. Vincent de Paul be modified to suit her particular situation and the American scene. In his own lifetime he saw her educational work flourish not only in Maryland but in Pennsylvania and New York as well.[32]

The most aesthetic monument to Carroll's cultural influence is the old Cathedral of the Assumption in Baltimore where he lies buried. At the very first meeting of the Baltimore trustees in 1795 a resolution was adopted, at Carroll's urging, to open subscriptions for a cathedral; but a decade passed before the cornerstone could be laid. The copper plate which commemorated the event bore the inscription: "The first stone of the Cathedral Church, to be erected for the honor of Almightly God . . . was placed the 7th day of July, 1806, by the Right Rev. John, Bishop of Baltimore." Meanwhile designs for the edifice were in the hands of Benjamin Henry Latrobe (1764-1820), the British born and educated engineer and architect who was already engaged in planning the national capitol at Washington. Although neither Latrobe nor Carroll lived to see this first cathedral completed, it still stands in Baltimore as an example of those powerful aesthetic impulses which permeated the culture of the early Republic and the men who strove so heroically to give them form.[33] In its integrity and simplicity of design the cathedral still testifies to the character and greatness of the man who lies beneath its high altar.

Style and stature — these were the characteristics of the Founding Fathers and of John Carroll in particular. He was a civilized man, a man of the world in the best sense of the term, he was accustomed to the best society of Europe and America and was always at ease in that society. It possessed the virtues of an aristocracy that was not snobbish but was based on the conviction that human life should be, wherever possible, embellished, ornamented with the human amenities. It was a fastidious culture — a culture of good taste. It was also a robust society, addicted to uproarious laughter. John Carroll's letters are filled with humor, and his friends retorted in kind.

John Carroll was, to his finger tips, a professional. The word has in our day become unpopular, but quite undeservedly so. It signifies, simply, excellence in

[31] Joseph W. Ruane, *The Beginnings of the Society of St. Sulpice in the United States, 1791-1829* (Washington, D.C., 1935), pp. 20-36.

[32] Annabelle M. Melville, *Elizabeth Bayley Seton, 1774-1821* (New York, 1951).

[33] Talbot Hamlin, *Benjamin Henry Latrobe* (New York, 1955), pp. 231-252.

performing one's chosen work. John Carroll had dedicated himself to the office of churchman; he worked at it with his whole being, with high skill, and in the face of all obstacles. In the sphere to which Carroll was called this was professionalism in the very finest sense. "While example and inspiration count for anything in the history of the American people the career of John Carroll will remain a very present reminder that love of civil justice, when predicated on love for God, and accompanied by unfailing charity toward fellowman, is as infallible a recipe for political happiness as our founding fathers intended to predict." [34]

[34] Melville, *John Carroll*, p. 287.

JOSEPH T. DURKIN, S. J.
AND
ANNABELLE M. MELVILLE

BIBLIOGRAPHY

Barker, Charles A. *The Background of the Revolution in Maryland.* New Haven: Yale University Press, 1940.

Beitzell, Edwin W. *The Jesuit Mission of St. Mary's County, Maryland.* Privately published, 1959.

Brent, Daniel. *Biographical Sketch of the Most Rev. John Carroll, Bishop and First Archbishop of Baltimore.* Baltimore: John Murphy, 1843.

Daley, John M. *Georgetown University: Origin and Early Years.* Washington, D.C.: Georgetown University Press, 1957.

Dalrymple, E. A., ed. *Narrative of a Voyage to Maryland by Father Andrew White, S.J.: An Account of the Colony of the Lord Baron of Baltimore.* Baltimore, 1874.

Foley, Henry. *Records of the English Province of the Society of Jesus.* London: Burns and Oates, 1875-1883.

Geiger, Sister Mary Virginia. *Daniel Carroll, a Framer of the Constitution.* Washington, D.C.: Catholic University of America Press, 1943.

Gerard, John. *Memorials of Stonyhurst College.* London, 1881.

Guilday, Peter. *English Catholic Refugees in the Low Countries.* London, 1914.

———. *The Life and Times of John Carroll, Archbishop of Baltimore (1735-1815).* New York: Encyclopedia Press, 1922.

Hamlin, Talbot. *Benjamin Henry Latrobe.* New York: Oxford University Press, 1955.

Hanley, Thomas O'Brien, S.J., ed. *The John Carroll Papers.* Notre Dame: University of Notre Dame Press, forthcoming.

Hughes, Thomas, S.J. *History of the Society of Jesus in North America.* 4 vols. New York: Longmans, Green, and Co., 1907-1917.

Melville, Annabelle M. *Elizabeth Bayley Seton, 1774-1821.* New York: Charles Scribner's Sons, 1951.

———. *John Carroll of Baltimore, Founder of the American Catholic Hierarchy.* New York: Charles Scribner's Sons, 1955.

Rowland, Kate M. *The Life of Charles Carroll of Carrollton, 1737-1832, with his Correspondence and Public Papers.* 2 vols. New York: G. P. Putnam's Sons, 1898.

Ruane, Joseph W. *The Beginnings of the Society of St. Sulpice in the United States, 1791-1829.* Washington, D.C.: Catholic University of America Press, 1935.

Shea, John Gilmary. *Life and Times of the Most Rev. John Carroll, Bishop and First Archbishop of Baltimore.* New York: John G. Shea, 1888.

Smith, Ellen Hart. *Charles Carroll of Carrollton.* Cambridge: Harvard University Press, 1942.

Spalding, H. S. *Catholic Colonial Maryland.* Milwaukee: Bruce Publishing Co., 1931.

Walsh, Richard, and Fox, William Lloyd. *Maryland, A History, 1632-1974.* Baltimore: The Maryland Historical Society, 1974.

Catalogue of the Exhibition

Painting gives us not only the persons, but the characters of great men. The air of the head and the mien in general give strong indications of the mind and illustrate what the historian says more expressly and particularly.[1]

The Face of a Family

The historian and the art historian work hand in hand when an art exhibition is being organized to illuminate an important chapter in history. The purpose of such an undertaking is to make a statement "expressly and particularly" about an era or an event and the principal figures who gave it life and substance. But the means for the statement are invariably within the art historian's province: sculpture, prints, drawings, the rich diversity of the decorative arts, as well as paintings — and above all, portraits in all media.

Anywhere So Long As There Be Freedom began with one portrait of Charles Carroll of Carrollton — a copy in oil of Robert Field's exquisite watercolor painted in 1803.[2] Discovery of one portrait of the Signer led to another — and another — and finally to his family. An extraordinary opportunity for an exhibition was in the making, for Charles Carroll of Carrollton's was one of the most frequently depicted faces in American history, and an impressive degree of contemporary documentation emerged to accompany the likenesses. When the focus was broadened to include the Signer's immediate family, the result was a history of portraiture in Maryland and Marylanders in portraiture from the Colonial era to the mid-19th century.

From the time that Cecil Calvert, second Baron Baltimore and first Lord Proprietor, received a charter from James II to the princely domain of Maryland in June 1632, the aristocratic roots of this colony were established. Almost from the beginning gentlemen landowners with substantial houses, a taste for elegant accoutrements, portraits included, and with the means to indulge this taste, formed an integral part of Maryland society. It followed naturally that European portraitists seeking careers in the New World should, at an early date, gravitate toward such a promising source of clients. The Carrolls were numbered among this distinguished gentry from 1688, with the arrival of the Third Lord Baltimore's[3] favorite, Charles Carroll the Settler. It also followed naturally that they, and the distinguished Maryland families to whom they were closely related,[4] would be foremost among the clients garnered by any artists plying their talents in the Proprietary Colony.

This, in brief, explains why Maryland can claim one of the most impressive chapters in American art history. It also explains how "Carroll" became synonymous with "portrait" in the annals of Maryland — the lifetime of the Signer alone covers almost a century of Maryland's painting history. His long life spanned six generations bearing the name of Carroll and of those families with whom they were connected by marriage. The Signer was born a decade before his grandmother Carroll's death and his great-grandchildren were arriving in profusion well before his own, but these last were not really sitting for their portraits in 1832. The richest selection of likenesses related directly to Charles Carroll of Carrollton, then, stems from the five generations, grandparents through grandchildren, and these are the focus of this study.

[1] Andrew Oliver, *Portraits of John and Abigail Adams.* (Cambridge, Mass.: The Belknap Press of Harvard University Press, 1967). Foreword, by Lyman Butterfield, [n.p.]

[2] Rather than giving catalogue numbers in the text, the reader is referred to the index of artists at the end of the book and the genealogy chart (facing p. xvi) which contains the numbers relating each subject to his or her catalogue entries.

[3] Charles Calvert, 3rd Lord Baltimore (1629-1715).

[4] The Carrolls intermarried frequently with the Darnall, Digges and Brooke families.

The tale of Carroll portraits begins in the first decade of the 18th century in the vicinity of the thriving port of Annapolis, the seat of Maryland's government from 1694 and the social and cultural center until Baltimore's rising prominence as a commercial and trade center snatched the honors away after the Revolution. Here, Justus Engelhardt Kühn and Gustavus Hesselius, the first two documented artists in Maryland history, introduced the decorative style of the late Europeon Baroque to America — and specifically to the colony of the Barons Baltimore. Both names are associated with the Settler and his generation.

The earliest record of the German-born Kühn in Maryland is December 3, 1708, when he made application to the Maryland General Assembly for naturalization.[5] He appears in various records of the Colony until the settlement of his estate in November 1717. All subjects attributed to Kühn are identified by family tradition as members of the closely related Digges, Darnall and Carroll families and, in each instance, an unquestionable provenance bears this out. The precise identity is, however, open to question in many instances. In addition, all works attributed to this artist do not appear to be from the same hand as his one signed and dated work, yet all those differing in style and technique cannot be assigned either to the same unknown hand or to Gustavus Hesselius, the only other *documented* painter working in Maryland during the early decades of the eighteenth century.

Gustavus Hesselius worked in Maryland from 1720 to 1726 and possibly as early as 1717. Again many of the attributions of Carroll family portraits to his hand are in doubt or are now disqualified. Both Kühn and Hesselius did definitely paint portraits within the family. Yet, consideration of all Carroll-related works traditionally associated with these two artists leads to an inescapable conclusion: there were other as yet unidentified painters working in Maryland at the time of Kühn and Hesselius. And these artists, as well, numbered the Carrolls among their clients. Thus, portraits of the first generation of Carrolls in Maryland open a Pandora's box of misattributions, reattributions, unexplored problems, and tantalizing possibilities which are presented in the catalogue as an invitation to the scholarly sleuth.

The second generation associated with the Carroll name in Maryland produced many portraits and few of the problems of Pandora's box, the only generation which can claim this distinction. The period was dominated, as was painting in the 1750's in all of Maryland, by the rococo sensibilities of one artist: John Wollaston. Documented in Maryland between 1753 and 1754, possibly present as early as 1752 or as late as 1755, Wollaston worked his way through the Carroll family from the Signer's parents to a fleet of cousins so extensive that the total number, including some not in the following catalogue, constitutes a notable percentage of the artist's more than three hundred American portraits. The Carrolls of Duddington, of Upper Marlboro, and of Rock Creek all figure prominently in this artist's work. If Charles Carroll of Carrollton himself had not been studying in France, a Wollaston would undoubtedly be added to his extensive list of portraits. The legacy which Wollaston left to Maryland and to

[5] J. Hall Pleasants, *Justus Engelhardt Kühn: An Early Eighteenth Century Maryland Portrait Painter* (Worcester, Mass.: Published by the Society, 1937).

the Carrolls reveals the polished work of an artist who could eloquently depict, if not the character, then certainly the affluent position of his sitters who wished to be presented in the gleaming satins and rich velvets he treated with perfection. The monotony of pose and costume, of background and accessories in the portraits seems not to have bothered Wollaston or his clients. He had mastered a formula which satisfied him and its elegance pleased America's budding aristocracy so much that no one seemed to object to the fact that only the face distinguished one canvas from another. In the case of the Carrolls even the face is sometimes indistinguishable.

Portraits of the third generation — that of Charles Carroll of Carrollton — extend from Wollaston to artists who were still working at the time of the Civil War, for example, Chester Harding and William James Hubard. The portraits of the family in this generation reflect the fact that the majority of prominent artists working in Maryland from the late Colonial period through the Jacksonian Era were not native born but constituted a distinguished group of visitors from other parts of America and abroad. They also reflect styles in American portraiture from Colonial stereotypes through the simplicity of the classical portrait formula of the Federal period to the full flowering of romanticism. In addition to the Wollastons of Charles Carroll's first cousins, his second cousin John Carroll sat to Gilbert Stuart and Rembrandt Peale and was also painted by Jeremiah Paul (though apparently not from life), and a handful of unknown artists. There is also a possibility that a portrait by John Wesley Jarvis may be waiting for discovery.

As for the Signer, it is known that he gave sittings from life, between childhood and old age, to thirteen artists: Sir Joshua Reynolds, Robert Field, Rembrandt Peale, Saint-Mémin, Charles Bird King, Charles Willson Peale, Robert Edge Pine, Anson Dickinson, Thomas Sully, Chester Harding, J. H. I. Browere, William James Hubard and one unknown from his years of school in France. This is a creditable record for a man who in old age, anyway, found "it is very irksom to set for my picture."[6] But even these sittings represent a small percentage of likenesses of Carroll painted within his lifetime. If one totals lost portraits, finished studies, replicas, early copies (some by outstanding artists such as Charles Willson Peale), and contemporary engravings, the total is very grand indeed. And then, the artists whose names have been linked with portraits of the Signer provide a tantalizing possibility and one of the many reasons which makes consideration of Carroll portraits such a fascinating puzzle. Are there portraits of Charles Carroll of Carrollton by John Trumbull, Gilbert Stuart, Joseph Wood and John Wesley Jarvis waiting to be discovered?

Charles Carroll's life divides neatly into three sections. The first ends with his return from his educational odyssey in Europe in 1765; the second encompasses his activities in public life from 1765 until his departure from the Maryland Senate in 1800; the third covers the years after retirement from politics, the years devoted to his multifarious business enterprises and the cultivation of his lands. His portraits are considered according to this tripartite division.

[6] CCC to Unknown Correspondent, November 15, 1827. Private Collection of a Descendant.

From the earliest period, only two portraits are recorded, one by an unknown artist and one executed in London by Sir Joshua Reynolds. Only the Reynolds is extant, the first likeness of the family documented as having been painted abroad — a circumstance which would be more common in the generation of the grand-children and which would lead to a preponderance of Marylanders in portraiture, rather than portraiture in Maryland. We know of a portrait by an unknown artist through a letter from his mother, Elizabeth Brooke, written while Charles was at the College of Louis-le-Grand in Paris:

> *... your picture is with me. I set great store by it for I think it has a great resemblance of you when ye was here. ... It is not so handsome as you was here. What Mr. Woppler says is here ye Limner has not done you justice.*[7]

The second third of his long life includes the deed for which he is generally known: the signing of the Declaration of Independence. It includes, as well, a development of great import in the history of Maryland and incidentally of her portraiture: the rise of Baltimore as the commercial and, as a result, the cultural and artistic center of the State." A village of only seven houses within [Mr. Carroll's] memory"[8] would be the setting for the greatest number of Carroll's portraits, in the last third of his life, and those of his children's generation. But this second third of the venerable Signer's long years, of vital importance historically, includes a dearth of portraits.

The Maryland-born artist Charles Willson Peale (1741-1827) painted him three times between his return from England in 1769 and about 1771. All of these are lost. John Trumbull (1765-1843) represented Carroll in two of his historical works of the Revolution: the famous *Declaration of Independence* and *General Washington Resigning his Commission* which were both composed well after the event. Trumbull's likenesses of Carroll do not relate to any known portraits of the Signer, and no study from life of Carroll by Trumbull has come to light.

There is evidence that the English settler in America, Robert Edge Pine (1730?-1788) painted an individual portrait of Carroll about 1785 when he painted a group portrait of the Carroll family. *The Departure of Charles Carroll Jr.* commemorates the departure of Charles Carroll of Homewood for his education at the English School in Liège, Belgium. If Pine did paint an individual portrait at the same time, it was probably destroyed by fire in 1803. *Congress Voting Independence* may have been started by Pine prior to his death in 1788, but the profile likeness of Carroll in that work is not based upon a known work attributed to Pine nor one by Edward Savage who later worked on the *Congress.* Thus, not a single life portrait of Carroll during this period is extant, and the lost Peales are the only ones which qualify with certainty as life portraits.

It is after 1800 that the real tide of portraits begins, and Carroll's appearance can be noted with regularity from Field's 1803 watercolor of him as a youthful

[7] Elizabeth Brooke to CCC, September 8, 1756. MS 206, MdHi.

[8] Basil Hall, *Travels in Canada, and the United States, in 1816 and 1817.* (London: 1818), Vol. II, p. 101.

and vigorous sixty-six to Hubard's portrayal of a delicate old gentleman well into his nineties.

Diminutive in size alone, of very great dimensions in achievement, the Signer was above all a modest, unassuming, conservative individual without a trace of vanity. In keeping with his character, there is no evidence that he ever solicited his own portrait. Every one known appears to be in answer to the wishes of his family or the request of the artists and public who sought him out.

In considering the portraits of the fourth generation, that of Charles Carroll's children and children-in-law, again, the artists one meets are the most distinguished working in Maryland at the time, including Robert Edge Pine, Gilbert Stuart, Robert Field, Saint-Mémin, Rembrandt Peale, Thomas Sully, C. B. King, and one attribution to Charles Willson Peale.

In parallel with the Signer's generation the majority are not native-born Marylanders again underscoring the fact that Maryland (especially at this time, Baltimore) was a popular field of artistic activity and an important cultural center which, in general, could not claim the most outstanding portraitists of the 18th and early 19th centuries as native sons. It is also curious to note the subordinate place which the women hold in this generation. Charles Carroll of Homewood and the sons-in-law, Richard Caton and Robert Goodloe Harper, claim several distinguished portraits, including a handsome bust of R. G. Harper by Raimondo Trentanove executed in Italy and foreshadowing the extensive activity in the next generation of Carroll family members painted abroad. There is no evidence that Gilbert Stuart, Saint-Mémin, Rembrandt Peale, or C. B. King ever painted their wives. The Sully of Harriet Chew is the only major portrait for the distaff side.

With the grandchildren, Carroll family portraiture in its most romantic flowering assumes aspects quite different from previous generations. Here the distaff side as a whole is represented by a more brilliant array of portraits than their husbands — at least one for each of the four Caton granddaughters, three of the four Carroll granddaughters, and the only surviving Harper granddaughter. Of the twenty recorded portraits of these eight, only two were painted in Maryland: the Sully of Emily Louisa Hinton Harper and the portrait of Emily Caton MacTavish which may be by the only native-born Baltimore artist for this generation: Philip Tilyard. The daughters of Charles Carroll of Homewood sat for their portraits in Philadelphia — almost all to Sully. Elizabeth, Marianne and Louisa Caton — "the Three American Graces" — set sail for Europe in 1816, conquered the hearts of an impressive array of English nobility, and added Sir Thomas Lawrence, Thomas Phillips, Andrew Robertson, Anne Mee, and Marie-Victoire Jaquotot to the extensive number of artists portraying the Carroll family. Within the family the balance was gradually shifting from portraiture in Maryland to Marylanders in portraiture.

Five generations, the Signer's grandparents through grandchildren, encompass the focus of this study. It might be expected then that the fact of these particular portraits would end with their execution and that the images would remain a unique reminder of the past. Two circumstances, however, have resulted in numerous progeny from the contemporary likenesses of Charles Carroll of Carrollton and his immediate family. Graphics constitute one. Not the numerous and very fine contemporary graphics which form such an important part of this study, but ones executed decades after the painting of the portraits and the decease of the subjects. And not just the Signer himself, who will continue to generate renewed interest at every possible anniversary of our Nation's birth from the event to infinity. In fact, there are mid-to-late nineteenth century engravings and lithographs of Daniel Carroll of Rock Creek, John Carroll, Harriet Chew Carroll, Mary Caton — and the Three American Graces. They are all latter day interpretations of the original portraits presented in this catalogue which show a continuous fascination not only with Carroll, but with his family. These graphics add immeasurably to the historical and romantic importance of the Carroll family in portraiture.

Copies constitute the second circumstance, resulting in an increase from the original portraits in this study which follows a geometric progression. It seems that copyists were actively engaged on this collection for a wide variety of reasons from the generation of Charles Carroll of Carrollton to the twentieth century. Copies were not limited to commissions for the family. Charles Willson Peale copied his son Rembrandt's portrait of the Signer for his Philadelphia Museum. Rembrandt Peale copied Lawrence's portrait of the Duke of Wellington apparently for his own use. Michael Laty copied Field's watercolor of the Signer for The Maryland Historical Society. Isaac L. Williams copied the Field-type portrait of the Signer for the American Colonization Society. The Carroll family, in their turn, were responsible for an enormous number of copies. The early and mid-nineteenth century ones have confused the story and confounded the art historian for generations, as they invariably descended to later generations as works from the original artist's hand. In some instances, we know the circumstances: Michael Laty made more than one copy from the Caton-MacTavish portraits in 1846 and 1847; the Signer's great-great grandson Harper Pennington, an artist by profession, is known to have made one copy of a Harper portrait in the 1880's and it is likely he made more; in the early part of this century, M. Calling Hall signed a copy of one of Sully's portraits, descending from Charles Carroll of Homewood's daughters and he is suspected of more activity within the family; and almost the entire MacTavish Collection was copied in Rome by an unknown artist in the 1920's or 1930's. In other instances the disposition of personal property in family wills provides clues concerning likely occasions for copying. The following catalogue includes the details.

Now, at last, five generations of Carroll family portraits appear to be quiescent — no longer burgeoning apace but vividly, temptingly providing the materials for an historical statement of portraiture in Maryland and Marylanders in portraiture made possible by a distinguished American family whose members were not avowed connoisseurs or professed collectors but who possessed, indeed, a passion for portraits. If our study raises more questions than it answers, that is all to the good.

Notes on the MacTavish Collection

Reference to The MacTavish Collection will be found throughout the catalogue. Dr. J. Hall Pleasants, in his monumental "Studies in Maryland Painting" on deposit at The Maryland Historical Society, laid the groundwork for an understanding of this extensive and complicated group of Carroll family portraits. The file numbers relating to each MacTavish collection portrait recorded by Dr. Pleasants will be found in the catalogue, and more complete details can be found in these files. However, evidence has come to light since Dr. Pleasants' death in 1957, and a further word of explanation seems in order.

Emily Caton MacTavish, youngest of Charles Carroll of Carrollton's Caton granddaughters, inherited directly from her grandfather a large percentage of his personal property and all of her mother's, Mary Caton's, personal property. Portraits were included in both inheritances. At her death in 1867, Emily Caton MacTavish left all of her family portraits and pictures to her granddaughter, Emily MacTavish, who later became a nun. The younger Emily's father, Charles Carroll MacTavish, Sr., specified in his will that, upon his death, his wife would be the guardian of their children's inheritance which they had received from their grandmother, Emily Caton MacTavish. These terms seem to have been carried out, as, at some later date, Mrs. Charles Carroll MacTavish, Sr., became custodian of the collection. It was deposited in her name at The Maryland Historical Society between 1879 and 1907. Between 1907 and 1912 the collection was shipped to Virginia Scott MacTavish, the younger Emily's sister, who never married and was living in Rome with her brother Charles Carroll MacTavish, Jr., at the time.

At her death in 1919, Virginia Scott MacTavish left the entire collection to her brother, Charles Carroll MacTavish, Jr., for life, with the stipulation that it be divided at his death between her cousins Charles Bancroft Carroll and Caton MacTavish. The collection was not inventoried at the time of her death so that the only indication of its contents are the listings in *The Maryland Historical Society Exhibition Catalogue 1848-1908* which record those paintings deposited by Mrs. Charles Carroll MacTavish, Sr. Charles Carroll MacTavish, Jr., married Mary Bergin in 1927 or 1928. There was no issue from this marriage. C. C. MacTavish, Jr. and Mary Bergin returned to America in 1933 retaining the apartment in Rome for an undetermined time. There are unsubstantiated reports that some works in the collection were brought back to America at this time and were received by the Baltimore Storage Company. The storage company cannot find any relevant records for this date. There are also rumors that some of the paintings were sold in Italy after 1933. In addition, in 1942, Mrs. Charles Carroll MacTavish, Jr., stated that the originals had been left in Rome, and only copies had been brought back to America. Apparently, after that date and probably between Mrs. MacTavish, Jr.'s death in 1942 and her husband's in 1948, a large majority were brought back to America, for some were sold at the Galton-Osborne Galleries in Baltimore reportedly on March 27, 1947, and others at Galton-Osborne Galleries in 1948. Also, in 1948 in Baltimore, at the time of Charles Carroll MacTavish, Jr.'s death, the collection was inventoried twice and appraised once prior to its division between Charles

Bancroft Carroll and Mary Carroll MacTavish, sole heir of Caton MacTavish. This division fulfilled the stipulation outlined in Virginia Scott MacTavish's will.

Factors which became apparent in 1948 have made the subsequent history of the MacTavish collection confusing in the extreme. For example, the three 1948 lists are not identical and none totally matches the entries in *The Maryland Historical Society Exhibition Catalogues* for 1879-1907. This would indicate changes in the composition of the collection between 1907 and 1948 and again, between the inventories and the appraisal in 1948. It would also support the persistent rumors of intermittent sales of originals in Rome after Virginia Scott MacTavish's death and of the execution of copies which were retained by the family.

The inventories reflect the mixture of originals, early copies, and 20th century copies contained in the collection, a fact of very great importance for several items in this catalogue. Apparently from the time of the Signer himself no distinction was made between a work by an artist's hand and a work after the artist. A Lawrence-type portrait was referred to as by Sir Thomas Lawrence, and it descended in the family as such, with the attribution as an original remaining undisturbed until the mid 20th century. Evidence to date, then, indicates:

(1) arrival of the collection in Rome intact by 1912;

(2) additions to the collection by copies between Virginia Scott MacTavish's death in 1919 and the return of the works to America during the period 1933-1948;

(3) sale in Italy of items in the collection at unknown dates after 1919;

(4) sale of items in Baltimore on March 27, 1947 at Galton-Osborne Galleries;

(5) anonymous sale of items in 1948 at Galton-Osborne Galleries;

(6) division of the remainder between Charles Bancroft Carroll and Mary Carroll MacTavish in 1948;

(7) sale by authority of Mary Carroll MacTavish of several items she inherited, immediately after the division in 1948 for which no circumstances are known (several of these works unlocated despite the gracious efforts on behalf of the former owner to reconstruct the circumstances of sale);

(8) intermittent sales after 1948 of items inherited by Charles Bancroft Carroll (details given in catalogue listing for these items);

(9) distribution of remaining unsold items to family members who wish to remain anonymous;

(10) destruction by fire in 1973 of several items inherited by Charles Bancroft Carroll.

These factors concerning each item in The MacTavish Collection are reflected in the catalogue entries. The inconsistencies and confusions in the provenance of these portraits, in turn, reflect our imperfect knowledge of the facts in each case. Every entry relating to this problem, however, is designated in its provenance as "part of The MacTavish Collection" if it is known to have existed prior to 1907 when removal of the original collection for shipment to Rome began, and as "The MacTavish Collection" if there is a possibility that it may have been executed after 1907.

NOTE: "MacTavish," "McTavish," and "Mactavish" are all accepted spellings for this name as each form has been used at various times by different family members. "MacTavish" has been used throughout this study as it was the form which John MacTavish, first of this family associated with the Carrolls, used in signing his will (see Baltimore City Wills, 1852. Folio 126, Book 25. Hall of Records, Annapolis).

References

Sources for MacTavish Note

1. Will of Charles Carroll of Carrollton. Hall of Records, Annapolis, Maryland. Accession number 19968.
2. Will of Mary Caton. Baltimore County Wills. 1846, Folio 295, Book 21. Hall of Records, Annapolis, Maryland.
3. Will of Emily MacTavish. Baltimore City Wills, 1867. Folio 27, Book 34. Hall of Records, Annapolis, Maryland.
4. Will of Virginia Scott MacTavish, Baltimore County Wills, 1922. Folio 23, Book 22. Hall of Records, Annapolis, Maryland.
5. List of paintings owned by Mrs. Charles Carroll MacTavish and on deposit in the Gallery of the Maryland Historical Society, 1907. On deposit at The Maryland Historical Society, Baltimore, Maryland.
6. List of paintings deposited at The Maryland Historical Society for Virginia Scott MacTavish by Alice G. Bergin, March 4, 1912. On deposit at The Maryland Historical Society, Baltimore, Maryland.
7. List of paintings withdrawn by Alice G. Bergin from The Maryland Historical Society on behalf of Virginia Scott MacTavish, October 7, 1912. On deposit at The Maryland Historical Society, Baltimore, Maryland.
8. Letter from Mary MacTavish (Mrs. Charles Carroll MacTavish, Jr.) to Ellen Hart Smith, February 6, 1942, on deposit Frick Art Reference Library, New York, New York.
9. Inventory of paintings which are to be divided between Charles Bancroft Carroll and Mary Carroll MacTavish; deposited at the Baltimore Storage Company in the name of Alice G. Bergin no date (1948?). In possession of a Carroll descendant.
10. Appraisal of The MacTavish Collection by Fidelity Appraisal Company, October 8, 1948. In possession of a Carroll descendant.
11. Inventory, dated November 10, 1948, of paintings from The MacTavish Collection deposited at the Peabody Institute. On deposit at Peabody Institute, Baltimore, Maryland.

Notes Concerning Portraits of the Carroll Family

The five generations of the Carroll family from Charles Carroll of Carrollton's grandparents through his grandchildren, are arranged chronologically according to their relationship to the Signer. The initials CC of A, CCC, and MDC below the subject headings and in the abbreviated references represent Charles Carroll of Annapolis, Charles Carroll of Carrollton, and Mary Darnall Carroll. To locate the portraits of a particular individual refer to the genealogical chart facing page xvi where the pertinent catalogue numbers are given under each name.

Portraits in the exhibition are numbered consecutively 1 through 90. Dimensions are in inches, height preceding width. Portraits related to a catalogue entry, but not in the exhibition, follow immediately; these include replicas, copies and variants. Additional portraits of each subject, not in the exhibition, will be found after the last catalogue listing for that subject. An effort has been made to cite all known portraits of subjects for the first four generations only. A representative selection of the outstanding engravers and lithographers has been cited. For the most part, those in later publications are not included.

As the emphasis is upon subject, not medium or artist, all likenesses of a particular individual are included together, whether oil portrait, miniature, silhouette, sculpture, or graphic work. A bibliographical index of artists (p. 303) indicates the total number of works in the exhibition by a particular artist.

For practical reasons, bibliographical references in the catalogue entries are shortened to include the author's last name or an abbreviated title if there is no author. The more complete reference is given in the Bibliographical Index at the end of the book.

As J. Hall Pleasants' "Studies in American Painting" are a particularly valuable source for the portrait itself, his file numbers are included. The complete Pleasants file is on deposit at The Maryland Historical Society, Baltimore (abbreviated as MdHi).

A limited provenance for each portrait is given, as its purpose is to indicate Carroll family ownership rather than a complete history of the object.

Ann C. Van Devanter

Charles Carroll of Carrollton and American Independence

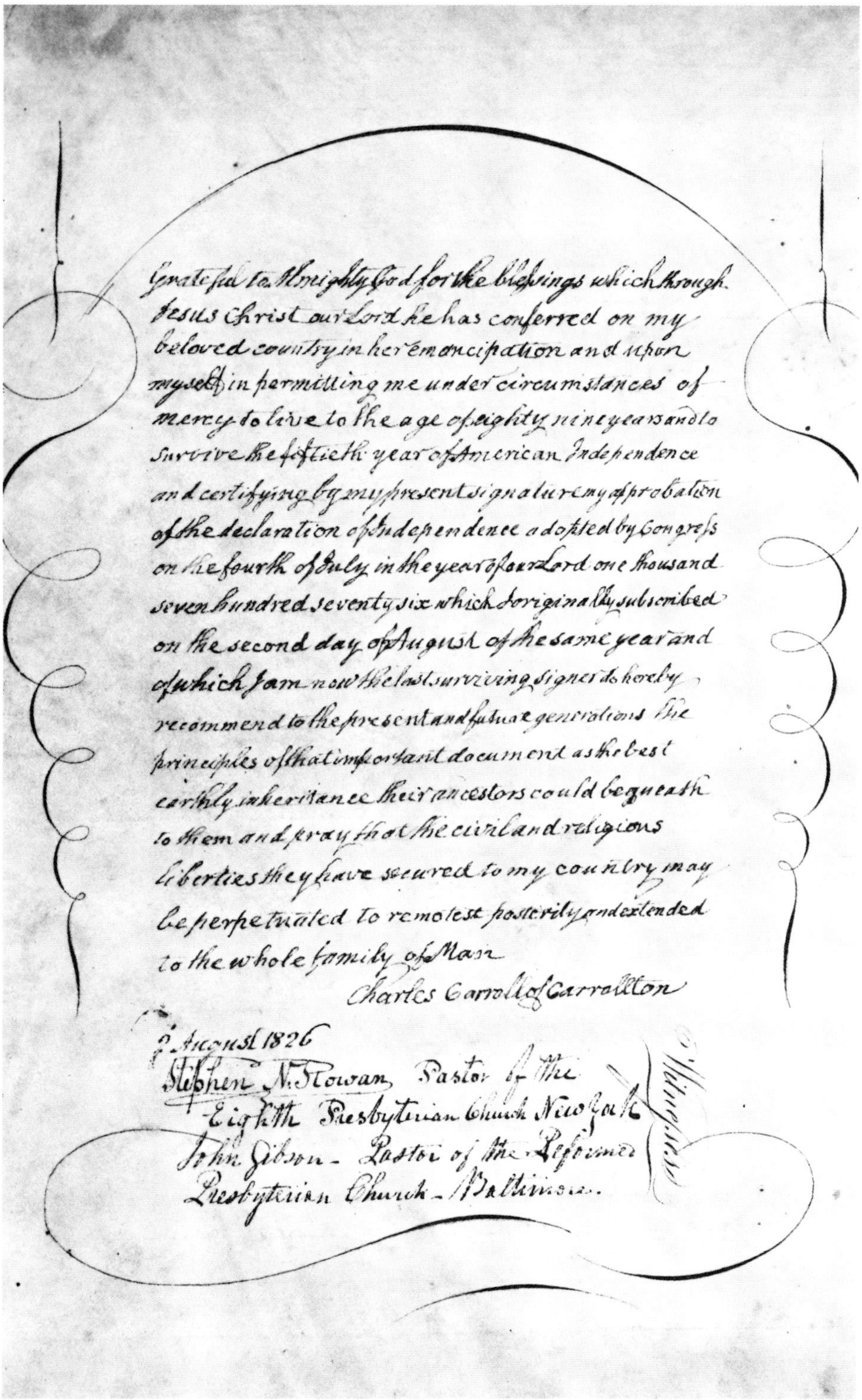
Grateful to Almighty God for the blessings which through
Jesus Christ our Lord he has conferred on my
beloved country in her emancipation and upon
myself in permitting me under circumstances of
mercy to live to the age of eighty nine years and to
survive the fiftieth year of American Independence
and certifying by my present signature my approbation
of the declaration of Independence adopted by Congress
on the fourth of July in the year of our Lord one thousand
seven hundred seventy six which I originally subscribed
on the second day of August of the same year and
of which I am now the last surviving signer I do hereby
recommend to the present and future generations the
principles of that important document as the best
earthly inheritance their ancestors could bequeath
to them and pray that the civil and religious
liberties they have secured to my country may
be perpetuated to remotest posterity and extended
to the whole family of Man

Charles Carroll of Carrollton

2 August 1826

Stephen N. Rowan, Pastor of the
Eighth Presbyterian Church New York
John Gibson - Pastor of the Reformed
Presbyterian Church - Baltimore.

Witnesses

Charles Carroll's Attestation in The Declaration of American Independence with the Certificate of Charles Carroll of Carrollton, the Last Living Signer of the Original Document

One volume, 32 pp., designed and executed by Isaac Bragg of Connecticut, bound by Joseph Forster of New York City; 15 13/16 x 12 7/8 inches

Presented to the Common Council of New York, July 4, 1828

Received by the New York Historical Society from the Common Council of New York City, March 14, 1889

New York Historical Society, New York

1.

CONGRESS VOTING INDEPENDENCE

Robert Edge Pine ? (1730?-1788) and Edward Savage (1761-1817)

Unsigned, ca. 1788-ca. 1818

Oil on canvas, 19 3/4 x 26 1/2 inches

The Historical Society of Pennsylvania, Philadelphia

Provenance: Purchased by Charles Henry Hart from the sale of Moses Kimball's Boston Museum, about 1892; purchased by subscription from him by the present owner in 1904.

Born in England, Robert Edge Pine emigrated to America in 1784 and worked in and out of Philadelphia until his death in 1788. The inventory of his estate in 1789 lists an unfinished picture of *The American Congress Voting Independence.* Charles Henry Hart states that Savage completed Pine's unfinished work (Hart, pp. 7 and 11-12). Edward Mulcahy (p. 85), on the other hand, produces evidence indicating that whatever Pine painted was destroyed by fire in 1803 or in 1807 and that this is a work completely executed by Savage although some of the individual portraits are based on works by other artists, including Pine.

> *The number of portraits reminiscent of other painters in his picture suggests that Savage may well have taken advantage of Pine's earlier effort to collect heads for his painting. Pine had a golden opportunity for such "head-hunting" when the Constitutional Convention met in Philadelphia in 1787* (Mulcahy, p. 89).

It is notable that the faces of four figures in the back, on the left, are unfinished. The only explanation for Savage leaving these faces incomplete would be that he was dependent upon the work of other artists for actual likenesses of these signers and did not wish to improvise. Furthermore, it is unusual for an artist to begin an engraving of a still unfinished work (see Cat. No. 2), which Savage, if he is the sole artist, did.

The painting "presents as true a picture of the Assembly Room of Independence Hall as we are ever likely to find" (Mulcahy, p. 91) even when comparing it to John Trumbull's *Declaration of Independence* (see Cat. No. 3). Pine's painting studio was in this room in 1784. If Savage's is the only hand in this work, we must assume either

that the room remained totally unchanged until at least 1796 when Mulcahy states that Savage could have begun the work or that Savage had an accurate model from which to copy.

Charles Carroll of Carrollton is the figure seated in the right foreground with his head turned to the right in full profile. This likeness is not based upon a known work by Pine. In fact, the source of this rather sketchy and abbreviated portrait of Carroll is rather a puzzle. Saint-Mémin's engraving after his portrait of Carroll (Cat. No. 23A) is a possibility as it would have been readily available, is close to the size of the image in the *Congress,* and there is a similarity in the profile which faces in the same direction. Another profile portrait (Cat. No. 24), also facing in the same direction, however, seems closely related to the Signer's likeness in the *Congress,* and it appears to date within the time period (1796?-1818) that Edward Savage was working on the painting.

RELATED WORK:
(Cat. No. 2)

2.

DECLARATION OF INDEPENDENCE

Edward Savage (1761-1817) after his painting which may have been begun by Robert Edge Pine ? (1730?-1788)

Engraving, plate started after 1796

Image size: 19 x 25 3/4 inches

The Johns Hopkins University, Baltimore

Edward Savage, portrait and historical painter and engraver, worked in Boston, New York City, and London before finally settling in Boston in 1801. He left the plate for this engraving unfinished at the time of his death. His son Edward Savage attempted to complete it without success. It is not known when this impression was pulled. It is presumably from the copper plate now in the Massachusetts Historical Society, and it may be from the Goodspeed printing of 1906.

3.

Declaration of Independence

Asher B. Durand (1796-1886) after John Trumbull A1756-1843)

Engraving, 1820-23

Legend: *Copyright secured according to the Act of Congress Decr. 20th 1820/The Declaration of the United States of America/ July 4th 1776/Painted by John Trumbull/Engraved by A. B. Durand*

Image size: 22 x 30 1/8 inches

Massachusetts Historical Society, Boston

John Trumbull, son of the Revolutionary Governor of Connecticut, studied painting with Benjamin West in London and became acquainted with Jacques-Louis David in Paris. His achievements were immense as a cartographer, an architect, a designer of medals, and an author, as well as landscape painter, portraitist, and the creator of the famous scenes of the American Revolution.

While in London studying with Benjamin West, Trumbull conceived his grand plan for a series of subjects from the Revolution. Probably the most famous of these is the *Declaration of Independence,* "composed and commenced" by Trumbull in West's London studio in 1786 (Morgan, p. 35) and completed in 1797. It is best known through the large version in the United States Capitol; Trumbull's sketch is in the collection of Yale University Art Gallery. In his catalogue of 1841, Trumbull writes of his painting:

> *To preserve the resemblance of the men who were the authors of this memorable act, was an essential object of this painting. . . . The artist . . . spared neither labour nor expense in obtaining his portraits from the living men. . . . The dresses are faithfully copied from the costume of the time, the present fashion of pantaloons and trowsers being then unknown among gentlemen.*
>
> *The room is copied from that in which Congress held their sessions at the time, such as it was before the spirit of innovation laid unhallowed hands upon it, and violated its venerable walls by modern improvement, as it is called.* (Morgan, pp. 35 and 38)

This engraving after Trumbull's work was the springboard for Asher B. Durand's highly successful career as an engraver. Trumbull was quite determined to have the painting engraved, but the cost of having it done by his first choice, the London en-

Plate 3A

graver James Heath, was so high that he sought the help of Durand who accepted the commission without the consent of his partner Peter Maverick. The partnership foundered on this point. Durand undertook the mammoth job in 1820; the engraving was published in 1823. The finished product pleased Trumbull to the extent that he wrote to the Marquis de Lafayette on October 20, 1823:

> *I have sent to you a small case containing a proof impression of a print which has been engraved here from my painting of the 'Declaration of Independence' by a young engraver, born in this vicinity, and now only twenty-six years old. This work is wholly American, even to the paper and printing, a circumstance which renders it popular here, and will make it a curiosity to you, who knew America when she had neither painters nor engravers nor artists of any kind, except those of* stern utility (Durand, p. 26).

Charles Carroll of Carrollton is the small figure seated in front of the door to the left with his head turned to the right. The source for Carroll's likeness in this work is not known. Despite the fact that Trumbull claimed to have painted the subjects from life sketches, except in specifically noted cases, a preliminary study of the Signer by Trumbull has not come to light.

Additional Painting:

(3A) *General Washington Resigning His Commission*, Annapolis, Maryland, December 23, 1783. John Trumbull (1756-1843). Unsigned, ca. 1816-1824. Oil on canvas, 20 x 30 inches. Yale University Art Gallery, New Haven.

This painting, along with *Declaration of Independence* (see Cat. No. 3), was part of Trumbull's series of Revolutionary War subjects. On December 24, 1824, he was paid by Congress for the large version of *General Washington Resigning* in the Rotunda of the Capitol; the small preliminary version was part of his gift to Yale University which carries the stipulation that should any item leave the University the entire bequest will be transferred permanently to Harvard.

Although generally considered one of Trumbull's poorer efforts, this painting is of particular interest to this exhibition because it includes not only a prominent portrait of Charles Carroll of Carrollton with his arm on the empty chair, but also of his two young daughters Mary (Mrs. Richard Caton) and Catherine (Mrs. Robert Goodloe Harper) who stand in front of him.

In addition to preliminary portrait studies, Trumbull is known to have used sketches of the Annapolis State House chamber in executing this work. The accuracy with which he depicted the setting has been borne out by twentieth century architectural research.

Portraits of Charles Carroll of Carrollton and His Family

CHARLES CARROLL THE SETTLER
("The Attorney General"), 1660-1720

(Paternal grandfather of CCC)

4.

Unknown artist or Justus Engelhardt Kühn ? (?-1717)

Unsigned, 1700-1720

Oil on canvas, 32 1/2 x 25 1/16 inches

The Maryland Historical Society, Baltimore

Provenance: By direct descent through Charles Carroll of Carrollton's granddaughter Emily MacTavish to Charles Carroll MacTavish, Jr.; part of The MacTavish Collection; sold at Galton-Osborne Galleries, Baltimore, on March 27, 1947, to The Maryland Historical Society

Reference: Pleasants, "Studies," no. 3066

There is no firm basis for the attribution of this portrait to Justus Engelhardt Kühn, and the portrait is dissimilar to Kühn's other known paintings. Attribution to Gustavus Hesselius (1682-1755) has been suggested, but there is a strength in the modelling of the face and a balance of the figure on the canvas which is not usually associated with this artist. Hesselius could have been in Maryland at the time this portrait was executed as he is documented as being in the colony by January 1719, over a year and a half before the Settler's death, and there are indications that he was making painting trips into Maryland as early as 1717. There are, however, other possibilities. For example, it could be that this portrait was painted by an as yet unidentified artist, working in Maryland, with great ability in delineating his sitter's character. Another possibility is raised by the fact that the Settler and his wife, like many of the prosperous early

PLATE 4A

colonists, visited Europe during the first decade of the 18th century. They could have had their portraits executed there, although, upon viewing this particular likeness identified as the Settler, it is doubtful that any artist in England or the Continent would have executed a portrait so austere in its conception.

Family tradition is the basis for identification of the subject of this portrait as Charles Carroll the Settler. It does not appear to be a companion piece to Cat. No. 5, a portrait identified as the Settler's wife, Mary Darnall Carroll. A 1720 inventory of the Settler's estate, unusual for its specific enumeration of each picture owned, lists "in the new Room . . . 3 Pictors being Mr. Carroll and his Spouse & Daughter" (MdHi, ms. 220, Liber X, Box 16). Another portrait of the Settler is listed in the "Dining room," indicating that there were two portraits of the Settler at the time of his death.

ADDITIONAL PORTRAIT OF CHARLES CARROLL THE SETTLER:
(4A) Justus Engelhardt Kühn ? (?-1717) or unknown artist after Kühn. Signed in script, left of center: *Kuhn*, date unknown. Inscribed at right of center: *AEtatis Sue/XLVIII.* Oil on canvas, 32 x 26 inches (oval, probably cut down from a rectangle). Private Collection of a Descendant. Provenance — by direct descent through Charles Carroll of Carrollton's grandson Charles Carroll of Doughoregan to the present owner. Reference: Pleasants, "Studies," no. 126.

According to family tradition, this portrait (Plate 4A) is believed to be Charles Carroll the Settler at a slightly younger age than Cat. No. 4, but the two subjects do differ considerably in appearance. In form and conception, this portrait suggests a companion piece to Cat. No. 5A, a portrait identified as the Settler's wife. The sitters' ages are inscribed on the canvases as 48 and 30, the ages of Charles Carroll the Settler and his wife in 1708. It is possible that these are the portraits referred to in the inventory of the Settler's estate as "Mr. Carroll and his Spouse."

The signature, lower left, is in script and is not similar to the one known signature of Kühn (Cat. No. 46A). It may have been the effort of a later restorer to fill in paint loss or to document an artist's name which the family had always associated with this likeness. The fact that the Settler was Administrator for Kühn's estate in 1717 proves an association between artist and sitter which could have resulted in a portrait.

This work has been relined and so heavily restored that it is not possible to determine without extensive laboratory examination whether or not it is a painting of the early 18th century. Restoration could account for alteration of features. In its present form it does not relate stylistically to the known works by Kühn.

Mrs. Charles Carroll, wife of the Settler (Mary Darnall), 1678-1742

(Paternal grandmother of CCC; Great-great aunt of MDC)

5.

Gustavus Hesselius ? (1682-1755)

Unsigned, 1717-1720

Oil on canvas, 30 1/8 x 25 3/16 inches

The Maryland Historical Society, Baltimore

Provenance: By direct descent through Charles Carroll of Carrollton's granddaughter Emily MacTavish to Mary Carroll MacTavish; part of The MacTavish Collection; sold to The Maryland Historical Society, 1949

Reference: Pleasants, "Studies," no. 3315

A question must be raised concerning the artistic attribution of this portrait. The face and some of the neck and shoulder are the only areas not so heavily overpainted as to obscure the original pigment. These do suggest Gustavus Hesselius, especially in the grey cast of the skin tones and the rather heavy handling of the facial features. The identity of the subject is according to family tradition. In the 1720 inventory of the Settler's estate, "Mrs. Charles Carrolls pictor £4" (MdHi, ms. 220, Liber X, Box 16) is listed as in the dining room. A second portrait of Mrs. Carroll was "in the new Room."

Mrs. Charles Carroll

Plate 5A

Additional portrait of Mrs. Charles Carroll:

(5A) Justus Engelhardt Kühn ? (?-1717) or unknown artist after Kühn. Unsigned, late 18th century. Inscribed above left shoulder: *AEtatis Sua[e?]/XXX.* Oil on canvas, 36 x 32 inches (oval, probably cut down from a rectangle). Private Collection of a Descendant. Provenance — by direct descent through Charles Carroll of Carrollton's grandson Charles Carroll of Doughoregan to the present owner. Reference: Pleasants, "Studies," no. 127.

The same points raised in the discussion of the portrait of Charles Carroll the Settler (Plate 4A) also apply to this likeness, believed to be his wife. Here there is no indication of a signature and again relining and heavy restoration make dating impossible without laboratory examination. This portrait has descended in the same branch of the family as a companion piece to Cat. No. 4A. The similar inscriptions on the two, corroborating the exact age of the Settler and his wife in 1708, suggest a correct identity for the subjects. 1708 also marks the first year that Justus Engelhardt Kühn is documented as being in Maryland.

CHARLES CARROLL OF ANNAPOLIS, 1702-1782

(Father of CCC; 1st cousin twice removed of MDC)

6.

Justus Engelhardt Kühn ? (?-1717)

Unsigned, ca. 1712

Inscribed on pedestal: *AEtatis Sua*[*e*]. *X*

Oil on canvas, 53 1/8 x 38 11/16 inches

The Maryland Historical Society, Baltimore

Gift of Mr. J. Gilman D'Arcy Paul, 1949

Provenance: By direct descent through Charles Carroll of Carrollton's granddaughter Emily MacTavish to Mary Carroll MacTavish; part of The MacTavish Collection; acquired by Mr. Paul who presented it to the present owner.

Reference: Pleasants, "Studies," no. 3308

This portrait was identified in the nineteenth century lists of The MacTavish Collection as "Charles Carroll 10 years old" (MdHi, *Catalogue of Exhibitions*, 1893). However, only two portraits of the Settler are listed in his 1720 inventory raising the possibility that the subject is another member of the Carroll, Digges, or Darnall family. The inventory does list a portrait of Daniel Carroll. Perhaps this is a likeness of Charles Carroll of Annapolis' brother, Daniel Carroll of Duddington as a boy.

In comparing this portrait with those of Ignatius Digges (Plate No. 46A), Eleanor Darnall (Cat. No. 14), and Henry Darnall III (Cat. No. 12), there are certain aspects which are dissimilar. For example, note the handling of the eyes and hair and the lack of architectural background, all of which contribute to an impression of an artist approaching his subject in a different manner. The elongation of the figure which is placed in a considerably more confined space, the bolder handling of detail, and the less rounded cast of the face when compared with the other portraits attributed to Kühn *suggest* a different hand at work. In addition, the canvas has been pieced, a feature atypical of Kühn's work, and there are indications of an original canvas larger than those usually used by Kühn: a tree has been cut off at the top edge and the deer's nose is very close to the left edge.

The older age of the subject and the effects of earlier restoration could, however, account for the differences, and a more detailed comparison between this portrait and that of Henry Darnall III (Cat. No. 12) where the two subjects are closer in dress and pose does suggest similarities — the silver collar on the deer in this portrait and on the slave in the Darnall portrait; details of costume, such as the drapery surrounding the figure, the stock, the shape of the tunic; the triangular motif of the architectural element to the right; and the almost identical stance and placement of hands. But the appearance of related and even identical elements in the portraits is not the conclusive proof that they are from the same hand. In the case of this portrait, the pervasive influence of English and Continental prints on Colonial American art and the early artist's dependence upon this source — frequently the identical one — must be carefully considered.

Ætatis Suæ. X.

7.

John Wollaston (fl. 1736-1767)

Unsigned, ca. 1753-1754

Oil on canvas, 50 1/8 x 40 3/16 inches

Private Collection of a Descendant

Provenance: By direct descent through Charles Carroll of Carrollton's daughter Mrs. Robert Goodloe Harper to the present owner

Reference: Pleasants, "Studies," no. 596

John Wollaston, London born and London trained, according to Charles Willson Peale, under a "noted drapery painter" (Sartain, p. 147) worked in New York, Maryland, Virginia, and Philadelphia between 1749 and 1759 and, after seven years in India, briefly reappeared in Charleston, South Carolina in 1767. He returned to London about that year.

Wollaston is documented in Maryland from March 15, 1753 when an anonymous admirer penned a rapturous verse "On seeing Mr. Wollaston's Pictures . . ." (*The Maryland Gazette*) until August 1754 when he is thought to have left for Virginia. As he was last documented in New York on April 1, 1752 and no record of him in Virginia before 1755 has come to light, it could be that Wollaston was in Maryland for a longer period of time than documentation would indicate, especially considering the number of impressive half-length Maryland portraits which are unmistakeably from the artist's hand. The Carroll family and their immediate connections represent a considerable number of the more than 55 Maryland sitters from Wollaston's hand including this likeness of Charles Carroll of Annapolis and that of his wife Elizabeth Brooke (Cat. No. 9). This elegant depiction of "the Squire," as he was known to his contemporaries, does justice not only to the subject as a distinguished man of property but also to the artist's consummate skill in the portrayal of textures and fabrics. Wollaston could eloquently depict if not the character then certainly the affluent position of his sitters. He produced, for his time, the most fashionable likenesses seen in the Maryland province (see Cat. Nos. 9, 11, 15, 44-48).

8.

John Wollaston? (Fl. 1736-1767) or John Hesselius? (1728-1778)

Unsigned, ca. 1753-1754

Oil on canvas, 30 x 25 inches

Private Collection of a Descendant

Courtesy of Kennedy Galleries, Inc., New York

Provenance: By direct descent through Charles Carroll of Carrollton's granddaughter Emily MacTavish to the present owner; part of The MacTavish Collection

Reference: Pleasants, "Studies," no. 1658; James Lane, "Studies in American Painting," June 5, 1958, on file at Kennedy Galleries, Inc.

It has been presumed that Wollaston painted this bust-length portrait of Charles Carroll of Annapolis during his documented trip to Maryland in 1753-1754. The English artist's characteristically elegant handling of textures, the highlights on velvet, and the full lighting of the face strongly suggest his style, as does the placement of the figure on the canvas. The possibility of attribution to John Hesselius, son of Gustavus, has been raised, but Wollaston appears most likely to be the artist in this instance.

RELATED PORTRAITS:

(8A) Unknown artist after John Wollaston (fl. 1736-1767). Unsigned, 19th century. Oil on canvas, 27 3/8 x 22 5/8 inches (oval). The Maryland Historical Society, Baltimore. This appears to be a 19th century portrait based on Cat. No. 8. The cast of the face is considerably altered, but the pose is identical.

(8B) Attributed to John Wollaston (fl. 1736-1767). Unsigned, ca. 1753-1754. Oil on canvas, 29 1/4 x 24 inches (sight). Private Collection of a Descendant. Provenance — by direct descent through Charles Carroll of Carrollton's grandson Charles Carroll of Doughoregan to the present owner. Reference: Pleasants, "Studies," no. 129. This portrait of Charles Carroll of Annapolis is similar to Cat. No. 8A, but the subject faces left instead of right. John Hesselius "by whom the greater part of the family portraits in the old mansions of Maryland was painted, and that in a respectable manner" (Dunlap, vol. I, p. 150) has been suggested in connection with this work as well as Cat. No. 8. It seems likely that Charles Carroll of Annapolis would at one time have engaged the services of John Hesselius, his talented and prosperous neighbor, husband of the widowed Mary Woodward of "Primrose Hill" and owner himself of the thousand-acre "Bellefield." He began working in Maryland during the 1750's and settled permanently in Anne Arundel County in 1759. During the late 1750's, Hesselius so closely copied Wollaston's style that, as it had been pointed out, it is often difficult to tell a Hesselius painting from a Wollaston. If this portrait is Hesselius' style, then it is indistinguishable from that of Wollaston.

(8C) Unknown artist after John Wollaston (fl. 1736-1767. Unsigned, late 19th or early 20th century. Oil on canvas, 34 x 28 inches (sight). Collection of Mr. and Mrs. Phillips Huntington Clarke. Provenance — part of The MacTavish Collection; sold in 1947 or 1948 to the present owner. This is a copy of Cat. No. 8B.

Charles Carroll of Annapolis

Mrs. Charles Carroll of Annapolis (Elizabeth Brooke), 1709-1761

(Half 1st cousin of CC of A; Mother of CCC; Great-aunt of MDC)

9.

John Wollaston (fl. 1736-1767)

Unsigned, ca. 1753-1754

Oil on canvas, 50 x 40 inches

The Detroit Institute of Arts

Mr. and Mrs. Walter B. Ford II Fund

Provenance: By direct descent through Charles Carroll of Carrollton's granddaughter Emily MacTavish to Charles Bancroft Carroll; part of The MacTavish Collection; sold at Kennedy Galleries, Inc., to The Detroit Institute of Arts, 1966

Reference: Pleasants, "Studies," no. 3314

Characteristic of John Wollaston's portraits is the limited number and similarity of dress styles depicted in his paintings, but there is a change in the costumes of his sitters after 1753. Either a trip home to England or a new shipment of mezzotints showing the latest London fashions could account for the new influences. Be that as it may, the characteristic stomachers, lace caps, and neck adornments of his New York ladies give way to the loose flowing, wasp-waisted dresses worn by Mrs. Carroll in one of the finest extant examples of the artist's rendering of fabrics.

Related portraits:

(9A) Attributed to John Wollaston (fl. 1736-1767). Unsigned, date uncertain. Oil on canvas, 49 1/2 x 38 inches (sight). Collection of Mrs. C. Dexter Pennington. Provenance — by direct descent through Charles Carroll of Carrollton's daughter Mrs. Robert Goodloe Harper to the present owner. Reference: Pleasants, "Studies," no. 595.

This portrait has been attributed to John Wollaston by J. Hall Pleasants and also by George C. Groce (p. 139 & repro. p. 143). It has descended in the family as a companion piece to Wollaston's portrait of Charles Carroll of Annapolis (Cat. No. 7). However, it may be an early copy of Cat. No. 9 or it was restored sometime in the past and traits characteristic of Wollaston have been obscured.

(9B) Unknown artist after Wollaston (fl. 1736-1767). Unsigned, probably early 20th century. Oil on canvas, 50 x 41 1/2 inches (sight). Collection of Mr. and Mrs. Phillips Huntington Clarke. Provenance — part of The MacTavish Collection; sold in 1947 or 1948 to the present owner.

A copy of Cat. No. 9, this portrait may be one of those made in Rome sometime prior to 1933.

Mrs. Charles Carroll of Annapolis

Henry Carroll, 1697-1719

(Brother of CC of A; Uncle of CCC; 1st cousin twice removed to MDC)

10.

Unknown English artist, formerly attributed to Justus Engelhardt Kühn ? (?-1717)

Unsigned, ca. 1707-1715

Oil on canvas, 61 1/4 x 41 13/16 inches

The Maryland Historical Society, Baltimore

Bequest of Miss Ellen C. Daingerfield

Provenance: By descent to Miss Daingerfield

Reference: Pleasants, "Studies," no. 516 (The sitter was formerly identified as Master Darnall or Arthur Darnall)

Although previously identified as Arthur Darnall, there is no record in the genealogies of a Darnall with that first name. Furthermore, Charles Carroll the Settler's inventory (MdHi, ms. 220, Liber X, Box 16) mentions a portrait of Henry Carroll. According to family tradition, the subject of the portrait died at sea which would suggest Henry Carroll, the Settler's eldest son, who, in the tradition of prosperous Catholic families, was sent as a young boy to attend the Jesuit college at St. Omer in French Flanders. He drowned at sea April 10, 1719, while returning home from legal studies at Gray's Inn, London. At the time of his death, both his brothers, Charles Carroll of Annapolis and Daniel Carroll of Duddington were studying at Douai. On July 7, 1719, the Settler writes: "Sons Charles and Daniel: I suppose you have before this time, had the afflicting news of your Brother's death within about six days saile of the Capes of Virginia as he was coming in" (Rowland, vol. I, p. 10).

This charming example of baroque portraiture illustrates greater sophistication than any work known to have been executed in Maryland in the early eighteenth century. It may well have been painted during Henry's long stay abroad. The question also comes to mind of visiting artists from Europe, one of whom may have ventured to Maryland for a brief, unrecorded stay before going perhaps to Virginia where portraits similar to this have been located.

Henry Carroll

Mrs. Daniel Carroll of Duddington I (Ann Rozier or Rozer), 1710-1764

(Sister-in-law to CC of A; Aunt by marriage of CCC; 1st cousin twice removed by marriage of MDC)

11.

John Wollaston (fl. 1736-1767)

Unsigned, ca. 1753-1754

Oil on canvas, 50 x 40 inches

Mr. and Mrs. Walter A. Slowinski

Provenance: By descent through Charles Carroll of Duddington to the present owner

Reference: Pleasants, "Studies," no. 1570

Mrs. Daniel Carroll of Duddington I (née Ann Rozier or Rozer) inherited the magnificent estate of Duddington upon which a large part of Washington, D.C., including the Capitol, now stands. Her husband, Daniel, second surviving son of the Settler, was the progenitor of the Carrolls of Duddington. Although a companion portrait of Daniel has not come to light, he too was undoubtedly painted by the artist of "the almond eyes." Family tradition states that this portrait was hidden in a fireplace during the War of 1812. An overzealous British soldier suspecting that an American was behind it slashed the canvas, destroying the right eye. This could explain the variation in features between this and the following portrait of the same subject.

Additional portrait of Mrs. Daniel Carroll of Duddington I:
(11A) John Wollaston (fl. 1736-1767). Unsigned, ca. 1753-1754. Oil on canvas, 49 1/8 x 39 1/2 inches (sight). Collection of Mr. Paul Madden. Provenance — by descent to the present owner. Reference: Pleasants, "Studies," no. 1847 (listed as owned by Mr. George Washington Young).

Although the cast of features in this portrait differs from Cat. No. 11, the nose and the distinctive cleft of the chin indicate that this is the same subject, an opinion confirmed by family tradition.

MRS. DANIEL CARROLL OF DUDDINGTON I

Henry Darnall III of "His Lordship's Kindness"
("the Attorney General"), 1702/1703—living 1788

(1st cousin of CC of A; 1st cousin once removed of CCC; Grandfather of MDC)

12.

Henry Darnall as a Child

Justus Engelhart Kühn (?-1717)

Unsigned, ca. 1710

Oil on canvas, 54 1/4 x 44 1/4 inches

The Maryland Historical Society, Baltimore

Bequest of Miss Ellen C. Daingerfield

Provenance: By direct descent to the sitter's great-granddaughter Miss Daingerfield

Reference: Pleasants, "Studies," no. 522

There is nothing in the history of American art which quite equals the group of children's portraits by Kühn (see Cat. No. 14 & Cat. No. 46A). This portrait is one of the finest works which can be unquestionably attributed to this artist. Family tradition is the basis for the identity of the sitter. Henry Darnall, about seven in this portrait, stands amidst a setting which speaks not of the realities of the family plantations, including "Darnall's Delight" (later called "the Woodyard") and "His Lordship's Kindness," but of the nostalgia and imagination of the artist's German homeland and his training in the traditions of the late International Baroque style. Yet the presence of the negro slave does illustrate an early Maryland custom among the great planters of presenting offspring with a slave as playmate in youth who would become a personal servant in maturity.

Henry, son of Henry Darnall II and Ann Digges, had a distinguished career which culminated with the position of Attorney General for the province of Maryland from 1751 to 1756. As Receiver of Revenues for Lord Baltimore, irregularities in his office necessitated his departure from Maryland. He spent his later years abroad.

MRS. HENRY DARNALL III (Anne or Ann Talbott or Talbot), before 1705-?

(1st cousin by marriage of CC of A; 1st cousin once removed by marriage of CCC; Grandmother of MDC)

13.

Unknown artist, formerly attributed to Gustavus Hesselius (1682-1755)

Unsigned, ca. 1722 ?

Oil on canvas, 29 15/16 x 25 inches

The Maryland Historical Society, Baltimore

Bequest of Miss Ellen C. Daingerfield

Provenance: By direct descent to the sitter's great-granddaughter Miss Daingerfield

Reference: Pleasants, "Studies," no. 475

Under date of November 17, 1722, the following entry appears in the Account Book (1720-1729) of John Digges:

> *"By payed Gus: Hesselis from drawing Mr. Darnalls and his Ladys Picture . . .*
> *9.10.8*
> (Library of Congress, Division of Manuscripts, p. 3).

The marriage settlement for Henry Darnall and Anne Talbot, said to be the niece and ward of Gilbert Talbot, Earl of Shrewsbury, is believed to be dated 1735 (Bowie, p. 242). Although they could have been married earlier, this does raise a question as to whether the above entry refers to them or other members of the extensive Darnall family.

No portrait of Henry Darnall by Hesselius exists. Dr. Roland Fleischer is certain that this portrait of Mrs. Henry Darnall III is not by Gustavus Hesselius (Fleischer, "Gustavus Hesselius"). In every detail its delicate rococo air is contrary to "the straightforward naturalism" of Hesselius. There is evidence of perhaps another as yet unidentified artist of great delicacy and charm working in Maryland in the second decade of the eighteenth century.

ADDITIONAL PORTRAIT OF MRS. HENRY DARNALL III:

(13A) *Anne Talbot as a child attended by a slave.* Unknown artist, formerly attributed to Gustavus Hesselius ? (1682-1755). Unsigned, early 18th century. Oil on canvas, 53 x 38 inches (sight). Formerly in the Private Collection of a Descendant, destroyed in fire in 1973, known through a photograph. Provenance — by direct descent through Charles Carroll of Carrollton's granddaughter Emily MacTavish to its last owner; part of The MacTavish Collection. Reference: Pleasants, "Studies," no. 3309; James Lane, "Studies in American Painting," June 6, 1958, on file at Kennedy Galleries, Inc.

The identity of both the subject and artist of this work are extremely doubtful. Family tradition has considered it to be a portrait of Anne Talbot although J. Hall Pleasants identified it as Mary or Eleanor Carroll, daughters of Charles Carroll the Settler. Its provenance definitely establishes it as a member of the Darnall, Digges or Carroll family. Its attribution to Gustavus Hesselius has been eliminated by Dr. Roland Fleischer.

MRS. HENRY DARNALL III

M RS. DANIEL CARROLL OF UPPER MARLBORO I (Eleanor Darnall), 1703/1704-1796

(1st cousin of CC of A; 1st cousin once removed of CCC; Great-aunt of MDC)

14.

Mrs. Daniel Carroll of Upper Marlboro I as a Child

Justus Engelhardt Kühn (?-1717)

Unsigned, ca. 1710

Oil on canvas, 54 1/16 x 44 3/16 inches

The Maryland Historical Society, Baltimore

Bequest of Miss Ellen C. Daingerfield

Provenance: By direct descent to Miss Daingerfield

Reference: Pleasants, "Studies," no. 515

The decorative charm of Kühn's work achieves its finest expression in this portrait identified by family tradition as Eleanor Darnall, daughter of Henry Darnall II of "Darnall's Delight," later called the "Woodyard," and Ann Digges. The artist has surpassed himself in echoing the formal splendor of the German Baroque manor against which the miniature Maryland lady and her dog are placed. As in most of Kühn's works, the exact age of the subject might be questioned. This portrait was probably painted at the same time as a similar one of her brother Henry Darnall III (Cat. No. 12).

15.

John Wollaston (fl. 1736-1767)

Unsigned, ca. 1753-1754

Oil on canvas, 32 3/8 x 24 3/4 inches

Private Collection of a Descendant

Provenance: By descent to present owner

Reference: Pleasants, "Studies," no. 2452

John Wollaston received so many commissions from the Carroll family, that the absence of portraits of particular subjects becomes the exception rather than the rule. Fortunately, Eleanor was not one of the exceptions. In this example, the English artist, who generally sacrificed depiction of character to a monotonous handling of pose and costume, background and accessories, and even features, has produced one of the finest character studies of his *oeuvre*. The serenity, intelligence and gracious dignity for which Eleanor was noted dominate this portrayal, while Wollaston's usual concentration on elegant accoutrements is considerably underplayed.

Related portraits:

(15A) Unknown artist after John Wollaston (fl. 1736-1767). Unsigned, probably late 19th century. Oil on canvas, 28 x 25 inches. Collection of Georgetown University, Washington, D.C. Provenance — collection of Miss Ellen C. Daingerfield, given to the present owner (prior to 1894). Reference: Pleasants, "Studies," no. 3505.
This is a copy of Cat. No. 15.

(15B) Unknown artist after John Wollaston (fl. 1736-1767). Unsigned, 19th century. Oil on canvas, 30 x 25 inches (sight). Presently unlocated; known through a photograph. Provenance — collection of Mr. Victor Spark. Reference: Pleasants, "Studies," no. 3416.
This is a copy of Cat. No. 15.

Charles Carroll of Carrollton 1737-1832

(1st cousin once removed of MDC through her mother Rachel Brooke; 2nd cousin once removed of MDC through her father Henry Darnall IV)

16.

Sir Joshua Reynolds (1723-1792)

Unsigned, 1762-1763

Oil on canvas, 30 1/4 x 25 1/4 inches

Collection of Mr. and Mrs. Paul Mellon, Upperville, Virginia

Provenance: By descent through Charles Carroll of Carrollton to Charles Bancroft Carroll; part of The MacTavish Collection; sold at Kennedy Galleries, Inc., to the present owner in 1971

Reference: Pleasants, "Studies," no. 1659

There is no question that Sir Joshua Reynolds painted Charles Carroll of Carrollton. On April 8, 1762, Charles Carroll of Annapolis wrote to his son in London:

> *I desire you will get your picture drawn by ye best hand in London; let it be a three quarter's length 30 in. x 25 in.; let it be put in a genteel gilt frame and sent me by ye next fleet carefully cased and packed* (Field, p. 64).

On March 22, 1763 Charles wrote his father from London:

> *I am to sit at 1 o'clock, being the second time for my picture. . . . my portrait without frame will come to 25 guineas, an extravagant price but you desired it should be done by the best hand: & 25 guineas is a fixed price for a 3/4 . . .* (MdHi, ms. 206, vol. I, no. 90).

Later that year, November 12, Charles wrote again:

> *My picture was done by Reynolds: tis a 3/4 length, a half length would come down to the knees . . .* (MdHi, ms. 206, vol. I, no. 100).

Joshua Reynolds created some question concerning the exact time at which the portrait was actually painted for in his ledgers he has an entry which reads:

> *1762/April 21*
> *Frame Pd. Mr. Chumly 21-0-0*
> *frame 3 1/2 Mr. Carrol case 5/21 frame 13.13.6*
> *I believe paid* (Cormack, p. 116)

In the Reynolds ledger the three preceding entries for other portraits are dated 1763; the one immediately following is for 1769, and the transcriber of the ledgers states that "the payments do not all seem to tally with the known portraits" (Cormack, p. 105). It is entirely possible that Sir Joshua, in fact, meant to enter 1763 instead of 1762. Certainly the above correspondence indicates that the order was placed in 1762 and the portrait completed in 1763. Be that as it may, we have a magnificent example of Joshua Reynolds' work, supreme in its capture of character.

In the 1760's Reynolds was experimenting with colored glazes on a bed of flake white which was not completely dried before the application of color, resulting in a later fading of color. That the fading of this portrait occurred at an early date is proved by a statement of the famous Baltimore collector Robert Gilmor, in the 1820's, in which he refers to

> *a portrait of old Mr. Carroll, by Reynolds, painted when he was in England; but it is much faded* (Dunlap, vol. III, p. 272).

Although this likeness of Carroll exhibits the fading tendency of the artist's colors, it does not detract from its beauty.

Related portraits:

(16A) Unknown artist after Sir Joshua Reynolds (1723-1792). Unsigned, 19th century. Inscription on label on back: *This painting was thought by Wm. M. Chase at time of sale (1912) to be about 150 years old. It is after the Sir Joshua Reynolds portrait painted in London and is perhaps a studio copy.* Oil on canvas, 21 x 16 1/2 inches. Private Collection of a Descendant. Provenance — bought by Oswald Jackson (or possibly by Louisa Carroll Thomas) in New York in 1912; by descent to present owner.

This copy after Cat. No. 16 differs considerably from the Reynolds in the cast of the features, but it is still without question based upon the original. The label on the back indicates it was in existence for sometime prior to 1912. It does not appear to be a late 18th century painting.

(16B) Unknown artist after Sir Joshua Reynolds (1723-1792). Unsigned, 20th century. Oil on canvas, size unknown. Presently unlocated, known to have existed from a letter, dated February 6, 1942, from Mrs. Charles Carroll MacTavish, Jr., to Ellen Hart Smith and now in the Frick Art Reference Library. Provenance — part of The MacTavish Collection.

17.

Robert Field (ca. 1769-1819)

Signed and dated above right shoulder: *RF/1803*

Watercolor on paperboard, 9 1/8 x 7 1/4 inches (oval)

Private Collection of a Descendant

Provenance: By descent through Charles Carroll of Carrollton's grandson Colonel Charles Carroll of Doughoregan to the present owner

Robert Field, "a handsome, stout, gentlemanly man, and a favourite with gentlemen" (Long, p. 150), was born in England and trained in engraving at the Royal Academy. He came to Philadelphia in 1794 after a brief stop in Baltimore. Between 1800 and 1805 the artist worked in Georgetown, Washington, D.C., and Maryland, after which he moved to Boston until 1808. In America, he produced, for the most part, the exquisitely finished miniatures and watercolors for which his work is noted. Although it is believed that some oils now attributed to Gilbert Stuart may be by Field, the artist's major work in oil seems to date after his move to Halifax, Nova Scotia, in 1808.

On August 9, 1803, Charles Carroll of Carrollton wrote his son:

> *Mr. Field has begun this day my picture; it is thought the resemblance will be strong. I shall offer him $40 which, if I am not mistaken you told me was his price for such a portrait of the size of the one he drew for M'Dowell* (MdHi, ms. 203).

On August 29, he wrote again to his son:

> *Your sister Caton thinks as you do, that Mr. Field has not given sufficient animation to my portrait. I think however it is well executed and all who have seen it, say the resemblance is striking; but in my opinion it conveys the idea of a much larger man than I am* (MdHi, ms. 203).

The "M'Dowell" to which Carroll refers in the first letter was Dr. John McDowell whose 1803 portrait, now in a private collection, is watercolor on cardboard, 9 x 7 1/4 inches, signed and dated above the left shoulder *RF/1803*. In 1927, in his major work on Field, Harry Piers deduced from the above information that the portrait of Carroll "will prove to be in water-colours" (Piers, p. 118).

About 1858, this watercolor of Carroll was taken to England by a descendant who married and remained there. With the Longacre engraving as the primary clue to its appearance, the watercolor was located in 1974. It is the finest extant likeness of the Signer between youth and very old age and, as such, has been the source of several copies as well as frequent reproductions.

Related portraits:
(Cat. Nos. 18-22)

18.

James B. Longacre (1794-1869), after Robert Field (ca. 1769-1819)

Legend: *Charles Carroll/of Carrollton./Drawn & Engraved by J. B. Longacre from a Painting by Field*

Engraving, image size: 4 x 3 5/16 inches

National Portrait Gallery, Smithsonian Institution, Washington, D.C.

It is this engraving, executed by James B. Longacre for John Sanderson's *Lives of the Signers* (vol. VII, 1827, p. 240) which provided the clue concerning the appearance of the original Field portrait of Carroll. It appears in every detail to be based upon Cat. No. 17, but it is not possible from the engraving alone to tell whether it is based upon a large scale oil portrait or a small watercolor. For years this has led to confusion concerning the form of the original Field, despite knowledge of Carroll's letters. That Carroll himself considered it an excellent likeness is indicated from the following unpublished letter written from Doughoregan Manor, November 15, 1827:

> *Gentlemen:*
> *I am much obliged to you for the regard you have expressed for my character in your letter of the 7th instant which have induced you to give my name to the splendid ship soon to be launched on the Merrimack. It is with regret that I do not comply with your request for my portrait, at my age it is very irksom to set for my picture & I have resisted the itterated importunities of my children to have one; be assured the expense is no consideration with me, nor cause of my refusal, impute it to what I have assigned.*
> *Mr. Longacre of Philadelphia has, or had several engravings admirably executed of my picture taken about 25 years since thought to be very like me at that time of my life. If in your estimation an engraving, such as described, will supply the place of a portrait by writing to Mr. Longacre I have no doubt he will furnish you with one* (Collection of a Carroll descendant).

There are four different versions of the Longacre engraving after Field (Stauffer, vol. II, p. 322), witnesses to its great popularity.

19.

Michael Laty (1826-1848), after Robert Field (ca. 1769-1819)

Signed lower left: *M. Laty. pinx*, 1846

Oil on canvas, 30 1/8 x 24 7/8 inches (oval)

The Maryland Historical Society, Baltimore

Provenance: Commissioned by Charles Carroll of Carrollton's daughter Mary Caton; presented on her behalf to the present owner by her daughter Emily MacTavish

Reference: Pleasants, "Studies," no. 485

This portrait is an exceptionally fine copy after the Field watercolor of Charles Carroll of Carrollton (Cat. No. 17). It shows a much greater degree of modelling in the facial structure than the other copies (Cat. No. 19A and 22) and has a stronger sense of direct focus in the eyes. It is known to have been painted after the original Field, for

Plate 19A

on May 6, 1846, the Signer's granddaughter Emily MacTavish wrote the following letter to The Maryland Historical Society:

I am requested by my Mother to present in her name, to the Maryland Historical Society, a Portrait of her late Father, Charles Carroll of Carrollton.

The Original Picture was painted by Field, early in the present century, when my Grandfather was about sixty years of age; and those members of the Association who are old enough to recollect the departed Patriot, at that period of his life will, I think, consider the resemblance a good one. —

The Painting, which is herewith sent, was executed by Mr. Laty, the young Baltimore Artist, referred to in the last Report of your President; and my Mother hopes it will prove an acceptable contribution to the Gallery of the Society. . . (MdHi, Correspondence Book I, 1844-1848).

Michael Laty's career had just begun when he died of typhoid at the age of 22. Almost his entire *oeuvre* consists of a few exceptionally fine copies of portraits by Gilbert Stuart, C. W. Peale, and, in this instance, Robert Field.

Related portraits:

(19A) Unknown artist, after Robert Field ca. 1769-1819) or Michael Laty (1826-1848). Unsigned, 19th century. Oil on canvas, 30 x 25 inches. Formerly in the private collection of a descendant; destroyed in a fire in 1973; known through a photograph. Provenance — by direct descent through Charles Carroll of Carrollton's granddaughter Emily MacTavish to the last owner; part of The MacTavish Collection. Reference: Pleasants, "Studies," no 1660; James Lane, "Studies in American Painting," February 16, 1969, on deposit at Kennedy Galleries, Inc.

Considerable controversy surrounds this copy after Field. It was published in 1892 as being by Robert Field (Bowen, p. 97) and was thought for some time to be the original Field upon which all other copies were based, but examination prior to its destruction indicated a mid-nineteenth century date. This time period would be compatible with the date 1858 when the watercolor was taken to England and when the family would logically have wanted a copy made for themselves. The portrait (Plate No. 19A), documented as being part of The MacTavish Collection, seems compatible with this thesis.

The prototype appears to be the copy executed by Laty after the Field watercolor (Cat. No. 19) and not the watercolor itself. Furthermore, by 1858, the Laty copy had been presented to The Maryland Historical Society and would have been available to this artist. Note, for example, the identical rendering of the stock and the hairline. The hair on the sides, the more rounded ear lobe, and the line of the cheek from the bottom of the right ear to the collar are just a few of the other features which differ from the Field original but which are exactly the same as the Laty. The frames are also identical. The MacTavish copy has a flatter, less modelled quality in the handling of the face when compared with the Laty. Nevertheless, this was a magnificent portrait of the Signer, and its destruction is a great loss to the iconography of Charles Carroll of Carrollton.

It was deposited at the Maryland Historical Society from 1893 to 1908 at which time it was shipped to Rome. By 1893 after its publication in Bowen, the attribution was changed to Gilbert Stuart as is evidenced by the listings in *The Maryland Historical Society Catalogues of Exhibitions 1848-1908*. In a list of The MacTavish Collection dated November 10, 1948, the attribution was changed back, as it should be, to "After Field."

(19B) Unknown artist after 19A. Unsigned, early 20th century. Oil on canvas, 30 1/4 x 25 1/4 inches (oval). Collection of the de la Boëssière Family. Provenance — given by Charles Carroll of Carrollton's great-great-granddaughter Virginia Scott MacTavish to Charles Carroll of Carrollton's great-great-great-grandaughter Amicie de la Grange on the occasion of her marriage to Comte Antoine de la Boëssière-Thiennes in 1809.

This portrait was undoubtedly copied, as a wedding present, from the previously mentioned MacTavish-owned copy of the Field portrait of Charles Carroll of Carrollton (Cat. No. 19A).

(19C) Unknown artist, formerly attributed to Thomas Sully ? (1783-1872). Unsigned, late 19th century. Inscribed on back: *Portrait of Charles Carroll of Carrollton an informal study from life by Thomas Sully of Philadelphia for large portrait was in 1871 in possession of Mrs. Carroll Jackson.* Oil on panel, 11 1/4 x 10 1/2 inches, approx. (oval). Private Collection of a Descendant. Provenance — by direct descent through Mrs. John Lee of "Needwood" to the present owner.

This portrait represents a most interesting puzzle in the Field-type portraits of Charles Carroll of Carrollton. The portrait inscribed on the back as in the possession of Mrs. Carroll Jackson is, in fact, Cat. No. 35, and this sketch, identified within the family for several generations as a Sully, is clearly derived from the Field-type portrait of Charles Carroll of Carrollton.

(Cat. Nos. 20-22)

20.

Henry Bryan Hall (1808-1884), after Michael Laty (1826-1848)
Legend: *Painted by M. Laty/Eng. by H. B. Hall/CHARLES CARROLL OF CARROLLTON*

Engraving, image size: 4 1/4 x 3 1/2 inches

The Maryland Historical Society, Baltimore

The Field-type portrait of Charles Carroll of Carrollton proved so continuously popular that there was a demand for a new engraving of it in the second half of the nineteenth century. This was probably executed by the elder Henry Bryan Hall who came to New York from London in 1850 and "etched a large number of portraits of men prominent in the Colonial and Revolutionary history of this country." (Stauffer, vol. I, p. 115). It is important to note that Hall engraved after the Laty copy (Cat. no. 19) of the Field watercolor.

Related portraits:
(20a) Unknown artist. No signature visible, probably early 20th century. Oil on canvas, 21 5/8 x 18 5/8 inches. St. Mary's Church, Annapolis.

A maverick piece, this portrait of Charles Carroll appears to be based on the H. B. Hall engraving (Cat. No. 20) after the copy by Michael Laty of the Field watercolor. It is interesting as an example of the durability and importance of the Field-type portrait of Carroll.

(Cat. No. 21)

21.

Unknown artist after Henry Bryan Hall (1808-1884)

Engraving, image size: 4 1/4 x 3 11/16 inches

The Maryland Historical Society, Baltimore

This engraving is similar to Cat. No. 20 but because there is no legend, the artist remains unidentified. It may be by Hall himself.

22.

Isaac L. Williams (1817-1895), after Robert Field (ca. 1769-1819)

Signed in lower right corner: *Painted by I. L. William[s]. Philad^{a}*, ca. 1840-1845.

Inscribed on back: *Charles Carroll of Carrollton/American Colonization Society/ Dr. H. L. E. Johnson, President/Recd. through Mr. Milton E. Ailes*

Oil on canvas, 30 1/8 x 25 1/16 inches

Collection of Mr. and Mrs. LeRoy Morgan

Provenance: Owned by the American Colonization Society until the Society was disbanded at which time the portrait was given to Joshua Evans who gave it to Charles Carroll Morgan, father of the present owner

Isaac Williams (he added the middle initial "L" to his name to distinguish himself from a neighbor) was a native of Philadelphia, and was considered by his contemporaries "in the front rank, with the pencil and brush, of our Commonwealth's artists" (Spindler, p. 262). He began exhibiting in his native city in 1837 and, after 1844, concentrated more on landscape than portraiture. He is listed in the Baltimore Directories for 1840, 1841, and 1845.

The listings for Williams in the Baltimore Directories would seem to suggest that he made this copy directly from Robert Field's watercolor of Charles Carroll of Carrollton (Cat. No. 17) during the period he worked in Baltimore, and it, therefore, would be the earliest copy. However, the Williams' portrait shows a certain dependence on the other copies (Cat. Nos. 19 and 19A) of the Field watercolor. In all of these copies, the stock is softened and rounded in the same manner and the hairline around the forehead is identically formalized into a more definite line. It is unlikely that two artists working independently would have effected the identical solution in changing these aspects of the original Field. As the Laty is the only copy documented as being directly after the Field, it was probably the source for the similar changes in the Williams as well as Cat. No. 19A. It is important to note that Laty preserves the oval form of the original watercolor while the Williams' portrait is a rectangle.

In any case, for a copy, the Williams' portrait is unusual in its vitality. Williams executed this portrait for the American Colonization Society, founded in 1816 "for Colonizing the Free People of Colour of the U.S." Charles Carroll was its President from 1828 to 1831.

Note Regarding the Copies after the Robert Field Portrait of Charles Carroll of Carrollton

It has been suggested that there was an intermediate, now missing, version between the Field watercolor and its copies, but existing evidence does not bear this out. This was first based upon references by Theodore Bolton to a Field oil of Charles Carroll of Carrollton (Bolton, p. 50). As the now destroyed copy of Field (Cat. No. 19A), belonging to Mrs. Charles Carroll MacTavish, was attributed to Field himself in a publication of 1892 (Bowen, p. 97) and after its removal from The Maryland Historical Society in 1907, it is believed that Bolton based his assumption of an oil by Field on this work.

The possibility of portraits by "Wood" and "Gilbert Stuart" being the missing links and, therefore, prototypes for the Laty, emerges from the listings in the *Maryland Historical Society Catalogues of Exhibitions (1848-1908)*. Although these listings may not be entirely accurate, we cannot totally discount them. A catalogue for 1848 lists a portrait of Charles Carroll of Carrollton by Laty, after Wood, owned by Dr. Edmondson; one for 1850 lists Charles Carroll of Carrollton by Laty, after Wood, owned by the Maryland Historical Society; by 1883, the catalogue listings revert back to the proper attribution and list Charles Carroll by Laty, after Field, owned by The Maryland Historical Society. If a "Wood" did paint a portrait of Charles Carroll of Carrollton, it vanished after 1850, and certainly a Laty copy after Wood has never been recorded.

From 1896 until 1907, there is the listing Charles Carroll of Carrollton by "M. Lati [sic] after G. Stuart" owned by The Maryland Historical Society. In addition, from 1893 to 1907, there appears in the Maryland Historical Society catalogues a listing for another portrait

of Charles Carroll of Carrollton by Gilbert Stuart owned by Mrs. Charles Carroll MacTavish. After 1907, the date for the removal of The MacTavish Collection from the Maryland Historical Society, no reference to a Laty after Gilbert Stuart occurs. A clue to what the "Gilbert Stuart" portrait looked like may be found in an illustration in *Century Magazine* for 1903 (vol. 43, p. 908) where the caption reads: "From the portrait after Gilbert Stuart, Maryland Hist. Soc'y." The frontispiece in Kate Mason Rowland's book, *Life and Correspondence of Charles Carroll of Carrollton* (vol. I) is also attributed to Gilbert Stuart (pp. xix-xx). Both portraits are, in fact, the Laty after Field (Cat. No. 19). This would indicate that the "Gilbert Stuart" referred to would be the similar MacTavish-owned copy after Laty (Cat. No. 19A). No reference to a portrait of Charles Carroll of Carrollton by Gilbert Stuart has appeared elsewhere.

23.

Charles Balthazar Julien Févret de Saint-Mémin (1770-1852)

Unsigned, 1804

Charcoal and white chalk on paper, 20 1/2 x 14 5/8 inches

The Maryland Historical Society, Baltimore

Gift of Dr. Clapham Pennington in Memory of Emily L. Harper and Emily L. H. Harper

Provenance: By direct descent through Charles Carroll of Carrollton's granddaughter Emily L. H. Harper to Dr. Pennington

Reference: Pleasants, "Studies," no. 591

Born in Dijon, France, and forced to flee as a result of the French Revolution, Saint-Mémin began his artistic career in 1796 in New York. With little professional training, but much ingenuity, he built himself a physiognotrace, a devise for tracing a lifesize profile, and a pantograph for reducing the portrait to a small diameter so that it could be engraved in miniature upon a copper plate. Between 1798 and 1810 he travelled from Boston to Charleston, South Carolina, doing profiles of everyone from George Washington to the Prince de Talleyrand. Wherever Saint-Mémin set up a studio, a procession of the fashionable and notable found their way to his door. Saint-Mémin returned to Dijon in 1814 and ended his days as director of the museum there.

Saint-Mémin's greatest period of activity in Maryland was in 1803 and 1804. It is during the latter year that he executed this likeness of Charles Carroll of Carrollton (Dexter, no. 332) at the age of 67. In 1805 Saint-Mémin was in and out of Washington, D.C., Georgetown, and Alexandria, but in 1806 he was preparing to leave Maryland for good for on December 11 of that year he announced in the *Federal Gazette and Baltimore Daily Advertiser:*

> *Likenesses engraved. The subscriber begs to leave to return his thanks for the liberal encouragement he has received during his residence in Baltimore, and as he is about to leave the city in a few weeks, he respectfully requests those whose likenesses he has begun, to call at his room that they may be finished before his departure.*

It is tempting to claim an interdependence between this portrait and the engraving after it and the other profile portraits of the Signer: the likenesses in *Congress Voting Independence* (Cat. No. 1); the Gobrecht medals (Cat. Nos. 26 and 27), and the portrait of an unknown artist (Cat. No. 24). It is impossible to state definitely, however, that the Saint-Mémin was, in fact, the source for them all.

Related portrait:

(23A) Charles Balthazar Julien Févret de Saint-Mémin (177-1852). Engraving, 1804. Image size: 2 3/16 inches in diameter. The Henry Francis du Pont Winterthur Museum, Wilmington, Delaware. This engraving would have been made from the copper plate incised by Saint-Mémin with the aid of his pantograph from his drawing of Charles Carroll (Cat. No. 23).

Plate 23A

Charles Carroll of Carrollton

24.

Unknown artist

Unsigned, early 19th century?

Oil on canvas, 24 x 18 1/2 inches

Private Collection of a Descendant

Provenance: Part of The Boston Museum Collection in 1892; purchased by a Carroll descendant at some later date.

In 1892 this portrait was published as belonging to the Boston Museum and was attributed to Rembrandt Peale (Bowen, facing p. 63). One wonders how this attribution was determined as the portrait is not suggestive of the artist's style. In examining the history of the Boston Museum, another artist with the same initials is suggested — Robert Edge Pine. Even though the modelling of the face and the conception of the head exhibit a strength and authority not customary in Pine's work, it is worth pursuing the association of his name with this portrait of Charles Carroll of Carrollton.

After Robert Edge Pine's death, the majority of his "Cabinet of Paintings" was purchased in 1789 by Daniel Bowen. An individual portrait of Charles Carroll of Carrollton was apparently in Pine's collection, for in 1795, when Bowen opened the Columbian Museum in Boston with an exhibition including his purchase of Pine paintings, number 38 in a list of the Columbian Museum was a portrait of Mr. Carroll of Maryland. In 1803 the Columbian Museum was destroyed by fire and after rebuilding, again burned in 1807. There is no evidence that Pine's portrait of Carroll survived these fires. The Columbian Museum was purchased by the proprietors of the New England Museum in 1825. In 1840/1841 the New England Museum, then under the proprietorship of Moses Kimball, became the first Boston Museum. It remained under Kimball's direction until 1892 when its dispersal began.

The fact that there was a portrait of Charles Carroll was known from the 1795 list. It seems likely that an effort was made to replace at least some of the works destroyed in the fire, and this is very likely that early replacement of the Carroll portrait. Possibly the artist employed to execute these replacements based his work on a readily available likeness of the Signer. The work which immediately comes to mind is the engraving by Saint Mémin (Cat. No. 23A), which faces in the same direction, but the finesse of execution of this much larger portrait casts some doubt on this assumption. On the other hand, Edward Savage who is said to have had a studio in Baltimore in 1810 (*250 Years of Maryland Painting* p. 31) worked on the *Congress Voting Independence* (Cat. No. 1). Could he possibly have had a hand in this work?

Knowing that the original portrait was by Robert Edge Pine, the initials "R P" became associated with the portrait. As the 19th century advanced these initials were interpreted to stand for the better known artist Rembrandt Peale, rather than Robert Pine whose name had fallen into obscurity. Unfortunately, relining had made examination of the original canvas impossible, but observation of the surface indicates that this is very likely an early 19th century work. An old label on the back of the stretcher is evidence that it was considered a work of some veneration in 1893:

> *World's Columbian Exposition, Chicago, 1893. For exhibition of American Retrospective Art*

No trace of the portrait existed between its publication in 1892 and the present. It came to light recently in the private collection of a descendant whose family remembers its purchase "sometime just before the turn of the century."

25.

Christian Gobrecht (1785-1844)

Original dies for Commemorative Medal Honoring Charles Carroll entering his 90th year.

Signed below shoulder, *Gobrecht. F.*, 1826

Inscribed on obverse: *To Charles Carroll of Carrollton*

Inscribed on reverse: UPON ENTERING HIS 90TH YEAR/SEPT XX MDCCCXXVI/THE SURVIVING SIGNER OF THE DECLARATION OF/INDEPENDENCE/AFTER THE 50TH/ANNIVERSARY

Steel, 2-13/16 inches in diameter

Private Collection

Provenance: By descent in the Carroll family until given to or purchased by an ancestor of the present owner

In honor of Charles Carroll's 89th birthday, September 19, 1826, the Carroll family commissioned Christian Gobrecht, engraver, die-sinker and medalist to design this medal. It has always been supposed that the medal was commissioned to honor the circumstance for which Carroll is most frequently remembered: last surviving Signer of the Declaration of Independence, for, on July 4, 1826, both John Adams and Thomas Jefferson, the only other two remaining Signers, had died. Although the striking of the medal was not completed until two years after the event it celebrates, through extant correspondence it is possible to trace the progress of the medals from the cast through the original dies illustrated here, to the planned disposition among the family. On June 6, 1828 Charles Carroll writes to his grandson of the same name: "I have received the model of the medal" (MdHi, ms. 203).

On August 30, 1828, the young Charles wrote the Signer:

> *I received this morning a letter from Gobrecht informing me that he had finished the dies and had submitted a specimen to Mr. Sully who pronounced the likeness and execution excellent. He wants money, but I think myself that it will be better not to pay him until the medals are received, as it may relax his energies— His part of the work is done, but I should like him to superintend the striking of the medals, which is done at the mint. If you think proper I will engage to pay him in October. The medals are promised for your birthday—a specimen in plaster has been sent on—as soon as I receive it I shall forward it to MacTavish* (MdHi, ms. 203).

And on the outside of this letter, the Signer himself has written:

> *2 Sept. wrote to him* [grandson Charles] *and send enclosed list of medals to be struck & how to be disposed of* (MdHi, ms. 203).

In spite of the striking similarity in pose and in the treatment of the hair to the Saint-Mémin drawing (Cat. No. 23) of the Signer, there are notable differences in the addition of a fur collar and in the treatment of the stock. The letter suggests that Thomas Sully had some hand in the design of this medal, possibly using the Saint-Mémin as a guide to the pose, as the two profiles face in the same direction, and taking the idea of the fur collar from Longacre's engraving (Cat. No. 18) after Field.

Related portraits:
(Cat. No. 26 & 27)

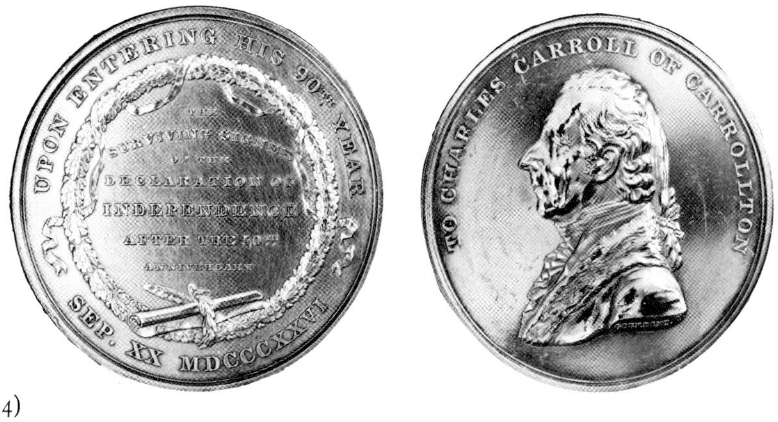

26.

Christian Gobrecht (1785-1844)

Medal

Signed below shoulder: *Gobrecht. F,* 1826

Inscribed on obverse: *To Charles Carroll of Carrollton*

Inscribed on reverse: UPON ENTERING HIS 90TH YEAR/SEPT XX MDCCCXXVI/THE SURVIVING SIGNER/OF THE/DECLARATION OF/INDEPENDENCE AFTER THE 50TH ANNIVERSARY

Gold, 2 inches in diameter

Collection of Richard Fuller Kimball

Provenance: By direct descent through Charles Carroll of Carrollton's daughter Mrs. Robert Goodloe Harper to the present owner

For his daughters, Mary and Kitty, and his grandsons Charles Carroll of Doughoregan and Charles Carroll Harper, Charles Carroll the Signer ordered gold medals (MdHi, ms. 203, September 2, 1828, enclosure). For the remaining thirteen family members he ordered silver. He does not include himself in the list!

27.

Christian Gobrecht (1785-1844)

Medal

Signed below shoulder: *Gobrecht. F,* 1826

Inscribed on obverse: *To Charles Carroll of Carrollton*

Inscribed on reverse: UPON ENTERING HIS 90TH YEAR/SEPT XX MDCCCXXVI/THE SURVIVING SIGNER/OF THE/DECLARATION OF/INDEPENDENCE AFTER THE 50TH/ ANNIVERSARY

Silver, 2 inches in diameter

The Baltimore Museum of Art
Adler and Hennage Funds 75.37.21

Provenance: By descent through the family of Charles Carroll of Duddington until purchased by the Museum

This medal is identical to Cat. No. 26 but in silver. Charles Carroll ordered this version for Mr. Caton, Mr. MacTavish, Mrs. MacTavish, Mrs. Mary Carroll, Mrs. Charles Harper, the Marchioness Wellesley, the Marchioness of Carmarthen, Miss Caton, Charles Carroll of Doughoregan's four sisters, and Miss Harper (MdHi, ms. 203, September 2, 1828, enclosure).

28.

Rembrandt Peale (1778-1860), formerly attributed to Charles Willson Peale (1741-1827)

Unsigned, ca. 1816-1819

Oil on canvas, 22 x 18 1/2 inches

The Baltimore Museum of Art

Bequest of Ellen H. Bayard 39.180

Provenance: By direct descent through Charles Carroll of Carrollton's granddaughter Mrs. Richard H. Bayard to Miss Ellen Bayard

Reference: Pleasants, "Studies," no. 20; *Peale's Museum Gallery of Oil Paintings*, Philadelphia, 1854 (Collection of the American Philosophical Society)

Although born in Bucks County, Pennsylvania, after his father C. W. Peale had settled his family in Philadelphia, Rembrandt Peale's associations with Maryland were extensive. In 1796 he established a museum in Baltimore with his brother Raphaelle which was abandoned three years later. In 1815 he returned from Philadelphia and built "The Baltimore Museum and Gallery of Fine Arts," patterned after his father's museum in Philadelphia and now the home of the present Peale Museum on Holliday Street. Peale's original museum was "an elegant rendezvous of taste, curiosity and leisure" (*Peale's Museum*, p. 3), which exhibited stuffed birds, Egyptian mummies and war-whooping Indians, along with a great variety of paintings, including the artist's own. Despite the efforts of his brother Rubens as manager, the Museum was not a financial success and Peale left Baltimore for good about 1822. Charles Carroll of Carrollton apparently had lent Rembrandt Peale $300 for the Museum. When the artist did not repay the loan, Carroll wrote the following:

> *I am unacquainted with Peal's circumstances, if unable to pay the debt from his own resources, he may on being sued find a friend to assist him* (New York Public Library, Arents Collection, CCC to Charles Ingersoll, April 8, 1825).

1816-1819 appear to be Peale's most active years of painting in Baltimore, and it is very likely that he executed this portrait during that period for his gallery of distinguished figures. The portrait bears the stamp of Rembrandt's finest work, but it was for years attributed to his father Charles Willson. Discovery in Philadelphia of a copy of the 1854 sale catalogue of Charles Willson's "Museum Gallery of Oil Paintings" with Rembrandt's own notations has corrected the attribution.

RELATED PORTRAITS:
(Cat. No. 29)

29.

Charles Willson Peale (1741-1827), after Rembrandt Peale (1778-1860)

Unsigned, 1823

Oil on canvas, 24 1/4 x 20 1/4 inches

Independence National Historical Park, Philadelphia

Provenance: Painted for Peale's Philadelphia Museum; purchased by the City of Philadelphia at the auction of the Museum's collection in 1854 (no. 133); on permanent loan from the City of Philadelphia

Reference: Pleasants, "Studies," no. 1636

It was inevitable that C. W. Peale would want a portrait of the distinguished Charles Carroll of Carrollton in his "Gallery of Great Men" which was later incorporated into the Independence Hall Collection. On May 25, 1823, he wrote his son Raphaelle from Annapolis:

> *I have some hopes that I may paint the portrait of old Mr. Carroll. He is 86 years old* (Sellers, 1952, p. 50).

According to Charles Coleman Sellers, "failing to get a sitting from life, he made a copy instead of a portrait by Rembrandt Peale at Baltimore" (Sellers, 1952, p. 50). This portrait is that copy which was executed after Cat. No. 28.

30.

Anson Dickinson (1779-1852)

Signed and dated lower right: *A. Dickinson/1824*

Miniature, watercolor on ivory, 3 1/4 x 2 5/8 inches

The Maryland Historical Society, Baltimore

Gift of Anita Hack Carroll Bleck, 1954

Provenance: From a Miss Thompson of Staunton, Virginia, two of whose sisters married direct descendants of Charles Carroll of Carrollton (Mary Carter Thompson to Governor John Lee Carroll and Caroline Thompson to Charles Carroll, VI, of Doughoregan) to Mrs. Bleck (Anita Hack), former wife of Charles Bancroft Carroll, great-great-great-grandson of Charles Carroll of Carrollton

Reference: Pleasants, "Studies," no. 3689

Born in Milton, near Litchfield, Connecticut, Anson Dickinson plied his miniaturist's trade from Montreal to Washington, D.C., between 1803 and 1851. According to one contemporary, Dickinson was

> *an artist of highly promising talents and of most amiable demeanor and engaging manners. . . . He is not a mere mechanic in his art but paints from his imagination. . .* (Kidder, p. vii).

Dickinson kept a list of over 1500 subjects painted during his long career; fortunately, the list has been preserved. From it and the newspapers as well, we know that Dickinson was in Maryland in 1824, 1828-1829, 1830-1831, and 1835.

Between dated entries for March 15 and April 1, 1824, appears the following notation in Dickinson's listing: "Mr. Carrol of Carlton 20" (Kidder, p. 29).

Comparison of the likeness of this miniature with the portrait by Rembrandt Peale (Cat. No. 28) of a few years earlier indicates that this is a finely rendered and accurate portrait of the venerable Signer in his 88th year.

31.

Thomas Sully (1783-1872)

Unsigned, 1826

Oil on canvas, 24 x 20 inches

Massachusetts Historical Society, Boston

Provenance: Given by the artist to Governor Thomas Swann of Maryland; sold at auction to George B. Chase who bequeathed it to the present owner in 1886

Born in Horncastle, England, and brought up in South Carolina, Thomas Sully made his reputation in Philadelphia where he lived from 1809 until his death, dominating the field of portraiture against stiff competition. He painted at a time when the demand for portraiture was such that John Neal (1793-1876), America's earliest art critic, remarked, "You can hardly open the door of a best room anywhere, without surprising, or being surprised by, the picture of somebody, plastered to the wall and staring at you with both eyes and a bunch of flowers" (Dickson, p. xxv).

Sully is known to have made several painting trips to Baltimore between 1820 and 1850. Whether one of these trips included execution of a life portrait of Carroll is not known, for there is indication that Carroll was in Philadelphia in 1826 (see Cat. No. 421 and the magnificent State House portrait (Cat. No. 37) was posthumous.

This study, not in Biddle and Fielding's transcription of Sully's Register, appears to be the first work Sully executed of Charles Carroll of Carrollton. It is a vividly, almost cruelly honest portrayal of a man in his ninetieth year and is probably Sully's character study from life. According to Sully's daughter, Blanche, "the design for the picture of Charles Carroll, was given to Governor Swann by Sully" (Bowen, p. 435).

Related portraits:
(Cat. Nos. 32-37)

32.

Thomas Sully (1783-1872)

Unsigned, 1826

Oil on canvas, 19 1/8 x 15 1/8 inches

Private Collection

Provenance: By descent to the great-great-grandson of Thomas B. Carroll; sold in April 1965 by M. Knoedler & Co., New York, to the present owner

This study is listed in Sully's Register, published by Biddle and Fielding, as number 292 under the name Charles Carroll of Carrollton: "Painted as a study for the whole length for the Marquis of Wellesley, begun May 22nd, 1826, finished May 25th 1826. Bust. Price $40.00." The family was obviously charged for this study, and it would have been released to them. It is a key piece in Sully portraits of Carroll for it appears to be the primary source for the Signer's head in all of the finished works (see Cat. Nos. 34B, 35 & 37).

33.

Thomas Sully (1783-1872)

Signed bottom center: *T. Sully*, 1826

Wash drawing on paper, 8 1/16 x 5 3/4 inches

Yale University Art Gallery, New Haven

The John Hill Morgan Collection

Provenance: Purchased about 1859 from the artist by Samuel P. Avery; returned by unknown means to the possession of the artist's granddaughter-in-law Mrs. A. M. Sully who sold it to John Hill Morgan; bequeathed by Mr. Morgan to the present owner in 1943.

It was Sully's habit to make several preliminary sketches for a major work such as the commission for the Marquess Wellesley (see Cat. No. 34B). Carroll's statement made in an 1827 letter that "at my age it is very irksom to set for my picture" (see Cat. No. 18) has been noted. Sully had obviously received a sitting from Carroll for the head (Cat. No. 31) but the rest of the composition still had to be realistically composed for Carroll's granddaughter Marianne and her husband the Marquess Wellesley. A letter of Sully's, dated July 31, 1859, on the back of this sketch indicates his solution to the problem without troubling the Signer unduly: "Dear Sir," he writes to Mr. Samuel P. Avery, "The sketch of Charles Carroll which you purchased of me was made in the room which Mr. Carroll usually occupied, & is a copy of the place. The person, was after a drawing I had made in pencil." It is not clear whether Sully sketched Carroll's room at Doughoregan or at the Caton house in Baltimore, but he did get "a copy of the place" with a slightly fanciful rendition of Carroll superimposed thereon. It became the basis for the Wellesley composition and remained in Sully's possession until about 1859.

34.

Thomas Sully (1783-1872)

Signed at bottom and again on back: *Thos Sully,* ca. 1826

Inscribed on back in pencil by a later hand: *1829/Charles Carroll of C.*

Watercolor on paper, 7 13/16 x 6 3/16 inches

The Walters Art Gallery, Baltimore

Provenance: Purchased in 1876 from the John Taylor Johnston sale by William T. Walters (no. 218). Bequeathed to the Walters Art Gallery

Reference: Pleasants, "Studies," no. 1983

Although Sully decided to retain the Queen Anne table of Cat. No. 33 in the background of the Wellesley portrait (Cat. No. 34B), this sketch reveals that he apparently recorded Carroll's room and a favorite chair from another angle.

Related portraits:

(34a) Thomas Sully (1783-1872). Unsigned, date unknown. Wash drawing, 4 1/2 x 3 1/8 inches. Presently unlocated; known through a photograph. Provenance — purchased by Erskine Hewitt in 1933 at the Ehrich Gallery; withdrawn from 1938 Hewitt sale. Reference: Pleasants, "Studies," no. 2582.

A small wash drawing showing a seated figure to just below the waist also appears to be a study for the "Marquis of Wellesley's" full-length portrait (Cat. No. 34b); it is a preliminary design for the composition and not a character study.

(34b) Thomas Sully (1783-1872). Unsigned, 1827. Oil on canvas, 81 1/8 x 51 1/4 inches. Thomas Gilcrease Institute of American History and Art, Tulsa, Oklahoma. Provenance — Commissioned by Charles Carroll of Carrollton for the Marquess Wellesley (letter, Sully to CCC, October 10, 1827, Archives of American Art, Smithsonian Institution, misc. ms. Sully); by descent to Charles Bancroft Carroll; part of The MacTavish Collection; sold in the 1950's through M. Knoedler & Co. to Thomas Gilcrease who deeded it to the City of Tulsa. Reference: Pleasants, "Studies," no. 1661.

Biddle and Fielding's transcription of Sully's register of paintings lists under Charles Carroll, "Full-length portrait painted for the Marquis of Wellesley, begun June 29th, 1827, finished August 21st, 1827. Size 58" x 94". Price, $500.00" (Biddle and Fielding, no. 293).

All evidence points to the fact that this portrait in the collection of the Gilcrease Institute (Plate 34b) is the Wellesley's portrait, the discrepancy in dimensions accounted for by the cutting down of the canvas at some time. It is the culmination of all the foregoing sketches — a perfect blending of Sully's careful planning from the incisive and penetrating character study to the details of pose and background.

On June 10, 1828 Charles Carroll wrote to his granddaughter Marianne of this portrait:

> *You write Sully's portrait fails in expression of my countenance, which, you fancy, spoke the idea of the mind before words gave it utterance; that look, which partial friends thought intelligent and expressive, has lost whatever lustre it once might have had* (MdHi. ms. 220).

(34c) Unknown artist, after Thomas Sully (1783-1872). Unsigned, Probably early 20th century. Oil on canvas, 96 x 62 inches (approx.). Formerly owned by Georgetown University, Washington, D.C.; destroyed in 1973 in a moving van accident. Plaque on frame read: *Charles Carroll of Carrollton (1737-1832) Given to Georgetown University by the Bergin Family in memory of Charles Carroll MacTavish and Wife Mary Bergin MacTavish.* Provenance — part of The MacTavish Collection.

This portrait was a copy of Cat. No. 34b.

PLATE 34B

35.

Thomas Sully (1783-1872)

Signed and dated left of center: *TS 1827*

Oil on canvas, 29 x 24 inches

Private Collection of a Descendant

Provenance: By descent through Charles Carroll of Carrollton's granddaughter Mrs. Isaac Rand Jackson to the present owner

Reference: Pleasants, "Studies," no. 3018

After completion of the commission for the Marquess Wellesley, Sully painted "for Mrs. Carroll" (Harriet Chew), Charles Carroll's daughter-in-law, this bust-length portrait, again based upon a preliminary study (Cat. No.32) for the Wellesley portrait. Begun September 29 and finished November 18, 1827 (Biddle and Fielding, no. 294), it is one of the finest character studies Sully ever painted. This was one sitter whom Sully carefully studied and whom he observed with profound respect and affection.

Related portraits:

(35a) Unknown artist after Thomas Sully (1783-1872). Unsigned, late 19th century. Oil on canvas, 30 x 24 inches (approx.). Formerly in the Private Collection of a Descendant; stolen in 1974; known through a photograph.

This portrait is an exact copy of Cat. No. 35.

(Cat. No. 36)

36.

Albert Newsam (1809-1864), after Thomas Sully (1783-1872)

Lithograph, 1832

Legend: *Ch Carroll of Carrollton/Painted by T. Sully in 1826 — Newsam Del. Childs Inman Lith.*[rs]*/Published by T. Sully & Childs & Inman, 1832. Philadelphia./Entered according to act of Congress in the year 1832 by Childs & Inman in the Clerks office of the District Court of the Eastern District of Pennsylvania.*

Image size. 12⅛ x 8 inches

Library of Congress, Washington, D.C.

This lithograph is after the bust-length portrait of Charles Carroll of Carrollton (Cat. No. 35).

37.

Thomas Sully (1783-1872)

Signed and dated lower left: *TS 1834*

Oil on canvas, 94 x 58 inches

State of Maryland

State House, Annapolis

Provenance: Commissioned by the State of Maryland in 1833 to be hung in the State House where it has remained since its completion in 1834

Reference: Pleasants, "Studies," no. 1054

Charles Carroll died November 14, 1832. Soon thereafter, the General Assembly of Maryland had passed the following resolution, which read in part:

> *That permanently to indicate to posterity a noble model of public spirit, and to keep alive to future ages of the Republic, the image of a useful life and glorious example; the Governor be and he is hereby requested to procure to be painted a full length likeness of the departed Charles Carroll, of Carrollton, to be placed in the Senate Chamber; the scene of his legislative labours; the theatre of that body, whose peculiar Constitution he framed, and the site of the sublime surrender of military authority, by the Father of our Country, with whose honours the deserts of Carroll are entwined* (Resolution, no. 90).

On January 2, 1834, the *Journal of Proceedings of the House of Delegates* notes, "We engaged Mr. Thomas Sully, a distinguished artist, to paint a full length likeness of the deceased" (pp. 74-75).

Sully began his commission for the State of Maryland October 22, 1833, and completed it January 27, 1834. The preliminary studies and sketches for the Marquess Wellesley's portrait provided the basis for this portrait. It is one of the most magnificent state portraits in American art — moving and eloquently expressive of the understated elegance which Carroll himself would have approved (Biddle and Fielding, no. 295).

Charles Carroll of Carrollton

38.
Asher B. Durand (1796-1886), after Chester Harding (1792-1866)
Engraving, ca. 1828-1833
Legend: *Painted by Harding/Eng. by A. B. Durand/CHARLES CARROLL OF CARROLLTON. Ch. Carroll of Carrollton* (facsimile signature)/[*JAMES HERRING NEW YORK. ENTERED ACCORDING TO THE ACT OF CONGRESS*]
Image size: 4 3/8 x 3 1/2 inches
The Maryland Historical Society, Baltimore
William Mozart Hayden Collection

Chester Harding, a backwoodsman, jack-of-all-trades turned fashionable portrait painter, had already worked in St. Louis and on the eastern seaboard and had achieved notable success in London when he made an important painting trip to Baltimore in 1828 where Charles Carroll of Carrollton was one of his most distinguished clients. As the following quotations testify, Harding's portrait of Carroll received considerable publicity in May and June of 1828, and the artist expected to receive orders for replicas of his portrait of the, then, last surviving Signer of the Declaration of Independence.

> *The lovers of the Fine Arts will be much gratified by a portrait of our venerable townsman, Charles Carroll of Carrolton by that distinguished artist, Mr. Harding. It is, perhaps, the best likeness of Mr. Carroll, and is, at all events, excellent. It may be seen, we learn, at Mr. Harding's room at the Athenaeum, between the hours of 1 and 2, and 5 and 7.* (American and Commercial Daily Advertiser, Baltimore, May 31, 1828)

> *We have seen at the Athenaeum in this city, at Mr. Harding's room, two superior portraits by this gentleman — one of the venerable CHARLES CARROLL OF CARROLLTON; the other of MR. WIRT, attorney general — they are both*

admirable likenesses, but that of Mr. Carroll is perhaps the most striking. The citizens of Baltimore will never have a better opportunity of procuring a full length portrait of this distinguished patriot, which placed in the Exchange or in some other public building, would redound to the honour of the city. We recommend the portrait as highly deserving their notice. (The Emerald and Baltimore Literary Gazette, June 7, 1828)

A comparison of extant portraits of Charles Carroll of Carrollton by Chester Harding with examples of those done after him indicates that there are two versions. Version I without hand and book is represented by Cat. No. 38. Cat. Nos. 39 and 40 represent Version II with hand and book. These Harding-type portraits of Carroll are mystifying, and, until there is a breakthrough on missing facts, suggestions concerning them must remain in part within the realm of speculation.

It is likely that Harding received only one sitting from Charles Carroll who stated in 1827 "it is irksom to set for my picture" (CCC to Unknown Correspondent, November 15, 1827, Private Collection of a Descendant). The artist, therefore, would presumably have made the portrait from life as simple as possible, concentrating on the head as in Version I and eliminating extra details, such as the hand and the book, that appear in Version II, the one which was probably executed later in the studio.

The only certain contemporary evidence of a handless Version I which survives is this engraving by Durand. The copyright date has not been determined, although it was completed prior to 1834 when it was published in *The National Portrait Gallery of Distinguished Americans*, compiled by James Herring and James B. Longacre (Vol. I, pl. 3). In the same year, William Dunlap wrote in his *History of The Rise and Progress of The Arts of Design in the United States:*

In a late letter from Horatio Greenough to Washington Allston, he says, that 'Durand's engraving after Harding's portrait of Charles Carroll, which he showed in a coffee house at Florence, quite astonished the Italians; they would hardly believe that it was executed by an American' (Vol. III, p. 64).

The Durand engraving complicates consideration of the Harding portraits of Charles Carroll. On May 30, 1828, apparently at the time his painting of Carroll was finished and displayed to the public, Harding wrote from Baltimore to the engraver, Asher Brown Durand (1796-1886) in New York:

I have just painted a portrait of the venerable Charles Carroll of Carrollton, and many of his friends have suggested the idea of having it engraved. The object of this note is to ascertain on what terms you would undertake to do it if you thought it worth undertaking at all.

I propose to have it engraved in line, with plate 7 x 9 inches, with a hand — the portrait is kit-Kat[?]. *I should wish it executed in your best style.*

As I have not the pleasure of knowing you personally I will refer you to S.F.B. Morse of your city. Should you be willing to engage in it, you will oblige me by letting me know your terms, when you could get it out etc. . . (Archives of American Art, Smithsonian Institution, Charles Henry Hart Autograph Collection, microfilm D5, 124-125).

The engraving which Durand produced lacks the hand requested by Harding, and comparison with Cat. Nos. 39 and 40 indicates that there are too many differences for Durand to have copied one of the known Version II portraits and merely to have cropped the hand which holds the book. For example, the dressing gown does not touch the neck at the same point; the top and fifth buttons of the vest are closed and the sixth button does not appear; the angles of the lapels and of the right arm are totally different; the treatment of the right shoulder is changed; and the right sleeve is much less full. Furthermore, all known examples of Version II measure approximately 36 x 28 inches, standard "kit cat" size as opposed to a standard bust length of 30 x 25 inches, the measurements of 38D, the only located, pre-20th century example of Version I.

Durand was noted for making accurate engravings after existing portraits.

As an engraver of flesh Mr. Durand stands unrivalled in America, and by his truth of drawing he gives portrait engraving all the advantages of the likeness preserved in the original paintings placed before him. His heads in Herring and Longacre's National Portrait Gallery are perfect representations of the painter's copies from nature (Dunlap, Vol. III, p. 64).

It does not seem plausible that Durand would have ignored the artist's instructions regarding the hand, and, in addition, would have created a radically different version of Harding's original which then became the prototype for examples of the Harding-type portraits presumed to be or known to be handless (Cat. Nos. 38A-38D). It is more likely that Durand had a painting from which to work and that it was handless in the manner of his engraving. No handless version is located which could be this prototype, but there is evidence that Durand did have one in New York (Cat. No. 38A), which is now lost.

RELATED PORTRAITS:

(38A) Chester Harding (1792-1866). Oil on canvas, dimensions unknown. Presently unlocated, known by a listing in *National Academy of Design Exhibition Record 1826-1860* (New York, 1943, p. 209). Provenance — Collection of Honorable S. Van Rensselaer, New York, 1829.

In 1829 a portrait of Charles Carroll owned by the "Hon. S. Van Rensselaer" (undoubtedly Stephen, member of Congress from New York) and painted by Chester Harding was exhibited at the National Academy of Design in New York (NAD *Record, p.* 209). Since Asher B. Durand and James Herring who copyrighted the engraving of Charles Carroll (Cat. No. 38) were also in New York, it seems likely that the portrait Van Rensselaer owned was the source for Durand's engraving. Presumably, then, the engraving (Cat. No. 38) is witness to the fact that Van Rensselaer's Harding was the handless version.

How would Van Rensselaer have acquired a portrait of Charles Carroll by Harding? Harding executed a portrait of Van Rensselaer in 1828 (Cowdry, p. 168). Harding's handless portrait from life of Carroll could have been in the artist's studio at the time, preparatory to his making the larger, more detailed studio replica. Van Rensselaer could have seen it there and then asked for a replica of Version I, as Harding had not completed Version II with hand and book. If this is the case, then Harding complied with Van Rensselaer's request, but he emphasized Version II in his letter to Durand as he considered it the more important and impressive work and preferred not to have Version I perpetuated. Durand, however, only had access to Version I.

(38B) Chester Harding (1792-1866). Oil on canvas, size unknown. Presently unlocated, known through a letter dated June 10, 1828, from Charles Carroll of Carrollton to Marianne Wellesley. Provenance — Charles Carroll of Carrollton to Emily MacTavish; part of The MacTavish Collection.

From Carroll's letter of June 10, 1828, we know that he gave Emily MacTavish a portrait by Chester Harding:

A Mr. Harding has lately drawn my portrait, a most striking, likeness of me in the ninety-first year of my life, the countenance with little meaning, the eyes dim and dull. I have given it to Emily MacTavish . . . (MdHi, ms. 220).

This portrait was very likely Harding's work from life which could have been seen by Van Rensselaer.

(38C) Abel Nichols after Chester Harding (1792-1866). Oil on canvas, size unknown. Presently unlocated, known through *The Maryland Historical Society Exhibition Catalogue* for 1879. Provenance — part of The MacTavish Collection.

The evidence of the existence of this painting is in the three portraits of Carroll recorded as by "Nichol" in the 1879 exhibition list of The Maryland Historical Society. None is marked "engr." or "eng.", the customary designation for engravings. Abel Nichols (1815-1860) studied with Harding in the early 1830's. It may be supposed that he made an early copy of Emily's painting (Cat. No. 38B) which he signed or which was otherwise firmly identified as being painted by him. Since Emily's original Harding was not signed and resembled the known "Nichol," all Harding-type portraits in the MacTavish branch of the family became known as by "Nichol" in the latter part of the 19th century. This would

Plate 38d

explain the fact that there is no mention of a Harding portrait in any of the Maryland Historical Society's exhibition lists. Both Emily's original Harding (Cat. No. 38b) and this "Nichol" copy are now lost. The third "Nichol" is Cat. No. 38d.

(38d) Unknown artist after Chester Harding (1792-1866). Unsigned, late 19th century. Oil on canvas, 29 3/8 x 24 1/2 inches. Private Collection of a Descendant. Provenance — part of The MacTavish Collection.

This portrait is a copy of the handless Harding-type portrait and appears to be late 19th century. It is undoubtedly the third copy called by "Nichol" in the 1879 exhibition list at The Maryland Historical Society. Although no Harding was ever recorded in the MacTavish Collection when it was deposited at the Maryland Historical Society between 1879 and 1912, it was the actual existence of this portrait and Cat. No. 38e in the possession of MacTavish descendants in 1948 which led to the realization that Harding portraits of Carroll had definitely been part of the collection.

(38e) Unknown artist after Chester Harding (1792-1866). Unsigned, ca. 1920-1933. Oil on canvas, 30 x 25 inches. Collection of Mr. and Mrs. Phillips H. Clarke. Provenance: part of The MacTavish Collection; sold in 1947 or 1948 to the present owner. Reference: Pleasants, "Studies," no. 1662.

A 20th century work, the portrait was probably executed in Rome in the 1920's or 1930's when many copies were made from portraits already in The MacTavish Collection.

(38f) Chester Harding (1792-1866). Signed right center: *Harding*, 2nd quarter of 19th century? Miniature, watercolor on ivory, 3 3/8 x 2 1/2 inches. Presently unlocated; repro. in *Charles Carroll of Carrollton* (BMA, 1937, p. 49). Provenance — previously in the Collection of Robert Garrett. Reference: Pleasants, "Studies," no. 1614.

From an extant photograph, it is not possible to discern the full signature on this lost miniature of the Harding-type, Version I portrait of Charles Carroll. According to a Frick Art Reference Library note of 1940 (175/10a), it looked like "L" or "JL" Harding. According to Dr. J. Hall Pleasants, the signature was simply "Harding." It appears closer to the Durand engraving than any of the known paintings, especially in the highlights on the hair. Also, the vest is reported as "plum color" rather than brown as in all of the known paintings, implying that the artist of this miniature did not know the coloring of the paintings and worked from the Durand engraving.

(38g) Henry Hoppner Meyer (ca. 1782-1847) after Chester Harding (1792-1866). Engraving. Image size: 4 x 3 inches. Legend: *Drawn by Hoppner Meyer from an original Painting/ Engraved by T. Illman/Charles Carroll of Carrollton (facsimile signature)/Entered according to act of Congress in the District Court, N.Y.* Library of Congress, Washington, D.C.

The source of this engraving is Version I of the Harding-type portrait of Charles Carroll.

39.

Chester Harding (1792-1866)

Unsigned, ca. 1828

Oil on canvas, 35 7/8 x 27 7/8 inches

National Gallery of Art, Washington, D.C.

Gift of Mr. and Mrs. Alexander Dallas Thayer, 1956

Provenance: It was owned at one time by R. H. R. Toland or Mrs. Benjamin Rush Toland of Philadelphia; to Ehrich Galleries of New York, ca. 1926; to another dealer; to McClees Gallery, Philadelphia, 1928, where Mr. Thayer purchased it; given to the present owner by Mr. Thayer.

Chester Harding's second version of Charles Carroll is the one the artist intended to perpetuate and to which the Baltimore newspapers (see Cat. No. 38) were probably referring. That the publicity did produce orders for this more impressive Version II is borne out by the existence of Cat. Nos. 39, 39A and 39B.

In this example of Version II the face is beautifully executed, and it could well be Chester Harding's carefully thought-out replica from a life study. In the three known examples of Version II, it should be noted that the hand does not appear to be from life, and the shoulder and arm do not have a realistic relationship to the figure, again raising the point that Harding may have painted from life only the head and shoulders of the Signer.

The provenance of this work is unclear, but it is entirely possible that it was originally ordered by a Baltimore citizen not connected with the Carroll family.

PLATE 39A

RELATED PORTRAITS:

(39A) Chester Harding (1792-1866). Unsigned, ca. 1828. Inscribed on label on back of frame: *D. Hoffman's property April 17, 1829.* Oil on canvas, 35 1/2 x 27 1/2 inches (sight). United States Capitol, Washington, D.C. Provenance — owned by a D. Hoffman in 1829; purchased from Mrs. Daniel Hoffman April 28, 1870, by the Forty-First Congress of the United States. There are differences between the Version II at the National Gallery (Cat. No. 39) and this one at the U.S. Capitol, for example, the chair and the opening at the top of the vest. The facial expression — actually the entire handling of the face — is slightly altered, creating a more formal conception, but both portraits appear to be studio replicas. A confusion surrounds the provenance of this painting. Is it possible that the name Daniel which occurs once in the correspondence concerning the purchase of the paintings by the U.S. Government is an error for David? Daniel Hoffman (1768-1842) of Baltimore who married Mary Schrote had no discernible connection to Charles Carroll of Carrollton; however, David Hoffman (1784-1854) who married Mary McKean was a prominent Baltimore attorney and was Charles Carroll of Carrollton's lawyer. There seems to be no connection between Daniel and David Hoffman. Of course, this could also have been an order from Harding's studio with no direct connection to the Carroll family.

(39B) Chester Harding? (1792-1866). Unsigned, ca. 1828. Oil on canvas, 30 x 28 inches. Private Collection of a Descendant. Provenance — by direct descent through Charles Carroll of Carrollton's grandson Charles Carroll of Doughoregan to the present owner. Reference: Pleasants, "Studies," no. 131. Closest to the U.S. Capitol Version II in facial expression, in the detail of the chair, and in the opening of the vest, this may be a studio copy after Cat. no. 39A rather than a studio replica — it does not appear to be from Harding's hand but is of the period. Carroll gave one Harding to Emily MacTavish. It seems logical that another member of the family might also have ordered a copy of Version II, which Harding entrusted to an assistant. It is unlikely that this would have been the source of the Nichol confusion (see Cat. No. 38C) as it descended in a different branch of the family not connected with the MacTavishes.

(Cat. No. 40)

40.

James B. Longacre (1794-1869), after Chester Harding (1792-1866)

Engraving, date unknown

Legend: *CHARLES CARROLL OF CARROLLTON/Engraved by James B. Longacre from a Painting by Chester Harding*

Image size: 11 3/8 x 7 5/8 inches

National Portrait Gallery, Smithsonian Institution, Washington, D.C.

The source of this engraving by James B. Longacre seems clearly to be the Chester Harding Version II portrait owned by the National Gallery of Art (Cat. No. 39). The date of this engraving and the reason Longacre undertook it are unknown. Longacre used the Asher B. Durand engraving (Cat. No. 38), and not his own, in his publication, *The National Portrait Gallery of Distinguished Americans.* One explanation for the Longacre engraving is the fact that it does match Harding's original specifications of "a hand" while the Durand engraving does not. Perhaps Harding approached Longacre after Durand failed to meet his exact requirements (see Cat. No. 38) or possibly Longacre may have considered it a good speculation due to the demand for portraits of Carroll as the last surviving signer of the Declaration of Independence. The Longacre work was apparently designed as a separate piece and not as a book illustration since it is listed in the artist's subscription book of orders, now unlocated.

We can only assume that this engraving is an enduring monument to the popularity of Harding's portrait of Charles Carroll of Carrollton, especially the version with the book, so important to Harding himself. It could be said that this portrait of Carroll was at one point on the way to becoming for Harding what the Athenaeum portrait of George Washington was for Gilbert Stuart.

RELATED PORTRAIT:

(40A) W. H. Mote (fl. 1830-1850), after James B. Longacre (1794-1869). Engraving, date unknown. Legend: *Engraved by W. H. Mote/CHARLES CARROLL/From a Print by Longacre after a Painting/by C Harding.* Image size: 5 1/16 x 4 inches. New York Public Library, New York.

W. H. Mote was an English portrait engraver. There is no evidence that he ever engraved in this country which would indicate that Harding's likeness of Carroll was even in demand abroad.

Charles Carroll of Carrollton

41.

William James Hubard (1807-1862)

Unsigned, 1830 or 1831

Oil on panel, 18 3/4 x 14 1/2 inches

The Metropolitan Museum of Art, New York

Rogers Fund, 1956/56.207

Provenance: By direct descent through Charles Carroll of Carrollton's granddaughter Emily MacTavish; part of The MacTavish Collection; purchased by the present owner

Born in England, W. J. Hubard came to America in 1824 with a traveling showman named Smith who exploited the young artist's considerable talents as a silhouette cutter. By the late 1820's he and Smith had parted and Hubard turned his interests to portrait painting. The years 1830-1831 find him enjoying great success among the prominent families of Baltimore, specializing in small cabinet portraits on panel. This likeness of Charles Carroll, the last of the Signer taken from life, is typical of Hubard's early work in its precise clarity, directness, and attention to detail. It embodies, as well, John H. B. Latrobe's description of Carroll as he remembered the Signer at about this age:

> *"Below the middle size, weak and emaciated, his voice thin and feeble, writing with a trembling hand, but always signing his name 'Charles Carroll of Carrollton'. . . . His hair was scant and white and silky, and his eyes especially were suggestive of great age. His complexion, however, was healthy. . . . His dress was the knee breeches of the old school, when I first recollect him, his waistcoat as long as we see in oldtime pictures, and I never saw him except in a loose roquelaure, something between a dressing gown and a frock coat . . . as one looked at Mr. Carroll, one saw a shadow from past days, when manner was cultivated as essential to a gentleman"* (Semmes, p. 215).

RELATED PORTRAITS:

(41A) Unknown artist after William James Hubard (1807-1862). Unsigned, date unknown. Oil on panel, 19 x 14 inches. Private collection of a Descendant. Provenance — part of The MacTavish Collection; purchased from the MacTavishes by the great-grandfather of the present owner, also a Carroll descendant.

Extant correspondence (on deposit, MdHi) proves that there were two versions of the Hubard portrait of Charles Carroll of Carrollton at The Maryland Historical Society in 1890: an original and a copy, both of which were part of The MacTavish Collection. A portrait based upon Cat. No. 41 was located in France in December 1974. Only study from a photograph has been possible but the technique appears to be much less distinct than Hubard's and details such as the crucifix are absent. This work, attributed to "Peale" by the MacTavishes, could well be the MacTavish copy mentioned in 1890.

(41B) William James Hubard? (1807-1862). Unsigned, date unknown (in existence in 1892). Oil on panel ?, size unknown. Presently unlocated; known through an illustration (Bowen, facing p. 97). Provenance — Collection of Mary Carroll Acosta, great-granddaughter of Charles Carroll of Carrollton.

In 1892 Clarence Bowen published a portrait of Charles Carroll (facing p. 97) "owned by Mrs. Mary C. Acosta . . . and deposited in the Maryland Historical Society." Bowen quoted a statement made by John H. B. Latrobe that:

> *Madame Acosta's is an admirable speaking and most characteristic likeness of Mr. Carroll by William J. Hubard. . . . Indeed, I knew the artist so well while he was in Baltimore, and was so familiar in Mr. Carroll's family at the time, that the probability is that I must have seen the work while it was in progress"* (Bowen, p. 434).

The portrait belonging to Madame Acosta, which was illustrated in Bowen, appears to be very similar to Cat. No. 41, but, since there is no indication that it was ever part of the MacTavish Collection, it may be a second copy after the Hubard.

Charles Carroll of Carrollton

42.

Endicott & Swett (in Balto. 1830-1831; in New York 1831-1834) after William James Hubard (1807-1863)

Lithograph, 1832

Legend: *CHARLES CARROLL OF CARROLLTON./Lithog. & Published by Endicott & Swett, New York. from the original picture by W. J. Hubard. Balto./Entered according to Act of Congress, in the year 1832, by Endicott & Swett, in the Clerks office of the District Court of the southern District of New York. mun[. . .]al*

Image size: 17 9/16 x 13 1/4 inches

The Maryland Historical Society, Baltimore

This lithograph is based upon William James Hubard's portrait of Charles Carroll (Cat. No. 41) and was published in the *New York Magazine* for August 21, 1832 with the following notation:

> *The copy-right of the original plate has been secured. We are informed that the family of venerable survivor of those who signed the Declaration of Independence consider this the most accurate likeness extant.*

Related portrait:

(42A) H. M. Snyder after Endicott and Swett (in Balto. 1830-1831; in New York 1831-1834). Signed lower right: *H. M. Snyder*, 1881. Image size: 5 x 3 7/8 inches. This woodcut after Cat. No. 42 was published in John Scharf's *History of Baltimore City and County* (vol. I, Baltimore: L. H. Everts, 1881), p. 317.

Additional Portraits of Charles Carroll of Carrollton:

(42B) Unknown artist, formerly attributed to John Vanderlyn (1775-1852). Unsigned, 1816?. Oil on canvas, 30 3/4 x 25 1/4 inches. Collection of The Johns Hopkins University, Baltimore. Provenance — purchased through Russell Sharpe from A. F. De Forest of New York in 1928 by Francis T. Garvan who gave it to the present owner. Reference: Pleasants, "Studies," no. 3361.

It has been said that this portrait was painted for President James Monroe, but there is no evidence to support this statement. In addition, this portrait does not appear to be by Vanderlyn, and it bears little resemblance to Charles Carroll of Carrollton, especially as he would have looked about 1816. It could be a highly idealized rendition of Carroll as he looked about the time of the 1803 Field portrait (Cat. No. 17).

(42C) Charles Bird King (1785-1862). Unsigned, 1816. Oil on canvas, 36 x 28 inches. Private Collection of a Descendant. Provenance — by direct descent through Charles Carroll of Carrollton's grandson Charles Carroll of Doughoregan to the present owner. Reference: Pleasants, "Studies," no. 130.

On August 31, 1816, Charles Carroll wrote to an unidentified correspondent, possibly Joseph Delaplaine (1777-1824):

> *My letter of the 6th, instant in answer to Mr. King's of the 29th of July, informed him I should be in Baltimore about the 20th December and remain there during the winter where I will sit to him for my portrait at any place in that city he may appoint.*
> (Pleasants, "Studies," no. 130).

This portrait stands as witness to the fact that Carroll did sit for King. It was commissioned by Joseph Delaplaine who had planned to include it in his *Repository of the Lives and Portraits of Distinguished American Characters*, Philadelphia, 1815-[16], probably for Volume II, Part II, which apparently was never issued.

(42D) John H. I. Browere (1792-1834). Unsigned, 1826. Plaster-cast life mask, 30 inches high. New York State Historical Association, Cooperstown, New York. Provenance — by direct descent in the artist's family; purchased in 1939 or 1940 by Stephen C. Clark for presentation to the New York State Historical Association in 1940.

Browere's greatest claims to fame are his life masks of distinguished Americans. On July 29, 1826, less than one month after Carroll had become the last surviving Signer of the Declaration of Independence he wrote from Doughoregan to the New York artist Archibald Robertson:

Mr. Browere has produced and read to me several letters from sundry most respectable personages; on their recommendation and at his request I sat to him to take my bust. He has taken it, and in my opinion and that of my family, and of all who have seen it, the resemblance is most striking. The operation from its commencement to its completion was performed in two hours, with very little inconvenience and no pain to myself.

This bust Mr. Browere contemplates placing, with many others, in a national gallery of busts. . . (Rowland, vol. 2, pp. 342-343).

Two days later, a notice appeared in the Baltimore *American and Daily Advertiser:*

Bust of Charles Carroll by J.H.J. [sic] Browere Esq. on exhibition at the Exchange.

The existence of this mask provides a unique opportunity to compare the accuracy of the three major portraitists of Carroll's last years: Sully (Cat. Nos. 34 & 35), Harding (Cat. No. 39), and Hubard (Cat. No. 41).

Plate 42d

(42e) Cast from Cat. No. 42d, ca. 1940. Bronze, 30 inches high. New York State Historical Association, Cooperstown, New York. Provenance — cast at the time Stephen C. Clark purchased original plaster cast from descendant of Browere for presentation to the New York State Historical Association.

(42f) Unknown artist. Unsigned, ca. 1876?. Plaster relief bust in shadow box frame, 6 inches high. Inscription on label on back: *Sold by/J. P. Van Eps. & Co./103 Pearl Street/New York/and by their Agents in the principal cities and towns throughout/the Union.* The Maryland Historical Society, Baltimore. Gift of Miss Ethel Miller. Reference: Pleasants, "Studies," no. 3211.

The justification for this object may well be the centennial of 1876 as the relief resembles a souvenir piece. No J. P. Van Eps & Co. is listed in New York; however, a painter by the name of Jacob Van Eps is listed in the New York directories from 1877 to 1881 as being at 227 Hudson Street.

(42g) Richard Edwin Brooks (1865-1919). Signed and dated: *Richard E. Brooks, Sc., Paris MCMII.* Bronze, figure: 84 3/4 inches high, base: 40 1/2 inches high. United States Capitol, National Statuary Hall Collection, Washington, D.C. Provenance — commissioned for the U.S. Statuary Hall. In 1896 a special Maryland State Commission was appointed to recommend subjects for statues to be placed in the U.S. Capitol and to suggest sculptors to execute them. In 1898 the Commission reported that Charles Carroll and John Hanson were their choices for the State of Maryland. Sometime after 1898 Brooks was chosen to execute the statues of Carroll and Hanson. The Carroll was completed in 1902 and was accepted for the U.S. Capitol Statuary Hall Collection in 1903.

(42h) Unknown artist, attributed by family tradition to John Wesley Jarvis (1812-1868). Unsigned, date unknown. Inscribed upper right: CHARLES CARROLL OF/CARROLLTON. Oil on canvas, size unknown. Private Collection. Provenance — by descent to the present owner. Th available photographs of this bust-length portrait would indicate that Jarvis did not have a hand in its execution. It appears to be a portrait of some age and, according to the owner, has been virtually ruined by poor restoration (see discussion under 42i).

(42i) Ellen Sully (1816-1896). Signed and dated at left: *ES 1836.* Inscribed upper right: *CHARLES CARROLL OF/CARROLLTON.* Oil on board, 24 x 20 inches. The Historical Society of Pennsylvania, Philadelphia. Provenance — presented by the Sully family to the Pennsylvania Colonization Society; presented by the Society to the present owner.

Plate 421

This portrait has always been considered a copy by Ellen Sully of the bust portrait executed by her father Thomas in 1827 (Cat. No. 35). The differences in pose, costume, and even the chair backs are too great to claim a connection between this and the elder Sully's portrait of Carroll. What this does resemble in almost every detail, including the exact block-letter form of the inscription, is the portrait attributed to Jarvis (Cat. No. 42H). The only notable difference is the handling of the hair. That portrait does not appear from a photograph to be of a quality which Ellen Sully would have sought to copy for the Pennsylvania Colonization Society. The question becomes "what were these two artists looking at?" For Ellen Sully, anyway, it was probably something in Philadelphia, and certainly something in existence prior to 1836, the year Ellen Sully's work was executed. Carroll's wig in the work attributed to Jarvis is reminiscent of the Revolutionary generation and not that of the Federal Republic. And the face could be that of a man in his late 40's or 50's. Could the prototype date from the 1770's or 1789's (too early for Jarvis, of course) or is the wig an anachronistic invention of the artist? In any case,, unless actual examination of 421 provides evidence not apparent in the photograph the interrelationship of the works attributed to Jarvis by family tradition and the Ellen Sully seem to indicate a missing prototype of Charles Carroll of Carrollton which was considered a fairly important likeness of the Signer in its day. Jarvis should be considered in a study of Carroll portraits since he was a popular and prominent artist in Baltimore between 1810 and 1813. His sitters constituted the closest associates of the Carroll family, and it is more than possible that a portrait of the Signer by Jarvis once existed.

(42J) Charles Willson Peale (1741-1827). Unsigned, 1826. Silhouette, 2 3/4 x 1 1/2 inches. Stamped under silhouette: Peale Museum. Inscribed on back: *This profileograph/done at Phila by/Charles W. Peale/1826/was given to Philip Thomas/President/B & O R.R. Baltimore, Md./from his esteemed friend and/advisor/Charles Carroll/Carrollton, Md./also of the B & O R.R.* Private Collection of a Descendant. Provenance — given to Philip Thomas by Charles Carroll of Carrollton; returned to the family by unknown means.

Mrs. Charles Carroll of Carrollton (Mary Darnall), 1749-1782

(First cousin once removed of CCC through his mother; Second cousin once removed of CCC through his father)

43.

Charles Willson Peale (1741-1827)

Signed and dated lower left on edge of table: *C. Peale pinx.*[t] *1771*

Oil on canvas, 30 3/4 x 25 inches

Collection of John D. Schapiro

Provenance: Commissioned for Edmond Jenings; by descent in the Jenings family until purchased by the Ehrich Galleries, New York, in 1923; acquired by Luke Vincent Lockwood prior to 1932; sold with Lockwood's collection, May 1954, at Parke-Bernet Galleries, Inc., New York; purchased by the present owner

Reference: Pleasants, "Studies," no. 1653 (subject listed at one time as "A Maryland Lady")

After the death in 1761 of Mrs. Charles Carroll of Annapolis, her niece, Rachel Brooke Darnall and Rachel's daughter Mary, then 12, went to live with Charles Carroll of Annapolis in the big house on Spa Creek. "Molly" was very much a member of the family circle when Charles Carroll of Carrollton returned from England in 1763; romance eventually flourished, and by 1767 he is writing to one of his intimate London friends Edmond Jenings of his bride to be:

> *She really is a sweet-tempered, charming, neat girl — a little too young for me I confess, but especially as I am of weak and puny constitution — in a poor state of health but in hopes of better . . .* (Rowland, vol. I, p. 84).

Charles and Molly were married in Annapolis on June 5, 1768.

Charles Willson Peale, a native of Maryland, holds an interesting place within the iconography of the Carroll family which extant portraits do not adequately illustrate. The artist was fortunate enough to capture the eye of John Beale Bordley who raised a subscription among several distinguished gentlemen of Maryland for Peale's study in London in 1767. Charles Carroll of Carrollton contributed 5 guineas. Between his return to Maryland in 1769 and his permanent settlement in Philadelphia in 1776, Peale in turn used his freshly polished skills to create a superb series of portraits of his supporters, their friends and associates which has left us an impressive record of the men who affected Maryland's role in the birth and establishment of our nation and their families as well. Charles Carroll was no exception. In Peale's list of portraits which appear to date between 1770 and 1775 we find the following entries:

> *3 Mr. Carrolls family half down 21.0.0*
> *2 Mr. Carroll 3/4 Mrs. Carroll 14.14.0*
> *the child 5.5*
> *Mr. Carrols Miniature 5.5*

Of the five likenesses on the list, this portrait of Mrs. Carroll is the only one whose present location is known. It is thought "probably" to be one of the separate portraits of Mr. and Mrs. Carroll that had been commissioned during Peale's study in England by Edmond Jenings. Extant correspondence proves that they were completed and received by Jenings.

Additional Portraits of Mrs. Charles Carroll of Carrollton:
(See discussion under Cat. No. 57E)

Charles Carroll of Duddington
(Also called of "Carrollsburg"), 1729-1773

(First cousin of CCC; second cousin once removed of MDC)

44.

John Wollaston (fl. 1736-1767)

Unsigned, ca. 1753-1754

Oil on canvas, 52 x 39 inches

Private Collection of a Descendant

Provenance: By descent to the present owner

Reference: Pleasants, "Studies," no. 781

This Charles Carroll was heir to several estates, including "Duddington Manor" through his mother Ann Rozier (or Rozer) and, through his father Daniel Carroll, "Clynmalira" and "Litterluna" which were both land grants made to his grandfather Charles Carroll the Settler. Daniel Carroll was known as "of Duddington" from his wife's legacy, and it is from him that the Duddington Carrolls descend.

Charles Carroll of Duddington married Mary Hill from Maryland in 1763. Reputedly an ardent sportsman, Charles of Duddington acquired the nickname "Trimbush" from his habit of trimming the tops of bushes with his whip while riding at breakneck speed.

As so frequently with the Carroll family, Wollaston produced a portrait in his most impressive format. The companion portrait of Mary is unlocated at present.

Additional portraits of Charles Carroll of Duddington:

(44A) John Wollaston (fl. 1736-1767). Unsigned, ca. 1753-1754. Oil on canvas, 51 x 41 1/2 inches. Collection of Mr. and Mrs. Richard L. Staples, Courtesy of Peter H. Davidson & Co., Inc., New York. Provenance — by descent to the present owner. References: Pleasants, "Studies," no. 134.

In this second, equally grand portrait by Wollaston, Charles Carroll is slightly differently posed and in different dress.

(44B) Attributed to John Wollaston (fl. 1736-1767). Unsigned, ca. 1753-1754 (?). Oil on canvas, 49 1/2 x 39 1/2 inches. Collection of a Descendant. Courtesy of Kennedy Galleries. Provenance — by descent to the present generation.

This is a slight variant in both pose and dress which appears to be based both on Cat. No. 44 and Cat. No. 44A.

Charles Carroll of Duddington

MARY CARROLL (Mrs. Ignatius Digges), 1730-1785

(First cousin of CCC; Second cousin once removed of MDC)

45.

John Wollaston (fl. 1736-1767)

Unsigned, ca. 1753-1754

Oil on canvas, 51 x 41 1/2 inches

Collection of Mr. and Mrs. Richard L. Staples

Courtesy of Peter H. Davidson & Co., Inc., New York

Provenance: By descent to the present owner

Reference: Pleasants, "Studies," no. 135

Daughter of Charles Carroll of Carrollton's uncle Daniel Carroll of Duddington and his wife Ann Rozier (or Rozer), Mary Carroll married in 1750 Ignatius Digges of "Melwood." Painted when she was hardly more than a bride, a portrait such as this could have inspired the following verse in *The Maryland Gazette* for March 15, 1753, the first documented date for Wollaston in Maryland:

EXTEMPORE:
On seeing Mr. WOLLASTON'S Pictures in Annapolis
By Dr. T. T.

Behold the won'drous Power of Art!
That mocks devouring Time and Death,
Can Nature's ev'ry Charm impart;
And make the lifeless Canvas Breathe.
The Lilly blended with the Rose,
Blooms gaily on each fertile Cheek. . . .

RELATED PORTRAITS:

(45A) Attributed to John Wollaston (fl. 1736-1767). Unsigned, ca. 1753-1754. Oil on canvas, 29 3/4 x 24 3/4 inches. Formerly in a Private Collection; destroyed in fire in 1973; known through a photograph. Provenance — by descent to Mrs. Richard S. Hill; bequeathed to James Morgan (1951); sold from Morgan estate by the C. & S. National Bank of Macon, Georgia, to unknown purchaser; consigned to Kennedy Galleries in 1963; destroyed by fire, 1973, while on loan from Kennedy to a private collection. Reference: Pleasants, "Studies," no. 1739 (listed as owned by James Ethelbert Morgan).

This painting was a bust length portrait of Mary Carroll Digges.

Mary Carroll

IGNATIUS DIGGES, 1707 or 1709-1785

(First cousin by marriage of CCC; First cousin twice removed of MDC)

46.

John Wollaston (fl. 1736-1767)

Unsigned, ca. 1753-1754

Oil on canvas, 50 3/4 x 41 3/4 inches

Private Collection of a Descendant, on deposit at The Maryland Historical Society, Baltimore

Provenance: By direct descent through the subject's grandson John Lee of "Needwood" to the present owner

Reference: Pleasants, "Studies," no. 1524

Ignatius Digges was the son of William Digges (d. 1740) of "Melwood" and his second wife Eleanor, widow of Philip Darnall (d. 1705; great uncle of Charles Carroll of Carrollton and great-great uncle of Mary Darnall Carroll). Mary Carroll of Duddington was Ignatius Digges' second wife. Although probably executed about the same time as the portrait of Mary (Cat. No. 45), they are not companion pieces.

Plate 46a

Additional portraits of Ignatius Digges:

(46a) *Ignatius Digges as a Child.* Justus Engelhardt Kühn (?-1717). Signed and dated on rail of balustrade to right: *Anno AEtatis Sua[e] 2 1/2 1710. E Kühn Feci[t].* Oil on canvas, 54 x 43 1/4 inches. Private Collection of a Descendant. Provenance — by descent through Charles Carroll of Carrollton's grandson Charles Carroll of Doughoregan to the present owner. Reference: Pleasants, "Studies," no. 123. This portrait of exceptionally fine quality is the only signed work by Kühn, and it serves as the basis for all attributions to the artist.

(46b) *Ignatius Digges as a Child.* Unknown artist after Justus Engelhardt Kühn (?-1717). Unsigned, date unknown. Oil on canvas, 54 x 44 inches. Inscribed on rail of balustrade to right: *Anno AEtatis Sua[e]* 2 1/2 1710. The Maryland Historical Society, Baltimore, Gift of Mrs. Thomas S. L. Horsey. Provenance — by descent to Mrs. Horsey; presented to the Society in 1962. Reference: Pleasants, "Studies," no. 1311.

This portrait is a copy of 46a.

Mrs. Daniel Carroll of Upper Marlboro II
(Eleanor Carroll), 1731/1732-1763
And her son, Daniel Carroll of Upper Marlboro III, 1752-ca. 1790

(First cousin of CCC; Second cousin once removed of MDC)

47.

John Wollaston (fl. 1736-1767)

Unsigned, ca. 1753-1754

Oil on canvas, 50 5/16 x 40 1/4 inches

The Maryland Historical Society, Baltimore

Gift of Dr. Clapham Pennington, 1925

Provenance: Purchased about 1867 from Judge Williamson Carroll of Little Rock, Ark. (a direct descendant) by Emily Harper (granddaughter of Charles Carroll of Carrollton, but no close relation to the sitter); inherited by her nephew Dr. Pennington.

References: Pleasants: "Studies," no. 538

Eleanor Carroll of Duddington, sister of Mrs. Ignatius Digges (Cat. No. 45) and of Charles Carroll of Duddington (Cat. No. 44), married her cousin Daniel Carroll in 1751. Her son Daniel III (also known as Daniel Carroll of Warburton), born a year later, appears with her here, one of a small number of infants depicted by Wollaston. Eleanor, according to a contemporary account,

> *. . . was bless'd with all the Qualifications that make the good Wife, tender Mother, kind Mistress, and affectionate Friend. Her benevolent Disposition, affability of Manners, and great good Sense, procured her the Friendship and Esteem of all her Acquaintance . . .* The Maryland Gazette, April 28, 1763).

Additional portrait of Mrs. Daniel Carroll:
(47A) John Wollaston (fl. 1736-1767). Unsigned, ca. 1753-1754. Oil on canvas, 30 1/8 x 24 5/8 inches. Private Collection of a Descendant. Provenance — by descent to the present owner. Reference: Pleasants, "Studies," no. 1523.

This is an exceptionally attractive bust-length portrait by Wollaston.

MRS. DANIEL CARROLL OF UPPER MARLBORO II
And her son, Daniel Carroll of Upper Marlboro III,

DANIEL CARROLL OF UPPER MARLBORO II (called of Rock Creek), 1730-1796

(Second cousin of CCC; First cousin once removed MDC)

48.

John Wollaston (fl. 1736-1767)

Unsigned, ca. 1753-1754

Oil on canvas, 50 3/4 x 40 5/8 inches

The Maryland Historical Society, Baltimore

Gift of Dr. Clapham Pennington, 1924

Provenance: Purchased about 1867 from Judge Williamson Carroll of Little Rock, Ark. (a direct descendant) by Emily Harper (granddaughter of Charles Carroll of Carrollton but no close relation to the sitter); inherited by her nephew Dr. Pennington.

Reference: Pleasants, "Studies," no. 539

Daniel Carroll of Rock Creek, brother of Archbishop John Carroll (see Cat. Nos. 50-56), was a distinguished member of the Revolutionary generation. He was a delegate to the Continental Congress (1781-1783), a Maryland state Senator (1782-1792), a delegate to the Constitutional Convention (1787), and a representative from Maryland to the First Congress of the United States (1789-1791). In 1791 George Washington appointed him one of the first three Commissioners to lay out the District of Columbia, a position he held until 1795. It was for this service that he was frequently identified as Daniel Carroll "Commissioner." This is an elegant companion piece to the portrait of Daniel's wife Eleanor (Cat. No. 47).

RELATED PORTRAITS:

(48A) Unknown artist after John Wollaston (fl. 1736-1767). Unsigned, probably late 19th century. Oil on canvas, 49 3/4 x 36 7/8 inches. Private Collection of a Descendant. Provenance — by descent to present owner. Reference: Pleasants, "Studies," no. 1552.

This portrait is a copy of Cat. No. 48.

(Cat. No. 49).

49.

Max Rosenthal (1833-1918) after John Wollaston (fl. 1736-1767)

Engraving, ca. 1885

Legend: *Max Rosenthal/Daniel Carroll/Signer of the Constitution of the United States /Danl. Carroll* (facsimile signature)

Image size: 5 15/16 x 3 15/16 inches

National Portrait Gallery, Smithsonian Institution, Washington, D.C.

This engraving is after the portrait of Daniel Carroll by John Wollaston (Cat. No. 48).

JOHN CARROLL, 1735-1815

(Second cousin of CCC; 1st cousin once removed of MDC)

50.

Unknown artist, formerly attributed to Robert Edge Pine? (1730?-1788)

Unsigned, ca. 1774-1775?

Oil on canvas, 29 x 25 inches

Private Collection of a Descendant

Courtesy of Kennedy Galleries, Inc., New York

Provenance: Part of The MacTavish Collection; by descent to the present owner, a Carroll descendant

Reference: Lane, "Studies in American Painting," on file at Kennedy Galleries, Inc.; Pleasants, "Studies," no. 1663

This portrait is identified by family tradition as John Carroll who was created first Bishop of North America in 1790 and Archbishop of Baltimore in 1808. Although no portrait of him is identified in *The Maryland Historical Society Exhibition Catalogues, 1848-1908,* where many of the pictures from The MacTavish Collection are listed, one is identified as "Rev. Mr. Carroll" on the inventory of MacTavish paintings made by the Peabody Institute in 1948.

Certain factors should be given consideration when examining this portrait. The color of the eyes in the portraits by Gilbert Stuart and Rembrandt Peale (Cat. Nos. 51 and 55) are blue. Here and in the Jeremiah Paul portrait (Cat. No. 52) they are brown. The Paul may have been executed after a study without color or an engraving. The sitter appears to be about thirty-nine to forty-one, John Carroll's age between his return from abroad in 1774 and his Mission to Canada in 1776. At that time he would have been wearing the lay clothing depicted here, as the suppression of the Jesuit order in 1773 and anti-Catholic sentiment in Maryland would have dictated. The style of coat could possibly date that early, but the shawl collar of the waistcoat did not come into vogue before the 1790's. By that time, Carroll would have been about sixty, older than the subject appears here, and he would most assuredly have had his portrait painted in the clerical vestments he had waited so long to wear publicly.

The question of artistic attribution is an open one. The overall effect of the portrait does suggest the Peale family but at present no decision in favor of a particular member of this famous American painting dynasty can be made. The work was at one time attributed to Charles Willson Peale by Professor James Lane who conducted the most exhaustive research on the portrait and compared it stylistically to the portrait of Colonel Stagg by Charles Willson Peale (Sellers, 1952, no. 819). James Peale has also been suggested. Between his return in the late spring of 1774 and 1776 John Carroll was not out of Maryland for sufficient time to have his portrait painted in any other location. Charles Willson and James Peale were in and out of Maryland in 1774 and 1775, the time when John Carroll would have worn lay clothing and when the age of the subject of this portrait and John Carroll would correspond. But the style most closely resembles that of Rembrandt Peale in the late 1790's. Rembrandt made his first youthful efforts at portraiture in 1791. By the late 1790's, when he was painting with the degree of finesse exhibited here, John Carroll was first Bishop of North America and over sixty. Two letters of Charles Willson Peale clearly indicate that Rembrandt was attempting to get a sitting for a portrait of John Carroll about 1800. There is evidence that this artist did get a sitting (see cat. No. 55). On the other hand, the high color in the cheeks is suggestive of the work of James Peale.

51.

Gilbert Stuart (1755-1828)

Unsigned, ca. 1803-1805

Oil on canvas, 29 x 24 inches

Georgetown University, Washington, D.C.

Provenance: Commissioned by Robert Barry of Baltimore; purchased by Lloyd N. Roger in 1838; by descent to his daughter; sold to Georgetown University in 1895

Reference: Pleasants, "Studies," no. 3461

Robert Barry, a devoted friend of John Carroll's, commissioned this portrait of Bishop Carroll for himself between 1803 and 1805, when Gilbert Stuart, the leading portraitist of the early American Republic, had a studio in Washington, D.C. at 7th and F Streets. Stuart's genius for isolating the essence of character is apparent in this deeply moving likeness of a man who

> *in the exercise of his sacred function . . . displayed a spirit of conciliation, mildness, and christian humility which greatly endeared him to those under his charge.*
>
> *His manners and deportment in private life were a model of the clerical character; dignified yet simple, pious but not austere. This secured him the affectionate attachment of his friends and the respect of all . . . (American and Commercial Advertiser,* Baltimore, December 4, 1915).

RELATED PORTRAITS:

(51A) Unknown artist after Gilbert Stuart. Portrait owned in 1926 by H. P. Chilton, Oyster Bay, New York. Presently unlocated; known through a photograph at Frick Art Reference Library, New York.

(51B) Unknown artist after Gilbert Stuart. Owned in 1929 by J. C. Goodfellow, Long Island, New York; then on loan to Georgetown Visitation Convent, Washington, D.C. Presently unlocated; known through a photograph at Frick Art Reference Library, New York.

(51C) Messrs. Bogle of Baltimore after Gilbert Stuart. An engraving for *Biographical Sketch of the Most Rev[erend] John Carroll . . .*, edited by John Carroll Brent (1843), frontispiece, 4 5/16 x 3 1/2 inches.

(51D) R. Dudensing after Gilbert Stuart. An engraving for *Lives of the Deceased Bishops of the Catholic Church in the U.S.* by Richard H. Clarke (1872), vol. I, frontsipiece, 4 1/4 x 3 1/2 inches.

John Carroll

52.

Jeremiah Paul ? (?-1820)

Unsigned, ca. 1806-1813

Oil on canvas, 30 7/8 x 25 1/4 inches

The Archdiocese of Baltimore

Reference: Pleasants, "Studies," no. 2208

William Dunlap, the "jovial and creative American Vasari," describes Jeremiah Paul as

> *One of the unfortunate individuals, who, showing what is called genius in early life, by scratching the lame figures of all God's creatures, on every thing that will receive chalk or ink, are induced to devote themselves to the fine arts, without the means of improvement, or the education necessary to fit them for a liberal profession. They arrive at a certain point of mediocrity, are deserted, and desert themselves* (Dunlap, Vol. II, p. 102).

Listed in the Baltimore Directories for 1807 and 1808, Paul was obviously in Baltimore by the previous year, as proved by a letter, dated July 9, 1806, from John Carroll to his friend James Barry. The Bishop writes that he is sending Jeremiah Paul to see the Gilbert Stuart portrait (Cat. No. 51), which Barry had commissioned, so that Paul can employ an artist to make an engraving. He indicates that Stuart himself will probably not get around to making one:

> *Mr. Paul is a painter of eminence, who has recommended himself very much by his performances here. He was anxious to take my portrait, with a view of engraving it, to which I would not consent, out of delicacy for Stuart — But as he [Stuart] will never probably execute his professed intention & Mr. Paul, a good judge, will employ an artist of great merit for the engraving, I have referred him to you for permission; requesting you at the same time to act with perfect freedom being no farther engaged to the bearer of this, [Paul] than to introduce him to, and inform you of his business.* (John Carroll to James Barry, Archives of the Archdiocese of Baltimore, 9c8).

Comparison of an engraving after "J. Paul" (Cat. No. 53) with the Stuart portrait of the Bishop is actually the strongest indication that Paul did go to Barry. Comparison of this oil portrait with the same engraving clearly indicates that Paul also had a hand in the oil portrait, if not as the artist, then certainly as a source for it. In 1813 Paul exhibited at The Pennsylvania Academy of The Fine Arts (Rutledge, p. 272) a portrait of Bishop Carroll (No. 95, p. 18). Since the *Cumulative Record* (Rutledge, p. 4) does not include engravings, this entry would suggest that Jeremiah Paul did execute an exhibitable oil portrait of John Carroll even though he did not get a sitting from life.

An examination of the canvas of this portrait attributed to Paul indicates that it could date from the period 1806-1813. However, in form, it radically differs from the Stuart which Paul was supposed to have copied. The pose, background, vestments, and eye color (blue in Stuart portrait; brown in this one) are all dissimilar. In fact, the only element which tellingly relates this to Stuart's work is the mannerism of the missing finger of the hand. Why is this portrait not closer in form to the Stuart? We may presume from John Carroll's letter that Paul's ultimate goal was an engraving. Paul could have made several different sketches from the Stuart for this purpose, and at a later date decided that he also wanted to execute an exhibitable

painting. He composed the painting from the sketches or drawings after the Stuart, making obvious and deliberate changes from the Stuart in order to be able to exhibit a portrait, as he did in 1813, without being accused of plagiarism. Actually the painting could have been executed after the engraving was published in 1812. That Paul's sketches intended as the basis for an engraving were without color could explain the fact that Carroll's eyes in the Stuart portrait are blue and in this one brown. The conclusion to be drawn is that this portrait is very possibly by Paul but does not serve as the basis for his famous engraving. Rather, it is an independent work from the same source: the artist's sketches or models for the engraving after the Stuart.

53.

William S. Leney, F.S.A. (1769-1831) and Benjamin Tanner, F.S.A. (1775-1848) after Jeremiah Paul (?-1820)

Engraving, 1812

Legend: *Painted by J. Paul./Engraved by W. S. Leney F.S.A./ & B Tanner F.S.A./ Reverendissimus/JOANNES CARROLL, S.T.D. ARCHIEPISCOPUS BALTIMORIENSIS PRIMUS/Entered according to Act of Congress the 9th day of April, 1812, by Benj*[n] *Tanner, of the State of Pennsylvania/The Most Reverend/JOHN CARROLL D.D./FIRST ARCHBISHOP OF BALTIMORE/Published 1st June 1812 by BENJAMIN TANNER Engraver. No. 74 South Eighth Street, Philadelphia.*
Image size: 21 1/2 x 17 5/8 inches

National Portrait Gallery, Smithsonian Institution, Washington, D.C.

This engraving clearly combines elements from both the Gilbert Stuart portrait of John Carroll (Cat. No. 51) and the portrait of the Bishop attributed to Jeremiah Paul (Cat. No. 52), although the mannerism of the missing finger in the hand found in both of the oil portraits is not perpetuated in this engraving. The head and the vestments are closely related to the portrait attributed to Paul (Cat. No. 52). In all other respects, the engraving is closer to the painting by Stuart, yet the legend clearly states "painted by J. Paul." The question is how were the head and vestments of the work attributed to Paul combined with the background and pose of the Stuart to produce the final version of the engraving? It is highly unlikely that Leney and Tanner would have created the composition themselves. Paul must have made a model, now lost, which more closely resembles the engraving as we know it, and this, not the painting attributed to Paul, is the basis for this engraving. The model, then, would have been based upon the Stuart which Paul was sent to see for that purpose but with sufficient differences in the head and vestments to make "painted by J. Paul" an accurate statement. Whether the hand was corrected by Paul or by Leney and Tanner cannot be determined.

RELATED PORTRAIT:
(Cat. No. 54)

JOHN CARROLL

54.

Henry Bryan Hall (1808-1884) after William S. Leney, F.S.A. (1769-1831) and Benjamin Tanner, F.S.A. (1775-1848)

Engraving, 1850-1884

Legend: *Painted by J. Paul/Eng^{d}. by H. B. Hall/JOHN CARROLL, D.D.*

Image size: 5 1/4 x 4 1/4 inches

National Portrait Gallery, Smithsonian Institution, Washington, D.C.

This engraving is after Cat. No. 53.

Related Portrait:

(54A) Samuel Hollyer (1826-1919) after William S. Leney, F.S.A. (1769-1831) and Benjamin Tanner, F.S.A. (1775-1848). Engraving, 1888. Legend: *Eng^{d} by S. Hollyer / Most Rev. John Carroll / Archbishop of Baltimore / Copyright by John G. Shea 1888.* Overall size: 9 15/16 x 6 1/16 inches. National Portrait Gallery, Smithsonian Institution, Washington, D.C.

This engraving may be after the Leney and Tanner (Cat. No. 53) or the H. B. Hall engraving (Cat. No. 54).

55.

Rembrandt Peale (1778-1860)

Unsigned, ca. 1809

Oil on canvas, 29 3/16 x 24 3/4 inches

The Archdiocese of Baltimore

The subject of this very fine portrait is now identified as John Carroll. On April 29, 1809 Charles Willson Peale wrote to Bishop Carroll: "My son Rembrandt told me that you had consented to sit to him sometime back" (Peale Papers, American Philosophical Society). On the same day he wrote to Rembrandt Peale in Baltimore: "I am sorry Bishop Carroll declines sitting for his portrait, because I know you would have made it a fine one" (Peale Papers, American Philosophical Society). But the Bishop must have relented, for in the copy of the Peale Museum Sale Catalogue of 1854 annotated by Rembrandt Peale, he has initialed entry no. 222, the portrait of John Carroll, indicating that he had painted it and not his father Charles Willson.

56.

John Sartain (1808-1897) after Joseph-Pierre Picot de Limoëlan Clorivière (1768-1826)

Mezzotint

Legend: *PAINTED BY I. P. DE C. / ENGRAVED BY J. SARTAIN. / The Most Rev. John Carroll / First Archbishop of Baltimore / Pub. by John Murphy, Baltimore /Copyright Secured*

Image size: 4 1/4 x 3 5/8 inches

The Maryland Historical Society, Baltimore

This engraving by John Sartain, one of the most prominent engravers of the day, is a record of the miniature of John Carroll by de Clorivière (Cat. No. 56A). De Clorivière, a member of the *petite noblesse*, officer in the Guards and ardent Royalist, was forced to flee France because of his part in a plot on Napoleon's life in 1800. He worked professionally as a painter from about 1803 to 1807 in Savannah, Charleston, and Baltimore where he entered the Sulpician Seminary of St. Mary's in the latter year. De Clorivière was ordained by Archbishop Carroll in 1812. He ended his days as priest and confessor to the Convent of the Visitation in Georgetown, D.C., and was venerated as its second father-founder. The completed facade of the Catholic Cathedral in Baltimore is shown in the background of the engraving.

RELATED PORTRAITS:

(56A) Joseph-Pierre Picot de Limoëlan de Clorivière (1768-1876). Miniature portrait. Presently unlocated; known through the engraving after the miniature and Rutledge, p. 76.

(56B) Unknown artist after Joseph-Pierre Picot de Limoëlan Clorivière (1768-1826). Engraving, image size: 3 7/16 x 2 7/8 inches.
Legend: *I. P. de C. pinx.*[t] */ A sculp.*[t] */ The Most Reverend / JOHN CARROLL, / Archbishop of Baltimore, / CATHOLIC METROPOLITAN / of the United States in N. America. / The first Bishop of Baltimore; consecrated A.D. 1790, / and raised to the dignity of Archbishop in 1810. / He was born in the State of Maryland, / on the 8th of Jan*[y] *1736* [*sic*] */ and died in Baltimore the 3rd of Dec.*[r] *1815*. The Maryland Historical Society, Baltimore./An engraving after Cat. No. 56A.

ADDITIONAL PORTRAITS OF JOHN CARROLL:

(56C) Unknown artist. Unsigned, 19th century. Miniature wax relief profile, 3 3/4 x 3 inches. The Maryland Historical Society, Baltimore, Gift of Mr. Joseph H. Bokel through Mrs. William H. Whitridge. Reference: Pleasants, "Studies," no. 1362.

(56D) Unknown artist, unsigned and undated. Miniature wax relief profile, 4 x 2 1/2 inches. The Maryland Historical Society, Baltimore.

(56E) Patience Wright (1725-1786). Inscribed across bottom: *RRJ Carroll ABB*. Wax relief profile, 3 3/4 x 2 1/2 inches. Presently unlocated; known through a listing in *Art in New Jersey From 1776-1876* (Montclair Art Museum, January 1-28, 1945, n.p. [51]).

Patience Wright who achieved great success in New York, Philadelphia, and London, is reputed to have executed a small wax profile of Bishop John Carroll. As Patience Wright did not rturn to America before her death and since Carroll was not ordained first Bishop of North America until six years after her death, it is rather unlikely that she did this profile model of Carroll. Wright's work was exhibited at the Montclair Art Museum in 1945, but the record of the owner at that time cannot be located.

MARY CARROLL (Mrs. Richard Caton), 1770-1846

(Eldest surviving child of CCC and MDC)

57.

Unknown artist after Robert Edge Pine (before 1730-1788)

Engraving, 1855

Legend: *MRS. RICHARD CATON, (Polly Carroll.)/From an original picture by R. E. Pine, in possession of/Mrs. MacTavish, Baltimore/New York, D. Appleton & C° 346 & 348 Broadway.*

Image size: 6 5/16 x 4 11/16 inches

The Maryland Historical Society, Baltimore

By all accounts "Polly" Carroll was so charming that she appeared beautiful without in fact being so. An English visitor to Baltimore in 1828 wrote that she was

> *one of the most accomplished persons, perhaps, in the world . . . Baltimore will never produce such another female. . . . She appears to be about sixty-five years of age; rather lusty, taller than the ordinary height, round face and very handsomely featured, but her manners were the most fascinating of any person I had ever known. Sweetness and grace mark her every word and gesture* (Semmes, p. 216).

It is unfortunate that the only surviving contemporary portrait of "Polly" Carroll is apparently the small head in the *Departure of Charles Carroll, Jr.* (Cat. No. 57F). This engraving after Cat. No. 57E appeared in Griswold's *The Republican Court . . .* (between pp. 208-209).

RELATED PORTRAITS:

(57A) Formerly attributed to Robert Edge Pine (before 1730-1788). Unsigned, before 1855. Oil on canvas, 29 x 24 1/2 inches (approx.). Presently unlocated; known through a photograph Provenance — part of The MacTavish Collection. Reference: Pleasants, "Studies," no. 1665. This portrait is based upon the head of Polly in the *Departure of Charles Carroll, Jr.* (Cat. No. 57F). Since the *Departure* was never owned by Mrs. MacTavish, this portrait probably served as the source of the engraving (Cat. No. 57) which would indicate that this painting was in existence prior to 1855, the date the engraving was published. It is not believed to be by Pine but was undoubtedly the prototype for 57B. It is considered a companion piece to a portrait of Richard Caton (Cat. No. 60A), also now unlocated.

(57B) Unknown artist after Robert Edge Pine (before 1730-1788). Unsigned, 20th century. Oil on canvas, 29 x 24 1/2 inches (approx.). Private Collection of a Descendant. Provenance — part of The MacTavish Collection. This portrait is a 20th century copy of Cat. No. 57A.

ADDITIONAL PORTRAITS OF MARY CARROLL CATON:

(57C) Attributed to Robert Field (ca. 1769-1819). Unsigned, ca. 1803. Miniature, watercolor on ivory, 3 x 2 1/4 inches. Destroyed in fire in 1973, known through a photograph. Provenance — by direct descent through the sitter's daughter Emily MacTavish to the last owner; part of The MacTavish Collection. Reference: Pleasants, "Studies," no. 3305.

There is a question that this miniature may not be Mary Carroll Caton, but her sister Catherine Carroll Harper. Unfortunately, the only certain likenesses of both Mary and Catherine, as young women, are the idealized renderings in Pine's *The Departure of Charles Carroll, Jr.* (Cat. No. 57F). At that time (1785), Catherine was only seven or eight. These factors make any definitive statement concerning identity extremely difficult, but the subject of this miniature does not closely resemble Mary from the few clues we have concerning her appearance. We know that Catherine was painted at least once for on September 22, 1817, Mary Diana Harper, her eldest daughter, then in France at school, writes to her father Robert Goodloe Harper: "I should like very much to have the portrait of my dear Mama" (MdHi, ms. 430). It does not seem likely that a young girl in school would ask that a large portrait be sent to her from Maryland. Mary Diana must have been referring to a miniature, perhaps this one. Regardless of the identity of the subject, this miniature strongly suggests attribution to Robert Field.

Mary Carroll

PLATE 57E

(57D) Attributed to Washington Allston (1779-1843). Signed and dated upper left: *W. Allston 1820.* Oil on canvas, 18 x 14 1/2 inches. Presently unlocated, known through a photograph. Provenance — unrecorded until bought by "a Rosenthal" in the Parke-Bernet Sale, New York, of the Lincoln Isham Collection and others on March 31, 1939. Reference: Pleasants, "Studies," no. 1917.

Consideration of the lives of the subject and artist makes it highly unlikely that this portrait is by Allston. It has been pointed out that this artist never signed his few portraits as boldly as was done in this canvas. Allston's portraits were mainly vehicles for practice or were personal mementos of family and close friends. After his return from Europe in 1818 and his settlement in New England, Allston did not make a business of accepting portrait commissions. The subject appears to be about 50 (Mary's age in 1820) with dark eyes and could be, from comparison with the scant clues concerning her appearance, Mary Caton.

(57E) Charles Willson Peale (1741-1827). Unsigned, ca. 1773. Oil on canvas, 22 1/2 x 18 inches. Private Collection of a Descendant. Provenance — unrecorded until purchased at auction at Sloane's Gallery, Washington, D.C., on February 11, 1903, by the mother of the present owner; sold as a portrait of Mrs. Richard Caton. Charles Coleman Sellers has written: "As this portrait of unusual dignity and charm is thoroughly typical of Peale's Colonial work, a doubt must be raised as to the identity of the subject. It has not had a continuous private ownership. It is so similar in size, style and coloring to the portrait of Charles Calvert . . . as to be a possible companion piece. Her face bears a striking resemblance to Peale's miniature of Martha Custis (Sellers, p. 52).

The subject of this portrait also bears a resemblance both to the engraving of Polly (Cat. No. 57), and to another Peale portrait identified as "probably" Mrs. Charles Carroll of Carrollton (Cat. No. 43). The former resemblance raises the possibility that this is Mrs. Richard Caton, painted at the time of her marriage in 1786 or a year or two before. The latter raises the possibility that this is another portrait of the Signer's wife.

PLATE 57F

ADDITIONAL PORTRAIT, *The Departure of Charles Carroll, Jr.:*
(57F) Robert Edge Pine (before 1730-1788). Unsigned, ca. 1785. Inscribed on the lid of trunk in lower right corner: *Mast Charles Carroll/Leige [sic] by the way of/London.* Oil on canvas, 60 x 80 inches. Private Collection of a Descendant. Provenance — by direct descent through Charles Carroll of Carrollton's grandson Charles Carroll of Doughoregan to the present owner.

This charming conversation piece memorializes the departure of Charles Carroll of Homewood to study at the English College in Liège, Belgium. A letter written by Charles Carroll of Carrollton to his London agents (New York Public Library; Arents Collection, July 31, 1785) reveals that young Charles departed from Georgetown (now District of Columbia) in early August of that year. The family members are identified from left to right as follows: "Nancy" [Anne] Darnall (d.1788) who was Molly Carroll's aunt and Charles Carroll's second cousin and who joined the Signer's household after his wife Molly died in 1782; Charles Carroll's two daughters — Mary and Catherine; the Signer himself; and then his son, Charles Carroll of Homewood. The suggestion that the figure of "Nancy" is, in fact, a posthumous portrait of Molly does not seem likely.

The heads of the subjects were painted on separate pieces of canvas and inserted into the whole. This was a frequent practice of the artist, who then engaged assistants, including his wife, to complete the rest of the painting. It is said that Pine was taking the likenesses of the Carrolls in the summer of 1785 after painting George Washington at Mount Vernon in April of that year (Hart, *Pennsylvania Magazine*, p. 9).

Richard Caton, 1763-1845

(Son-in-law of CCC and MDC)

58.

Attributed to Gilbert Stuart (1755-1828)

Unsigned, 1803-1805

Oil on canvas, 28 11/16 x 23 3/4 inches

Private Collection of a Descendant

Provenance: By direct descent through the sitter's daughter Emily MacTavish to the present owner; part of The MacTavish Collection

Reference: Pleasants, "Studies," no. 3310

Born in Liverpool, England, Richard Caton settled in Baltimore about 1785. By March 1787 Charles Carroll of Carrollton was forced to write his second cousin Daniel Carroll of Duddington (1764-1849), the "cousin long-legs" of his daughter Mary's childhood, who had asked for Mary Carroll's hand:

> *As the intelligence I am going to give you may make some alterations in your plans, although disagreeable, I must impart it to you. My daughter, I am sorry to inform you, is much attached to, and has engaged herself to, a young English gentleman of the name of Caton. I do sincerely wish that she had placed her affections elsewhere, but I do not think myself at liberty to control her choice, when fixed on a person of unexceptionable character. My assent to this union is obtained on two conditions: that the young gentleman shall extricate himself from some debts which he has contracted, and shall get into a business sufficient to maintain himself and a family . . .* (Eberlein & Hubbard, p. 359 and Stirling, p. 1058).

Richard and Mary were married November 25, 1787. The dashing groom never managed to extricate himself from debt to the end of his days, although he was entrusted with the considerable management of his father-in-law's financial affairs! This portrait from the MacTavish Collection, attributed to Gilbert Stuart by family tradition, shows the handsome Caton in middle age.

Related portrait:
(Cat. No. 59)

59.

Charles Volkmar [Wolkmar] (ca. 1809-1892), formerly attributed to Richard Caton Woodville (1825-1855)

Signed and dated lower left: *Wolkmar/1846*

Oil on panel, 10 3/4 x 8 3/8 inches

The Maryland Historical Society, Baltimore

Gift of Mr. J. Gilman D'Arcy Paul, 1949

Provenance: By direct descent through the sitter's granddaughter Emily MacTavish; part of The MacTavish Collection; purchased from Mary Carroll MacTavish by Mr. Paul for presentation to the present owner

Reference: Pleasants, "Studies," no. 3312

Recent laboratory examination revealed the signature of Charles Volkmar and the date 1846 on this portrait. Charles Volkmar was a portrait and landscape painter who was born in Germany about 1809 and came to Baltimore in 1836. He was also known as a retoucher and restorer of old, faded or mutilated canvases. This incisive character study was painted by Volkmar when Richard Caton was in his eighties.

Related Portrait:

(59a) Unknown artist. Unsigned?, date unknown. Oil on canvas, 11 x 8 inches. Presently unlocated; known through a 1948 family inventory of The MacTavish Collection. Provenance — part of The MacTavish Collection.

A second portrait of Richard Caton, the same size as Cat. No. 59, is listed on the 1948 inventory but is not recorded elsewhere. Its listing may be an error.

60.

Edward Weber & Co. (ca. 1835-ca. 1851) after Charles Volkmar (1809-1892)

Lithograph, ca. 1835-1851

Legend: *Lith. by E. Weber & Co Balt^{o}.*

Inscribed on mount: *Richd Caton* (facsimile signature)

Image size: 7 1/8 x 6 7/16 inches

The Maryland Historical Society, Baltimore

Gift from the J. Gilman D'Arcy Paul Estate, 1972

This engraving is clearly after Charles Volkmar's portrait of Richard Caton (Cat. No. 59). It was the inscription on the engraving's mount that corrected the identity of the subject of Volkmar's portrait as family tradition had considered it a likeness of John MacTavish.

There is a photograph of this engraving with J. Hall Pleasants "Studies," no. 3312 showing the legend *R. Caton Woodville pinx^{t}.* on the left and directly opposite it on the right, *Lith. by E. Weber & Co Balt^{o}.* At present no engraving can be located which includes both parts of the legend. The one illustrated here has been trimmed, but evenly. Therefore, it is not possible to see how the left side of the legend could have been cut off.

Additional Portrait of Richard Caton:

(60A) Attributed to Robert Edge Pine (1730?-1788) Unsigned, ca. 1787. Oil on canvas, 25 x 21 inches (oval). Presently unlocated; known through a photograph. Provenance — by direct descent through the sitter's daughter Emily MacTavish to Mary Carroll MacTavish; part of The MacTavish Collection; sold, circumstances unknown. Reference: Pleasants, "Studies," no. 1664.

The sitter has been identified by family tradition as Richard Caton. The portrait is of a young man in his mid or late twenties as Caton would have been about 1787, but it does not appear to have been painted that early. A photograph of this portrait taken about 30 years ago shows it to be a companion piece of the head of Mary Caton attributed to Robert Edge Pine (Cat. No. 57A). The subject does not bear resemblance to known portraits of Richard Caton, and the style does not appear to be that of Pine.

(60B) Attributed to Robert Edge Pine. Unsigned. Oil on canvas 24 x 20 inches (oval). Presently unlocated; listed as part of The MacTavish Collection.

In several of the lists of The MacTavish Collection, there is mention of this oval portrait of Richard Caton which is identical in size to (Cat. No. 60A). No evidence has come to light regarding this portrait.

Charles Carroll of Homewood, 1775-1825

(Only surviving son of CCC and MDC)

61.

Charles Balthazar Julien Févret de Saint Mémin (1770-1852)

Unsigned, 1800

Charcoal and white chalk on paper, 20 3/8 x 14 3/4 inches

The Baltimore Museum of Art 39.183

Bequest of Ellen H. Bayard

Provenance: By direct descent through the sitter's daughter Mrs. Richard Henry Bayard to Ellen H. Bayard

Reference: Pleasants, "Studies," no. 21

This portrait of Charles Carroll of Homewood has been dated 1800 (Dexter, no. 333). Since almost all of Saint-Mémin's subjects for that year are Philadelphians, this portrait must have been executed in Philadelphia where he married Harriet Chew on July 17, 1800.

Related Portraits:

(61A) Charles Balthazar Julien Févret de Saint-Mémin. Engraving, 1800. 2 1/2 inches in diameter (oval, image size). Collection of the Daughters of the American Revolution Museum, Washington, D.C.

Saint-Mémin charged gentlemen $25 for a handsome profile portrait, a copper plate, and twelve engravings. This is one of the engravings that would have been included with Cat. No. 61.

CHARLES CARROLL OF HOMEWOOD

62.

Robert Field (ca. 1769-1819)

Signed and dated lower left: *RF/1800*

Miniature, watercolor on ivory, 3 x 2 1/4 inches (oval)

Private Collection of a Descendant

Provenance: By direct descent through the sitter's daughter Mrs. Isaac Rand Jackson to the present owner

This exceptionally fine example of a Robert Field miniature reveals the "corpulent" tendencies of the Signer's only son who inherited every advantage, little of his father's steadiness but was adept at spending his father's money, especially on the beautiful house from which he took his name. The date on the miniature is the year of Charles Carroll of Homewood's marriage to Harriet Chew. It is not a companion piece to the Field miniature of his wife (Cat. No. 63) which is dated the same year but is not the same size and differs substantially in the background.

Additional portrait of Charles Carroll of Homewood:
(62A) Rembrandt Peale (1778-1860). Unsigned, ca. 1798. Oil on canvas, 30 x 25 inches (sight). Private Collection of a Descendant. Provenance — given by the sitter to Mary Wallace; bequeathed to her daughter Mary Walker Ranken. Charles Carroll of Homewood was a young man in his early twenties and had recently returned from his education abroad when he sat for this portrait — a superior example of Rembrandt Peale's early work. A letter pasted on the reverse of the portrait states:

Charles Carroll of Carrollton, Junior, Esqr. This is his likeness — which he gave to Mary Wallace — and which she received on Monday, Jan. 28, 1799. —
Drawn by Mr. Rembrandt Peal [sic] — when Mr. Carroll was 22 years old, and Mary Wallace gives this to her daughter Mary Walker Ranken at her decease.

How this portrait returned to the Carroll family is not known. Whether the Mary Wallace who married Colonel T. W. Veazey in 1812 at Elkton is the Mary Wallace referred to in the above letter has not been determined.

Mrs. Charles Carroll of Homewood (Harriet Chew), 1775-1861

(Daughter-in-law of CCC and MDC)

63.

Robert Field (ca. 1769-1819)

Signed and dated right of center: *RF/1800*

Miniature, watercolor on ivory, 3 3/4 x 2 3/4 inches (oval)

Private Collection of a Descendant

Provenance: By direct descent through the sitter's daughter Mrs. Isaac Rand Jackson to the present owner

The few extant portraits of Harriet Chew, daughter of Benjamin Chew, Chief Justice of Pennsylvania, are witness to her beauty. Her charm was as famous for, when George Washington sat to Gilbert Stuart, it is said that he would urge Harriet to accompany him. The President said her conversation "should give his face its most agreeable expression" (Griswold, p. 412). This charming miniature, painted at approximately the same time as her husband's (Cat. No. 62), shows her in 1800, the year she was married.

64.

Thomas Sully (1783-1872)

Signed and dated lower left corner: *TS 1822*

Oil on canvas, 30 x 25 inches

Collection of Mrs. John R. Sabina

Provenance: By direct descent through Charles Carroll of Carrollton's granddaughter Mrs. Richard Henry Bayard to the present owner

Reference: Pleasants, "Studies," no. 1981

Thomas Sully's contribution to the iconography of the Carroll family is great indeed. The Signer himself would come later (see Cat. Nos. 31-37), but in 1822 the artist was extremely busy in and around Harriet Carroll's household which was then in Philadelphia (see Cat. Nos. 82, 82A, 83 & 86A). She and Charles Carroll of Homewood had separated in 1816 and she had gone back to Philadelphia with her children, much of the contents of Homewood, and the everlasting devotion and support of her father-in-law Charles Carroll of Carrollton.

The entry for this portrait (no. 291) in Biddle and Fielding's transcription of Sully's Register reads:

> *Portrait begun May 16th, 1822, finished July 6th, 1822. Bust.*
> *Signed TS 1822. Price $100.00*

Almost fifty, presumably sadder and wiser, Harriet is still a great beauty whose fascination is not lost on the artist. There is less of Sully's saccharine prettiness here and more of a sensitively expressed character than one usually finds in his work.

Additional portraits of Mrs. Charles Carroll of Homewood:

(64A) John Trumbull (1756-1843). Unsigned, 1793. Inscription on piece of paper on back: *Harriet Chew/daughter of Bertr Chew Esq. of/Philadelphia/Painted by/J. Trumbull 1793/ at Phila.* Miniature, oil on panel, 4 x 3 3/16 inches (sight). Yale University Art Gallery, New Haven. Provenance — purchased from the artist by the present owner. Reference: Pleasants, "Studies," no. 2010.

The identity of the subject of this miniature has always been unquestioned; however, the subject is pictured with red hair and blue eyes, and Harriet is known to have had very dark hair and dark eyes.

(64B) Unknown artist after John Trumbull (1756-1843). Engraving, 1855. Legend: *MRS. CHARLES CARROLL. JUN./(Harriet Chew)/From an original picture by John Trumbull. in the/Trumbull Gallery, Yale College, New Haven.* Image size: 6 5/16 x 3 11/16 inches. The Maryland Historical Society, Baltimore.

This engraving was included in *The Republican Court or American Society in the Days of Washington* (Griswold, p. 355) as was that of "Polly Caton" (Cat. No. 57). Although the engraving is based upon Cat. No. 64A, the subject is turned slightly to the left as in Sully's portrait, rather than facing front as in the miniature.

Mrs. Charles Carroll of Homewood

CATHERINE CARROLL (Mrs. Robert Goodloe Harper), ca. 1778-1861

(Youngest daughter of CCC and MDC)

No portrait beyond childhood located (see Nos. 57C, 57F & 65)

Catherine, wife of Robert Goodloe Harper, might be termed the mystery figure of Charles Carroll of Carrollton's immediate family. We catch glimpses of "Kitty" in family correspondence after her marriage in 1801 — the births, illnesses and deaths of her children (only two out of six reached adulthood); her visitings back and forth to her father and her "Sister Caton" (Mrs. Richard Caton); her concern that her dashing husband was being too gay without her in Washington when he was elected to the U.S. Senate in 1816; the burdens of Oakland, the beautiful estate her father had bought for her after her marriage; and her health which she always considered precarious. Unfortunately, no portrait beyond childhood has been located.

ROBERT GOODLOE HARPER, 1765-1825

(Son-in-law of CCC and MDC)

65.

Charles Balthazar Julien Févret de Saint-Mémin (1770-1852)

Unsigned, 1799

Charcoal and white chalk on paper, 20 1/2 x 14 1/2 inches

The Maryland Historical Society, Baltimore

Gift of Dr. Clapham Pennington in Memory of Emily Harper and Emily Harper Pennington, 1926

Provenance: By descent through Charles Carroll of Carrollton's grandson Charles Carroll Harper or granddaughter Emily L. H. Harper to Dr. Pennington

Reference: Pleasants, "Studies," no. 571

Charles Carroll at first did not approve of Robert Goodloe Harper as a husband for his youngest daughter, Catherine, even though the Signer's consent to the match was helped by the extensive written autobiography he demanded from Harper. Harper finally garnered sufficient honors to satsfy just about anyone, even though his financial situation, in the typical fashion of the Signer's children and in-laws, necessitated considerable support from his father-in-law.

Son of a Virginia cabinetmaker, Harper represented South Carolina in the Federal Congress from 1795 to 1801. He married "Kitty" Carroll in 1801, moved to Baltimore and became one of the most distinguished lawyers of his day. Harper was made a Major-General in the War of 1812. He was elected to the U.S. Senate in 1816 but resigned almost immediately to run as the Federalist Candidate for Vice-President.

This portrait of Robert Goodloe Harper by Saint-Mémin (Dexter, no. 453) was drawn while he represented South Carolina in the U.S. Congress. The artist's rendering hints at Harper's pomposity, which some observers noted, but does not reveal that he was a superb and persuasive orator, a social lion, and a dandy. He appeared at Monroe's Inaugural Ball in great splendor, his clothes of the latest fashion "perfumed like a milliner, with a large knot of black ribbon on each shoe" (Wharton, p. 135).

RELATED PORTRAIT:
(Cat. No. 66)

66.

Charles Balthazar Julien Févret de Saint-Mémin (1770-1852)

Engraving, 1799

Image size: 2 inches in diameter

Private Collection of a Descendant

Provenance: By descent through Charles Carroll of Carrollton's grandson Charles Carroll Harper or granddaughter Emily L. H. Harper to the present owner

As was Saint Mémin's practice, he charged $25 for a profile portrait, a copper plate, and twelve engravings. This engraving would have accompanied his drawing of Robert Goodloe Harper (Cat. No. 65). There are four locks of hair in the back of the frame. According to family tradition the whitish blond hair is that of Charles Carroll of Carrollton; the two circular locks of light and dark brown hair are that of Robert Goodloe Harper and his son Charles Carroll Harper; and the smaller reddish brown circular lock is that of a Harper child who died at a young age.

67.

Robert Field (ca. 1769-1819)

Unsigned, 1800-1801

Miniature, watercolor on ivory, 2 11/16 x 2 1/8 inches

The Maryland Historical Society, Baltimore

Gift of Dr. Clapham Pennington, 1929

Provenance: By descent through Charles Carroll of Carrollton's grandson Charles Carroll Harper or granddaughter Emily L. H. Harper to Dr. Pennington

Reference: Pleasants, "Studies," no. 1370

This miniature of Robert Goodloe Harper, like the Saint-Mémin drawing (Cat. No. 65), was painted while Harper was a South Carolina Congressman in Washington, D.C. Mrs. Thornton of that city wrote in her diary, December 26, 1800: "had the drawing room prepared for Mr. Field to paint in as he expects Mr. Harper to sit" (Piers, p. 151). Perhaps this very fine example of Field's work was a gift for Kitty, Harper's bride-to-be.

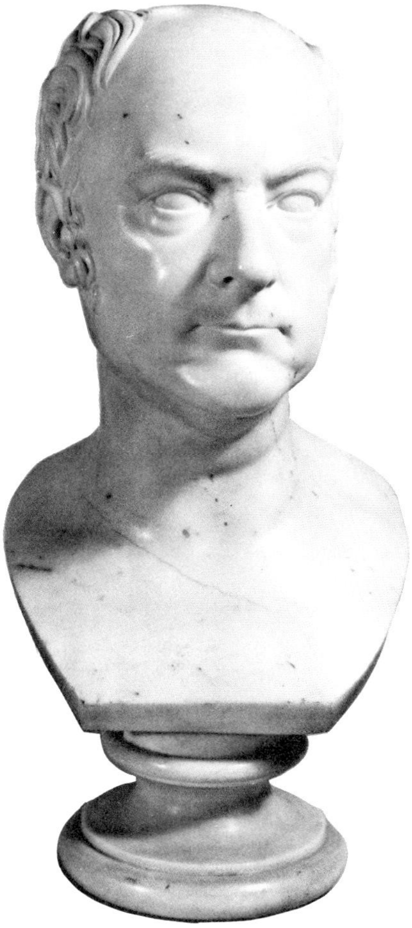

68.

Raimondo Trentanove (1792-1832)

Signed and dated along back of shoulder: *R: Trentanove, Fece Roma 1819*

Marble, 20 inches high

The Maryland Historical Society, Baltimore

Deposited by Dr. Clapham Pennington, 1927

Provenance: By descent through Charles Carroll of Carrollton's granddaughter Emily L. H. Harper to Dr. Pennington

In 1818 when Catherine and Robert Harper made their grand tour of Europe, this impressive bust of General Harper was executed in Rome by the young Italian sculptor Raimondo Trentanove, the favorite pupil of Canova. In a letter from Charles Carroll Harper, Robert's son, to his sister Emily, he refers to "the busts of my father" (MdHi, ms. 431, Box 10), presumably this marble and plaster model (Cat. No. 68A). In the same letter, he says that he hopes Emily can persuade their mother Catherine to sit for Greenough in Florence. There is no evidence that their mother complied.

Related portrait:

(68A) Raimondo Trentanove. Signed and dated along back of shoulder: *R: Trentanove, Fece Roma 1819*. Plaster cast of marble bust, 21 inches high. The Maryland Historical Society, Baltimore. This is the model for Cat. No. 68.

69.

Charles Bird King ? (1785-1862) or unknown artist, formerly attributed to J. W. Jarvis or Rembrandt Peale

Unsigned, ca. 1817 or ca. 1825

Stencilled on back: *Presented by Mr. William Read to Mr. William C. Pennington and Miss Emily L. Harper on the day of their marriage Dec. 7, 1853*

Oil on canvas, 29 13/16 x 24 3/4 inches

Collection of Edward Norriss Kimball, Jr.

Provenance: From the sitter to Mr. William G. Read (1800-1878), a brilliant lawyer who trained under Robert Goodloe Harper; gift of Mr. Read to Mr. and Mrs. W. C. Pennington to the present owner

Reference: Pleasants, "Studies," no. 594

In 1817, Charles Bird King exhibited a portrait of Robert Goodloe Harper "Painted for Joseph Delaplaine" at the Pennsylvania Academy of the Fine Arts (Sixth Annual

Exhibition, p. 12). Delaplaine had commissioned a portrait of Harper as well as one of the Signer (Cat. No. 42c) for his *Repository of the Lives and Portraits of Distinguished American Characters* (Philadelphia, 1815-[16]). The portrait illustrated here could be the work of Charles Bird King, but it is not typical of his style. On April 8, 1826, Charles Carroll Harper sent his grandfather the Signer an account of the bills he had paid toward settling his father's estate. In the accounting he lists "my father's portrait 41.00" (Collection of a Descendant). This reference suggests there must have been two portraits of Robert Goodloe Harper, one by King and one by an unknown artist.

Related portrait:
(69A) Robert Goodloe Harper Pennington (1854-1920) after Charles Bird King (?) or unknown artist. Unsigned, ca. 1885. Oil on canvas, 30 x 20 inches. The Maryland Historical Society, Baltimore. Gift of Miss Emily Louisa Hinton Harper, 1885. Reference: Pleasants, "Studies," no. 2812.

This copy was painted about 1885 by the subject's great-grandson, an artist by profession, who was known to have painted several copies of family portraits.

Elizabeth Caton (Lady Stafford), 1787-1862

(Eldest daughter of Mr. and Mrs. Richard Caton; Granddaughter of CCC and MDC)

70.

Thomas Phillips, R.A. (1770-1845)

Unsigned, ca. 1829

Oil on canvas, 34 5/8 x 26 7/8 inches

Private Collection

Provenance: By descent in the Stafford family until acquired by another Carroll descendant

In May 1816 Richard and Mary Caton's three daughters — Elizabeth, Louisa, and Marianne — and Robert Patterson, Marianne's husband, sailed for England on a European odyssey which changed all their lives. They embarked with impressive letters of introduction, the most important one from the Bagots. Sir Charles Bagot was British Minister to Washington and a relative by marriage of the first Duke of Wellington and his eldest brother, Marquess Wellesley.

Marianne's future stepdaughter, Hyacinthe Littleton, daughter of Marquess Wellesley, said that they were

> . . . *introduced to the Wellesley Circle by the Bagots. . . .* En attendant *the Duke of Wellington fell violently in love with her* [Marianne] *and it was the amusement of all London. She was evidently much pleased with the éclat of the thing but always behaved very correctly* (Butler, pp. 511-512).

The malicious English diarist Mr. Creevey wrote:

> *It is not amiss to see these sisters . . . not content with passing themselves off for tip-top Yankees . . . to* me *too, who remember their grandfather, old Caton, a Captain of an Indiaman in Liverpool, their father an adventurer to America, and know their two Aunts now at Liverpool . . . who move in about the* third rate *society of the town* (Butler, p. 497).

Creevey aside, "The American Graces" or "The Three Graces" (see Cat. No. 70B), as they became known in London society, were introduced to the Prince Regent and to everyone of consequence in London and Paris and almost immediately their letters home were full of descriptions of festivities in their honor, of long visits to such distinguished personages as The Earl of Leicester of Holkham, known as "Coke of Norfolk," and, above all, to the Duke of Wellington who had become their champion and from whom the little entourage was never far — whether at Cheltenham, England, in the summer of 1816, or at Wellington's French Occupation headquarters in Cambrai in 1817, or Mont-Saint-Martin, his house in the French countryside nearby. The Signer received a letter from Betsy describing their introduction to the King and Royal Family of France in February 1817 and commenting on "the long trains bordered with silver and gold and other concomitant circumstances" (Field, p. 189). The Signer was especially pleased with the attentions of the Duke of Wellington: "His affability is charming, for his attentions to my granddaughters. I feel most thankful" (Field, p. 189).

Although Marianne has always been referred to as the eldest of "The Three Graces," Elizabeth's birth date of May 30, 1787, was recently located and precedes the baptismal date of September 21, 1788 recorded for Marianne. Elizabeth, twenty-nine when she went abroad, was described by a contemporary British chronicler as

> *tall and remarkably graceful, with eyes of dark grey, expressing quickly both feeling and intelligence. She was more highly cultivated in literature than her sisters and her society was more largely sought by men of letters and the statesmen and thinkers of the time than by the ordinary beaux of society, for her mental qualities were brilliant and attractive* (*Baltimore American*, October 1, 1939).

It is through Elizabeth's letters that we learn so much of the Duke of Wellington and his interest in Charles Carroll's family. On March 5 of 1817, for example, she writes from the Duke's château near Cambrai:

> *The Duke of Wellington is all kindness and attention to us. I have just returned from riding with him. He mounted me on his fine horse Copenhagen which he rode during the battle of Waterloo* (MdHi, ms. 431, vol. 2).

Elizabeth never returned to America. In 1836, at the Church of St. Roche in Paris, she married Sir George William Jerningham, 8th Baron Stafford. There were no children from this marriage. "Betsy" lived at Costessey (or Cossey) Park, Norfolk, where this portrait of her remained into the present century. Thomas Phillips, a popular British portraitist in the first half of the 19th century, honors in his portrait of Elizabeth his reputation for portraits "characterized by simplicity of style and truthful finish, solid and carefully executed" (*Dictionary of Artists*, 1970, p. 331).

Until recently, it was believed that no individual likeness of "Betsy" still existed.

Discovery of a photograph of this portrait in the National Portrait Gallery, London, provided the clue which led to its discovery.

The only known portrait of the 8th Baron Stafford is a small pastel by Daniel Gardner. It shows the subject as a boy and is still in the possession of the Stafford family.

RELATED PORTRAITS:
(70A) Samuel Freeman (ca. 1773-1857) after Thomas Phillips R. A. (1770-1845). Engraving, published by Fisher, Son and Co., 1829. Size unknown. Collection of Comte Florian de Kergolay.

This engraving is based upon Cat. No. 70.

ADDITIONAL PORTRAIT, *The Three Graces:*
(70B) William Edward West ? (1788-1857). Unsigned, after 1824. Oil on canvas, 22 x 27 inches. Private Collection of a Descendant. Provenance — given to a Carroll descendant by a Carroll cousin; descended to the present owner. Reference: Pleasants, "Studies," no. 1982.

This portrait of "The Three Graces" was undoubtedly painted aftr 1824 when three of the Caton daughters had settled in England. The three figures here appear to be quite fancifully rendered and the "portraits" do not appear to be drawn from life. It has been attributed to William Edward West although it does not do justice to this artist's style. It is known, however, that, while in Paris in 1824-1825, a long-standing friendship developed between the artist and the "Three American Graces." Washington Irving visited West's Paris studio on different occasions when "Mrs. Patterson" and "Miss Caton" were sitting to him, and West was a member of their circle after he settled in England in 1825. That same year Marianne was engaged to Marquess Wellesley and Elizabeth Caton wrote to West in October:

> *My sister desires me to ask you if, she wishes to have her portrait and Lord Wellesley's taken, whether you would come to Ireland to do it in the course of the winter* (Dunn, p. 663).

The Caton sisters have been linked with a conversation piece entitled *The Muses of Painting, Poetry, and Music* (Collection of the Corcoran Gallery of Art, Washington, D.C.) which is attributed to West. The figures of the Muses bear no resemblance to the firmly identified portraits of the Caton sisters.

ADDITIONAL PORTRAIT OF ELIZABETH CATON:
(70C) Unknown artist. Engraving. Additional information unknown. Presently unlocated; known by an illustration in the *Baltimore American*, September 24, 1939.

This portrait differs in so many respects from Cat. No. 70 that it would seem to indicate another likeness of Elizabeth.

MARIANNE CATON (née Mary Anne; First, Mrs. Robert Patterson; Second, Marchioness Wellesley), 1788-1853

(2nd daughter of Mr. & Mrs. Richard Caton; Granddaughter of CCC and MDC)

71.

Marie-Victoire Jaquotot [Jaquetot and Jacquet] (1778-1855) after Sir Thomas Lawrence (1769-1830)

Signed and dated on back: *Victoire Jaquotot/pinxit/Paris 1818*

Inscribed on back in Elizabeth Caton's handwriting: *Belongs to Miss Caton*

Miniature, enamel on ivory, 3 1/4 x 2 3/4 inches

Collection of the Eighth Duke of Wellington

Provenance: In possession of the Dukes of Wellington

Marianne was reputed to be the most beautiful of "The American Graces." As a young girl in 1806, the acknowledged Belle of Baltimore married Robert Patterson (no portrait known), brother of the ill-fated Betsy who became Napoleon's sister-in-law for a brief period. Robert accompanied his wife and sisters-in-law to England in 1816, but he proved "rather an impatient traveller" (MdHi, mss. 431, December 1816) and little was said about him. All words were reserved for the Graces, especially Marianne. Byron patterned his Zuleika after her — "The might, the majesty of loveliness" (Stirling, p. 1034). Thomas Coke, Earl of Leicester of Holkham, referred to Marianne as ". . . a most beautiful and lovely woman . . . [whose] fascinating and lively deportment . . . will speak for itself" (Stirling, p. 1063). The Prince Regent upon meeting her is said to have exclaimed, ". . . is it possible that the world can produce so beautiful a woman!" (Stirling, p. 1063). And the Duke of Wellington wrote to Mrs. Arbuthnot:

> *I don't think I have been blinded by my partiality for her when I state that in disposition, temper, sense, acquirements and manners she is equal if not superior to any Woman of any country with whom I have ever been in Society* (Butler, p. 513).

Indeed "the Duke's romantic attachment to the lovely Marianne Patterson was no fabrication" (Longford, p. 46).

Marianne returned to Europe a widow in 1823, her husband Robert having died in the fall of 1822. On October 29, 1825, she married the Duke of Wellington's older brother, Marquess Wellesley who was then Lord Chancellor of Ireland. Wellington was undone by the news but remained Marianne's devoted friend and admirer to the end of his life.

Marie-Victoire Jaquotot painted this miniature of Marianne from a portrait of her by Sir Thomas Lawrence which the Duke of Wellington commissioned in 1816 or 1817. Lawrence must have painted Marianne's portrait in London, as the artist was apparently not in France before May 1817 when Wellington is known to have given Lawrence a partial payment for this portrait (see Cat. No. 71A). It also seems apparent that Wellington must have had the Lawrence portrait with him in France where he was stationed as Commander-in-Chief of the occupation forces, for this miniature was painted in Paris and is an exact copy of the portrait even to the precise details of the necklace and bracelet.

The inscription on the back of this miniature indicates that it may have been painted for Marianne's sister Elizabeth. At some future date, it must have been returned to the Duke's family.

Related Portraits:

(71A) Sir Thomas Lawrence (1769-1830). Unsigned, 1817. Oil on canvas, 30 x 25 inches. Collection of the Eighth Duke of Wellington. Provenance — Commissioned by the first Duke of Wellington; in continuous possession of the Dukes of Wellington. Reference: Pleasants, "Studies," no. 3407. This portrait is referred to in a copy of a memorandum to Sir Thomas Lawrence in the Duke's hand dated 9th May, 1817, which reads in part:

> *For my Picture for Mrs. Patterson £ 78.15*
> *Mrs. P's for me £ 52.10*
> (Wellington Private Correspondence, p. 158)

And again, July, 1817:

> *4th July, 1817, Paid £ 158.7 for the second half of my Picture for Mrs. Patterson and of her Picture for me and the Frames.*
> (Wellington Private Correspondence, p. 158)

(71B) Attributed to Sir Thomas Lawrence (1769-1830). Unsigned, ca. 1817. Oil on canvas, size unknown. Formerly Collection of Emily MacTavish; destroyed or presently unlocated; known through newspaper description on November 27, 1823 (see discussion). Provenance — deposited by Marianne at the Caton's house in 1823, part of The MacTavish Collection. When Marianne came home from Europe in the late spring of 1818, she brought with her a portrait of herself and one of the Duke of Wellington "by Lawrence." When she returned to Europe in 1823, she left the two portraits in Maryland, a fact confirmed by a memo in the Peale Museum, Baltimore:

> *Portraits — Duke of Wellington and Mrs. Patterson ditto. Mrs. Patterson left with other articles of furniture at Mrs. Caton's Jan. 2, 1823*

That the portrait of Marianne referred to in the memo was thought to be by Lawrence is indicated in the catalogue of the Second Annual Exhibition of the Peale Museum (1823) where No. 144, a portrait of Mrs. Robert Patterson by Sir Thomas Lawrence, is listed as belonging to Mrs. Patterson (*Rendezvous For Taste*, p. 35).

A notice in the *Baltimore American and Commercial Advertiser* for November 7, 1823, describes the portrait of Marianne, then on exhibition at the Peale Museum:

> *This is a beautiful picture. . . . The arms are not well drawn and want ease; the pearl necklace inimitable; the drapery tasteful and elegant.*

The wording of this notice is important, for the Duke of Wellington's portrait (identical to Cat. No. 71) does not have either drapery or pearl necklace, while the later portrait of Marianne (Cat. No. 72) does not show enough arm to merit a comment concerning this feature of the portrait, and it was probably not executed at this date. This indicates a variant, destroyed or now unlocated. The next mention of a "Lawrence" portrait of Marianne in Maryland was in 1828, five years after her return to Europe when her grandfather wrote to her: "I never cross, my dear Mary, your portrait by Sir Thomas Lawrence, without thinking it represents one I shall never see again" (MdHi, mss. 220, June 10, 1828). And Fanny Kemble at the Catons in January 1833 mentions seeing a "loving picture by Lawrence of the eldest of the three beautiful sisters, the daughters of Mrs. Caton" (Crawford, pp. 252-253). The continuous listing of this portrait as "by Lawrence" does not necessarily mean it was from his hand but could indicate that it is of the Lawrence type or from his studio.

72.

Sir Thomas Lawrence (1769-1830)

Unsigned, ca. 1825

Oil on canvas, 30 x 25 inches

From the Collection of Mr. William A. Dickey, Jr.

Lent by Mr. and Mrs. C. Edward Walter

Provenance: Bequeathed by the Marchioness Wellesley to her sister Lady Stafford and after her death to the 8th Baron Stafford; by descent in the Stafford family until its sale in London about 1913. It was resold twice again before being purchased by Mr. Dickey from Wildenstein and Co. about 1950; by descent to Mrs. Walter.

Marianne, Marchioness Wellesley, glittered as Vicereine of Ireland and afterwards as Lady of the Bed-Chamber to Queen Adelaide, whose husband William IV succeeded George IV in 1830. She died in her grace-in-favour apartment at Hampton Court, retaining "traces of her former beauty" to the end, although "bowed down by dropsied disease" (Perrine, p. 6). Marianne had no children by either marriage.

Soon after her second marriage, Marianne sat to Lawrence for a second portrait. It was three quarters finished at the time of Lawrence's death but was probably completed in his studio before it was delivered to her in 1831 (Garlick, p. 76).

In her will Marianne (Hall of Records, Annapolis, Baltimore City Wills, NH 26, pp. 227ff.) left this portrait to her sister Elizabeth, Lady Stafford, and directed that it go to Lord Stafford after Elizabeth's death.

Related Portraits:

(72A) Unknown artist after Sir Thomas Lawrence (1769-1830). Unsigned, date unknown. Oil on canvas, 30 x 25 inches. Private Collection of a Descendant, Courtesy of Kennedy Galleries, Inc., New York. Provenance — gift from Marchioness Wellesley to her nephew Charles Carroll MacTavish, Sr., in 1853; part of The MacTavish Collection; by direct descent to the present owner.

In the summer of 1853, months before her death, Marianne wrote Ella Scott MacTavish, the bride of her nephew Charles Carroll MacTavish as follows:

> *Tell him [Charles] I shall send him my picture by Sir Thomas Lawrence which hung In Ld Wellesleys room at Kingston House. He must promise me to burn the one you have at Carrollton for I should not like such a Sign Post to go down to posterity* (MdHi, mss. 216, Box 2).

As we know that the Staffords received their portrait of Marianne's second sitting to Lawrence (Cat. No. 72), it must be presumed that the one sent to Charles MacTavish was an early copy, possibly a studio copy of Cat. No. 72. This portrait (Cat. No. 72A) is quite possibly the one which Marianne sent. That she says "by Lawrence" may not necessarily mean by the *hand* of Lawrence. The "Sign Post" to which she refers would most likely have been the portrait Marianne left in Maryland (Cat. No. 71B). Either the "Sign Post" is presently unlocated or it was destroyed as she requested (see discussion, Cat. No. 72C).

(72B) Unknown artist after Sir Thomas Lawrence (1769-1830). Unsigned, prior to 1902. Oil on canvas, 30 x 25 inches. The MacTavish Collection; presently unlocated, known through an illustration in Field, facing p. 198, and through a photograph on file at the Frick Art Reference Library, New York (no. 22-11/0). Provenance — part of The MacTavish Collection. Reference: Pleasants, "Studies," no. 1666.

This, according to Pleasants and the Frick Art Reference Library note, is the portrait which Virginia Scott MacTavish referred to as being by Lawrence and which she left to Charles Carroll MacTavish, Jr., for life and after his death to the Metropolitan Museum of Art. In 1948, it was rejected by the Metropolitan as a copy. It is now unlocated. This varies from the other portraits related to the second sitting of Marianne in the substitution of a landscape background for the drapery.

(72C) Unknown artist after Sir Thomas Lawrence (1769-1830). Unsigned, date unknown. Oil on canvas, 30 x 25 inches. Presently unlocated; known through an illustration in *Rendezvous for Taste*, p. 24. Provenance — part of The MacTavish Collection.

In 1893, there were three portraits of the Marchioness Wellesley from the Collection of Mrs. Charles Carroll MacTavish listed in the *Maryland Historical Society Exhibition Catalogues 1848-1908*. Two are "by Lawrence" and one is "after Lawrence." There are two interpretations concerning the three entries in the 1893 list. The determining factor is whether or not the "Sign Post" was destroyed. If it was not, then the two portraits listed as "by Lawrence" would most likely be Cat. No. 71B, the variant that Marianne brought home with her in 1818 and which remained in Maryland, and Cat. No. 72A, the portrait Marianne sent to her nephew Charles Carroll MacTavish, Sr. There is evidence that the family considered both of these portraits to be "by Lawrence." The third listing would refer to Cat. No. 72B, the portrait published in Field in 1902 and offered to the Metropolitan.

Since Cat. No. 72C is only known through a poor reproduction, it is difficult to date this portrait, but it could be 20th century. It could have been done in Rome in the 1920's or 1930's when other MacTavish portraits were copied. However, if it is 19th century, then Cat. No. 71A, the "Sign Post," was destroyed. Cat. No. 72A, Cat. No. 72B, and this portrait, Cat. No. 72C, would be three portraits listed in 1893.

(72D) Sir Thomas Lawrence (1769-1830). Unsigned, ca. 1817. Drawing on canvas, dimensions unknown. Presently unlocated; known through Garlick (1962-1964, p. 247). Provenance — Lawrence sale, Christie's, June 19, 1830, no. 401; bought by Bt. Hixon.

PLATE 72F

(72E) Sir Thomas Lawrence (1769-1830). Unsigned ?, date unknown. Pencil and colors, 19 3/4 x 15 3/4 inches (oval). Presently unlocated; known through a catalogue of a sale "Properties of Duke of Leeds," Christie's, June 20, 1930. Provenance — Collection of Louisa Caton, Duchess of Leeds.

These two portraits (Cat. Nos. 72D and 72E) could be studies for the known portraits of Marianne or they could be clues to the format of the variant (Cat. No. 71B).

(72F) Andrew Robertson (1777-1845). Unsigned, date unknown. Inscribed on back: *Marianne, 2nd wife of Marquess Wellesley, K. G.* Miniature, watercolor, 7 1/4 x 5 1/4 inches. Collection of the Eighth Duke of Wellington. Provenance — Collection of Alfred Montgomery; to the present owner.

This miniature by Robertson is illustrated here as it occupies an interesting place in the iconography of Marianne. The only likeness known to have been engraved, it has been the most frequently reproduced portrait of her from the late 19th century and is, therefore, the image of her most widely known.

Alfred Montgomery was a close personal friend of the Marquess Wellesley and of Marianne. How the miniature came back to the Dukes of Wellington is not known.

(72G) T. A. Dean (fl. 1818-1840) after Andrew Robertson (1777-1845). Engraving, 19th century. Legend: *THE MOST NOBLE MARIANNE. / MARCHIONESS OF WELLESLEY. / Engraved by DEAN from a Miniature by Mrs [sic] ROBERTSON / London, Published by Edward Bull, 26, Holles Street.* National Portrait Gallery, London.

This is an engraving of Cat. No. 72F.

ARTHUR GERALD WELLESLEY, First Duke of Wellington, 1769-1852

(Brother-in-law of Marianne Caton)

73.

Sir Thomas Lawrence (1769-1830)

Unsigned, ca. 1814

Oil on canvas, 36 x 28 inches

The Wellington Museum, London

Provenance: Bequeathed by the Marchioness Wellesley (Marianne Caton) to the Second Duke of Wellington, 1853. Formerly at Stratfield Saye House; became National property in 1947

Arthur Wellesley, first Duke of Wellington, through "The American Graces," became closely involved with the Carroll family for three decades. It all started in the summer of 1816 when the Duke and the Caton-Patterson entourage were at Cheltenham, England. In 1817 and 1818, a great number of the letters which Betsy and Louisa wrote home to Maryland were from Mont-Saint-Martin, the Duke's house near Cambrai, France. In March 1818 Lady William Russell wrote from Paris to a friend:

> *Lord Kinnaird is here,* fra mille quai, *and the Duke of Wellington looks horridly ill,* si dice *that it is not the present* combinazione *but love; that he declares he never knew the meaning of the word until he saw Mrs. Patterson, and her departure for America* déchire son tendre coeur *in a terrible manner. He really looks mighty sick* (Butler, p. 497).

Wellington entertained Robert and Kitty Harper at Cambrai in 1818; when Marianne returned to America, still a married woman, he wrote long letters ending with such phrases as "God Bless you my dear Mrs. Patterson" and signed "Ever Yours most affectionately, Wn." He corresponded with the Signer Charles Carroll who sent him as a gift a copy of Durand's engraving (Cat. No. 3) after Trumbull's *Declaration of Independence* (New York Public Library, Arents Collection, CCC to Wm. Murdock, Esq., March 3, 1824). In 1845, when the American Graces' niece Mary Wellesley MacTavish married the Honorable Henry George Howard, the wedding took place at the Duke's London mansion, Apsley House, and he gave her away as he had her aunt Louisa twenty-seven years before (MdHi, Diehlman File).

This magnificent portrait of the Duke of Wellington by Sir Thomas Lawrence has always been dated 1814, or at the latest 1815, and is without a doubt the one that Marianne left at her death to the second Duke of Wellington. This does raise the question as to what portrait the Duke was referring to in his memo to Lawrence in 1817: "my picture for Mrs. Patterson" (*Wellington Private Correspondence,* p. 158).

An original of the Duke by Sir Thomas Lawrence was a very special gift to Marianne, and it is unlikely that she would have left it behind when she returned to Maryland in 1818, presumably for good. She also brought home a copy (Cat. No. 71B) of her portrait by Lawrence as the Duke of Wellington had commissioned the original (Cat. No. 71A) for himself.

Evidence of the fact that she brought a portrait of the Duke of Wellington to Maryland and that it was an original Lawrence is the following item in the Baltimore *American and Commercial Advertiser* for October 23, 1822 regarding certain items in the first annual exhibition of the Peale Museum:

> *140. Wellington, from Sir Lawrence. A fine picture — but remarkable, chiefly for being, by Lawrence. The style is beautiful, and the work, allowing somewhat for trick and foppery, both in the painter and the subject, is full of the master.*

Marianne left this portrait of the Duke with her parents Mr. and Mrs. Richard Caton prior to her return to Europe in 1823 (see memo, Cat. No. 71). On November 7, 1823, a review in the same newspaper of the second annual exhibition of the Peale Museum mentions the portrait by Lawrence of the Duke of Wellington on exhibit. The "proprietor" [owner] is Mrs. Patterson who had already returned to Europe.

In his *History of the Rise and Progress of the Arts of Design* (vol. III, p. 272, 1833), William Dunlap quotes the distinguished Baltimore collector Robert Gilmor as saying that there were two Lawrences at Mr. Caton's which must have been the Lawrence portrait of the Duke and the copy of Marianne's portrait by Lawrence considered to be an original or a product of Lawrence's studio. In the inventory of Mary Caton's effects (Hall of Records, Annapolis, Baltimore County Inventories, D.M.P. no. 59/1847-1848) dated 1847-48 is listed "Portrait of Wellington (Lawrence) $100.00." There is only one other portrait appraised for $25.00 and all other "paintings," "prints," 'pictures," "busts and casts," fifty-three in number, are appraised from 63¢ to $5.00. This is certainly proof that the portrait of the Duke of Wellington was indeed considered to be in a special class and much more so than that of Marianne which is not enumerated. Sometime after this inventory was made the portrait must have been returned to Marianne in England who then bequeathed it to the second Duke of Wellington.

RELATED PORTRAITS:

(73A) Rembrandt Peale (1778-1860) after Sir Thomas Lawrence (1769-1830). Unsigned, ca. 1819. Oil on canvas, 35 1/2 x 26 3/4 inches. The Museum of Fine Arts, Boston. Provenance — Collection of the Boston Museum and Gallery of Fine Arts, ca. 1841; Gift of the owners of the Boston Museum.

On June 9, 1822, Charles Willson Peale wrote his son Rubens of Rembrandt Peale:

> ... *by a catalogue of the Exhibition I find he has exhibited the portrait of Lord Wellington (a fac simile) he says* (Charles Willson Peale Letterbook, American Philosophical Society).

This portrait (Cat. No. 73A) is the facsimile referred to in Peale's letter.

(73B) Michael Laty (1826-1848) after Sir Thomas Lawrence (1769-1830). Signed and dated on back: *Laty pinx May/1847*. Oil on canvas, 36 x 29 inches. Formerly in The MacTavish Collection; destroyed by fire in 1973; known through a photograph. Provenance — by descent through Charles Carroll of Carrollton's granddaughter Emily MacTavish; part of The MacTavish Collection. Reference: Pleasants, "Studies," no. 1668.

After Mrs. Richard Caton's death in 1846 and before the portrait of the Duke of Wellington by Sir Thomas Lawrence was sent to Marianne in England, Michael Laty was commissioned to make a copy of the Lawrence portrait. Only one portrait of the Duke of Wellington is ever listed as being part of The MacTavish Collection in *The Maryland Historical Society Exhibition Catalogues, 1848-1908,* and it is recorded as being "by Lawrence." There is reason to believe that this was the copy by Laty for it was thought to be an original Lawrence by the family as recently as 1948. Under the will of Virginia Scott MacTavish, the Laty copy was left to her brother Charles Carroll MacTavish, Jr., for life and then to the Metropolitan Museum of Art. In 1948 when the "Lawrence" enumerated in Virginia Scott MacTavish's will was presented to the Metropolitan, it was rejected as a copy when the inscription on the back was discovered after the frame was removed. In a November 10, 1948, list of The MacTavish Collection, made when the collection was at the Peabody Institute, there is mention of this portrait, and it is correctly reattributed to Michael Laty.

It is interesting to note that Michael Laty was commissioned to make this copy the year after he was requested to make a copy of the Robert Field watercolor of Charles Carroll of Carrollton (Cat. No. 19).

(73C) Unknown artist after Sir Thomas Lawrence (1769-1830). Unsigned, 20th century. Oil on canvas, 36 x 29 inches. Hampton National Historic Site, Towson, Maryland. Provenance — The MacTavish Collection.

This copy, probably after the Laty, was undoubtedly made in Rome by the MacTavishes in the 1920's or 1930's. It is listed as a "modern copy" in the inventory of The MacTavish Collection made on November 10, 1948, when the collection was at the Peabody Institute.

(73D) W. H. Pyne ? (1769-1843) after Sir Thomas Lawrence (1769-1830). Unsigned; date unknown. Oil on canvas, 36 x 29 inches. Collection of the Peabody Institute, Baltimore. Presently unlocated; known through a 1956 Peale Museum Catalogue listing; no reproduction known.

In 1956 a portrait of the Duke of Wellington lent by the Peabody Institute was exhibited at the Peale Museum. It was not part of The MacTavish Collection and is presently unlocated. W. H. Pyne was an English watercolor painter who devoted the latter part of his career mainly to the literature of art. He is not known for making copies of oil portraits. It seems that either the attribution of the artist or the identity of the subject is incorrect.

Richard Colley Wellesley, Second Earl of Mornington, Marquess Wellesley, 1760-1842

(Grandson-in-law of CCC and MDC; Brother of the First Duke of Wellington)

74.

Sir Thomas Lawrence (1769-1830)

Unsigned, 1813

Oil on canvas, 52 x 40 3/4 inches

Her Majesty Queen Elizabeth II

Provenance: Presented by the Marquess Wellesley to Queen Victoria

Richard Colley Wellesley, eldest brother of the 1st Duke of Wellington and, by inheritance, Second Earl of Mornington, was created Marquess Wellesley in 1799 in recognition of an already distinguished career as a Member of Parliament, Junior Lord of the Treasury, and finally as Governor-General of India. The aging Wellesley had been Lord Lieutenant of Ireland for four years when he married his second wife, Marianne Patterson. She reigned in splendor as Vicereine of Ireland until 1828 when Wellington became Prime Minister and forced the resignation of his brother due to differences concerning British attitudes toward Ireland. Brilliant, and with every possible opportunity, the elder brother had not in the end made the most of his talents. Wellington's characterization of him when he learned of the impending marriage (he had reputedly introduced them in the first place) was not wide of the mark:

> . . . *Ld Wellesley was a man totally ruined; when he quitted Ireland, which he must soon do, he wd not have a house to take her to, or money to keep a carriage; that he had not a shilling in the world, &, moreover, was of a most jealous disposition, a violent temper & that he had entirely worn out his constitution by the profligate habits of his life* (Longford, p. 114).

But Marianne, of whom Wellesley's son-in-law said "a better person does not live . . . ill humour and prejudice seem quite foreign to her nature" (Butler, p. 561), from all reports, made quite a success of the situation. Wellesley was Lord Steward of the Royal Household in 1832-1833, again Lord-Lieutenant of Ireland in 1833-1834, and Lord Chamberlain in 1835.

This impressive portrait of Wellesley shows him in court dress, with the Order and Ribbon of the Garter, the Star of the Garter and the Garter with Lesser George. Lawrence had told the English diarist Farington in 1811 that Wellesley had

> *ruined His fortune by His excessive expences on Women. — With all his abilities He has so great a share of vanity, that at the age of abt. 53 Lawrence has noticed when His Lordship sat to him for His Portrait, that His Lips were painted* (Farington *Diary*, vol. VI, p. 258).

Related Portraits:

There are several replicas or copies of this portrait, notably at Eton College, Windsor; Ampleforth (formerly at Beningbrough); in the Oriental Club, London; in the Castle, Dublin; and from the collection of E. H. Riches, in the Foreign Office, London. Another descended in the family of the sitter's widow until presented to His Majesty King George VI by Sir Algernon Law in 1940.

It has been engraved numerous times, including among others, a mezzotint by C. Turner, 1815; a stipple engraving by G. Adcock, 1829; a line engraving by P. Lightfoot, 1839; a mezzotint by S. Cousins, 1842; a line engraving by G. Cook, 1846.

(74A) Unknown artist after Sir Thomas Lawrence (1769-1830). Unsigned, date unknown. Oil on canvas, 17 1/2 x 15 1/2 inches. Presently unlocated; known through The MacTavish Collection lists and inventories. Provenance — by descent through Charles Carroll of Carrollton's granddaughter Emily MacTavish; part of The MacTavish Collection. Reference: Pleasants, "Studies," no. 1667. Only one portrait of Marquess Wellesley appears in The MacTavish Collection lists between 1893 and 1948.

Louisa Caton (First, Lady Hervey-Bathurst; Second, Duchess of Leeds), ca. 1791-1874

(Third daughter of Mr. and Mrs. Richard Caton; Granddaughter of CCC and MDC)

75.

Sir Thomas Lawrence (1769-1830)

Unsigned, ca. 1817

Oil on canvas, 35 7/8 x 27 3/4 inches

The Art Museum, Princeton University, Princeton, New Jersey

Provenance: Estate of Lady Wimborne, 1928; presented to the present owner by Mrs. Donald Geddes, 1950

This voluptuous portrait of Louisa Caton was painted by Sir Thomas Lawrence while she was married to her first husband Felton Elwell Hervey-Bathurst. The youngest of "The Three Graces" and the first to make an English match, Louisa was, according to an early chronicle

> *small of stature, but of a beautiful figure, light and agile in all her movements, her conversation gay and playful, but commonplace. She had, however, her own peculiar charms, although in manners she differed from her sisters (Baltimore American,* October 1, 1939).

Her husband Felton Elwell Hervey-Bathurst had been Wellington's Aide-de-Camp at Waterloo. He and Louisa met within the Duke's circle not long after her arrival in Europe and were married at Apsley House, April 24, 1817, the Duke of Wellington giving the bride away. After the wedding, "Hervey" was posted to Cambrai, France, as secretary to Wellington. Throughout the rest of 1817 and into 1818 the Duke's house at Mont-Saint-Martin became the center of activity for the Caton girls and when they were not present, they never seemed to be far from Wellington's thoughts. Louisa wrote to her uncle Robert Goodloe Harper on June 28, 1817:

> *He* [the Duke] *writes to me always in the most affectionate manner. My sisters say he spoils me, indeed if I was his own child he could not appear more fond of me* (MdHi, ms. 431).

Louisa was a widow by October 1819. In 1828 she married Francis Godolphin d'Arcy Osborne, Marquess of Carmarthen who, two years later, became 7th Duke of Leeds. She had no children by either marriage.

Additional Portrait of Louisa Caton:

(75a) Mrs. Anne Mee (1791-1874). Unsigned ?, 1828-1838. Miniature, watercolor on ivory, 4 inches. Presently unlocated; known through a listing for a sale at Sotheby Co. on July 3, 1961. Provenance — purchased by a dealer named Clayton.

After Louisa married for the second time, Mrs. Anne Mee, a talented miniaturist and a favorite of George IV, must have painted her portrait.

(75b) James Thomson (1788-1850) after Mrs. Anne Mee (1791-1874). Engraving, date unknown. Legend: *The Rt. Hon. Louisa Catherine / Marchioness of Carmarthen / Engraved by Thomson from a Miniature by Mrs. Mee / Publ. by Edward Bull & Clinton, 26 Nollis St.* Size unknown. Presently unlocated; known through a photograph on file at the National Portrait Gallery, London.

This engraving after the miniature by Mrs. Mee which dates to the late 19th century became the recognized likeness of Louisa as it was reproduced in various publications.

Louisa Caton

Sir Felton Elwell Hervey-Bathurst, Bart., 1782-1819

(Grandson-in-law of CCC and MDC)

76.

Attributed to Thomas Heaphy (1775-1835)

Unsigned, 1813-1819

Oil on canvas, 50 x 40 inches

Collection of Frederick John Hervey-Bathurst

Provenance: By descent to the present owner

Louisa's husband "Hervey" was born Felton Elwell Hervey and assumed the name Bathurst from his mother's family in 1801. He was Aide-de-Camp to the Prince Regent as well as the Duke of Wellington, and in 1818 he was created a Baronet. One of the best eye-witness accounts of the Battle of Waterloo is the lengthy one he wrote Charles Carroll of Carrollton about 1817 ("Contemporary Letter on the Battle of Waterloo," *Nineteenth Century* Magazine, March 1893).

Thomas Heaphy, the artist to whom this portrait is attributed, was a talented watercolorist and portrait painter whose popularity for a time rivalled that of Sir Thomas Lawrence. In 1812 the Duke of Wellington invited Heaphy to the British camp in the Peninsula to paint the portraits of the English officers. Heaphy remained until the end of the Peninsular Campaign in 1814. The artist may have completed this portrait of Hervey in his London studio upon his return from Spain. Preliminary work could not have been done before the Battle of Vittoria in 1813 where Hervey lost his arm.

Related Portraits:

(76A) Attributed to Thomas Heaphy (1775-1835). Unsigned, 1813-1819. Oil on canvas, 51 x 40 inches. The Provost & Fellows of Eton College, Windsor. Provenance — probably gift of Felton Elwell Hervey-Bathurst's parents to the Head Master Dr. George Heath; given by Dr. Heath to the College.

This portrait shows Hervey in the uniform of the 15th Light Dragoons and is a version of Cat. No. 76 which does not include medals.

(76B) Thomas Heaphy (1775-1835). Signed and dated 1819. Watercolor, 24 x 18 inches. Collection of Frederick John Hervey-Bathurst. Provenance — by descent from the sitter to the present owner.

Thomas Heaphy also painted a watercolor of Sir Hervey-Bathurst. As a photograph was not available, it is not known whether this watercolor relates to the two oil portraits.

Additional Portraits of Sir Felton Elwell Hervey-Bathurst:

(76C & 76D) Among the most tantalizing of the unlocated works connected with the Carroll family are the Sir Thomas Lawrence portraits of Hervey-Bathurst. In the Executor's list of unfinished or undelivered portraits in his studio compiled after Sir Thomas Lawrence's death, No. 352 is "A Portrait of the late Sir Felton Hervey." The claimant was "Lady (Felton) Hervey now Marchs of Carmarthen," and notation is made that it was delivered to her July 22, 1830 along with No. 353, a Portrait of Hervey "in crayons" and No. 354, "A Spanish Portrait of the Duke of Wellington (Garlick, 1962-1964, p. 310). This last is the famous Goya now in the National Gallery, London. What Lawrence was doing with it we don't know, as Wellington had given it to Louisa as a gift and she left it to the 8th Duke of Leeds. The two Lawrence portraits of Hervey remain a mystery.

Sir Felton Elwell Hervey-Bathurst

FRANCIS GODOLPHIN D'ARCY OSBORNE, 7th Duke of Leeds, 1798-1859

(Grandson-in-law of CCC and MDC)

77.

Unknown artist

Lithograph, 1838

Legend: *Published 18th Sept. 1838, by T. McLean, 26 Haymarket, London / A. Ducote's Lithogr, 70, S^e^ Martins Lane*

Image size: 9 3/4 x 12 5/16 inches

Trustees of the British Museum, London

Louisa's second husband, Francis Godolphin d'Arcy Osborne, then Marquess of Carmarthen, was seven years her junior when they married, April 24, 1828. This match drew forth envious comment from Betsy Patterson who wrote home:

> *Louisa has made a great match. He is very handsome, not more than twenty-eight, and will be a Duke with thirty thousand a year. . . . The Duke of Leeds, they say, is, of course, very angry at his son's marriage with Louisa* (Stirling, p. 1072).

But quite the opposite sentiments prevailed in Louisa's family. Charles Carroll wrote to Marianne from Doughoregan June 10, 1828:

> *I congratulate you and our whole family on Louisa's marriage with Carmarthen.*
> *The choice he has made is a proof of discernment in discovering in Louisa attractions to make him a happy husband. I feel most grateful to Lord Wellesley in acting, as he has done, the part of a tender parent in bestowing Louisa's hand on the Marquis* (MdHi, ms. 220).

In July 1838, on the death of his father, Carmarthen succeeded to "the family honours" which included the following titles, in addition to Marquess of Carmarthen: Duke of Leeds, Earl of Danby, Viscount Latimor of Danby, Baron Conyers of Hornby Castle and Osborne of Kiveton, and Viscount Osborne of Dunblane. Carmarthen and Louisa lived in splendour at Hornby Castle and at Kiveton Park.

No full scale portrait of the 7th Duke of Leeds has been located and Louisa's second husband, reputedly one of the handsomest and most dashing "catches" of his day, must be represented by this small lithograph which was published as part of a series of equestrian portraits.

ADDITIONAL PORTRAITS:

(77A) Mrs. Anne Mee (1791-1874). Unsigned ?, date unknown. Watercolor on ivory; 7 1/8 inches. Presently unlocated; known through a listing in catalogue for a sale at Sotheby & Co., July 3, 1961; purchased by a dealer named Clayton.

Francis Godolpin D'Arcy Osborne

Emily Caton (Mrs. John MacTavish), 1793 ? -1867

(Youngest daughter of Mr. and Mrs. Richard Caton; Granddaughter of CCC and MDC)

78.

Unknown artist

Unsigned, ca. 1825

Oil on canvas, 36 1/4 x 28 1/4 inches

On Deposit at The Peale Museum, Baltimore

Courtesy of The Sisters of the Good Shepherd

Provenance: Believed to have been given by the sitter to the Sisters of the Good Shepherd

Emily who might be remembered as the sister of the "Three American Graces" or simply as the other Caton daughter was, in fact, her grandfather's favorite. It was Emily who stayed home in Maryland and managed the Signer's households at Doughoregan and in Annapolis until "Folly Quarter" was completed for her in 1832; it was Emily who read evening after evening to her grandfather in his old age and who took her mother to live with her at "Folly Quarter" when Mary was too old and blind to manage the big house in Baltimore; it was Emily who nursed Charles Carroll of Homewood in his last illness; it was Emily who produced the only Caton grandchildren. Finally, it was Emily who inherited the great, tangled, mystifying MacTavish Collection of paintings which have confused and confounded so many for so long.

This is the only portrait of her ever recorded, and it is not certain who painted it. Philip Tilyard (1785-1830) has been suggested from a stylistic assessment of the portrait. This artist was known to have painted many prominent Baltimore Catholics within Emily's circle, but the attribution is not firm. Regardless of who painted this portrait, it is a superb character study. Emily is shown at about 40 years of age as plain, dowdy, serene, serious, and capable. She was destined to reign in Maryland, never far from home for long — or from her "dear Grandpapa."

John MacTavish, ca. 1787-1852

(Grandson-in-law of CCC and MDC)

79.

William James Hubard (1807-1862)

Unsigned, 1829-1832

Oil on panel, 20 x 14 1/2 inches

The Maryland Historical Society, Baltimore

Provenance: By direct descent to Mary Carroll MacTavish; part of The MacTavish Collection

Reference: Pleasants, "Studies," no. 3311

Born and educated in Scotland, John MacTavish came to Canada about 1808 to try his hand in business, moved on to Baltimore in 1816, and on August 15 of that year was married at "Doughoregan Manor" to Charles Carroll of Carrollton's youngest Caton granddaughter, Emily. After the wedding the MacTavishes returned to Montreal to live, but John, called by Emily her "excellent husband Mac," (MdHi, no. 431, May 22, 1817) brought a dreadfully homesick wife back to Maryland by 1819, never to leave again. In 1828 John inherited the estate of his uncle Simon MacTavish, reputedly the richest man in Montreal and head of the firm of MacTavish, Frobisher & Company, the supply house and virtual directorate of the Great North West Company. For the last seventeen years of his life John MacTavish was "the highly esteemed Consul of Her Britannic Majesty for the State of Maryland — an office which he filled with distinguished honor . . ." (*Baltimore American and Commercial Daily Advertiser*, Baltimore, June 22, 1852).

William James Hubard undoubtedly painted this portrait of John MacTavish during the same period that he executed his portrait of Charles Carroll of Carrollton (Cat. No. 41). The two works provide us with different examples of Hubard's settings for his charming cabinet pieces: interior and exterior, each sufficiently detailed to speak volumes about the subject. Obviously, John MacTavish was a sportsman and a bit of a dandy.

Additional portrait of John MacTavish:

(79a) Attributed to Charles Bird King (1785-1862). Unsigned and undated. Oil on canvas, 40 1/2 x 30 1/2 inches. Presently unlocated; known through a photograph. Provenance — by direct descent to Mary Carroll MacTavish; part of The MacTavish Collection; sold. Reference: Pleasants, "Studies," no. 3313.

This portrait was sold in Baltimore about 1948. Unfortunately, the former owner cannot remember the circumstances of the sale.

Charles Carroll of Doughoregan ("the Colonel"), 1801-1862

(Eldest child and only surviving son of Mr. and Mrs. Charles Carroll of Homewood; Grandson of CCC and MDC)

80.

William Edward West (1788-1857)

Unsigned, 1838-1840

Oil on canvas, 36 x 27 1/2 inches (sight)

Private Collection of a Descendant

Provenance: By direct descent to the present owner

References: Pleasants, "Studies," no. 132

Born in Lexington, Kentucky, William Edward West began his career in Natchez, Mississippi. He worked in Italy, France, and England between 1819 and 1838, the year he came to Baltimore. He was settled in New York by 1840 and, from about 1855 until his death, he worked in Nashville, Tennessee.

This portrait of Charles Carroll of Doughoregan was probably painted while the artist was working in Baltimore. It is far more typical of West's elegant and romantic works than the group portrait of "The Three Graces" (Cat. No. 70B) which has been considered part of his *oeuvre.*

Charles Carroll of Doughoregan studied in Paris with his cousin Charles Carroll Harper between 1817 and 1819. In 1825 he married a cousin, Mary Digges Lee (1794-1859). Since Charles Carroll of Doughoregan's father died in 1825, seven years before the Signer's own death, he inherited the Manor directly from his grandfather. His life was devoted to the maintenance and improvement of the great estate which had been acquired by his great-great-grandfather Charles Carroll the Settler.

Charles Carroll of Doughoregan

MARY SOPHIA CARROLL (Mrs. Richard Henry Bayard), 1804-1886

(Third surviving child of Mr. and Mrs. Charles Carroll of Homewood; Granddaughter of CCC and MDC)

81.

Augustin-Amant-Constant-Fidèle Edouart (1789-1861)

Unsigned, 1840

Inscribed on paper below figure: *Mrs. Richard H. Bayard, Wilmington, Delaware, August 15th, 1840*

Inscribed on back: *Mrs. Richard H. Bayard, Wilmington, Delaware. Saratoga Springs, 15th Aug. 1840*

Inscribed on label on back: *This Silhouette of Mrs. Richard H. Bayard was cut by August Edouart during his visit to the United States 1839-1849. Arthur S. Vernay, 12 East 45th St. New York*

Silhouette; paper: 9 x 3 3/4 inches

Private Collection of a Descendant

Provenance: By direct descent to the present owner

This charming silhouette provides a vivid impression of Mary Sophia as a fashionable matron. It was executed by the French silhouettist who came to America in 1839 using the name August Edouart and who pursued an enormously successful career from Massachusetts to New Orleans until his return to France in 1849.

Charles Carroll of Homewood's daughters were brought up in Philadelphia by their mother, Harriet Chew, after their parents' separation in 1816. Mary Sophia, the second daughter, married the dashing Richard Henry Bayard of Wilmington in 1820. She

> *was a woman who possessed beauty and brilliancy in rare degree . . . At Washington, when the great statesmen of the country were at their zenith, Mrs. Bayard shone in society. Her home was frequented by such men as Webster, Calhoun, Clay and Choate. Her conversational powers . . . charmed these distinguished men. . . . Her beauty was no less marked than her brilliancy. It is said that at one time she was the loveliest woman in Washington city. (Baltimore Sun,* March 1886, Diehlman File, MdHi).

82.

Thomas Sully (1783-1872)

Unsigned, 1822

Inscribed on back of frame: *Mrs. Bayard. Daughter of Charles Carroll of Homewood, granddaughter of Charles Carroll of Carrollton. . . .*

Oil on canvas, 31 x 26 inches (sight)

Private Collection of a Descendant

Provenance: By direct descent to the present owner

Sully began a portrait of Mary Sophia (Biddle and Fielding, no. 103) and one of her husband (Cat. No. 83) on May 15, 1822; hers was completed July 2nd of that year. Although there are two known Sully likenesses of Mary Sophia (see also, Cat. No. 82A), the portrait referred to in Biddle and Fielding is presumed to be this one since it is most closely related to her husband's portrait (Cat. No. 83).

Additional Portrait of Mary Sophia Carroll:

(82A) Thomas Sully. Unsigned, ca. 1822. Oil on canvas, 29 x 19 inches (oval). Private Collection of a Descendant. Provenance — by direct descent to the present owner.

This portrait of Mary Sophia, traditionally dated 1822, appears to represent her at just about the same age as Cat. No. 82. Although one portrait of her is listed in Biddle and Fielding's transcription of Sully's Register, neither the identification of the subject nor the artistic attribution are in question. It is entirely possible that Sully painted this for her mother Harriet Chew Carroll, whose portrait (Cat. No. 64) was being painted by the artist at about the same time.

RICHARD HENRY BAYARD, 1796-1868

(Grandson-in-law of CCC and MDC)

83.

Thomas Sully (1783-1872)

Signed and dated lower right: *TS 1822*

Oil on canvas, 29 x 24 inches

The Baltimore Museum of Art 39.179

Bequest of Ellen H. Bayard

Provenance: By direct descent to Miss Bayard

References: Pleasants, "Studies," no. 25

Mary Sophia Carroll married on December 20, 1820, a young man who was to become outstanding as a statesman and politician: Richard Henry Bayard. Born in Wilmington, a distinguished lawyer in his native state, he entered politics in 1832 when he was elected mayor of Wilmington. From 1836 to 1839 and 1840 to 1845 he was in the U.S. Senate, and in between Senate terms he served as Chief Justice of Delaware. Bayard was *chargé d'affaires* to Belgium from 1850 to 1853.

In addition to his many distinctions it is apparent from Sully's portrait that Richard Henry Bayard was very handsome indeed, even taking into account that it was "a rule and a habit with Sully never to send a disagreeable portrait from his easel" (Tuckerman, p. 63). Sully began this portrait on May 15, 1822, the same day as Mary Sophia's (Cat. No. 82). It was completed July 6 (Biddle and Fielding, no. 102).

RELATED PORTRAITS:

(83A) Unknown artist after Sully. Other information unknown. Presently unlocated; known through Frick Art Reference Library (no. 121-6/U). Provenance — formerly Collection of City Hall, Wilmington, Delaware.

A copy after Cat. No. 83

84.

Unknown artist

Unsigned, ca. 1825

Miniature, watercolor on ivory, 2 1/8 x 1 3/4 inches

The Baltimore Museum of Art

Bequest of Ellen H. Bayard 36.47.54

Provenance: By direct descent to Miss Bayard

A beautiful example of the miniaturist's art, it is not known who painted this portrait of Richard Bayard, although the artist made the sitter as dashing as Sully had done.

Additional Portrait of Richard Henry Bayard:

(84a) Joseph Alexis Bailly (1825-1883). Signed and dated *A Bailly/1868.* Plaster bust, 22½ inches high. The Maryland Historical Society, Baltimore. The marble bust to be executed from this cast has not been located, if, in fact, it was made. It shows Bayard in the last year of his life — a victim of the ravages of time, but nevertheless a noble figure.

Bailly was a Parisian-born wood carver and sculptor who came to America in 1848. After two years of travelling between New Orleans, New York City, Philadelphia, and Buenos Aires, he settled in Philadelphia, where he worked first as a wood carver and wax modeller, later as a portrait sculptor.

JOHN LEE OF NEEDWOOD, 1788-1871

(Grandson-in-law of CCC and MDC)

85.

Joseph Wood (1778-1830)

Unsigned, ca. 1820

Oil on paper on board, 8 7/8 x 7 inches

Private Collection of a Descendant

Provenance: By direct descent to the present owner

References: Pleasants, "Studies," no. 2824

On June 5, 1832, Harriet Carroll (see Cat. No. 86A) married John Lee, son of Governor Thomas Sim Lee of Maryland. Educated by private tutors and at Harvard University, John Lee was elected as a Democrat to serve in the eighteenth U.S. Congress from 1823 to 1825, but his principal occupation was management of his estate "Needwood" in Frederick County, Maryland. Lee was a proponent of both the Baltimore and Ohio Railroad and the Chesapeake and Ohio Canal.

Born on a farm near Clarkstown, New York, the artist, Joseph Wood, was in partnership in New York City with John Wesley Jarvis between 1802 and 1810, was then on his own until 1813 when he moved to Philadelphia, and finally settled in Washington, D.C. in 1816. Wood is listed in the Baltimore Directories for 1819 and 1824. He could have executed this portrait of John Lee in either Baltimore or Washington. Wood painted portraits and miniatures, having received instruction in the latter from Edward Greene Malbone (1777-1807), considered one of the finest miniaturists of his day. This cabinet piece in its small and precise rendering reveals the influence of the miniaturist's art.

Louisa Catherine Carroll (Mrs. Isaac Rand Jackson), 1809-? And Her Child

(Fifth child of Mr. and Mrs. Charles Carroll of Homewood; Granddaughter of CCC and MDC)

86.

Attributed to Thomas Sully (1783-1872)

Unsigned, 1834-1844

Oil on canvas, 27 1/2 inches in diameter

Private Collection of a Descendant

Provenance: By direct descent to the present owner

Biddle and Fielding's transcription of Sully's Register (no. 892) lists a portrait of Mrs. Isaac Rand Jackson which was exhibited in the New York Loan Exhibition of Sully portraits in 1895. In neither the transcription nor the list for the Exhibition is there a mention of a child being included in the portrait. The subject is identified by family tradition. Since Mrs. Jackson's descendants cannot recall any individual portrait of Louisa and one is not known to exist, it must be presumed that this is Biddle and Fielding's no. 892.

Louisa married Isaac Rand Jackson on January 17, 1833. Their five children were born between 1833 and 1842. The child in this portrait remains unidentified by the family, so that the portrait could have been painted between 1834 and 1844.

Additional Portraits of Louisa Catherine Carroll with Harriet Carroll (1808-?):

(86a) Attributed to Thomas Sully (1783-1872). Oil on canvas, 30 x 48 inches (sight). Presently unlocated; stolen from the private collection of a descendant; known through a photograph. Provenance — by direct descent to the last owner.

In 1822 when Sully recorded his portraits of the subjects' mother, sister, and brother-in-law, (Cat. Nos. 64, 82, and 83) Harriet Carroll (right) and Louisa (left) would have been fourteen and thirteen respectively. It is probable that this portrait of them was painted at that time. It is the only known likeness of Harriet Carroll, later Mrs. John Lee of "Needwood." In the 1895 New York loan exhibition of Sully portraits, a painting listed as "Jackson, Mrs. Isaac Rand [Louisa] and Mrs. John Lee [Harriet]" was included. Biddle and Fielding no. 894 is listed as "Jackson, Mrs. John Lee" with the following note: "the authors have not been able to see No. . . 894; it was exhibited in 1895 at the Loan Exhibition of Portraits in New York and was owned by Mrs. Oswald Jackson, of New York." There was no Mrs. John Lee Jackson in the family. Biddle and Fielding's no. 894 is probably this portrait, but the mystery is intensified by the fact that Sully's original manuscript register (Historical Society of Pennsylvania, Philadelphia) does not appear to list a portrait matching this description, although the attribution has not been questioned.

(86b) M. Calling Hall after Thomas Sully (1783-1872). Unsigned, early 20th century. Inscribed on back: *Granddaughters of Charles Carroll of/Carrollton/Louisa and Harriet Carroll/Copy by M. Calling Hall/Portrait by Thomas Sully.* Oil on canvas, 36 x 18 inches (approx.). Private Collection of a Descendant. Provenance — commissioned by the mother-in-law of the present owner.

This portrait is a copy of Cat. No. 86a.

ISAAC RAND JACKSON, 1804-1842

(Grandson-in-law of CCC and MDC)

87.

Unknown artist

Unsigned, ca. 1835

Inscribed on back: *Isaac Rand Jackson / Born 1804 in Newburyport / Married 1833 at Philadelphia / Louisa Catherine Carroll / Died 1842 at Copenhagen / While Representing the / United States of America / at the Court of Denmark*

Miniature, watercolor on ivory, 2 1/2 x 2 inches

Private Collection of a Descendant

Provenance: By direct descent to the present owner

This miniature and the information included in the inscription are all we really know about Isaac Rand Jackson, except the names and birth dates of his five children and the fact that the Jacksons lived in Philadelphia. According to family tradition, Isaac was "quite a man about town."

Charles Carroll Harper, 1802-1837

(Only surviving son of Mr. and Mrs. Robert Goodloe Harper; Grandson of CCC and MDC)

88.

Charles Bird King ? (1785-1862)

Unsigned, ca. 1830-1836

Oil on canvas, 28 1/2 x 24 1/2 inches

Collection of Mrs. Andrew Matthew McCrone

Provenance: By direct descent to the present owner

Reference: Pleasants, "Studies," no. 593

Charles Carroll Harper, only surviving son of Kitty and Robert, showed great promise of following in his father's footsteps as a statesman before his untimely death. Although he did not hold elective office, he ran for the Maryland House of Delegates in 1826, and he was Secretary of the American Legation at Paris in 1829-30 and again at the time of his death. He married Charlotte Chiffelle of Charleston, South Carolina, of whom no portrait is known. Harper's obituary described him as

> *a rare combination of exalted and highly cultivated intellect, amiability of disposition, and unremitting kindness and urbanity of deportment. A gentleman in the most enlarged sense of the term, he commanded by his intelligence the respect of all, while his kindness and mildness of manner in the various relations of life gained for him the love and esteem of those who were so fortunate as to enjoy his acquaintance (Baltimore American and Commercial Daily Advertiser,* August 9, 1837).

The artistic attribution of this portrait has never been recorded by the family. Recently, however, a scholar who has made an extensive study of Charles Bird King has tentatively stated from a photograph that it is most suggestive of King's style.

89.

Thomas Crawford (1813 ?-1857)

Signed and dated on back of shoulder: *T. Crawford, fec.[t] Rome — 1838*

Marble, 29 1/2 inches high

The Baltimore Museum of Art

Gift of Caroline Dexter Pennington 32.26.1

Provenance: By direct descent to Mrs. Caroline Dexter Pennington

Thomas Crawford served his apprenticeship with the New York city stonecutting firm of Frazee & Launitz. In 1835 he went to Rome, the first of many American sculptors to settle there in the mid-19th century. For the remainder of his life his studies were located in the Eternal City. Crawford

> *had begun his career in Rome as a student adhering to a flagging neoclassicism. . . . But his earliest portraiture had shown the naturalism that in the late 1840's began to eclipse Thorwaldsen's neoclassical spell. . . . With this naturalism he was able to blend that serene yet dramatic character that he had learned in his early days in Rome. And though he died at the early age of forty-four, he had done much to advance the art and profession to where the sculptor was respected as a man of great talent, even of genius* (Craven, p. 135).

The Harpers were travelling in Italy shortly before Charles Harper's death. That this handsome likeness is dated 1838, the year after he died, can only be explained by the fact that it was actually executed from a model made prior to his death. There is no doubt that a bust of Harper was executed, for it is mentioned in his sister Emily Harper's will.

Emily Louisa Hinton Harper, 1812-1892

(Youngest and only surviving daughter of Mr. and Mrs. Robert Goodloe Harper; Granddaughter of CCC and MDC)

90.

Thomas Sully (1783-1872)

Signed and dated on back: *TS 1853*

Oil on canvas, 24 x 20 inches

Private Collection of a Descendant

Provenance: By descent from the sitter to the present owner.

Reference: Pleasants, "Studies," no. 592

Emily Harper lived all her long life as

> *one of the most honored Ladies . . . in Baltimore. . . . The best society of this country and Europe has been graced by the presence of Miss Harper; but in the homes of the poor she is as well known as in the gilded saloons of fashion* ("Social Athens of America," p. 34).

Her portrait by Sully was begun February 15, 1853 at Baltimore and was finished April 24 (Biddle and Fielding, no. 740). Emily was a handsome woman of 41 at the time. As a young girl, her brother described her as

> *. . . so gay, so gentle in her disposition, so thoughtless — I might say, that she yields rather than is convinced, obeys rather than believes; there is so much elasticity in her spirits, that an impression is soon obliterated* (Charles Carroll Harper to Robert Goodloe Harper, MdHi, ms. 431, February 22, 1823).

Emily Louisa Hinton Harper

The Carroll Family: An English Lifestyle in America

In preparation of this publication and exhibition, an intense search was made for a representative group of furniture from the 18th and early 19th century that could be associated with the first three generations of the Carroll family in America — Charles Carroll the Settler, Charles Carroll of Annapolis, and Charles Carroll of Carrollton. Unfortunately, the extensive correspondence with other museums and historical societies as well as with over a hundred Carroll descendants did not uncover the quantity of Queen Anne, Chippendale and Federal furniture that must have either been made in or imported to Maryland in the 18th century and early 19th century. The results are not totally unexpected, especially in Maryland and Virginia where the absence of original 18th century furnishings is the pattern in American decorative arts. In the particular example of the Carroll family, it was, in addition, the numerous divisions of inheritance as well as changes of fortune that have contributed to the lack of identification of furnishings owned by them.

As the Carroll house in Annapolis was emptied of its contents by the time of the tax assessment of 1820, any furniture that was to have survived from this house would have been moved to Doughoregan or dispersed among the children and grandchildren. Under the terms of the will of Charles Carroll of Carrollton, his grandson Charles Carroll of Doughoregan and his granddaughter Emily Caton MacTavish were the recipients of all the household effects, including portraits, silver, and furniture contained in Doughoregan Manor. Later in the 19th century, much of the furniture and silver left Doughoregan Manor through marriage or by inheritance. Some of the furnishings undoubtedly went to Europe with other possessions. It is known, for example, that many of the objects bequeathed to Emily Caton MacTavish were to journey to Rome in the late 19th century with a group of family portraits and silver. Only the portraits and the silver were to return to America after the Second World War.

However, what we lack in physical evidence of the original furnishings in the Carroll houses is compensated by the records of the three generations of Carrolls that have survived in the collections of The Maryland Historical Society and elsewhere. Unlike other Maryland or even American families, these first generations of the Carroll family in Maryland were each of considerable property and affluence. The inventory made of the estate of Charles Carroll the Settler in 1720 must be one of the most extensive and revealing of early 18th century America.[1] The Settler had made his will in 1718 which was probated eight days after his death on July 20, 1720. Rather than providing the usual inventory of the estate, his heirs and executors chose to post a bond on the estate for the sum of £60,000 sterling.[2] This sum would indicate that the Settler, along with such men as Richard Bennett of Maryland, William Byrd and King Carter of Virginia, would number among the richest men in the Chesapeake Bay area. This is an important discovery, for it had always been assumed that the great Carroll fortune was almost totally amassed by Charles Carroll of Annapolis. The 1720 inventory was kept with the Carroll papers and is written in a bound ledger whose unfilled pages were used by Charles Carroll of Carrollton to record his accounts in the early 19th century. Here

[1] Inventory of Charles Carroll, the Settler. Carroll Papers MS 220, Liber X, Box 16. MdHi.

[2] Anne Arundel County Testamentary. Proceedings, Liber 24, f. 283. Hall of Records, Annapolis.

is provided a room by room inventory of the dwelling in Annapolis. The inventory creates a large house of perhaps 11 or more principal rooms and the expected private chapel. In the old hall there were, besides three old oval tables, one "scrutoire," a chest of drawers, and a pair of old tables, chairs, and one "marble," probably a statue. A dining room is named as such which is very rare for the period. Contained therein are 12 tall back leather chairs, three oval tables, one tea table, two card tables, one looking glass, four pair of sconces, and one clock. Here also are designated four portraits — Mr. Henry Carroll, Mr. Charles Carroll, Mr. Daniel Carroll, and Mrs. Mary Carroll (see discussion, Cat. Nos. 4, 5, and 10).

In the inventory, the plate, consisting of flatware, porringers, tankards, canns, flagons, and other holloware pieces, was valued slightly in excess of 448 pounds. The monumental flagon, included in this exhibition, (Cat. No. 92) was valued at £28 4s. and by family tradition was presented to Charles Carroll the Settler, by the Fourth Lord Baltimore. The flagon was made in London in 1715 by Joseph Ward, the year Charles Carroll the Settler went to England and acted as Executor of the Third Lord Baltimore's estate. Also listed are ten house servants in Annapolis, his ship "Experiment" and its furnishings as well as a chariot and harness for four horses which he left to his wife.

Of great interest is the designation of a chapel with its contents of furniture and of religious articles. This open listing in such an inventory, as well as the presence of monstrances, a ciborium, a tabernacle, and four sets of vestments in white, red, green and purple, indicates that the practicing of Catholicism in 18th century Maryland was not as underground as one might expect. The vestments themselves would have been for Jesuit priests who must have made the circuit to the Carrolls and to Maryland's other leading Catholic families.

Included in the inventory is a listing of all the goods in the Settler's store house. Like William Byrd of Virginia and Richard Bennett of Maryland, Charles Carroll the Settler was a store keeper in stock quantities of luxury items to be sold in Maryland and the tidewater areas of the Chesapeake. In reading the list, particularly noting the types of dry goods, every imaginable item is included — cotton and penniston, broad-cloth, silk poplin, persian silks, fine shalloon, holland and garlicks; shoes and boots by the dozens; fine haberdashery, including ribbons and handkerchiefs; women's silk girdles by the dozens; 32 wigs, mostly bobbed; kid gloves for young lads and boys, etc., etc. One wonders exactly who were his clientele, as Annapolis in this period was not a town sufficient in population or wealth to support such luxuries. The Settler also had on hand more utilitarian items, such as guns, saddles, stationery, glass and earthenware, window glass, brass lanterns, diamond glass and window lead bands for casement windows, 1054 bushels of salt and 10,692 gallons of rum contained in 62 hogsheads, 45 tierces, and 8 barrels.

Since Charles Carroll of Annapolis had but one heir in Charles Carroll of Carrollton, there was no inventory of his estate, nor have any body of letters or orders through English agents that would cast light on his household furnishings survived. There is only one exception. While a student at the Inner Temple in London, Charles Carroll of Carrollton was befriended by a distant relative, a Mr. Christopher Bird, who was obviously an agent for or in the

CHOCOLATE POT
George II, London, 1738-1739
Maker: John Swift
Cat. No. 98

manufacture of marble chimney pieces. In April of 1760, Charles Carroll of Carrollton wrote his father in Annapolis inquiring if there might be a market in Maryland or in the Chesapeake area for marble mantel pieces.[3] Not quite a year later, he again wrote his father advising him that "Mr. Bird sent by the fleet a venture of marble tables; I hope the event will answer his expectations. . . . The Marble Slab you ordered goes with the tables [meaning by the same fleet]."[4] Perhaps one of these tables found its way to the house on Spa Creek or to Doughoregan Manor.

However, there are numerous articles of silver included in this exhibition that were once the property of Charles Carroll of Annapolis. It is as one might expect in 18th century Maryland and Virginia: plate of English origin and of the highest quality. In 1734 he must have ordered from England numerous pieces of matching silver of which a chocolate pot, two card trays, and a large tray or salver (Cat. Nos. 96-98) survive. The maker was John Swift of London,

[3] CCC to CCA, April 10, 1760, MS 206, MdHi.

[4] CCC to CCA, March 28-29, 1761, MS 206, MdHi.

Covered Flagon
George I, London, 1715-1716
Maker: Joseph Ward
Cat. No. 92

and the Carroll arms surrounded by a decorative cartouche are masterfully engraved on each piece. It is also known that the total evaluation of the plate for the house in Annapolis was slightly in excess of £1296 when a list of the silver was delivered to the tax assessor in Annapolis on April 28th, 1779.[5] It is interesting to note that some of the plate listed in the Settler's inventory of 1720 is repeated here. For example, the flagon of 1715 (Cat. No. 92) is recorded as weighing 81 troy ounces and 6 penny weights.

Eighteenth century Annapolis was not devoid of crime, at least not of petty thievery. In both 1749 and 1750 Charles Carroll of Annapolis advertises for

[5] MS 220, MdHi.

plate either lost or stolen from his house on Spa Creek. The advertisement is particularly revealing in that it refers to an article of silver as old, thus indicating that it was obviously inherited from his father, as well as documenting Charles Carroll of Annapolis' own description of the family crest:

> *Lost or stolen from the dwelling house of Charles Carroll Esq. of the city of Annapolis about ten days ago, one old silver mugg holding above a half a pint with a coat of arms engraved thereon — a sword erect between two lyons rampant, likewise three silver spoons with a crest on each, being of a falcon with wings extended standing on a stump having a branch on each side.*[6]

One of the most important documents is the letterbook of Charles Carroll of Carrollton for the years 1771-1833 which is now in the Arents Collection of the New York Public Library. It is from this that we learn of the mode of life of Charles Carroll of Carrollton and his father, before the latter's death in 1786, at the house at Annapolis and at Doughoregan Manor. It reveals a complete dependence on and/or a choice of English manufacture for nearly every aspect of their lives. It is unfortunate not to have the space to discuss all the subjects presented in this letterbook. Just prior to the Revolution, Charles Carroll of Carrollton was responsible for the habitation, clothing, and feeding of over 500 people which included his family, free men, artisans, craftsmen, and slaves at Doughoregan and his other plantations. Each spring literally thousands of yards of the best Welsh cotton and the best German "oznabrig" would be ordered for clothing his slaves. "Groon german strong" and green penniston would be ordered for "the servants in livery and the housemaids."[7] Woolen material and other warmer fabrics would in turn be ordered in the same quantity in the fall.[8]

During the Revolution, Charles Carroll established a small linen manufacture at Doughoregan, but it is unlikely that he could have supplied the needs of his large plantation. In the fall of 1791, he wrote to a Mr. Josiah Burr of New Haven, Connecticut, in reference to material that he had obviously provided, "I have no other fault to find with the Connecticut oznabrig with which you have supplied me for these two years past, than that it is too narrow for men full grown."[9] In the same letter he goes on to order over 2000 yards of this same material. Every implement necessary and known to the laborious agricultural pursuits is contained in these orders even to the manufacturer of a mechanical turnip slicer.[10] The garden seed orders could provide an index of those seeds that were available and which were imported at an early date to Maryland and America.[11]

[6] *The Maryland Gazette,* November 8, 1749, Hall of Records, Annapolis.

[7] New York Public Library, Arents Collection 50767, March 20, 1783. This and following footnotes in reference to this letterbook will contain only the date of the order or correspondence as the letterbook is not paginated. Where the complete date is included in the text the reference will not be footnoted.

[8] Ibid; December 14, 1782.

[9] Ibid; November 7, 1791.

[10] Ibid; January 14, 1774.

[11] Ibid; October 8, 1771, September 21, 1772 and September 20, 1773.

Side Chair
Queen Anne, Maryland or
Pennsylvania, ca. 1750
Cat. No. 122

The numerous pages of orders for English goods sent from Annapolis or Elkridge to the agents in London always called for large supplies of drugs and medicine. Time and time again, Charles Carroll of Carrollton implored that, for the health and safety of his family and slaves, these drugs and medicines be fresh and of the very best quality.[12]

From the Arents letterbook, it is known that prior to the Revolution and its consequent trade embargo on all furniture, silver, and other household items Charles Carroll of Annapolis and Charles Carroll of Carrollton would have ordered, by preference, through agents in England. The Carrolls could well afford the best and would not have been satisfied with the local Annapolis product. In silver, perhaps teaspoons would have been purchased from a local silversmith, or a cabinetmaker may have been employed to provide straight chairs

[12] Ibid; January 8, 1775.

or tables, such as the rather plain, obviously locally made, Maryland Chippendale chair included in this exhibition (Cat. No. 125). But of all the silver located that dates prior to the Revolution and belongs to descendants of the Carroll family, none is of American manufacture, and even after the Revolution the large majority still seems to have been ordered and imported from England.

A buyer in America, such as Charles Carroll of Carrollton, was to some extent ordering and buying an unknown commodity. He could rely on the taste of his London agent, and, as in the case of Charles Carroll, could continually admonish or remind the agent that he wanted his money spent well and, more specifically, in Charles Carroll's own words, on objects of "taste and value."[13] The agents may have shuddered or winked at each other when the long and involved orders came from their client in Maryland. Through his entire life Charles Carroll of Carrollton always felt that he had to be on top of any business operation and certainly to have the last word. He rarely ordered one thing or a list of objects without an accompanying remark or instruction. In the case of stationery he would add "please give particular charge that the paper is not greasy"[14] or in the case of cheshire cheese, the last received was "too bad for even the servants to eat."[15] He was not usually satisfied with any of the goods subsequently received at Elkridge or Doughoregan. He was not adverse to immediately returning them to London for full credit, both for their cost and that of the return shipping, reminding his London agents that "the shop keepers in London are so apt to ship off to America their refuse goods."[16] Just on the eve of the outbreak of the Revolution in August of 1774, he was to write to his agents "I shall not import next year a coppers worth from England."[17]

There are many orders during this fifty odd year period covered by correspondence in the Arents letterbook that are relative to a study of the household furnishings ordered for the house at Annapolis and Doughoregan Manor as well as their interior decoration. In the context of this catalogue and specifically in connection with certain objects gathered for this exhibition we can only mention the most salient examples. There seems to have been a great deal of activity in acquiring household furniture in the period from about 1771-1774. In 1771 an entire set or suite of furniture was ordered for what would seem to be a newly completed or refinished room in the Annapolis house.[18] Room dimensions with ceiling heights are given that could be for the two panelled drawing rooms on the first floor of the old brick section of the house at Annapolis or possibly a room of similar dimensions in the frame wing on the eastern end. Ordered for the room were two handsome gilt girandoles of two lights each, four crimson curtains (the given dimensions match those of the windows in the existing Annapolis house), one fashionable sofa with twelve chairs to match, two pier glasses "to be as fashionable and handsome as can be purchased for fifteen guineas each. The carving and guilding to conform with

13 Ibid; October 26, 1771.

14 Ibid; October 8, 1771.

15 Ibid; September 21, 1772.

16 Ibid; March 1, 1773.

17 Ibid; August 17, 1774.

18 Ibid; October 26, 1771.

the girandoles . . . to be of a solid kind, it has been found by experience that slight carving will neither endure the extremes of heat or cold nor the rough treatment of negro servants." One Turkey carpet (the measurements again conform to the drawing room in the Annapolis house) is ordered and it is noted that "if a turkey carpet cannot be procured exactly in these dimensions, or near it you are advised to procure one of the best kind of Axminster, Wilton, or any other English manufactury." Included in this order were andirons, a fender, and fire tools, all to fit a marble chimney piece ordered at the same time, and two fashionable card tables with "no superfluous carving about them." After the listing of the above mentioned objects is a notation "all the furniture above described for the same apartment." Also included in the same letter, with the exact dimensions given, is an order for "one best painted black and white floor cloth" with specific instructions from Charles Carroll of Carrollton to send the carpet and floor cloth on a roller "if they will stow well." There is an order for "a very good eight day clock in a neat plain mahogany case to stand in a hall of 10 feet and a half pitch, N. B. Apply for this clock to Mr. Monkhouse, clockmaker in Gloucester Street near Queen Square and say the clock is for Charles Carroll Esq. in Maryland." This clock is owned by a Carroll descendant. In 1771 when the clock was ordered, Charles Carroll of Carrollton had been home for five years, and the inscription on the dial reads John Scott, Successor to John Monkhouse. There was ordered at the same time twelve yards of scotch carpeting for use on a stairway, and a hall lantern for "the house at Patapsco" referring to Doughoregan near Elkridge on the Patapsco. In September of 1772, perhaps referring to the painted floor cloth ordered nearly one year earlier Charles Carroll of Carrollton writes as follows, "the floor cloth you sent me for my house in Annapolis is hardly fit to lay on any floor owing to the paints coming off and that for my house in Elkridge is almost as bad."[19] There are other orders for painted floor cloths indicating their use and acceptance in principal rooms in the late 18th century as well as numerous orders for Turkey carpets which seem to be in each instance more desirable, at least as far as the Carrolls were concerned, than Axminsters, Wiltons, or other carpets of English manufacture. Even when ordering Turkey carpets Charles Carroll could not help himself from giving detailed instructions such as "Mr. Johnson is requested to examine well this carpet to see that it is clear of puckers which Turkey carpets often have and which besides being ugly occasions them to wear out sooner in such places. . . ."[20]

The furniture orders were usually equally specific. In 1772 he had ordered two substantial square mahogany tables, "exactly of a height and so contrived as upon occasion to be fixed together to make one table"[21] and in January of 1775, "a very neat night chair, with its furniture formed with such a deception as to appear anything but what it really is . . . but not troublesome to use."[22]

At the same time, an order was sent to the London agents for "thirty-six common plates to be of the neatest plain make and of the very best pewter.

[19] Ibid; September 21, 1772.

[20] Ibid; February 9, 1784.

[21] Ibid; October 16, 1772.

[22] Ibid; January 8, 1775.

Writing Desk
George III, English, ca. 1770
Cat. No. 123

SAUCEBOAT
George III, London, 1771-1772
Maker's name not traced
Cat. No. 104

My crest to be engraved on them all, which may be had of Mr. Deard in Piccadilly." Also to be bought of John Deard were "two strong neat genteel silver tureene ladles, one neat strong punch ladle, all to best finished and no work that will harbor dust."

During the Revolution the London agents moved their operation to Nantes in France, and foodstuffs, wines, and dry goods continued to be ordered through them. However, during this period in France there is no specific mention of household goods such as china, silver, glass, furniture, etc. When he had some respite from his revolutionary activities, Charles Carroll of Carrollton might have introduced himself to the wares of American craftsmen. But by 1783 the agents Wallace, Johnson, and Muir were back in London, and the following year the drawing room of the house at Annapolis was obviously done over in a newer and more fashionable taste. Ordered for the windows were blue silk and stuff damask window curtains, all these "made up in the newest taste with carved corniches, fringe, tossils, lines, hooks & c (etc.) that is proper for them."[23] Matching damask was ordered to re-upholster the sofa and a new Turkey carpet for the floor. In February 1785 there was a lengthy order and discussion for a harpsichord that resulted in the harpsichord included in this exhibition (Cat. No. 128).[24] Charles Carroll wrote:

> *I have been informed that a Mr. Kirkman is by much the best Harpsichord maker in London I would therefore have your Mr. Johnson buy the Harpsichord of Kirkman — Mr. Bromner of whom the Harpsichord miscellany is to be bought is a very good judge of instruments, and I wish he would choose one for me — It must be quite plain without any finery or inlaid work*

[23] Ibid; February 9, 1784.

[24] Ibid; February 8, 1785.

about it which the cabinet makers call I believe finneering — because such will not stand the great and sudden changes and extremes of heat and cold of this climate.[25]

It would seem that Mr. Kirkman was too busy to make a harpsichord in the prescribed time for Mr. Carroll. The Carroll harpsichord included here was made by the London firm of Burkat Shudi and Johannes Broadwood and is dated on its interior 1788. In the late 18th century, it did take approximately three years to make such a special order instrument. A harpsichord of such size and with a double keyboard is unusual in America for this period.

In November of 1785 Charles Carroll wrote the following to his London agents, "Gentlemen I send by Captain Johns of the *Nonesuch* an old silver tankard which I would have melted into a new one of the same size and shape with my coat of arms and crest engraven on it as the old one."[26] Among the Carroll silver located for this exhibition is a silver tankard (Cat. No. 105) in style of the early 18th century. It is engraved with the Carroll coat of arms and crest. However, it bears the London hallmark for the year 1785, and the maker is Hester Bateman.

Covered Tankard
George III, London, 1785-1786
Maker: Hester Bateman
Cat. No. 105

[25] Mr. Kirkman was undoubtedly either Jacob or Abraham Kirkman, harpsichord makers in London. Mr. Bromner would be Robert Bremner, music publisher in London in the late 18th century.

[26] Charles Carroll letterbook, op. cit., November 14, 1785.

In 1792 one of the parlors in the house at Annapolis was again redone.[27] The material ordered for the curtains, the sofa, and twelve matching chairs, was a crimson damask of silk and worsted. For whichever room in the house it might have been, there was also ordered "a floor cloth of the pattern following, let it be handsomely painted and very strong." The pattern given was that of the rug's dimensions not design. In 1793 again for a room 20 feet square and most certainly for either the brick or frame sections of the house in Annapolis (since there are no rooms of these exact dimensions at Doughoregan) there were ordered "four elegant furniture chintz window curtains with cornices, for a parlour," the curtains . . . "long lined and trimmed with handsome rich coloured fringe and tassels, the pattern large, rich, and uncommon, . . . an elegant Wilton carpet drab ground with a small mixture of crimson in the pattern."[28] At the same time and again from England were ordered two large silver tureens and stands for soup. In the same order and beyond the exact categories of furniture and its discussion, but nonetheless of interest to us, were "two high raised ornaments for a table of confectionary in the form of a temple or arbour." In 1798 there was ordered "one genteel substantial silver cross for the table called a sliding X. N.B. the crest of my arms to be engraved thereon."[29] This exact dish cross has been located among the collections of the Daughters of the American Revolution Museum in Washington, D. C. but unfortunately could not be borrowed for this exhibition. In the last years of the 18th and early 19th century substantial silver orders were still being placed through the agents in England as well as older silver sent abroad for repair and replacement. Knives and forks are ordered by the dozens during this period as well as numerous holloware pieces all again too numerous to mention here.

For our purposes, in addition to the orders for furniture and silver, it is those orders for earthenware and porcelain that are most valuable. In 1775, besides 36 white stone chamber pots, there was ordered a service of Queens china to consist of about 150 pieces.[30] Accompanying the order were Charles Carroll of Carrollton's instructions that "this service is to be of the newest pattern but no ways decorated so as to harbor dirt." In December 1772, he had placed through his agents a very special order.[31] There is no hint as to the exact manufacturer desired, but that Charles Carroll of Carrollton intended it to be made to order is verified by the small illustrations in the order showing the various sizes and shapes of the china desired. In 1793 he is still ordering "blue and white nankin tea china, richly guild."[32] The earthenware and porcelain orders rather than those for silver diminish and all but disappear at the Revolution. Undoubtedly, by that time, the finest of English and European porcelain was being imported to America and could be purchased in Annapolis and Baltimore and elsewhere. Included in this exhibition are representative examples from a

[27] Ibid; April 18, 1792.

[28] Ibid; June 22, 1793.

[29] Ibid; October 9, 1798.

[30] Ibid; January 8, 1775.

[31] Ibid; December 20, 1772.

[32] Ibid; June 22, 1793.

SIDE CHAIR
Federal, Baltimore, ca. 1790
Cat. No. 129

large set of Spode China known as Charles Carroll's service, most likely referring to his great years of entertainment at Doughoregan in the first three decades of the 19th century. Remnants of this large service are owned by various descendants of Charles Carroll of Carrollton. Each of the plates and soup plates are decorated with different sea shell designs and date from about 1819 (see Cat. No. 142).

The inventory made of Charles Carroll of Carrollton's estate after his death in 1832[33] cannot be deemed accurate. In many instances, the inventory shows certain rooms of the house to be partially furnished. It would seem that some of the objects had been removed by the time of the inventory. It is possible that part of the furnishings were given by Charles Carroll before his death to his children and grandchildren. In addition, there is the often repeated family story that Emily Caton MacTavish did not attend the funeral services for her

[33] Inventory of the Estate of Charles Carroll of Carrollton, April 1, 1833. MS 205. MdHi.

Hunt Board
Federal, Baltimore, ca. 1790
Cat. No. 136

grandfather in Baltimore, and, when the funeral cortege finally reached Doughoregan Manor, she was seen driving one, or, perhaps as the story goes, one of three wagon loads of furniture and other objects being taken from Doughoregan across the fields to her house, Folly Quarter.

Most of the pieces of furniture in this exhibition cannot be documented through the Arents letterbook. The well known and beautifully carved classical style side chairs (Cat. Nos. 129 and 130) and the two matching card tables (Cat. Nos. 131 and 132) have always been said to have been first owned by Charles Carroll of Carrollton and are of Baltimore, or at least Maryland manufacture. One of the chairs is owned by a Carroll descendant, but most of this famous set has found its way into public institutions.

A pair of English side chairs (Cat. No. 124) in the Adam style and a breakfront (Cat. No. 126) have been borrowed from a Carroll descendant and seemingly are original furnishings from the Annapolis house or Doughoregan Manor although they were removed from the latter early in this century. A splendid huntboard (Cat. No. 136) and side chairs (Cat. Nos. 134 and 135), dating from the last years of the 18th century are by family tradition said to have been used at Doughoregan Manor during Charles Carroll of Carrollton's lifetime.

William Voss Elder, III

Silver *

91. Douter

William III

Maker: John Ladyman

London Hallmarks for 1700-01 and *LA* in monogram below a crown, in shaped cartouche, above rim

Carroll Crest (Hawk with wings folded) one side

Height: 4½ inches; width: 1⅝ inches

Mrs. Andrew Matthew McCrone

92. Covered Flagon

George I

Maker: Joseph Ward

London Hallmarks for 1715-16 and *WA* separated by an anchor in a shaped reserve, below rim of flagon and on underside of cover; maker's mark also appears separately on handle

Carroll Arms on front, partially obscured by the addition of a 19th century spout; the Crest (Hawk with wings folded) appears on center of cover

Height: 14⅛ inches; width: 11⅛ inches

Private Collection

93. Dessert Spoon

George I

Maker's name not traced

London Hallmarks for 1725-26 and *W/W* in shaped reserve, on back

Carroll Crest (Hawk with wings elevated) on back

Length: 7 13/16 inches

Private Collection of a Descendant

Courtesy of Kennedy Galleries, Inc., New York

94. Caster

George II

Maker: Samuel Wood

London Hallmarks for 1758-59 and *S·W* in circular reserve, on bottom and on flange of top section

Carroll Crest (Hawk with wings elevated) on neck

Height: 6 5/8 inches; diameter: 2 1/2 inches

The Maryland Historical Society, Baltimore

Gift of Anita Hack Carroll Bleck, 1954

* Unless otherwise noted, the objects included in the listings of silver, furniture, and memorabilia were inherited by and are still owned by descendants of Charles Carroll of Carrollton, his children, and his grandchildren.

95. Pair of Casters

George II

Maker: Samuel Wood

London Hallmarks for 1758-59 and *S·W* in circular reserve, on bottom and on flange of top section

Carroll Crest (Hawk with wings elevated) on neck of each caster

Height: 5 3/8 inches; diameter: 1 3/4 inches

The Colonial Williamsburg Foundation

This pair of casters was first sold in Baltimore in 1907, with the note, "once the property of the father of Charles Carroll of Carrollton with his crest engraved." Part of an original set of three, the larger caster is Cat. No. 94.

96. Pair of Salvers

George II

Maker: John Swift

London Hallmarks for 1738-39 and *I·S* in beaded circular reserve, on bottom (maker's mark is partially overstruck by an *A* on one salver)

Carroll Arms in cartouche in center of each; no Crest

Height: 1 1/16 inches; diameter: 6 1/2 inches

The Maryland Historical Society, Baltimore

Gifts of Nancy Howard Venable and Priscilla Dorsey Howard

These salvers are by the same maker as Cat. 97 and 98 and have identically engraved Coats of Arms. They are seemingly part of a set. At one time, both salvers were in possession of Mrs. Venable. How and when they passed from Carroll ownership is unknown.

97. Salver

George II

Maker: John Swift

London Hallmarks for 1738-39 and *I·S* in beaded circular reserve, on bottom

Carroll Arms in cartouche in center (badly worn); no Crest

Height: 1 3/8 inches; diameter: 12 9/16 inches

Private Collection of a Descendant

Courtesy of Kennedy Galleries, Inc., New York

98. Chocolate Pot

George II

Maker: John Swift

London Hallmarks for 1738-39 and *I·S* in beaded circular reserve, on bottom

Carroll Arms in cartouche on side; no Crest

Height: 10 3/4 inches; width: 8 5/8 inches

Estate of Miriam Perkins Carroll Norris

99. Knives and Forks (ten of each)
George III
Maker's name not traced, England ca. 1765
Lion passant on top or bottom; *J H* in square reserve on opposite side
Carroll Crest (Hawk with wings elevated) on front of handle
Knives, length: 10 3/4 inches
Forks, length: 8 3/4 inches
The Baltimore Museum of Art
Darnall Fund 75.37.1-.20
These knives and forks were purchased from a descendant of Charles Carroll of Duddington.

100. Marrow Scoop
George III
Maker's name not traced
London Hallmarks for 1760-61, on back
Carroll Crest (Hawk with wings elevated), on back
Length: 8 13/16 inches
Private Collection of a Descendant

101. Salver
George III
Maker: Robert Rew or Richard Rugg
London Hallmarks for 1761-62 and *R·R* in rectangular reserve, on back
Digges Arms impaling those of Carroll in cartouche, in center; no Crest
Height: 1 3/8 inches; diameter: 13 1/4 inches
Private Collection of a Descendant
This salver was owned by Ignatius Digges of "Melwood Park," Prince George's County, and his wife Mary Carroll.

102. Chocolate Pot
George III
Makers: Thomas Whipham and Charles Wright
London Hallmarks for 1761-62 and *C·W, T·W* crossed-joined in oval reserve, on bottom
Digges Arms impaling those of Carroll in cartouche, on side; no Crest
Height: 10 1/2 inches; diameter 7 3/4 inches
Private Collection of a Descendant
The chocolate pot was owned by Ignatius Digges of "Melwood Park," Prince George's County, and his wife Mary Carroll.

103. Pair of Wine Coasters

George III

Maker: Francis Spilsbury, Jr. (probably)

London Hallmarks for 1767-68 and *F·S* in shaped reserve, on inside of bottom (date letter and maker's mark partially obliterated on one)

Carroll Arms on side of each in cartouche; no Crest

Height: 1 13/16 inches; diameter 4 5/8 inches

The Maryland Historical Society, Baltimore

Gift of Mrs. B. Frank Newcomer, 1975

When this pair of wine coasters was purchased in 1907 by the donor's mother-in-law, the bill of sale stated that they had belonged to Charles Carroll of Annapolis.

104. Sauceboat

George III

Maker's name not traced

London Hallmarks for 1771-72 and *G·S* in rectangular reserve, on bottom

Carroll Crest (Hawk with wings elevated) on side

Height: 5 3/4 inches; width: 7 1/4 inches

Private Collection of a Descendant

105. Covered Tankard

George III

Maker: Hester Bateman

London Hallmarks for 1785-86 and *HB* in shaped reserve, below rim

Carroll Arms on front, partially obscured by the addition of a 19th century spout; no Crest

Height: 8 inches; width: 10 1/4 inches

Estate of Miriam Perkins Carroll Norris

106. Fork (one of twelve)

George III

Maker: Thomas Wallis

London Hallmarks for 1789-90 and script *TW* in rectangular reserve, on back

Carroll Crest (Hawk with wings elevated) on back

Length: 8 1/4 inches

Private Collection of a Descendant

Courtesy of Kennedy Galleries, Inc., New York

107. Goblet (one of two)

George III

Maker: William Bayley (probably)

London Hallmarks for 1791-92 and *W B* in rectangular reserve (bady worn), below rim

Carroll Arms and Crest (Hawk with wings elevated) on side of each

Height: 6 1/8 inches; diameter: 3 3/4 inches

Private Collection

108. Salver
George III
Maker: Robert Salmon
London Hallmarks for 1791-92 and *R S* in rectangular reserve, on bottom
Carroll Arms and Crest (Hawk with wings elevated) in center
Height: 1 5/8 inches; diameter: 15 15/16 inches
Private Collection of a Descendant
Courtesy of Kennedy Galleries, Inc., New York

109. Oval Tray
George III
Maker: Robert Jones
London Hallmarks for 1799-1800 and *RJ* in rectangular reserve, on bottom
Carroll Arms and Crest (Hawk with wings elevated) in the center (added ca. 1828)
Length: 31 1/4 inches
The Trustees of the Tenth Duke of Leeds Will Trust
This tray was originally owned by Francis Godolphin D'Arcy Osborne, 7th Duke of Leeds, and Louisa Caton, Duchess of Leeds.

110. Pair of Candlesticks
George III
Maker: John Green & Co., Sheffield, England
Sheffield Hallmarks for 1800-01 and *IG&C* in rectangular reserve, on base; *11 oz. 14 dw* engraved on base of one; *11 oz. 16 dw* engraved on base of other
Carroll Crest (Hawk with wings folded) on base
Height: 12 1/4 inches; diameter: 5 11/16 inches
Estate of Miriam Perkins Carroll Norris

111. Tablespoon (one of six)
American, ca. 1800
Maker: Standish Barry, Baltimore, working 1784-1810
SB in rectangular reserve, on back
Carroll Crest (Hawk with wings elevated) on front
Length: 8 3/4 inches
Private Collection of a Descendant
Courtesy of Kennedy Galleries, Inc., New York

112. Sugar Tongs
American, ca. 1800, probably Baltimore
Maker unknown
R M C engraved in oval at bend
Length: 6 11/16 inches
The Maryland Historical Society, Baltimore
Gift of Mrs. Herbert M. Brune, Sr., 1952
These sugar tongs were originally owned by Richard and Mary Caton, son-in-law and daughter of Charles Carroll of Carrollton. They were given by their daughter, Louisa Caton, Duchess of Leeds, to the donor's father-in-law.

113. Porringer
George III
Maker: John Moore
London Hallmarks for 1802-03 and *I M* in circular reserve, on bottom
Carroll Crest (Hawk with wings elevated) on top of flat handle
Height: 2 9/16 inches; width: 9 1/8 inches
Private Collection of a Descendant

114. Cake Basket
George III
Maker: William Frisbee
London Hallmarks for 1806-07 and *W F* in shaped reserve, on base
Engraved with the Arms of Richard, Marquess Wellesley
Width: 13 1/2 inches
The Trustees of the Tenth Duke of Leeds Will Trust
This cake basket was originally owned by Marianne Caton Patterson, Marchioness Wellesley, granddaughter of Charles Carroll of Carrollton, and her second husband, Richard Colley, Marquess Wellesley.

115. Serving Spoon
George IV
Makers: William Ely, William Fearn & William Chawner
London Hallmarks for 1809-10 and *WE/WF/WC* in rectangular reserve, on back
MacTavish Crest (Boar's head) on front
Length: 12 inches
Private Collection of a Descendant

116. Fork (one of two)
George IV
Maker's name not traced
London Hallmarks for 1827-28 and *BD* in rectangular reserve, on back
Carroll Crest (Hawk with wings elevated) on front
Length: 6 3/4 inches
Private Collection of a Descendant
Courtesy of Kennedy Galleries, Inc., New York

117. Teaspoon (one of five)
George IV
Maker: Jonathan Hayne
London Hallmarks for 1828-29 and script *JH* in oval reserve, on back
Carroll Crest (Hawk with wings elevated) on front
Length: 5 5/8 inches
Private Collection of a Descendant
Courtesy of Kennedy Galleries, Inc., New York

118. Knife (one of nine)
George IV
Maker's name not traced
Sheffield Hallmarks for 1828-29 and *J·R* in rectangular reserve, on handle; steel blades and replacements
Carroll Crest (Hawk with wings elevated) on front of handle
Length: 10 1/8 inches
Private Collection of a Descendant
Courtesy of Kennedy Galleries, Inc., New York

119. Fork (one of three)
American, ca. 1830
Maker: Andrew Ellicott Warner, Baltimore, working 1805-70
A·E·W in shaped reserve, *11* and *2* in separate rectangular reserves with clipped corners, on back
Carroll Crest (Hawk with wings elevated) on back
Length: 8 1/4 inches
Private Collection of a Descendant
Courtesy of Kennedy Galleries, Inc., New York
These forks were made to match Cat. No. 106

120. Fork (one of three)
American, ca. 1830
Maker: Andrew Ellicott Warner, Baltimore, working 1805-70
A·E·W in shaped reserve, Head of Liberty and *11* in rectangular reserves with clipped corners, on back
MacTavish Crest (Boar's head) on back
Length: 6 3/4 inches
Private Collection of a Descendant
Courtesy of Kennedy Galleries, Inc., New York

121. Pitcher
American, ca. 1830
Maker: Andrew Ellicott Warner, Baltimore, working 1805-70
A·E·Warner in shaped reserve, Head of Liberty, *11* and *2* in rectangular reserves with clipped corners, on bottom
Carroll Crest (Hawk with wings elevated) on front
Height: 9 3/4 inches; width: 8 1/4 inches
Private Collection of a Descendant
Courtesy of Kennedy Galleries, Inc., New York

Furniture and Other Household Objects

122. SIDE CHAIR

Queen Anne, ca. 1750

Maryland or Pennsylvania

Walnut

Height: 41 inches; width: 20 1/2 inches; depth: 17 inches

Joan Pennington Overturf

This side chair, according to family tradition, was originally owned by Charles Carroll of Carrollton. The date of manufacture would indicate it could also have been used by Charles Carroll of Annapolis.

123. WRITING DESK

George III, ca. 1770

English

Mahogany

Height: 32 inches; width: 42 inches; depth: 26 inches

Private Collection

This writing desk, according to family tradition, was owned by Charles Carroll of Carrollton. It was purchased by the present owners from Carroll descendants in Howard County early in this century.

124. SIDE CHAIR (one of two)

George III, ca. 1770

English

Mahogany

Height: 37 5/8 inches; width: 21 7/8 inches; depth: 19 1/4 inches

Private Collection of a Descendant

On October 26, 1771, Charles Carroll of Carrollton ordered through agents in London furniture, mirrors, curtains, a carpet, and other items for a room in his Annapolis house. Specified was "one fashionable sopha with 12 chairs to match" (Arents Collection s0767, New York Public Library). These chairs were in use at Doughoregan Manor until the first decades of this century and stylistically could be part of this 1771 order.

125. SIDE CHAIR

Chippendale Style, ca. 1770-80

Maryland

Mahogany

Height: 37 1/2 inches; width: 21 7/8 inches; depth: 20 1/2 inches

The Maryland Historical Society, Baltimore

Gift of Miss Bertha Cohen and her nieces, Mrs. D. Grigsby Long, Mrs. Harriet Cohen Coale, and Mrs. Arnold Burges Johnson, 1920

A brass plate on the chair reads: "Charles Carroll of Carrollton, presented by his granddaughter Miss Harper to her friend, Dr. Joshua I. Cohen, Baltimore." Numerous identical chairs are still in the possession of a Carroll descendant.

126. BREAKFRONT BOOKCASE

George III, ca. 1775

English

Mahogany with satinwood inlay

Height: 111 1/2 inches; width: 81 inches; depth: 23 1/4 inches

Private Collection of a Descendant

According to family tradition, this breakfront bookcase was used at Doughoregan Manor and remained there until the early part of this century.

127. HIGH POST BED

Chippendale, ca. 1780

Maryland, possibly Annapolis

Mahogany and tulip poplar

Height: 91 inches; width: 43 1/2 inches; length: 81 inches

Mr. & Mrs. Robert R. O'Donnell

This high post bed, most likely originally of a larger size, is said to have been owned by Charles Carroll of Carrollton. It descended through the line of Charles Carroll of Homewood.

128. HARPSICHORD

English, ca. 1788-89

Burkat Shudi & Johannes Broadwood, London

Inscribed above the keyboard: *B.S. et J.B., patent no. 955 Londoni fecerunt 1789/Great Pulteney Street/Golden Square;* inscribed underneath soundboard: *John Broadwood 1788*

Mahogany with maple veneer, brass fittings and casters (An early photograph indicated a porcelain plaque above the keyboard with painted Carroll Arms and Crest)

Height: 37 3/8 inches; width: 37 13/16 inches; length: 97 5/16 inches

Groton School, Groton, Massachusetts

Gift of Fanny Reed Hammond, 1939

The alleged ownership by Charles Carroll of Carrollton of this harpsichord began with its exhibition at the Centennial Celebration in Philadelphia in 1876. Entry number 266 in the 1876 *Official Catalogue* reads: "Knabe, Wm. & Co., Baltimore, Md. — Grand, square and upright pianos; a harpsichord made by Tschudi & Broadwood for Charles Carroll of Carrollton" (Part I. Dept. II, Manufacturers, p. 333). In February of 1785, Charles Carroll of Carrollton ordered a harpsichord from his agent in London, suggesting the maker be Kirkman; but apparently the instrument was made to special order by Burkat Shudi and Johannes Broadwood. Ownership and history are recorded in *Furniture of the Olden Time* by F. C. Morse (Macmillan Company, New York, 1902, reprint 1937) where it is noted that the harpsichord was owned by Charles Carroll of Carrollton in 1789, stored in a loft of an old building at St. John's College, Annapolis, in 1828 and discovered there in the late 19th century. There were numerous other owners prior to its acquisition by Fanny Reed Hammond, who in turn gave it to Groton School.

129. Side Chair

Federal, ca. 1790

Baltimore

Mahogany with satinwood inlay

Height: 36 7/8 inches; width: 20 7/8 inches; depth: 18 5/8 inches

The Baltimore Museum of Art

Museum Purchase, Louis Untermyer Fund 57.43

This chair is one of a large set of undetermined number. Some of these chairs are in major museums and private collections. Others are still retained by Carroll descendants (see Cat. No. 130), attesting to their purported original ownership by Charles Carroll of Carrollton. Two card tables, one each of an original two pairs, repeat the string inlays and carved bell-flower design (Cat. No. 131 and 132). They also have a tradition of Carroll ownership.

130. Side Chair

Federal, ca. 1790

Baltimore

Mahogany with satinwood inlay

Height: 36 7/8 inches; width: 20 7/8 inches; depth: 18 5/8 inches

Private Collection of a Descendant

For a discussion of this chair, refer to Cat. No. 129.

131. Card Table

Federal, ca. 1790

Baltimore

Mahogany with satinwood inlay

Height: 29 1/16 inches; width: 30 11/16 inches: depth: 15 inches (closed)

Mr. and Mrs. Harry B. Dillehunt, Jr.

The present owner of this and the following card table is descended from a William E. Hooper, a contemporary and sometime business associate of Charles Carroll of Carrollton. Family tradition suggests that William E. Hooper received the original two pairs of card tables from Charles Carroll of Carrollton. One table from each pair (see also Cat. No. 132) has descended to the present owners.

132. Card Table

Federal, ca. 1790

Baltimore

Mahogany with satinwood inlay

Height: 29 1/8 inches; width: 30 13/16 inches; depth: 15 inches (closed)

Mr. and Mrs. Harry B. Dillehunt, Jr.

For a discussion of provenance, see Cat. No. 131.

133. Side Chair (one of two)
Federal, ca. 1790
Baltimore
Mahogany
Height: 37 inches; width: 20 1/2 inches; depth: 17 inches
Private Collection of a Descendant
These side chairs are part of a large set which was originally used at Doughoregan Manor. Armchairs and other side chairs from the set are still owned by various Carroll descendants.

134. Side Chair (one of two)
Federal, ca. 1790
Baltimore
Mahogany
Height: 37 1/8 inches; width: 19 3/4 inches; depth: 16 3/4 inches
The Baltimore Museum of Art
Gift of Mrs. Francis White, from the Collection of Mrs. Miles White, Jr.
73.76.214.1 & .2
According to members of the Carroll family and to notes made by the late Mrs. Miles White, Jr., a set of chairs (see also Cat. No. 135) and a huntboard (Cat. No. 136) were in use at Doughoregan Manor in the late 18th century. These three pieces were purchased by Mrs. White from a Carroll descendant.

135. Side Chair
Federal, ca. 1790
Baltimore
Mahogany
Height: 37 1/8 inches; width: 19 3/4 inches; depth: 16 3/4 inches
Private Collection of a Descendant
This chair is from the same set as Cat. No. 134.

136. Huntboard
Federal, ca. 1790
Baltimore
Mahogany with satinwood inlay
Height: 31 1/8 inches; width: 68 1/2 inches; depth: 23 3/4 inches
The Baltimore Museum of Art
Gift of Mrs. Francis White, from the Collection of Mrs. Miles White, Jr.
73.76.220
For a discussion of this huntboard, refer to Cat. No. 134.

137. Pembroke Table
Federal, ca. 1790
Maryland
Mahogany with satinwood inlay
Height: 28 3/8 inches; width: 35 3/8 inches; length: 46 15/16 inches (open)
Mr. and Mrs. Bryden B. Hyde
This table was purchased at a Boucher family sale in Annapolis with a memorandum stating that it had been used in the library of the Carroll house on Spa Creek.

138. PORTABLE DESK AND TILL

Early 19th century

American

Mahogany with brass mounts
Carroll Crest (Hawk with wings elevated) on brass shield in center of lid.

Height: 6 13/16 inches; width: 19 1/8 inches; depth: 11 3/4 inches

Mr. Samson Feldman and Miss Sadie B. Feldman

This desk was acquired by the present owners through purchase.

Other provenance is not available.

139. ELEPHANT CLOCK

Louis XV style, early 19th century

French

Maker unknown

Gilt brass and enamel

Height: 15 3/4 inches; width: 12 3/8 inches; depth: 7 inches

The Baltimore Museum of Art

Bequest of Ellen H. Bayard 39.198

In the will of the donor, a Carroll descendant, this clock is listed as first belonging to Charles Carroll of Carrollton.

140. THE MILL

American, ca. 1790-1800

Artist unknown

Oil on canvas, 20 3/8 x 29 5/8 inches

Hammond-Harwood House Association, Annapolis

This painting was purchased from an art dealer in 1950; at that time, the original owner was stated as Charles Carroll of Carrollton.

141. EGGNOG PITCHER

English, ca. 1800

Cream-colored earthenware

Height: 11 1/2 inches; width: 12 7/16 inches

Mr. and Mrs. Bryden B. Hyde

When the eggnog pitcher was purchased by the present owner, an accompanying memorandum stated: "To my friend Robert L. Preston from Jany S. Taliaferro, Feb. 6, 1910. This pitcher came out of the old pantry at my uncle A. M. Smith's old mansion in Baltimore and came from the Baltimore home of Charles Carroll of Carrollton, when his effects were sold 40 or 50 years ago." Similar pitchers with alleged Carroll ownership survive in other private collections.

142. Plates and Platter from a Dinner Service

English, ca. 1819

Maker: Josiah Spode, II

Private Collection of a Descendant

This large, bone china service was owned by Charles Carroll of Carrollton and used at Doughoregan Manor in the early 19th century before and after his death in 1832. Many pieces remain in the possession of Carroll descendants. Each of the plates and soup plates is decorated in the center with painted shells of fanciful designs, and the cobalt blue border is overlayed with a kelp design in gilt.

Memorabilia

143. Snuff Box

French or English, mid-18th century

Maker unknown

Silver and tortoise shell

Height: 13/16 inches; length: 3 inches; width: 2 inches

Private Collection of a Descendant

The oval-shaped snuff box has a tortoise shell bottom and top. Applied to the top in silver, with the tortoise shell as a background, is a scene of a stag hunt, more French than English in character. According to family tradition, the snuff box belonged to Charles Carroll of Carrollton.

144. Seal

English or American, late 18th or early 19th century

Maker unknown

Ivory, silver, and bloodstone

Carroll Coat of Arms and Crest (Hawk with wings elevated) on face of seal with motto: *UBICUNQUE* [*sic*] *CUM LIBERTATE*

Overall length: 3 5/8 inches; diameter of handle: 1 1/4 inches

Face of seal (oval): 7/8 x 13/16 inches

The Maryland Historical Society, Baltimore

Gift of Anita Hack Carroll Bleck, 1952

This seal was obtained by Mrs. Bleck from a member of her first husband's family.

145. Knee Buckle

Probably French, late 18th century

Maker unknown

Paste, silver, and steel

Span: 2 13/16 inches; width: 13/16 inches

The Maryland Historical Society, Baltimore

Gift of Mrs. J. Albert Key, 1966

This knee buckle was presented to The Maryland Historical Society as belonging to Charles Carroll of Carrollton. The exact relationship of the donor to the Carroll family is unknown.

146. Watch and Chatelaine

French or Swiss, ca. 1780

Maker unknown

Gold with Geneva enameling, split pearls on front and back bezels, split pearls and seed pearls on chatelaine; original red leather case.

Swiss verge movement; casemaker's initials stamped on stem: *B F 7234*; monogram on seal suspended from chatelaine with engraved *JCC* or *ICC*

Watch, height to stem: 2 3/4 inches; diameter: 2 inches

Chatelaine, length: 9 5/16 inches

Mrs. Edmund R. Purves

According to family tradition, although in conflict with the perhaps later engraved initials on the chatelaine, this watch belonged to Charles Carroll of Carrollton and descended through the line of Charles Carroll of Homewood.

147. Scholastic Medal

American, 1805

Maker unknown

Gilt ten-pointed star

Engraved on one side: *Miss / Louisa C Caton / at Mrs. Keets' / ACADEMY. / Novr. 23^{d}. /1805*; on other side over an engraved artist's palette and brushes: *Genius / Rewarded.*

Width: 4 inches

Private Collection of a Descendant

148. Fob Seal

English or American, ca. 1800-10

Maker unknown

Carnelian and gold

Patterson Crest (A Pelican in her piety) and initials *RP* (Robert Patterson) engraved on seal

Length: 1 1/6 inches; width: 7/8 inches; diameter: 3/16 inches

The Maryland Historical Society, Baltimore

Gift of Mrs. Andrew Robeson, 1949

This fob seal was given to the Society by the great-granddaughter of Edward Patterson, brother of Robert Patterson who was the first husband of Marianne Caton, granddaughter of Charles Carroll of Carrollton.

149. Watch

Paris, ca. 1818

Maker: Abraham Louis Breguet (1747-1823)

Inscribed on dial: Breguet

Overall length: 2 3/8 inches; diameter: 2 3/16 inches

Sir Frederick Hervey-Bathhurst, Bart.

This watch was purchased in Paris by Sir Felton Elwell Hervey-Bathurst who married Louisa Caton, granddaughter of Charles Carroll of Carrollton. By tradition, it was obtained when the Duke of Wellington and his aide-de-camp Hervey-Bathurst went together to Breguet's in Paris where they purchased similar gold watches.

150. Pair of Shoe Buckles

Paris, 1819

Maker's name not traced

Standard mark for 1819, *OR* in rectangular reserve, *ROG / DOU / BLE* in rectangular reserve, and *IG* stamped on side of buckle

Gold and steel

Span: 2 7/16 inches; width: 1 3/4 inches

The Maryland Historical Society, Baltimore

Gift of Mr. Edmund Law Rogers Smith, 1948

A note, originally attached to the buckles by the donor, stated that they belonged to Charles Carroll of Carrollton.

151. FOB SEAL

English or American, ca. 1820

Maker unknown

Gold and carnelian

Bayard Arms and Crest (A Horse, *rampant*, couped) and Motto: *HONOR ET JUSTITIA*

Length: 1 1/16 inches; width: 7/8 inches; height: 1 3/8 inches

The Baltimore Museum of Art

Bequest of Ellen Howard Bayard 36.47.62

The donor was descended from Charles Carroll of Carrollton through the Signer's granddaughter Mary Sophia Carroll who married Richard Henry Bayard of Wilmington, Delaware.

152. SPECTACLES

American, early 19th century

Maker unknown

Silver

Length (extended): 6 inches; width: 4 3/8 inches

Mrs. Andrew Matthew McCrone

The eye glasses or spectacles, according to family tradition, were owned and used by Charles Carroll of Carrollton.

152. WATCH

Paris, ca. 1820

Maker: House of Breguet (most likely made by a student of Abraham Louis Breguet, 1747-1823)

Gold case, silver dial, and blue steel hands; original crystal has been replaced; quarter-hour repeating movement

Marked on dial: *BREGUET*; marked on inside of back: *1626*; an indecipherable mark in lozenge inside of back

Overall length: 3 inches; diameter: 2 13/16 inches

Private Collection

This watch was owned by Charles Carroll of Carrollton.

154. PENDANT TRIPLE FOB SEAL

American or English, early 19th century

Maker unknown

Gold, sardonyx, carnelian, and bloodstone

On sardonyx seal: figure of a woman mourning over a funeral urn and on plinth: *SOUVENIR*; on carnelian: the MacTavish Crest (Boar's head), the initials *Jm^{c}T*, and the motto *NON OBLITUS*; on bloodstone: a Stag's Head Crest, the initials *DM^{c}G*, and motto: *BE MINDFUL.*

Length: 2 1/2 inches; width: 1 5/8 inches

Private Collection of a Descendant

This triple fob seal, made into a pin at a later date, has descended in the MacTavish family. The initials *JM^{c}T* stand for John MacTavish who married Emily Caton, granddaughter of Charles Carroll of Carrollton.

155. RING

English or American, ca. 1825

Maker unknown

Gold and bloodstone

Engraved in Hebrew: *They Asked The Peace of Jerusalem;* inside band: *C.C.B. to R.H.B.*

Diameter: 3/4 inches; stone: 9/16 inches square

The Baltimore Museum of Art

Gift of Ellen Howard Bayard 36.47.65

The initials *R.H.B.* are those of Richard Henry Bayard who married Mary Sophia Carroll, the granddaughter of Charles Carroll of Carrollton.

156. LOCKET

American, early 19th century

Maker unknown

Gold, glass, and hair

Inscribed on back: *From Charles Carroll of Carrollton;* a lock of his hair is knotted under glass on the front.

Diameter: 1 3/16 inches

The Maryland Historical Society, Baltimore

Gift of Mrs. Robert E. Lee Williamson, 1946

This locket is said to have been given by Charles Carroll of Carrollton to his friend and neighbor Barney Dean, a collateral ancestor of the donor's husband in whose family the locket descended.

157. BADGE COMMEMORATING THE LAYING OF THE CORNERSTONE OF THE BALTIMORE AND OHIO RAILROAD

Baltimore, 1828

Maker: Medairy and Bannerman So. (John Medairy and William W. Bannerman, in business together, 1827-1831)

Silk, printed with a portrait of Charles Carroll of Carrollton and legend: *IN / Commemoration of the / Breaking of Ground for the / BALTIMORE & OHIO RAIL ROAD / Performed / by / CHARLES CARROLL OF CARL^{T}. / Last Surviving Signer of the / Declaration / of Independence / July 4th 1828*

Length: 7 1/2 inches; width: 3 inches

The Maryland Historical Society, Baltimore

Gift of Mrs. Walter W. Hooper, 1931

Other badges commemorating the same event were decorated with likenesses of George Washington and Benjamin Franklin.

158. CRUCIFIX

English or American, early 19th century

Ebony cross, ivory figure

Height: 20 inches; width: 10 inches

Private Collection of a Descendant

According to family tradition, this crucifix was the property of Charles Carroll of Carrollton. A remarkably similar crucifix appears in the background of William James Hubard's portrait of Carroll (Cat. No. 41).

Notes To Bibliography

Two of the essays in the catalogue are accompanied by their own bibliographies which provide important source material for the study of Charles Carroll of Carrollton and John Carroll. Those sources which were specifically used in the preparation of the catalogue listings have been repeated here.

With the exception of Charles Carroll of Carrollton, the literature on the Carroll family is scant, and the only extensive and reliable sources are the manuscripts cited.

The Selected Bibliography is divided into the following sections: Manuscripts Consulted, Newspapers Consulted, General Sources: Subjects, General Sources: Artists, and Selected Bibliography on Artists. The numbers following bibliographical entries refer to the relevant catalogue entry.

Unless a more detailed bibliography appears under the name of an artist, it may be assumed that biographical information on the artist was taken from the general references.

Selected Bibliography and Index of Artists

MANUSCRIPTS CONSULTED

MARYLAND HISTORICAL SOCIETY, Baltimore
Charles Carroll of Carrollton Correspondence, MS 215
Charles Carroll of Carrollton Correspondence with son, MS 203
Charles Carroll of Carrollton Inventory of Real Estate, MS 205
Charles Carroll of Carrollton Journal, 1792-1802, MS 209
Charles Carroll of Carrollton Letterbooks, MS 203.1
Carroll-Harper Papers, MS 1225
Carroll-MacTavish Papers, MS 220
Carroll Papers, MS 206
Correspondence between Charles Carroll of Annapolis and Charles Carroll of Carrollton
Carroll Papers, MS 216
Carroll-Purves Papers, MS 1227
Caton-Hoffman Papers, MS 1229
Mary Diana Harper Letters, MS 430
Harper-Pennington Papers, MS 431
Correspondence Books I, 1844-1848

LIBRARY OF CONGRESS, Division of Manuscripts
Carroll Family Papers

NEW YORK PUBLIC LIBRARY
Arents Collection
Thomas A. Simms Collection (Daniel Carroll of Duddington)

ARCHIVES OF AMERICAN ART, SMITHSONIAN INSTITUTION
Charles Henry Hart Autograph Collection, microfilm
Df, 1124-1125
Miscellaneous, MS Thomas Sully, 1827

AMERICAN PHILOSOPHICAL SOCIETY
Peale Papers
Peale Letterbook

NEWSPAPERS CONSULTED

The Maryland Gazette
American and Commercial Daily Advertiser
The Emerald and Baltimore Literary Gazette
Baltimore American and Daily Advertiser
Federal Gazette and Daily Advertiser
Baltimore American
The Maryland Journal and Baltimore Advertiser
Morning Chronicle and Daily Advertiser
The Republican [Easton]

General Works Consulted: Subjects

The Baltimore Museum of Art. *Charles Carroll of Carrollton (1737-1832) and His Family; An Exhibition of Portraits, Furniture, Silver, and Manuscripts at The Baltimore Museum of Art September 19-October 30, 1937.* Baltimore: Under the Auspices of the United States Commission for the Celebration of the Two Hundredth Anniversary of the Birth of Charles Carroll of Carrollton, 1937. cat. nos. 4A, 5A, 7, 9A, 12, 14, 23, 37, 38F, 39B, 42C, 46A, 47, 48, 57F, 62B, 64, 66, 67, 70B, 80.

The Baltimore Museum of Art. *Two Hundred and Fifty Years of Painting in Maryland, May 11-June 17, 1945. Baltimore:* The Baltimore Museum of Art, 1945.

Bowie, Effie Gwynn. *Across the Years In Prince George's County.* Richmond: Garrett and Massie, 1947.

Brent, John Carroll, ed. *Biographical Sketch of the Most Rev. John Carroll, First Archbishop of Baltimore: With Select Portions of His Writings.* Baltimore, John Murphy, 1843.

Field, Thomas Meagher, ed. *Unpublished Letters of Charles Carroll of Carrollton, and of His Father, Charles Carroll of Doughoregan.* New York: The United States Catholic Historical Society, 1902.

Geiger, Sister Mary Virginia. *Daniel Carroll, A Framer of the Constitution.* Washington, D.C.: The Catholic University of America, 1943.

Griswold, Rufus Wilmot. *The Republican Court or American Society in the Days of Washington.* New York: D. Appleton and Co., 1855.

Gurn, Joseph. *Charles Carroll of Carrollton.* P. J. Kennedy & Sons, 1932.

Hanley, Thomas. *Charles Carroll of Carrollton.* Washington, D.C.: Catholic University Press, 1970.

Keidel, George Charles. *Catonsville Biographies, a Series of Personal Sketches.* Catonsville, Maryland, 1915.

Land, Aubrey. *The Dulanys of Maryland.* Baltimore: Maryland Historical Society, 1955.

Longford, Elizabeth. *Wellington: Pillar of State.* New York: Harper & Row, Publishers, 1972.

Maryland Historical Magazine. Vol. I, March 1906, to Vol. LXX, 1975.

McGrath, Francis Sims. *Pillars of Maryland.* Richmond: Dietz Press, 1950.

Perrine, William. "The Baltimore Belle Who Made The Most Brilliant Match of Any Girl in America," *The Ladies' Home Journal,* January, 1901, p. 5ff.

Rowland, Kate Mason. *The Life of Charles Carroll: 1737-1832.* New York: G. P. Putnam's Sons, 1898.

Sanderson, John. *Biography of the Signers to the Declaration of Independence.* 9 vols. Philadelphia, R. W. Pomeroy, 1827.

Semmes, John. *John H. B. Latrobe and His Times 1803-1891.* Baltimore: The Norman, Remington Co., 1917.

Semmes, Raphael. *Baltimore as Seen by Visitors.* Baltimore: Maryland Historical Society, 1953.

Smith, Ellen Hart. *Charles Carroll of Carrollton.* Cambridge, Mass.: Harvard University Press, 1942.

Stirling, A. M. W. "A Transatlantic Invasion of 1816," *The Nineteenth Century,* Dec., 1909, pp. 1058-1075.

Wharton, Anne Hollingsworth. *Salons Colonial and Republican.* Philadelphia: Benjamin Blom, Inc., 1900; reissued 1971.

Wharton, Anne Hollingsworth. *Social Life in the Early Republic.* Philadelphia: J. B. Lippincott & Co., 1902.

GENERAL WORKS CONSULTED: ARTISTS

Baltimore Directories, 1796, 1799, 1800-1804, 1807-1808, 1810, 1812, 1814-19, 1822-24, 1827, 1829, 1831, 1833, 1835-38, 1840-1842, 1845, 1847-1848.

The Baltimore Museum of Art. *Charles Carroll of Carrollton (1737-1832) and His Family; An Exhibition of Portraits, Furniture, Silver, and Manuscripts at The Baltimore Museum of Art September 19-October 30, 1937.* Baltimore: Under the Auspices of the United States Commission for the Celebration of the Two Hundredth Anniversary of the Birth of Charles Carroll of Carrollton, 1937, cat. nos. 4A, 5A, 7, 9A, 12, 14, 23, 37, 38F, 39B, 42C, 46A, 47, 48, 57F, 62B, 64, 66, 67, 70B, 80.

The Baltimore Museum of Art. *Two Hundred and Fifty Years of Painting in Maryland, May 11-June 17, 1945.* Baltimore: The Baltimore Museum of Art, 1945.

Dictionary of National Biography. London: Oxford University Press, 1959-1960.

Dictionary of American Biography. New York: C. Scribner's Sons, 1928-1936.

Fielding, Mantle. *American Engravers Upon Copper and Steel.* New York; reprint ed. Bunt Franklin, 1966.

Groce, George, and Wallace, David. *Dictionary of Artists in America 1564-1860.* New Haven: Yale University Press, 1957.

Long, Basil S. *British Miniaturists.* London: The Holland Press, 1966.

Maryland Historical Magazine, Vol. 1, 1906, to Vol. LXX, 1975.

Pleasants, J. Hall. "Studies in Maryland Painting." The Maryland Historical Society: Baltimore, Maryland.

Prime, Alfred C. *The Arts and Crafts in Philadelphia, Maryland and South Carolina, 1786-1800.* Topsfield, Mass., 1932.

Schidlof, Leo R. *The Miniature in Europe in the 16th, 17th, 18th, 19th Centuries.* Graz: Akademische Druck-V. Verlagsonstalt, 1964.

Thieme, Ulrich, and Becker, Felix. *Allgemeines Lexikon Der Bildenden Künstler von der Antike bis zur Gegenwart.* Leipzig: Verlag von Wilhelm Engelmann, 1910.

ALLSTON, WASHINGTON
Attributed to: cat. no. 57D

The Lincoln Isham Collection and Others Sale, March 31, 1939. New York: Parke-Bernet Gallery, 1939.

Pleasants, J. Hall. "Studies in Maryland Painting." No. 1917-cat. no. 57D. On deposit Maryland Historical Society, Baltimore.

BAILLY, JOSEPH ALEXIS
Cat. no. 84A

BOGLE, MESSRS. (probably James Bogle, ca. 1817-1873, and Robert Bogle, ca. 1817-?)
Cat. no. 51C

BROWERE, JOHN H. I.
Attributed to: cat. no 42D
After: cat. no. 42E

Hart, Charles H. *Browere's Life Masks of Great Americans.* New York: Doubleday, 1899. Cat. no. 42D

Millard, Everett L. "The Browere Life Masks." *Art in America* (April 1950): 69-80, 128. Cat. no. 42D

Rowland, Kate Mason. *The Life of Charles Carroll: 1737-1832.* New York: G. P. Putnam's Sons, 1898. Cat. no. 42D

BROOKS, RICHARD EDWIN
Cat. no. 42G

Information on file, Office of the Architect, U.S. Capitol, Washington, D.C.

CRAWFORD, THOMAS
Cat. no. 89

Craven, Wayne. *Sculpture In America.* New York: Thomas Y. Crowell Co., 1834.

Will of Emily Louisa Hinton Harper, Private Collection of a Descendant

DEAN, THOMAS A.
Attributed to: cat. no. 72G

DE CLORIVIERE, JOSEPH-PIERRE PICOT DE LIMOELAN
Attributed to: cat. no. 56A
After: cat. no. 56

Rutledge, Anna Wells. "A French Priest, Painter and Architect in the United States: Joseph Pierre Picot de Limoëlan de Clorivière." *Gazette Des Beaux-Arts,* vol. XXXIII (March 1948): 159-76.

DICKINSON, ANSON
Cat. no. 30

Frick Art Reference Library notes, New York. 175-10D[2]. Cat. no. 30.

Kidder, Mary Helen. *List of Miniatures Painted by Anson Dickinson, 1803-1851.* Hartford: Connecticut Historical Society, 1937. Cat. no. 30.

Pleasants, J. Hall. "Studies in Maryland Painting." No. 3689—Cat. no. 30. On deposit Maryland Historical Society, Baltimore.

Rutledge, Anna Wells. *Cumulative Record of Exhibition Catalogues, The Pennsylvania Academy of the Fine Arts, 1807-1870, The Society of Artists, 1800-1814, The Artists' Fund Society, 1835-1845.* Philadelphia: The American Philosophical Society, 1955.

DUDENSING, RICHARD
Cat. no. 51D

DURAND, ASHER B.
Cat. nos. 3, 38.

Craven, Wayne. "Asher B. Durand's Career As An Engraver." *American Art Journal,* vol. 3. no. 1 (1971):39-71.

Dunlap, William. *A History of The Rise and Progress of the Arts of Design in the United States.* New York, 1834; reprint ed., New York: Dover Publications, Inc., 1969. Cat. no. 38.

Durand, John. *The Life and Times of Asher B. Durand.* New York: Kennedy Graphics, Inc., Da Capo Press, 1970.

Hendricks, Gordon. "Durand, Maverick and the *Declaration.*" *American Art Journal,* vol. 3, no. 1 (1971):58-71.

Herring, James and James B. Longacre. *The National Portrait Gallery of Distinguished Americans.* Philadelphia: James B. Longacre, 1836. Cat. no. 38.

Lawall, David B. "Asher B. Durand: His Art and Art Theory in Relation to His Times." Ph.D. dissertation. Princeton University, 1966.

Morgan, John Hill. *Paintings by John Trumbull at Yale University.* New Haven: Yale University Press, 1926.

Rutledge, Anna Wells. *Cumulative Record of Exhibition Catalogues, The Pennsylvania Academy of the Fine Arts, 1807-1870, The Society of Artists, 1800-1814, The Artists' Fund Society, 1835-1845.* Philadelphia: The American Philosophical Society, 1955.

Stauffer, David McNeely. *American Engravers Upon Copper and Steel.* New York: The Grolier Club of the City of New York, 1907. Nos. 679—Cat. no. 3; no. 566—Cat. no. 38.

Stewart, Robert G. *A Nineteenth-Century Gallery of Distinguished Americans.* Washington, D.C.: National Portrait Gallery, Smithsonian Institution Press, 1969.

Edouart, Augustin-Amant-Constant-Fidele
Cat. no. 81

Endicott & Swett (George Endicott, 1802-1848 and Moses Swett, ca. 1826-1837)
Cat. no. 42.
After: cat. no. 42A

Field, Robert
Cat. nos. 17, 62, 63, 67
Attributed to: 57C
After: cat. nos. 18, 19, 19A, 19B, 19C, 20, 20A, 21, 22

Bolton, Theodore. *Early American Portrait Painters in Miniature.* New York: Frederic Fairchild Sherman, 1921. Cat. nos. 17, 19A.

Bowen, Clarence Winthrop, ed. *The History of the Centennial Celebration of the Inauguration of George Washington as First President of the United States.* New York: D. Appleton and Co., 1892.

Lane, James. "Studies in American Painting." Feb. 16, 1969. On deposit Kennedy Galleries, Inc. Cat. no. 19.

The Maryland Historical Society Catalogues of Exhibitions, 1848-1908. Cat. no. 19.

Piers, Harry. *Robert Field, Portrait Painter in Oils, Miniature and Water-colours and Engraver.* New York: Frederick Fairchild Sherman, 1927. Cat. no. 17.

Pleasants, J. Hall. "Studies in Maryland Painting." Nos. 19, 485, 1370—cat. no. 67; no. 1660—cat. no. 19A; no. 3305—cat. no. 57C. On deposit Maryland Historical Society, Baltimore.

Sanderson, John. *Biography of the Signers to the Declaration of Independence.* 9 vols. Philadelphia: R. W. Pomeroy, 1827. Cat. no. 18.

Smith, Justin H. "The Prologue of the American Revolution," pt. V: "The Fortune of War," *The Century Illustrated Monthly Magazine,* vol. 65, N.S. vol. 43, (Nov. 1902-April 1903).

Wharton, Anne Hollingsworth. *Salons Colonial and Republican.* Philadelphia: Benjamin Blom, Inc., 1900; reissued 1971.

Wehle, Harry B. "American Miniatures 1730-1850," *A Biographical Dictionary of the Artists,* by Theodore Bolton: 83-84.

Freeman, Samuel
Cat. no. 70A

Gobrecht, Christian
Cat. nos. 25, 26, 27

Darrach, Charles G. "Christian Gobrecht, Artist and Inventor," *Pennsylvania Magazine of History and Biography,* vol. XXX (July 1906):355-8. Cat. nos. 25, 26, 27.

Rutledge, Anna Wells. *Cumulative Record of Exhibition Catalogues, The Pennsylvania Academy of the Fine Arts, 1807-1870, The Society of Artists, 1800-1814, The Artists' Fund Society, 1835-1845,* Philadelphia: The American Philosophical Society, 1955. Cat. nos. 25, 26, 27.

HALL, M. CALLING
Cat. no. 86B
No reference located.

HALL, HENRY BRYAN
Cat. nos. 20, 54
After ?: cat. no. 54A

Stauffer, David McNeely. *American Engravers Upon Copper and Steel.* New York: The Grolier Club of the City of New York, 1907.

HARDING, CHESTER
Cat. nos. 38A, 38B, 38F, 39, 39A, 39B
After: cat. nos. 38, 38C, 38D, 38E, 38F, 38G

The Baltimore Museum of Art. *Charles Carroll of Carrollton (1737-1832) and His Family: An Exhibition of Portraits, Furniture, Silver, and Manuscripts at The Baltimore Museum of Art September 19-October 30, 1937.* Baltimore: The Baltimore Museum of Art under the Auspices of the United States Commission for the Celebration of the Two Hundredth Anniversary of the Birth of Charles Carroll of Carrollton, 1937. Cat. no. 38F.

Cowdry, Mary Bartlett. *National Academy of Design Exhibition Record, 1826-1860.* New York, 1943. Cat. no. 38A.

Dunlap, William. *A History of the Rise and Progress of the Arts of Design in the United States.* New York, 1834; reprint ed., New York: Dover Publications, Inc., 1969. Cat. no. 38.

Frick Art Reference Library notes, New York. No. 121-13a—cat. no. 38E; 121-5b—cat. no. 39B; 121-5c—cat. no. 39; 175-10a—cat. no. 38F; 121-6e—cat. no. 39A.

The Maryland Historical Society Catalogues of Exhibitions, 1848-1908. Cat. nos. 38B, 38C, 38D.

Pleasants, J. Hall. "Studies in Maryland Painting." No. 131—cat. no. 39B; no. 1614—cat. no. 38F; no. 1662—cat. no. 38E. On deposit Maryland Historical Society, Baltimore.

Rutledge, Anna Wells. *Cumulative Record of Exhibition Catalogues, The Pennsylvania Academy of the Fine Arts, 1807-1870, The Society of Artists, 1800-1814, The Artists' Fund Society, 1835-1845.* Philadelphia: The American Philosophical Society, 1955.

Stewart, Robert G. *A Nineteenth-Century Gallery of Distinguished Americans.* Washington, D.C.: National Portrait Gallery, Smithsonian Institution Press, 1969.

White, Margaret E., ed. *A Sketch of Chester Harding, Artist, Drawn By His Own Hand.* New York: Houghton Mifflin Co., 1928.

HEAPHY, THOMAS
Cat. no. 76B
Attributed to: cat. no. 76, 76A

Whitley, William Thomas. *Thomas Heaphy (1775-1835) First President of the Society of British Artists.* London: The Royal Society of British Artists' Art Club, 1933.

HESSELIUS, GUSTAVUS
Hesselius ?: cat. no. 5
Formerly Attributed to: cat. no. 13, 13A

Fleischer, Roland Edward. "Gustavus Hesselius." Ph.D. dissertation, The Johns Hopkins University, 1964. Cat. nos. 13, 13A.

Fleischer, Roland Edward. "Gustavus Hesselius: A Study of His Style." *American Painting to 1776: A Reappraisal.* Winterthur, Delaware: Winterthur Conference Report, 1971.

Frick Art Reference Library notes, New York. No. 122-6E—cat. no. 13.

Lane, James, "Studies in American Painting." June 6, 1958. On deposit Kennedy Galleries. Inc., New York. Cat. no. 13A.

Philadelphia Museum of Art. *Gustavus Hesselius 1682-1755.* Philadelphia: Philadelphia Museum of Art Under the Auspices of the Pennsylvania 300th Anniversary Commission, 1938.

Pleasants, J. Hall. "Studies in Maryland Painting." No. 475—cat. no. 13; no. 3309—cat. no. 13A; no. 3315—cat. no. 5. On deposit Maryland Historical Society, Baltimore.

Hesselius, John
Hesselius?: cat. no. 8
Reference to: cat. no. 8B

Doud, Richard Keith. "John Hesselius: His Life & Work. A thesis submitted to the faculty of the University of Delaware, June 1963.

Doud, Richard Keith, ed. "John Hesselius, Maryland Limner," *Winterthur Portfolio 5.* Charlottesville: University Press of Virginia, 1969.

Samuel Hollyer
Cat. no. 54A

Hubard, William James
Cat. nos. 41, 79
After: cat. nos. 41A, 41B, 42

Bowen, Clarance Winthrop, ed. *The History of The Centennial Celebration of the Inauguration of George Washington as First President of the United States.* New York: D. Appleton and Co., 1892. Cat. no. 41A.

Dunlap, William. *A History of the Rise and Progress of the Arts of Design in the United States.* New York, 1834; reprint ed., New York: Dover Publications, Inc., 1969.

Frick Art Reference Library notes, New York. No. 121-1V. Cat. no. 41.

Gardner, Albert Ten Eyck. "Southern Monuments: Charles Carroll and William James Hubard." *The Metropolitan Museum of Art Bulletin* (Summer 1958): 19-23.

Gardner, Albert Ten Eyck, and Stuart P. Feld. *American Paintings: A Catalogue of the Collection of the Metropolitan Museum of Art.* New York: The Metropolitan Museum of Art, 1965.

McCormack, Helen G. *William James Hubard, 1807-1862.* Richmond: The Valentine Museum, For the Virginia Museum of Fine Arts, 1948.

Pleasant, J. Hill. "Studies in Maryland Painting." No. 3311—cat. no. 79. On deposit Maryland Historical Society, Baltimore.

Rutledge, Anna Wells. *Cumulative Record of Exhibition Catalogues, The Pennsylvania Academy of the Fine Arts, 1807-1870, The Society of Artists, 1800-1814, The Artists' Fund Society, 1835-1845.* Philadelphia: The American Philosophical Society, 1955.

Jaquotot, Marie-Victoire
Cat. no. 71

Bénézit, E. *Dictionnaire critique et documentaire des Peintres, Sculpteurs, Dessinateurs et Graveurs.* Librarie Gründ, 1955.

JARVIS, JOHN WESLEY
Attributed by family tradition to: cat. no. 42H
Formerly attributed to: cat. no. 69
After ?: cat. no. 42I

Dickson, Harold E. *John Wesley Jarvis, American Painter, 1780-1840.* New York, 1949.

KING, CHARLES BIRD
Cat. no. 42C
King?: cat. no. 88
King ? or Unknown Artist: cat. no. 69
After ?: cat. no. 69A

Bowen, Clarence Winthrop, ed. *The History of the Centennial Celebration of the Inauguration of George Washington as First President of the United States.* New York: D. Appleton and Co., 1892.

Frick Art Reference Library notes, New York. No. 121-6J. Cat. no. 42C.

Pennsylvania Academy of Fine Arts, Sixth Annual Exhibition. Cat. no. 69.

Pleasants, J. Hall. "Studies in Maryland Painting." No. 130—cat. no. 42C; no. 593—cat. no. 88; no. 594—cat. no. 69; no. 2812—cat. no. 69A. On deposit Maryland Historical Society, Baltimore.

Rowland, Kate Mason. *The Life Of Charles Carroll: 1737-1832.* New York: G. P. Putnam's Sons, 1898.

Rutledge, Anna Wells. *Cumulative Record of Exhibition Catalogues, The Pennsylvania Academy of the Fine Arts, 1807-1870, The Society of Artists, 1800-1814, The Artists' Fund Society, 1835-1845.* Philadelphia: The American Philosophical Society, 1955.

KUHN, JUSTUS ENGELHARDT
Cat. nos. 12, 14, 46A
Formerly attributed to: cat. no. 10
Unknown or Kühn: cat. no. 4 (?), 4A, 5A, 6
After: cat. no. 46B

Dunlap, William. *A History of the Rise and Progress of the Arts of Design in the United States.* New York, 1834; reprint ed., New York: Dover Publications, Inc., 1969.

Frick Art Reference Library notes, New York. No. 122-11a—cat. no. 5A; no. 1B3-1C—cat. no. 12.

The Maryland Historical Society Catalogue of Exhibitions 1893-1908. Cat. no. 6.

Pleasants, J. Hall. "Justus Engelhardt Kühn: An Early 18th Century Maryland Portrait Painter." *Proceedings of the American Antiquarian Society,* Oct. 1936.

Pleasants, J. Hall. "Studies in Maryland Painting." No. 123—cat. no. 46A; no. 126—cat. no. 4A; no. 127—cat. no. 5A; no. 515—cat. no. 14; no. 516—cat. no. 10; no. 522—cat. no. 12; no. 1311—cat. no. 46B—3066—cat. no. 4; no. 3308—cat. no. 6. On deposit Maryland Historical Society, Baltimore.

LATY, MICHAEL
Cat. nos. 19, 73B
After: cat. nos. 19A, 19B, 20

Bowen, Clarence Winthrop, ed. *The History of the Centennial Celebration of the Inauguration of George Washington as First President of the United States.* New York: D. Appleton and Co. 1892. Cat. no. 19A (listed as by Field).

Frick Art Reference Library notes, New York. No. 121-14a—cat. no. 19; no. 121-6a—cat. no. 73B.

Lane, James. "Studies in American Painting." Feb. 16, 1969. On deposit Kennedy Galleries, Inc., New York. Cat. no. 19A.

The Maryland Historical Society Catalogues of Exhibitions, 1848-1908. Cat. nos. 19A, 73B.

Pleasants, J. Hall. "Studies in Maryland Painting." No. 485—cat. no. 19; no. 1660—cat. no. 19A; no. 1668—cat. no. 73B. On deposit Maryland Historical Society, Baltimore.

LAWRENCE, SIR THOMAS
Cat. nos. 71A, 72, 72D, 72E, 73, 74, 75, 76C, 76D
Attributed to: cat. no. 71B
After: cat. nos. 71, 72A, 72B, 72C, 73A, 73B, 73C, 73D, 74A

Dunlap, William. *A History of The Rise & Progress of The Arts of Design in the United States.* New York, 1834; reprint ed., New York: Dover Publications, Inc., 1969.

Field, Thomas Meagher, ed., *Unpublished Letters of Charles Carroll of Carrollton, and His Father, Charles Carroll of Doughoregan.* New York: The United States Catholic Historical Society, 1902.

Frick Art Reference Library notes, New York. No. 222-6V—cat. no. 71A; 221-5K—cat. no. 73.

Garlick, Kenneth. *A Catalogue of Paintings, Drawings and Pastels of Sir Thomas Lawrence. Glasgow:* University Press, 1964. Cat. nos. 76C, 76D.

Garlick, Kenneth. *Sir Thomas Lawrence.* London: Routledge and Degan Paul, 1954.

The Maryland Historical Society Catalogues of Exhibitions, 1848-1908. Cat. nos. 71A, 72A, 72B, 72C, 73B, 73C, 74A.

Pleasants, J. Hall. "Studies in Maryland Painting." Nos. 1666—cat. no. 72B; no. 1667—cat. no. 74A; no. 1668—cat. no. 73B; no. 3407—cat. no. 71A. On deposit Maryland Historical Society, Baltimore.

Properties of Duke of Leeds. Catalogues of sale. London: Christie's 1930. Cat. no. 72E.

Rendezvous For Taste. Baltimore: The Peale Museum, 1956. Cat. nos. 71B, 72C, 72D.

Wellington, Arthur Wellesley. *A Selection From the Private Correspondence of the 1st Duke of Wellington.* London: Dropmore Press. ed. by the Duke of Wellington. Printed for the presentation to the members of Roxburghe Club, 1952. Cat. nos. 71A, 73.

Wellington, Gerald Wellesley, 7th Duke of. *The Iconography of the First Duke of Wellington.* London: J. M. Dent & Sons Ltd. 1935.

Williams, D. E. *Life and Correspondence of Sir Thomas Lawrence.* London: Henry Colburn and Richard Bentley, 1831.

LENEY, WILLIAM S., F.S.A. and BENJAMIN TANNER, F.S.A.
Cat. no. 53
After: cat. nos. 54, 54A

Stauffer, David McNeely. *American Engravers Upon Copper and Steel.* New York: The Grolier Club of the City of New York, 1907. No. 1722—cat. no. 53.

LONGACRE, JAMES B.
Cat. nos. 18, 40
After: cat. no. 40A

Herring, James and, Longacre, James. *The National Portrait Gallery of Distinguished Americans.* Philadelphia: 1834. Cat. no. 18.

Rutledge, Anna Wells. *Cumulative Record of Exhibition Catalogues, The Pennsylvania Academy of the Fine Arts, 1807-1870, The Society of Artists, 1800-1814, The Artists' Fund Society, 1835-1845.* Philadelphia: The American Philosophical Society, 1955.

Sanderson, John. *Biography of the Signers to the Declaration of Independence.* 9 vols. Philadelphia: R. W. Pomeroy, 1827.

Stauffer, David McNeely. *American Engravers Upon Copper and Steel.* No. 1954—cat. no. 18; no. 1953—cat. no. 40. New York: Grolier Club of the City of New York, 1907.

Stewart, Robert G. *A Nineteenth-Century Gallery of Distinguished Americans.* Washington, D.C.: National Portrait Gallery, Smithsonian Institution Press, 1969.

Mee, Mrs. Anne
Cat. nos. 75A, 77A
After: cat. no. 75B

Meyer, Henry Hoppner
Cat. no. 38G

Mote, W. H.
Cat. no. 40A

Stauffer, David McNeely. *American Engravers Upon Copper and Steel.* New York: The Grolier Club of the City of New York, 1907.

Newsam, Albert
Cat. no. 36

Nichols, Abel
Cat. no. 38C

The Maryland Historical Society Catalogue of Exhibitions, 1879. Cat. no. 38C.

Paul, Jeremiah
Paul ?: cat. no. 52
After: cat. nos. 53, 54, 54A

Dickson, H. E. "A Note on Jeremiah Paul," *Antiques* (June 1949):392-393.

Dunlap, William. *A History of The Rise and Progress of the Arts of Design in the United States.* New York, 1834; reprint ed., New York: Dover Publications, Inc., 1969.

Frick Art Reference Library notes No. 121-6a—cat. no. 52.

Pleasants, J. Hall. "Studies in Maryland Painting." No. 2208—cat. no. 52. On deposit Maryland Historical Society, Baltimore.

Rutledge, Anna Wells, ed. *Cumulative Record of Exhibitions Catalogues, The Pennsylvania Academy of the Fine Arts, 1807-1870, The Society of Artists, 1800-1814, The Artists' Fund Society, 1835-1845.* Philadelphia: The American Philosophical Society, 1955.

PEALE, CHARLES WILLSON

Cat. nos. 29, 42J, 43, 57E

Formerly attributed to: cat. nos. 28, 50

XVII & XVIII Century American Furniture & Paintings. The Celebrated Collection Formed By the Late Mr. and Mrs. Luke Vincent Lockwood: Public Auction Sale, cat. no. 1521 of Parke-Bernet Galleries, Inc., New York, May 13, 14, 15, 1954. Cat. no. 43.

Hanley, Thomas. *Charles Carroll of Carrollton.* Washington, D.C.: Catholic University Press, 1970.

Peale's Museum Gallery of Oil Paintings . . . Public Sale . . . Oct. 6, 1854 . . . M. Thomas and Sons, Auctioneers. . . . Philadelphia: Owen, 1854. Cat. no. 28.

Pleasants, J. Hall. "Studies in Maryland Painting." No. 1636—cat. nos. 28, 29; no. 1653—cat. no. 43. On deposit Maryland Historical Society, Baltimore.

Rowland, Kate Mason. *The Life of Charles Carroll: 1737-1832.* New York: G. P. Putnam's Sons, 1898.

Sellers, Charles Coleman. *Portraits and Miniatures by Charles Willson Peale.* Philadelphia: American Philosophical Society, 1952. Cat. no. 29.

PEALE, REMBRANDT

Cat. nos. 28, 55, 62A, 73A

Formerly attributed to: 24, 69

After: cat. no. 29

Antiques (May 1970):708.

Bowen, Clarence Winthrop, ed. *The History of the Centennial Celebration of the Inauguration of George Washington as First President of the United States.* New York: D. Appleton and Co., 1892. Cat. no. 24.

Frick Art Reference Library notes, New York. No. 121-14 0^4. Cat. no. 28.

Peale's Museum Gallery of Oil Paintings . . . Public Sale . . . Oct. 6, 1854 . . . M. Thomas and Sons, Auctioneers. . . . Philadelphia: Owen, 1854. Cat. nos. 28, 55.

Pleasants, J. Hall. "Studies in Maryland Painting." No. 20—cat. no. 28; no. 1636—cat. no. 29; no. 594—cat. no. 69. On deposit Maryland Historical Society, Baltimore.

Rendezvous For Taste: Peale's Baltimore Museum 1814-1830. Baltimore: The Peale Museum, 1956.

Rutledge, Anna Wells. *Cumulative Record of Exhibition Catalogues, the Pennsylvania Academy of the Fine Arts, 1807-1970, The Society of Artists, 1800-1814, The Artists' Fund Society, 1835-1845.* Philadelphia: The American Philosophical Society, 1955.

Sellers, Charles Coleman. *Portraits and Miniatures by Charles Willson Peale.* Transactions of the American Philosophical Society, Philadelphia, vol. 42, pt. 1, 1952.

PENNINGTON, ROBERT GOODLOE HARPER

Cat. no. 69A

PHILLIPS, THOMAS, R.A.

Cat. no. 70

After: cat. no. 70A

A Dictionary of Artists of the English School. Amsterdam: G. W. Hissink and Co., 1970. Cat. no. 70.

Harper's New Monthly Magazine. vol. LXI, no. CCCLXIV, Sept. 1880. Cat. no. 70A.

PINE, ROBERT EDGE
Cat. no. 57F
Attributed to: 57A, 60A, 60B
Pine?:1
After: 57, 57B
Unknown after Pine: 24

Bowen, Clarence Winthrop, ed. *The History of the Centennial Celebration of the Inauguration of George Washington as First President of the United States.* New York: D. Appleton and Company, 1892. Cat. no. 24.

Broadside: Columbian Museum, Near the Mall, Boston. Printed at D. Bowen's Ornamental Printing Office [1801]. On deposit at the Bostonian Society, Boston. Cat. nos. 1, 24.

Broadside: 100 Elegant Paintings. Boston [1799]. On deposit at the Bostonian Society, Boston. Cat. no. 24.

Broadside: Columbian Museum, Head of the Mall. Boston, [1799]. On deposit at the Bostonian Society, Boston. Cat. no. 24.

Broadside: Columbian Museum, Head of the Mall. Boston, 1795. On deposit at the Bostonian Society, Boston. No. 38—Cat. no. 24?

Columbian Museum. Exhibition List 1795. Collection of the Bostonian Society, Boston, Mass.

Frick Art Reference Library notes, New York. Nos. 222-11D—cat. no. 57A; 275-11T—cat. no. 57C; 112-12A—cat. no. 57D.

Griswold, Rufus Wilmot. *The Republican Court or American Society in the Days of Washington.* New York: D. Appleton and Company, 1855. Cat. nos. 57, 57A.

Hart, Charles Henry. "*The Congress Voting Independence:* A Painting by Robert Edge Pine and Edward Savage in the Hall of the Historical Society of Pennsylvania." *Pennsylvania Magazine of History and Biography,* vol. 29 (1905):1-14. Cat. nos. 1, 57F, 24.

Maryland Historical Society. *Catalogue of Exhibitions, 1848-1908.* Cat. nos. 57A, 57B, 60A, 60B.

Mulcahy, James M. "*Congress Voting Independence:* The Trumbull and Pine-Savage Paintings." *Pennsylvania Magazine of History and Biography,* vol. 80 (1956):74-91. Cat. no. 1.

Peale, Rembrandt. "Reminiscences Desultory." *The Crayon,* vol. III (1856):5. Remarks on Robert Edge Pine.

Pleasants, J. Hall. "Studies in Maryland Painting." Nos. 1664—cat. no. 60A; 1665—cat. no. 57A.

PYNE, W. H.
Pyne?: Cat. no. 73D

Rendezvous For Taste. Baltimore: The Peale Museum, 1956.

REYNOLDS, SIR JOSHUA
Cat. no. 16
After: cat. nos. 16A, 16B

Armstrong, Sir Walter. *Sir Joshua Reynolds: First President of the Royal Academy.* New York: Charles Scribner's Sons, 1900.

Bowen, Clarence Winthrop, ed. *The History of the Centennial Celebration of the Inauguration of George Washington as First President of the United States.* New York: D. Appleton and Co., 1892.

Cormack, Malcolm. transcriber. "The Ledgers of Sir Joshua Reynolds." *Walpole Society Annual*, vol. 42, 1970. Cat. no. 16.

Cotton, William. *Sir Joshua Reynolds, and His Works. Gleanings From His Diary, Unpublished Manuscripts, and From Other Sources.* London: Longman, Brown, Green, Longmans, and Roberts, 1856.

Dunlap, William. *A History of the Rise and Progress of the Arts of Design in the United States.* New York, 1834; reprint ed., New York: Dover Publications, Inc., 1969.

Frick Art Reference Library notes, New York. No. 221-14J[2]. Cat. no. 16.

Pleasants, J. Hall. "Studies in Maryland Painting." No. 1659—cat. no. 16. On deposit Maryland Historical Society, Baltimore.

Waterhouse, Ellis K. *Reynolds.* New York: Phaidon, distributed by Praeger, 1973.

Wharton, Anne Hollingsworth. *Salons Colonial and Republican.* Philadelphia: Benjamin Blom, Inc., 1900; reissued 1971.

ROBERTSON, ANDREW

Cat. no. 72F

After: cat. no. 72G

Dunlap, William. *A History of the Rise and Progress of the Arts of Design in the United States.* New York, 1834; reprint ed., New York: Dover Publications, Inc., 1969.

ROSENTHAL, MAX

Cat. no. 49

SAINT-MEMIN, CHARLES BALTHAZAR JULIEN FEVRET DE

Cat. nos. 23, 23A, 61, 61A, 65, 66

Bowen, Clarence Winthrop, ed. *The History of the Centennial Celebration of the Inauguration of George Washington As First President of the United States.* New York: D. Appleton and Co., 1892.

Frick Art Reference Library notes, New York. No. 557-3A[4]. Cat. no. 23.

Norfleet, Fillmore. *Saint-Mémin in Virginia: Portraits and Biographies.* Richmond: The Dietz Press, 1942.

Pleasants, J. Hall. "Studies in Maryland Painting." No. 21—cat. no. 61; no. 571—cat. no. 65; no. 591—cat. no. 23. On deposit Maryland Historical Society, Baltimore.

Saint-Mémin, Charles Balthazar Julien Févret de. *Collection of Portraits.* New York: Elias Dexter, 1862. Cat. nos. 23, 62A, 65, 66.

SARTAIN, JOHN

Cat. no. 56

SAVAGE, EDWARD:

Cat. nos. 1, 2

Reference to: 24

Hart, Charles Henry. "*The Congress Voting Independence:* A Painting by Robert Edge Pine and Edward Savage in the Hall of the Historical Society of Pennsylvania." *Pennsylvania Magazine of History and Biography.* vol. 29 (1905):1-14. Cat. nos. 1, 2.

Mulcahy, James M. "Congress Voting Independence: The Trumbull and Pine-Savage Paintings." *Pennsylvania Magazine of History and Biography*, vol. 80 (1956):74-91. Cat. nos. 1, 2.

Stauffer, David McNeely. *American Engravers Upon Copper and Steel.* New York: The Grolier Club of the City of New York, 1907. No. 2759—cat. no. 2.

Snyder, Henry M.
Cat. no. 42A

Scharf, John. *History of Baltimore City and County.* Baltimore: L. H. Everts, 1881. Cat. no. 42A

Stuart, Gilbert
Cat. no. 51
Attributed to: cat. no. 58
After: cat. nos. 51A, 51B, 51C, 51D
Reference to: cat. no. 22

Archives, Georgetown University, Dept. of Art History. Cat. no. 51.

Dunlap, William. *A History of the Rise and Progress of the Arts of Design in the United States.* New York, 1834; reprint ed., New York: Dover Publications, Inc., 1969.

Frick Art Reference Library notes, No. 121-7 E4. Cat. no. 51.

Mount, Charles Merrill. *Gilbert Stuart.* New York: W. W. Norton, 1964.

Park, Lawrence. *Gilbert Stuart: An Illustrated Descriptive List of His Works.* New York: W. E. Rudge, 1926. Cat. nos. 51, 51A, 51B.

Pleasants, J. Hall. "Studies in Maryland Painting." No. 3310—cat. no. 58; no. 3461—cat. no. 51. On deposit Maryland Historical Society, Baltimore.

Wharton, Anne Hollingsworth. *Salons Colonial and Republican.* Philadelphia: Benjamin Blom, Inc., 1900; reissued 1971.

Whitley, William T. *Gilbert Stuart.* Cambridge, Mass.: Harvard University Press, 1932.

Sully, Ellen
Cat. no. 42I

Sawitzky, William. *Pennsylvania Historical Society.* Catalogue, descriptive and critical, of the paintings and miniatures in the Historical Society of Pennsylvania. Philadelphia: The Historical Society of Pennsylvania, 1942. Cat. no. 42I.

Frick Art Reference Library notes, No. 121-14a. Cat. no. 42I.

Sully, Thomas, Cat. nos. 31, 32, 33, 34, 34A, 34B, 35, 37, 64, 82, 82A, 83, 86A, 90
Attributed to: 86
Formerly attributed to: 19C
After: 34C, 35A, 36, 83A, 86B

The Baltimore Museum of Art. *Two Hundred and Fifty Years of Painting in Maryland.* Baltimore: The Baltimore Museum of Art, 1945.

Biddle, Edward and Mantle Fielding. *The Life and Works of Thomas Sully (1783-1872).* Philadelphia: Privately printed, 1921. reprint ed. New York: Kennedy Graphics, 1970. Nos. 292—cat. no. 32; 293—cat. no. 34B; 294—cat. no. 35; 291—cat. no. 64; 103—cat. no. 82; 102—cat. no. 83; 892—cat. no. 86; 894—cat. no. 86A; 740—cat. no. 90.

Bowen, Clarence Winthrop, ed. *The History of the Centennial Celebration of the Inauguration of George Washington as First President of the United States.* New York: D. Appleton and Co., 1892. Cat. no. 31.

Dickson, Harold E., ed. *Observations on American Art, Selections From the Writings of John Neal (1793-1876),* State College: The Pennsylvania State College, 1943. Cat. no. 31.

Frick Art Reference Library notes, New York. No. 121-14F^5—cat. no. 32; 121-14x^2—cat. no. 19c; 121-1T—cat. no. 33; 121-6J^2—cat. no. 34A; 121-1Z—cat. no. 34B; 121-14K^5—cat. no. 35; 121-1V—cat. no. 37.

Hart, Charles Henry. "Thomas Sully's Register of Portraits 1801-1871." Vol. XXXII (1908):385ff, *Pennsylvania Magazine of History and Biography.*

Pleasants, J. Hall. "Studies in Maryland Painting." Nos. 25—cat. no. 82; 592—cat. no. 90; 1054—cat. no. 37; 1661—cat. no. 34B; 1981—cat. no. 64; 1983—cat. no. 34; 2582—cat. no. 34A; 3018—cat. no. 35.

Proceedings, Massachusetts Historical Society, 2nd Series, vol. II, p. 261; vol. III, p. 282.

Rutledge, Anna Wells. *Cumulative Record of Exhibition Catalogues, The Pennsylvania Academy of the Fine Arts, 1807-1870, The Society of Artists, 1800-1814, The Artists' Fund Society, 1835-1845.* Philadelphia: The American Philosophical Society. 1955.

Tuckerman, Henry T. *Book of the Artists; American Artist Life.* reprint ed. New York: Carr, 1966. Cat. nos. 82, 83.

Wharton, Anne Hollingsworth. *Salons Colonial and Republican.* Philadelphia: Benjamin Blom, Inc., 1900. Reissued 1971.

Thomson, James
Cat. no. 75B

Trentanove, Raimondo
Cat. no. 68, 68A

Trumbull, John
Cat. nos. 3A, 64A
After: 3, 64B

Dunlap, William. *A History of the Rise and Progress of the Arts of Design in the United States.* New York, 1834; reprinted, New York: Dover Publications, Inc. 1969.

Durand, John. *The Life and Times of Asher B. Durand.* New York: Kennedy Graphics, Inc., Da Capo Press, 1970.

Frick Art Reference Library notes, New York. No. 175-11G—cat. no. 64A.

Griswold, Rufus Wilmot. *The Republican Court or American Society in the Days of Washington.* Cat. nos. 64A, 64B.

Morgan, John Hill. *Paintings by John Trumbull at Yale University.* New Haven: Yale University Press, 1926. Cat. nos. 3, 3A.

Pleasants, J. Hall. "Studies in Maryland Painting." Nos. 2010—cat. no. 64A; 1986—cat. no. 3A. On deposit Maryland Historical Society, Baltimore.

Sizer, Theodore. *The Works of Colonel John Trumbull.* New Haven: Yale University Press, 1950. Cat. nos. 3, 3A, 64A.

Sizer, Theodore, ed. *The Autobiography of John Trumbull.* New Haven: Yale University Press, 1953.

Vanderlyn, John
Formerly attributed to: cat. no. 42B

Frick Art Reference Library notes, New York. No. 121-6B. Cat. no. 42B.

Pleasants, J. Hall. "Studies in Maryland Painting." No. 3361—cat. no. 42B. On deposit Maryland Historical Society, Baltimore.

Volkmar, Charles
Cat. no. 59
After: cat. no. 60

"Artists in Baltimore, Some Interesting Facts Regarding A Noted Painter," *Baltimore American*, March 10, 1889.

Grubar, Francis S. *Richard Caton Woodville, An Early American Genre Painter.* Washington: Corcoran Gallery of Art, 1967.

Pleasants, J. Hall. "Studies in Maryland Painting." No. 3312—cat. no. 59. On deposit Maryland Historical Society, Baltimore.

Weber, Edward & Co.
Cat. No. 60

West, William Edward
Cat. no. 80
West?: cat. no. 70B

Dunlap, William. *A History of the Rise and Progress of the Arts of Design in the United States.* New York, 1834; reprint ed., New York: Dover Publications, Inc., 1969.

Dunn, N. P. "An Artist of the Past," *Putnam's Monthly*, Sept. 1907: 658-669. Cat. nos. 70B, 80.

Pleasants, J. Hall. "Studies in Maryland Painting." No. 132—cat. no. 80; no. 1982—cat. no. 70B. On deposit Maryland Historical Society, Baltimore.

Williams, Isaac L.
Cat. no. 22

The Annual Reports of the American Society for Colonizing the Free People of Colour of the United States. Vol. 11-20, 1828-1836. New York: Negro University Press; reprinted 1969.

Spindler, Adaline B. "Isaac L. Williams, Artist and Painter," *Lancaster Historical Society* (Nov. 1, 1912): 261-269. Cat. no. 22.

Wollaston, John
Cat. nos. 7, 9, 11, 11A, 15, 44, 44A, 45, 46, 47, 47A, 48
Attributed to: cat. nos. 8, 8B, 9A, 44B, 45A
Formerly attributed to: cat. no. 9B
After: cat. nos. 8A, 8C, 15A, 15B, 48A, 49

Dunlap, William. *A History of the Rise and Progress of the Arts of Design in the United States.* New York, 1834; reprint ed., New York: Dover Publications, Inc., 1969.

Frick Art Reference Library notes, New York. No. 121-13B—cat. no. 8; no. 121-15—cat. no. 8B; no. 122-5K—cat. no. 11A; no. 122-5I—cat. no. 11; no. 122-11J—cat. no. 15; no. 121-11C—cat. no. 44; no. 121-6X—cat. no. 44.

Georgetown University College Journal, vol. 22, p. 65 (Mrs. Daniel Carroll of Upper Marlborough).

Groce, George C. "John Wollaston (fl. 1736-1767): a Cosmopolitan Painter In the British Colonies," *The Art Quarterly*, vol. XV (Summer 1952): 133-148. Cat. nos. 7, 9, 9B, 11, 11A, 15, 44, 44A, 45, 46, 47, 47A, 48

Lane, James. "Studies in American Painting." June 5, 1958. On deposit Kennedy Galleries, Inc., New York. Cat. no. 8.

Maryland Historical Society Catalogues of Exhibitions 1848-1908.

Pleasants, J. Hall. "Studies in Maryland Painting." No. 129—cat. no. 8B; no. 134—cat. no. 44A; no. 135—cat. no. 45; no. 538—cat. no. 47; nos. 539, 595—cat. no. 9A; no. 596—cat. no. 7; no. 781—cat. no. 44; no. 1523—cat. no. 47A; no. 1524—cat. no. 46; nos. 1552, 1570—cat. no. 11; no. 1658—cat. no. 8; no. 1739—cat. no. 45A; no. 1847—cat. no. 11A; no. 2452—cat. no. 15; no. 3314—cat. no. 9; no. 3416—cat. no. 15B; no 3505—cat. no. 15A. On deposit Maryland Historical Society, Baltimore.

Sartain, John. *Reminiscences of a Very Old Man*. New York: D. Appleton & Co., 1899.

Wharton, Anne Hollingsworth. *Salons Colonial and Republican*. Philadelphia: Benjamin Blom, Inc. 1900; reissued 1971.

Wood, Joseph

Cat. no. 85

Pleasants, J. Hall. "Studies in American Painting." No. 2824—cat. no. 85. On deposit Maryland Historical Society, Baltimore.

Woodville, Richard Caton

Formerly attributed to: cat. no. 59

Grubar, Francis S. *Richard Caton Woodville, An Early American Genre Painter*. Washington: Corcoran Gallery of Art, 1967.

Designed by Gerard A. Valerio
Composed in Palatino by Service Composition, Inc.
Printed on Cortlea Cover and Patina text by Schneidereith & Sons
Binding by Optic Bindery
Edition: 3000

Photography Credits:

Cortland V. D. Hubbard, Cat. Nos. 62, 63, 64; Joseph Szaszfai, Cat. Nos. 86, 87; Herbert Bose, Cat. Nos. 81, 82. Cat. No. 74 is reproduced by gracious permission of Her Majesty The Queen.